CW01379241

Chinese Landscapes

Chinese Landscapes

THE VILLAGE AS PLACE

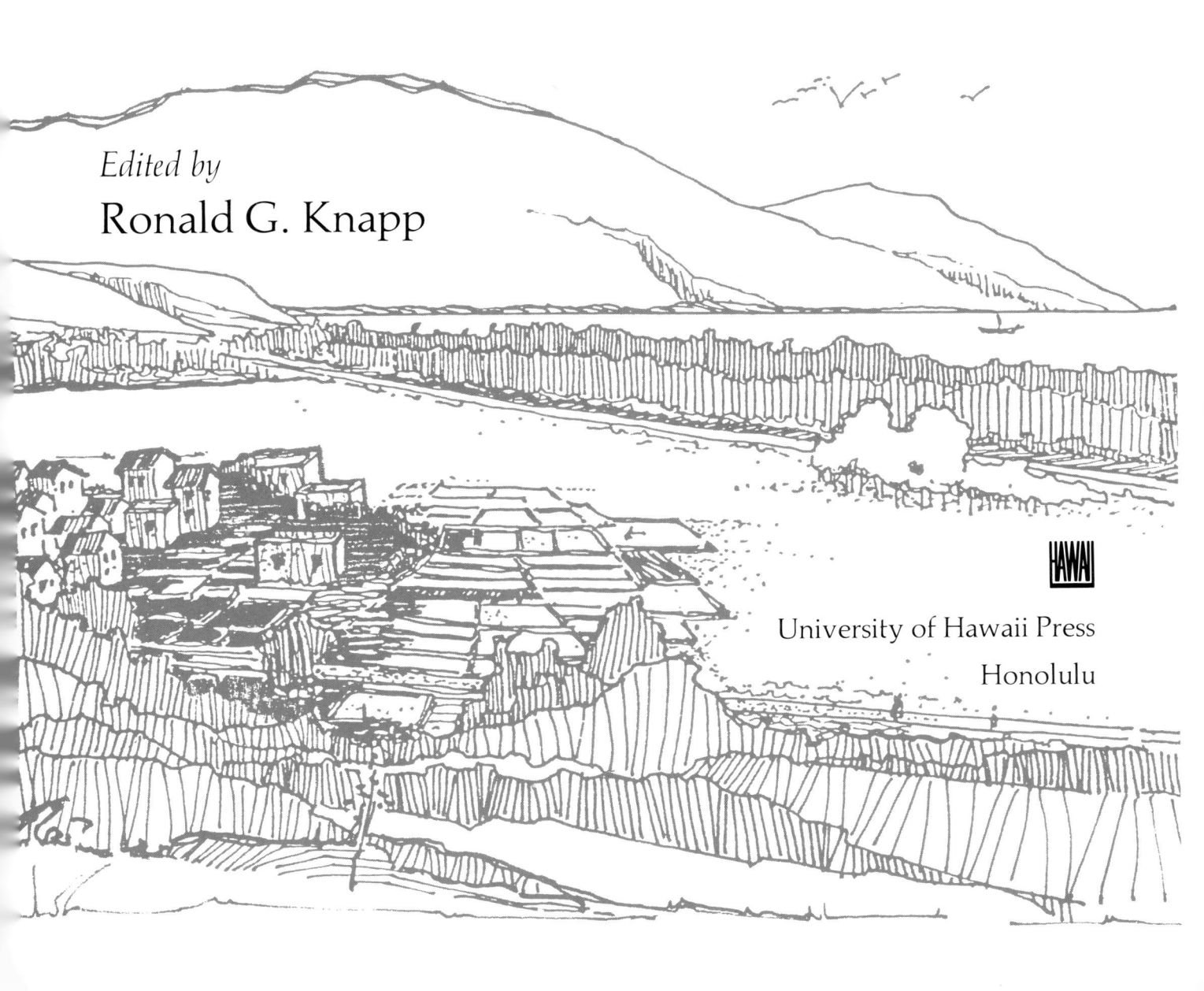

Edited by
Ronald G. Knapp

University of Hawaii Press

Honolulu

© 1992 University of Hawaii Press
All rights reserved
Printed in the United States of America
97 96 95 94 93 92   5 4 3 2 1

Library of Congress Cataloging-in-Publication Data

Chinese landscapes : the village as place / edited by Ronald G. Knapp.
    p.   cm.
   Includes bibliographical references and index.
   ISBN 0-8248-1413-4
   1. Rural geography—China.   2. Villages—China.   I. Knapp, Ronald G., 1940-   .
GF656.C48   1992
307.72'0951—dc20   91-42252
                                                          CIP

Title page illustration by James P. Warfield.

University of Hawaii Press books are printed on acid-free paper and meet the guidelines for permanence and durability of the Council on Library Resources

CONTENTS

Acknowledgments / vii

A Note on Chinese Romanization / ix

1. Village Landscapes / 1
   RONALD G. KNAPP

2. China's Rural Settlement Patterns / 13
   JIN QIMING AND LI WEI

3. Village *Fengshui* Principles / 35
   FAN WEI

4. Changing Village Landscapes / 47
   RONALD G. KNAPP AND SHEN DONGQI

Tradition

Tradition: Introductory Perspectives / 75

5. Sheung Wo Hang Village, Hong Kong: A Village Shaped by *Fengshui* / 79
   PATRICK H. HASE AND LEE MAN-YIP

6. Xiqi Village, Guangdong: Compact with Ecological Planning / 95
   JONATHAN HAMMOND

7. Chawan Village, Guangdong: Fishing and Farming along the South China Sea / 107
   JAMES P. WARFIELD

8. Hongcun Village, Anhui: A Place of Rivers and Lakes / 119
   SHAN DEQI

vi   **Contents**

9. Dangjia Village, Shaanxi: A Brilliant Pearl / 129
   LIU BAOZHONG

10. Zhouzhuang, Jiangsu: A Historic Market Town / 139
    JOSEPH C. WANG

11. Yachuan Village, Gansu, and Shimadao Village, Shaanxi: Subterranean Villages / 151
    GIDEON GOLANY

12. Hekeng Village, Fujian: Unique Habitats / 163
    OLIVIER LAUDE

13. Cangpo Village, Zhejiang: A Relict with a Future? / 173
    RONALD G. KNAPP

Transition

Transition: Introductory Perspectives / 189

14. Dazhai Village, Shanxi: A Model Landscape / 193
    CHRISTOPHER L. SALTER

15. Suburban Weigang, Jiangsu: A Transformed Village / 211
    GREGORY VEECK

16. Lincun Village, Fujian: Harmony between Humans, Environment, and the Supernatural / 221
    HUANG SHU-MIN

17. Fengjiacun Village, Shandong: A Corporate Community / 233
    STEWART ODEND'HAL

18. Dacaiyuan Village, Henan: Migration and Village Renewal / 245
    NANCY JERVIS

19. MaGaoqiao Village, Sichuan: Habitat in the Red Basin / 259
    STEPHEN ENDICOTT

20. Longlin Village, Hainan: Cash Crops and New Houses / 269
    CATHERINE ENDERTON AND WEN CHANGEN

21. Hsin Hsing Village, Taiwan: From Farm to Factory / 279
    RITA S. GALLIN AND BERNARD GALLIN

References / 295

Contributors / 307

Index / 311

ACKNOWLEDGMENTS

The preparation of this collection of essays, covering so much territory from so many perspectives, depends on portraying in words and illustrations the sense of place in China's countryside, and thus it presented special challenges and opportunities. The strength of *Chinese Landscapes: The Village as Place* arises from the imagery of the participating authors. I appreciate their willingness to participate in this multi-disciplinary effort to comprehend China's rural landscapes.

I owe a special debt to Camy Fischer, whose original drawings and maps, as well as improvements to the illustrations of others, add an important visual dimension to the book.

I'd like to acknowledge the guidance and concern of many at the University of Hawaii Press who have helped bring four of my books to life. Patricia Crosby, editor for two of my books, more than anyone has helped guide this collection to its current form. Her concern, clarity, and gentle prodding are all appreciated.

The careful copyediting of Susan Stone has made it possible to maintain consistency with my two books on Chinese vernacular architecture. I am thankful also for Cheri Dunn's able guidance of the manuscript through the production phases.

A NOTE ON CHINESE ROMANIZATION

Chinese terms are romanized in the *pinyin* system throughout this volume. Terms found in the Hong Kong chapter have added romanization in the Yale system for colloquial Cantonese and those in the Taiwan chapter in the Wade-Giles system for standard Chinese. The romanization of place names in Hong Kong and Taiwan follows conventional usage rather than utilizing *pinyin* spellings.

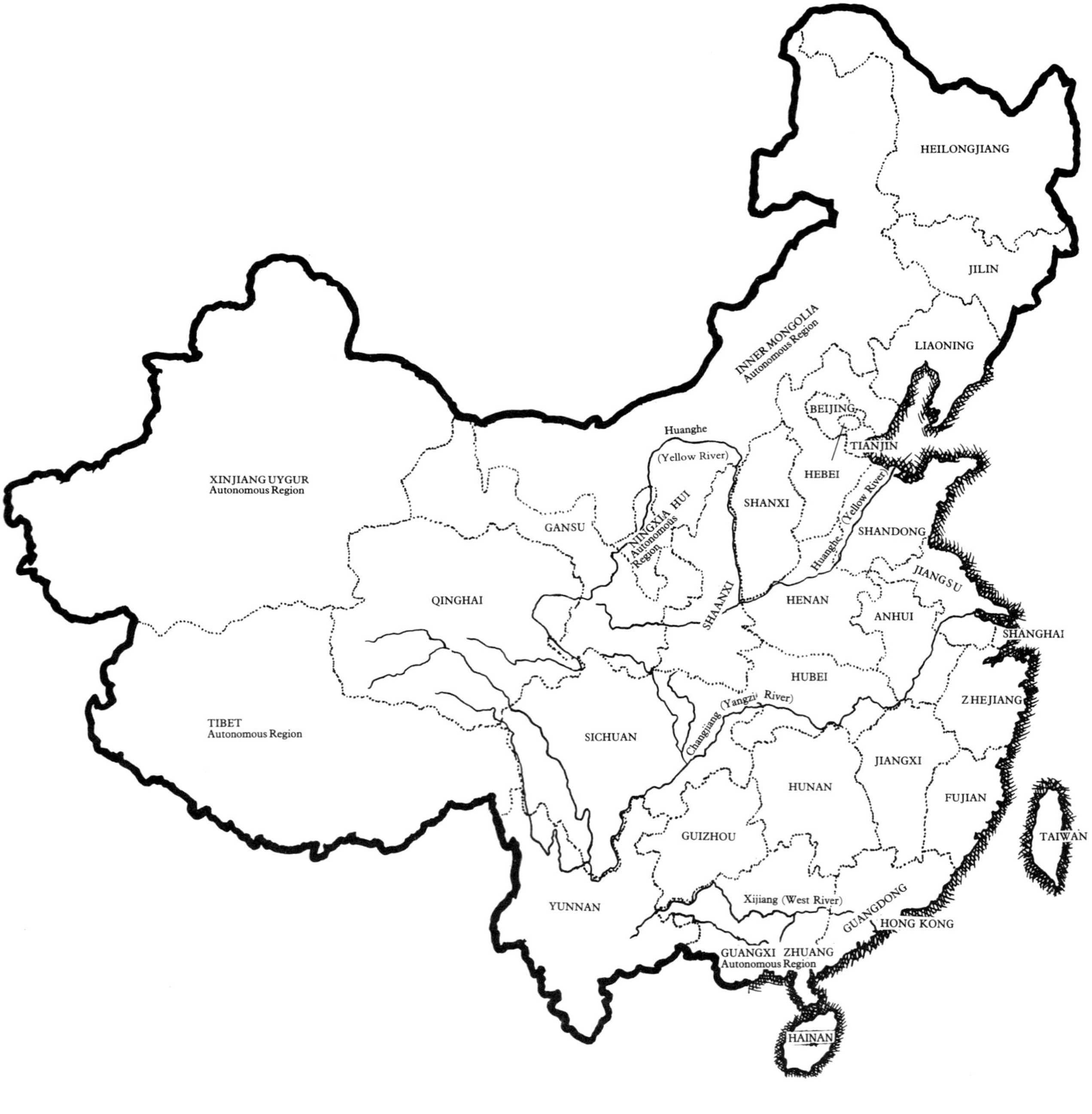
HEILONGJIANG
JILIN
LIAONING
INNER MONGOLIA
Autonomous Region
BEIJING
TIANJIN
HEBEI
Huanghe
(Yellow River)
XINJIANG UYGUR
Autonomous Region
GANSU
NINGXIA HUI
Autonomous
Region
SHANXI
SHANDONG
Huanghe
(Yellow River)
JIANGSU
QINGHAI
HENAN
ANHUI
SHAANXI
SHANGHAI
HUBEI
Changjiang (Yangzi River)
ZHEJIANG
TIBET
Autonomous Region
SICHUAN
JIANGXI
HUNAN
FUJIAN
TAIWAN
GUIZHOU
Xijiang (West River)
GUANGDONG
HONG KONG
YUNNAN
GUANGXI ZHUANG
Autonomous Region
HAINAN

Chinese Landscapes

Figure 1.1. The eighteen case-study villages discussed in the "Tradition" and "Transition" sections of *Chinese Landscapes*.

CHAPTER 1

Village Landscapes

RONALD G. KNAPP

GEOGRAPHERS and others have written much about the diverse physical environments and varied cultural landscapes forming the complex mosaic of China. That Chinese villages differ from one area of the country to another is a truism, a fact travelers and scholars often have commented on. The dry North China Plain is one of the "two Chinas" noted by George B. Cressey (1934, 13). John King Fairbank writes that here "one sees in summer an endless expanse of green fields over which are scattered clusters of darker green, the trees of earth-walled villages. It is like the view of our Middle West, where farmsteads and their clumps of trees are dispersed at rough half-mile intervals. But where our corn belt has a farm, on the North China plain there is an entire village. Where one American farmer's family lives with its barns and shed among its fields in Iowa or Illinois at a half-mile interval from its neighbors roundabout, in [north] China an entire community of several hundred persons lives in its tree-studded village, at a half-mile interval from neighbor villages" (1983, 2). Villages of many sizes have always appeared planted like islands among the fields, with taupe tamped earth walls clearly demarcating settlement from the surrounding fields.

Villages throughout the better-watered and topographically more irregular areas south of the Yangzi River have always been more visually diverse and numerous than those in the north. Although there were also large villages—even surpassing in population and physical size those of north China—dispersed households in hamlets have always been found in great number. Commenting on central China during the mid-nineteenth century, M. Huc remarked that if "you travel along the roads, you would be led to believe the country much less populous than it really is. The villages are few and far between, the waste lands so considerable that you might at times fancy yourself in the deserts of Tartary. But traverse the same province by the canals or rivers, and the aspect of the country is entirely changed. Often you pass great cities, containing not less than two or three millions of inhabitants, whilst smaller towns and great villages follow each other in almost uninterrupted succession" (1855, 2:98). Writing disparagingly of rural habitats, Huc said that the villages in Hubei, on the one hand, "have in general a very poor and wretched appearance" (1855, 2:297). In Sichuan, on the other hand, "the aspect of the villages, and even the farms, bears witness to the comfortable circumstances of their inhabitants" (1855, 1:289-290). Hsiao reminds us that even if Huc "exaggerated the opulence of Szechwan [Sichuan] or underestimated the productivity of the soil of Hupeh [Hubei]," he clearly saw how differences arose from "geographical conditions" (1960, 13-14). Others such as Alicia B. Little at the turn of the century and Richthofen, who witnessed China after the depredations of the Taiping rebellion more than a quarter century earlier, sketched the diversity of village conditions as the Qing dynasty reached its nadir (1908; 1903).

There is indeed a bewildering variety of settlement forms in the Chinese countryside. Chinese rural households, as they have since the neolithic period, continue to live in one of myriad villages that vary greatly in size and composition. By late traditional times, there emerged, in addition to village settlements, large numbers of rural markets, termed "standard market towns" by Skinner, that linked villagers to a hierarchically nested and dense network of central places—in effect structurally altering longstanding fundamental patterns of residence and opportunity in the countryside (1964, 3-43). The proliferation of local markets over the last millennium was, as Elvin notes, a consequence as well as a cause of an increasingly specialized and commercialized rural economy (1973, 169). It is true that many such local markets have been small in scale and periodic in operation, convening only for a few hours at a fixed site according to a regular schedule. Yet, even though given shape by rural trading, standard market towns and their dependent areas came in time to have important social dimensions, becoming culture-bearing units in Chinese society. The geometry of such patterns allowed that a peasant "was a member of two communities: his village and the marketing system to which his village belonged" (Skinner 1971, 272). Following Skinner's usage, the term "village" is generally used in this volume to describe nucleated or compact settlements that do not contain a market. The broader term "village communities" is used to describe dispersed as well as nucleated residential patterns that do not support markets. The literature on rural China, however, is not always consistent in the usage of the term "village." Even market towns (*jizhen*), for example, are sometimes described as "villages" (Spencer 1940, 48). For the most part, as Philip C. C. Huang has pointed out, "the village marked off not only the boundaries of residence, but also to some extent the boundaries of production and consumption" (1985, 23). Regional variations in village form and composition have been shaped generally by ecological differences as well as patterns of commercialization.

For the most part, a village is a mappable spatial domain with identifiable characteristics relating to residence and work. The most common Chinese terms used to identify village settlements are *cun* and *zhuang*, which are used as generic character suffixes to form specific toponyms for rural settlements. A great many Chinese villages incorporate the surname of the dominant lineage in the village. Many *cun* and *zhuang*, however, take their names from local conditions, reflecting the spontaneity of settlement and the need to name a space and thus transform it into a place. Such names document simple locational considerations such as a site at the mouth of a stream, on a slope, in a mountain pass, or in a gulch; topographical characteristics such as a nearby stream, ridge, bay, embankment, or hill; cultural features with identification linked to a temple, well, customs barrier, garrison, pagoda, or bridge; compass directions as well as the numbers one to ten; size (large and small), position (upper and lower), and age (new and old), among other characteristics. Specific examples are discussed in the chapters that follow. (A general treatment of Chinese place names is Spencer 1941, 90-92.)

Besides the seemingly ubiquitous *cun* and

zhuang, other Chinese characters have been frequently appended to village names that reflect the nature of early settlement, the scale of habitat, or the addition of some marketing function, among other factors. Some of these characters are only used locally or regionally—a subject that deserves more etymological treatment than it has been given. Along the northern and southern margins of the country, one encounters many rural settlements that have the character *bao, ying,* or *zhai* as part of their names. Most of these settlements likely arose from peasant pioneer and/or military colonization in areas in which settlers encountered hostile indigenous groups (for a map showing the distribution of such settlements, see Voon 1969, 40; Yin 1988, 6-7). Similarly, *tun* is a common term indicating the past stationing of troops at a defensive post that evolved into a common rural settlement. The specialized local usage of *zhuang* in the region around Beijing to indicate imperial "estates" reflects the extension of official control into the hinterland beyond the capital. Here also, the raising of horses to meet the needs of military expeditions and border patrols in north China brought about rural settlements tied to pastures *(chang)* and corrals *(quan)* that became part of place names.

Small hamlets that together make up a village community often use localized terminology in their names. Many such examples can be found in the Jiangnan region, where *da* or *dai* is used to indicate a small canalside group of houses, or in Sichuan, where *ba, yuanba,* or *yuanzi* signifies a fragmented residential cluster set amidst or surrounded by a grove of bamboo.

For many Chinese villages, the transition from a purely residential setting to one with some trading functions—however tentative and small-scale—is suggested in the name. The addition to a place name of a character suffix such as *chang*, used especially in Sichuan and Guizhou, or *ji*, found particularly in the region straddling the borders of eastern Henan, southern Hebei, southwestern Shandong, northern Jiangsu, and northern Anhui, as well as *xu* in southern Hunan, western Jiangxi, southern Fujian, Guangdong and Guangxi, shows clearly regional patterns of usage and functional change relating to periodic markets. A comprehensive study of the historical and contemporary usage of these characters as well as *jie, pu, dian, hang, jizhen, shi, fang,* and other similar forms may offer evidence of the artificiality of many provincial borders, the striking linguistic and other cultural differences that exist within individual Chinese provinces, as well as the evolution of rural marketing patterns. Many rural settlements that long ago lost the atmosphere of a bucolic village and were transformed into actual towns or cities never abandoned the character or characters that today reveal their more humble patrimony.

In the People's Republic of China today, a dichotomous classification based on a set of administrative criteria divides all settlements into urban and rural. Cities *(chengshi)* and officially designated towns *(jianzhi zhen)* make up the urban sector, whereas villages *(nongcun)* and undesignated towns *(fei jianzhi zhen)* or simply market towns *(jizhen)* make up the rural sector. The simplicity of this classification, however, often masks the reality of the differences one encounters in rural China, especially concerning the designated and undesignated towns, in which designation as "an urban place" has often been a political decision based on tax advantages. For most rural Chinese, the closest true urban center is one of the county towns *(xiancheng)*, each of which is the seat of the county government.

Over the past decade, Chinese planners have championed the role of small towns in China's rural development as a strategy to forestall the blind migration of farmers into large cities by providing opportunities for nonagricultural employment in their home areas. This strategy has been accompanied by a rapid increase in the number of designated towns from 2,664 in 1982 to some 9,130 in 1985, increasing to more than 10,000 today—inserting a matrix of sanctioned urban places into China's countryside. Stimulating this rapid growth in designated towns was a relaxation of criteria for designation as a *jianzhi zhen* by provincial governments in the early 1980s and officially in 1984 by the national government. To be officially designated as a town, a settlement had to be either a seat of county government; a seat of township government *(xiang)* in which the total population of the township was below 20,000, with 2,000 nonagricultural persons resident in the township seat; or a seat of township government where the total population of the township exceeded 20,000, with the number of nonagricultural persons living in the township seat in excess of 10 percent of the total population. Formal designation places the settlement at the lowest echelon of the urban hierarchy. As a result of designation as a town, county governments assume financial responsibility for much of the welfare and investment in the town, although in reality limited financial resources usually limit the actual amounts available. "From the perspective of prospective candidates for town designation, it is more than a matter of mechanically reacting to some tightened or loosened urban criteria; it also involves weighing the incentives and disincentives in gaining town status. Although there are ample reasons for becoming a designated town, there are also circumstances that discourage some well-qualified settlements from wanting to be counted as towns in the formal sector" (Lee 1989, 782).

Chinese Landscapes portrays the rich variety of rural settlements in China. Written by anthropologists, architects, geographers, historians, a sociologist, and a veterinary ecologist, the following chapters attempt to make sense of individual Chinese villages as *places* of habitation, work, and leisure. The emphasis throughout the book is on comprehending the spatial patterns and the context of these basic behaviors, which when taken together constitute the village ensemble. Some Chinese villages are compact and ordered, many more are sprawling and chaotic, and still others are only hamlets of a handful of households. Whatever the village form, environmental, economic, social, and technical factors have interacted to mold and define the changing rural settlement landscape. These factors are explored throughout the book.

In the exploration of Chinese village landscapes in this book, three general chapters set the stage for the individual chapters that follow. Jin Qiming and Li Wei in Chapter 2 survey the broad types of nucleated and dispersed settlements in China, systematically examining villages using different criteria such as morphology, shape, size, internal structure, and general economic function. After a topical review, the authors present the main features of eleven rural settlement regions that Jin Qiming has identified for China.

Chapter 3 by Fan Wei assesses the principles that underlie the morphology of many Chinese villages. This chapter is an antidote to the common Western perception that the internal geometry of villages in north or south China is without pattern, mazelike, with "no trace of design" (Smith 1899, 8–9). Indifference to regularity and lack of uniformity stemmed, according to one observer, from "the fact that villages were natural growths" (Hsiao 1960, 12). A commonly accepted simple evolutionary explanation may be summarized as follows: Villages "developed just as circumstances happen to make them. . . . The first settler built his dwelling where he thought best; another followed his example. It was necessary to have a path to get to these and soon . . . another path, or a continuation of the first, running, it may be, at sharp angles. Other houses, other paths, other streets; but no system about them" (Browne 1901, 195).

Although it may appear that villages in general display a lack of orderliness, a great many rural settlements indeed have an "order" derived from geomancy, or *fengshui*. Fan Wei in his chapter and several authors of later chapters reveal that Chinese practices of siting demonstrate an environmental awareness, a regard for recurring patterns of nature, and the imposition of an order. Villagers themselves, as well as Chinese poets, painters, and planners, continue to speak of the creative ways in which Chinese peasants over millennia have manipulated space in order to create village landscapes of beauty and practicality.

Chapter 4 by Ronald G. Knapp and Shen Dongqi surveys the changing landscapes of Chinese villages on the mainland in the four decades since 1949, emphasizing the role of national politics in the People's Republic of China in setting directions for the restructuring of rural settlements as well as in general rural construction and planning. The geometry and morphology of the countryside in the PRC have changed substantially over the past four decades. Many villages no longer occupy their original sites, having been demolished and rebuilt elsewhere in a style alien to tradition. Others echo the past yet are no longer simply a collection of residences for local peasants but transitional settlement forms in which the residents are both farmers and factory workers. Whereas most traditional rural settlements emerged during centuries of small-scale agricultural development, slowly changing from century to century, today many are changing rapidly and are clearly planned. Throughout China's countryside during the 1980s, the scale and speed of village landscape transformation were unprecedented. This chapter excludes the political and economic factors affecting village change in Taiwan and Hong Kong, a topic that deserves parallel treatment.

Eighteen village studies form the core of *Chinese Landscapes*, ranging across China from the dry north to the humid areas of southeastern and southwestern China. The village studies are divided between two sections, called "Tradition" and "Transition," depending on the emphasis of the author. This division must not be seen simply as contrasting static conditions with changing conditions, however. Although tradition may be contrasted with modernity, such a simplistic binary opposition has only limited utility, as the chapters taken together clearly indicate. All of the villages presented in this book exist in the modern world and reflect in one way or another the impingement of this world. Still, some village forms are more suggestive of their past than others. It is this suggestion of antecedence that helped determine whether a village was placed in the "Tradition" or the "Transition" section.

Different disciplinary perspectives and the length of experience within a studied village have resulted in different emphases from chapter to chapter. Lee Man-yip, the coauthor with Patrick Hase of the chapter on Sheung Wo Hang in Hong Kong, was born and continues to live in the village, a fourteenth-generation descendant of the founder. The view from the inside is strengthened by the authors' recognition and use of the rich historical data sources available for the region and their acknowledgment of field work by others in nearby areas during recent decades.

Shan Deqi, writing on Hongcun in Anhui, and Liu Baozhong, writing on Dangjia in Shaanxi, with their students and colleagues, have surveyed, mapped, and photographed what they and others consider to be some of China's most beautiful and best-preserved villages. Comparatively little affected by the currents of political campaigns, these villages provide us at the end of the twentieth century with more than echoes of China's past; they explicitly are China's past. It is important that the efforts of these architect authors to gain support for historic preservation be acknowledged and assisted. With a similar intent, the architect Joseph Wang examines Zhouzhuang, a historic market town in Jiangsu province, calling attention to traditional design features that fit the settlement to an area cut by extensive canals. My own description of Cangpo in Zhejiang sketches a village that has been unable to join the many Chinese villages undergoing radical change in appearance and function over the past decade.

Gideon Golany's chapter on Yachuan in Gansu and Shimadao in Shaanxi has been extracted from his more comprehensive studies of how subterranean dwellings in China relate to similar earth-sheltered habitats elsewhere in the world. Jonathan Hammond and James Warfield draw on their talents as architects to document and evaluate the traditional private and public spaces of Xiqi, a farming village, and Chawan, a fishing village, in Guangdong province. Similarly, Olivier Laude, well traveled in China's countryside, returned to Fujian to photographically document the richness and color of life in villages with some of China's most extraordinary dwelling units, the castlelike building complexes of the Hakka.

As Christopher L. Salter has done so well previously, he examines in his chapter China's most (in)famous village, Dazhai in Shanxi province, and its role as a model for landscape transformation. Nancy Jervis, writing on Dacaiyuan in Henan, first visited the village in 1972, returning there several times between 1981 and 1984 for research. Huang Shu-min writes of Lincun village in Fujian and Gregory Veeck of Weigang in Jiangsu from the perspective of long-term access to their respective villages in the preparation of Ph.D. dissertations. Stephen Endicott, born in China, began his interviews and research in the Sichuan countryside in 1980–1981, returning to MaGaoqiao in 1986 and 1988. Catherine Enderton, a geographer, returned to Hainan specifically to reappraise and organize her earlier impressions of a distinct village in subtropical China. Stewart Odend'hal's work on Fengjiacun village in Shandong is part of an ongoing multidisciplinary collaborative project that is documenting and analyzing a village of north China, an area insufficiently examined in the literature. His perspective as a veterinary ecologist draws attention to elements little acknowledged by most visitors to Chinese villages. Bernard and Rita Gallin, the authors of the chapter on Hsin Hsing in Taiwan, write of a village they have studied on an ongoing basis for more than three decades, clearly an extraordinary time frame in viewing village transition. Their chapter reveals the general impact of economic and demographic changes on the physical and social lives of villagers as well as suggests similarities and differences with mainland patterns.

Each author was asked to present what might be called "the setting" for his or her village. Where possible, the factors originally considered in the site selection for the village—access to water, drainage, directional orientation, regard for terrain, proximity to fields, security, junction of land or water routes, for example—are described. Other questions addressed include the following: Does the village site itself or do the individual parts of the village (e.g., houses) reveal a sensitive understanding of local environmental patterns? Does it appear that villagers are mindful of slope, drainage, prevailing winds, and exposure to the sun? To what degree do these conform with *fengshui*? The villages described by Huang Shu-min in Fujian, Liu Baozhong in Shaanxi, Patrick Hase and Lee Man-yip in Hong Kong, Jonathan Hammond in Guangdong, and myself in Zhejiang portray the varied application of traditional *fengshui* principles and environmental adaptation in very different parts of the country. Each author examines private and public spaces —as well as the sights, colors, sounds, and in some cases even the smells of individual villages. To the degree possible, the spatial extent of the village is presented. Each village chapter is illustrated with maps, drawings, and photographs to clarify the village as place.

Where information is available, the historical background of each village—its origin and changes over time—is presented. However, for most Chinese rural settlements, such details cannot be determined precisely. The stories villagers tell of the settlement process are often wrapped in legends tied to tales of refugees who, fleeing famine and warfare, were dispersed throughout the country in search of unoccupied land on which to acquire rights of settlement in order to start anew. Sometimes whole villages moved in response to perceived geomantic shortcomings of a current site (Hayes 1963, 143-144). Describing the creation of villages in the New Territories of Hong Kong, David Faure tells us that

the act of settling is one for which the villager does have a clear concept. . . . He associates it with the process by which an ancestor comes from afar, decides to make his home in a locality, shelters himself first in makeshift thatched sheds, and then replaces them gradually with brick or stone houses. In the process, he acquires the right to build houses, to reclaim waste land for cultivation, to gather fuel from the hillsides, to have access to his fields and houses, and to be buried eventually in a proper grave, if necessary, nearby. He raises a family, and passes these rights on to his descendants, who become the lineage now settled at the village. (1986, 1-2)

For some villages, genealogies of long-resident families, with their general record of births, marriages, and deaths of at least male progeny, provide a skeletal answer to questions concerning the original settlement and the vagaries of village life over time. Genealogies, in addition, sometimes include a succinct description of a family's origin, a listing of notable ancestors who through education and position brought status and wealth to a lineage, the acquisition or loss of property, as well as a discussion of the ancestral hall that is the repository for the memorial tablets of distant members (Hayes 1985, 79-81). For most villages, however, it is only a "general memory" of such movements that villagers use to date the arrival of their ancestors at a settlement site. As Margery Wolf tells us for Hotien village in Taiwan, listening to the elderly, "who have both the time and the interest to speculate about the past," helps historical reconstruction "from half-remembered stories of their own aged parents and grandparents" (1968, 11-12). Similarly, "walking the Chinese countryside to learn the lessons it still has to tell us about the past" (Golas 1980, 314) has aided many of the authors in tracing the origins and history of villages discussed in these chapters.

Access to water is an especially significant element in the choice of a village site and a factor that has contributed to a variety of rural settlement forms (Huang 1985, 55-57, 64-66; 1990, 145-147). On the North China Plain, strategically located shallow community wells, rarely exceeding ten meters in depth, anchored large villages to particular sites. Such wells provided the water to meet domestic needs and thus constrained the size of the residential complex. The ecological importance and fragility of fixed wells was nonetheless often ignored by villagers, who allowed the pollution of domestic wells by draft animals (Smith 1899, 28). In villages of southern China, where access to water sources was easier, a single village often embraces several separate residential clusters that draw water either from multiple wells, canals, ponds, or streams. Complementing a stream that threaded through Nanqing village in Guangdong province, for example, were some thirty small ponds, located so rainwater would drain into them to provide for the daily needs of villagers and for irrigation as well (Yang 1959, 10). Functions often were mixed, however, as in Phoenix village, Guangdong province, where water sources were frequently polluted because drinking water was drawn from locations along streams where others were washing clothes or toilet buckets, and from wells surrounded by filthy mud holes draining into them. Kulp found these unsanitary conditions to come "first from ignorance of the value of public sanitation and second, from carelessness" (1925, 59). Today, as in Half Moon village in the suburbs of Beijing, water increasingly is pumped from a common well and then distributed by flexible pipe to a "dragon's head" spigot within each village courtyard. But even in this relatively prosperous suburban area, just half a mile from Half Moon village, villagers carry water from a common village well to their homes, where the water is used sparingly for cooking, washing, and laundering, after which it is recycled to water the kitchen garden (Chance 1984, 27). Each of the authors in this volume addresses the question of water sources, and some the disposal of human waste.

Village dwellings have almost uniformly been described in the past by Western writers as inadequate in terms of sanitation and aesthetics. According to Arthur H. Smith, writing at the end of the nineteenth century, mountain dwellings were "dark, damp, and unwholesome at all seasons of the year," and cave dwellings were "quite free from any form of ventilation, a luxury for which no provision is made in the construction of a Chinese dwelling" (1899, 8–9). Poorly made bricks, even when fired, often broke easily when they were handled and, according to Smith, were "like well-made bread, full of air-holes," which served as tubes "by which the bibulous bricks suck up moisture from below, to the great detriment of the building of which they generally form merely the foundations, or perhaps the facings" (1899, 9). The authors in this volume explore the forms that dwellings take in their villages using photographs and line drawings. However, this book goes beyond the editor's previous books on Chinese vernacular architecture, which focused on individual dwellings (Knapp 1986; 1989).

Many Chinese villages barely stand out from the physical environments within which they have arisen, with only blurred boundaries marking areas of residence from adjacent cultivated land. In Sichuan, as discussed in Chapter 19, small hamlets of bamboo, wattle and daub houses are found placed among stands of bamboo amidst the rice fields; although all is the result of human action, the ensemble gives the appearance of a completely natural environment. Even where vegetation is less lush, such as on the North China Plain, the horizontality of earthen ochre walls of dwellings ties village settlements to the bare alluvial soil from which they are built.

Under normal peaceful conditions, Chinese villages in the past were relatively open to the outside world, but circumstances often led to fortification of villages and a clear delineation of settlement from the surrounding fields. G. William Skinner has posited a cyclical theory to explain wall building around many villages as an architectural response to unsettled conditions, with dynastic decline and attending banditry and rebellion prompting a process of community closure that frequently ended in the raising of village walls, patterns which differed from one area of the country to another (Skinner 1971, 280). This cycle of village fortification has been described well for Nian villages in the region north of the Huai River in Anhui and Jiangsu provinces, where continuing instability from the 1850s through the 1930s led to the transformation of open village forms into strongholds (Chiang 1954, 32–39; Perry 1980, 88–94). Some of these fortified villages were but temporary refuges, earthen forts occupied at night by poor villagers, who slept in huts made of wheat stocks. But where the wealth of affluent landowners made it possible, some fortifications in the 1930s in northern Jiangsu were quite substantial, with multiple walls of brick and stone, parapets, moats, and corner towers. Although the walls around most northern Chinese villages no longer exist, having been razed as stability replaced conflict, fragments of old walls and moats, such as those of Fengjiacun described in Chapter 17, echo the recurring instability of the past century.

Fortified or semifortified settlements were built in southeastern China by the Hakka in southwestern Fujian province, as discussed in Chapter 12, as well as in neighboring areas of Guangdong, Jiangxi, and Guangxi provinces. Much of this construction came in response to communal feuding between rival lineages or surname groups as well as interlineage conflict throughout the eighteenth and nineteenth centuries (Freedman 1958, 105–113; 1966, 104–117; Lamley 1977; 1990). The architectural evidence of past conflict between and among single-lineage villages continues to be evident in the massively fortified villages and watchtowers that remain throughout the rural landscapes of southeastern China.

Chinese villages and towns, however, generally have lacked conspicuous architectural built forms and spaces, such as the towers, broad plazas, imposing churches and courthouses, or other large public buildings found widely in the West. The most prominent building spaces found in Chinese villages and towns traditionally were temples *(simiao)* and lineage or clan halls, sometimes called ancestral halls *(zongci* or *citang)*. Structurally, they generally differed little from common dwellings, although in scale and ornamentation they often stood apart. In many Chinese villages, both northern and southern ones, the presence of a stunningly large tree with a broad area of shade, perhaps near the shrine to the local earth god *(tudigong)*, a bridgehead, or the area around a well or along a canal or pond, provided an area for common activity, a focus for identity, and perhaps a name. In Kaixiangong, studied by Fei Hsiao-tung, informal gatherings in the summer evenings were noted at the four bridgeheads (1939, 19). A larger open area, such as that formed where two roads meet, might provide a venue for children to play or, as in Half Moon village outside Beijing, a place for villagers of all ages to join together on summer evenings to watch television (Chance 1984, 27–28). Conspicuous forms that are the signature of individual villages are noted where appropriate, and an assessment is made of their community significance.

The space requirements of traditional rural economic practices characteristic of the region in which the villages are located are generally presented in the chapters that follow. In many villages, there are specific areas set aside for threshing, winnowing, drying, and storing crops. In others, space such as the flat roofs of dwellings, roads, and temple courtyards are "borrowed" for such purposes. These space requirements vary from area to area and reflect the different seasonal demands of grain, vegetable, tea, and silk production, for example. Specialty products of some villages as well as cottage industries may suggest other space uses. In many villages, there appears to be an incessant adjustment of space as activities seasonably compete for the limited space available. Each chapter explores the daily and seasonal activities found in a village and discusses how land and water transport are reflected in the layout and accessibility of the village.

The spatial extent of descent groups structured the patterns of social and religious organization found within many villages. In Guangdong and Fujian, large so-called lineage or clan villages traditionally provided a comprehensive exclusiveness not found in more heterogeneous villages (Freedman 1958; 1966). The clustering of kinsmen, when examined carefully, reveals the territorial separation of common descent groups, as seen, for example, in the fourfold division of Hotien village in Taiwan (Wolf 1968, 12). The spatial clustering of descent groups is not examined in this book, however.

In the past, in many of the atomistic village communities of rural China, relatively small temples or shrines were constructed to a *tudigong,* a tutelary deity whose dominion was a specified locale. Tudigong, sometimes called the "Earth God," traditionally was viewed by Chinese peasants as a low-level territorial bureaucrat to whom they reported births, marriages, and deaths. Tudigong then transmitted this information to his superiors in the multilayered pantheon. More than intermediary scribe and recorder, Tudigong also was a source of advice and assistance to peasants as they dealt with their daily lives. The shrines of *tudigong* often were associated with magnificent old trees or odd rock formations, as shown in the chapter on Sheung Wo Hang. Distinctive natural sites in many villages provided not only the locus of informal interaction among villagers but also an aesthetic focus. Usually modest in scale, the *tudigong* shrine was usually of cut stone or fired brick and rarely exceeded a meter in height. Incense and other offerings reveal the level of interaction between the villagers and this tutelary deity. In larger villages, the distribution of shrines to *tudigong* may be used as an index of village spatial organization. Although many such shrines were destroyed in the decades after 1949, many remain in Chinese villages, especially in the south.

The realms "administered" by individual *tudigong* shrines frequently were nested within an overlapping territorial hierarchy that had as its focus a larger, more elaborate, and more comprehensive temple. Such temples enabled the performance of ritual that took the individual beyond the household, beyond the locale governed by Tudigong, to an expanded level of social interaction even across lines of kinship. Such higher-order temples, such as the Shangdigong temple described by Margery Wolf in Taiwan, were supported by all villagers. Once a year, the image of the god, Shangdi, was set into a sedan chair and, accompanied by firecrackers and cymbals, given a tour of inspection of all sections of the village under his administration (1968, 13). These territorial gods served as metaphors for the civil system of authority, at once inhabiting and defining villages and village subdivisions (see Feuchtwang 1974). Temples may be found any place in Chinese villages but are frequently on the periphery, not because rituals were not central to Chinese life, but because most ritual activities traditionally were centered within the residence. Fei comments that "it would be more correct to regard the temples as the residences of priests and gods, who are not only segregated some distance from the ordinary people but are also separated from everyday community life except on special ceremonial occasions" (1939, 21). The absence of temples in most of the villages discussed in the chapters that follow reflects the extensive destruction of such structures in the decades after 1949.

Most Chinese villages today are hybrid places. In the past in many villages—especially those rich from locally produced grain or cottage industries such as silk production, or even those having benefited from the wealth of degree-earning officials or successful merchants—cyclical festivals centered on temples and shrines as well as ceremonies held within ancestral halls or within the home added a texture to villages as places that bound together time and space. In the decades after 1949, political campaigns in the People's Republic of China destroyed the social fundamentals of many of these activities, declaring them feudal superstitions and discrediting the lineage basis supporting many of them. The dismantling, destruction, or reassigned use of temples, shrines, monuments, and ancestral halls, among other vernacular forms, throughout China's countryside created spatial and social vacuums. In many villages today, however, not only are still-standing ancestral halls and temples being cleared of workshops that occupied them in recent decades, but new ceremonial facilities are also being built, as can be seen in Longlin and Cangpo villages. In many cases, only tentative steps are being taken toward restoration, as local officials in many locales continue to forbid the rituals that would breathe life back into the forms that continue to stand as mere cultural artifacts.

Over the centuries, most Chinese villages grew only slowly, with each generation of villagers bequeathing a cultural landscape not too different from the one it had itself inherited. Until recently, neither technological innovation nor intervention from outside the village contributed to rapid changes in most mainland Chinese villages. In recent decades, however, as sketched in Chapter 4, the pace of change has quickened in many villages. How individual Chinese villages are changing is addressed by most authors represented in this volume, many of whom look at the ways in which political movements since 1949 have contributed to changes in village form and morphology. Over the past decade, a seemingly unrelenting building craze or "building fever" (*jianfang re*), as the Chinese term it, has brought about the alteration not only of individual village buildings but also overall village form. In the mid-1980s, most Chinese villages carried out a planning exercise that resulted in a map of the current village and a planning map for the year 2000. These maps represent an attempt to reorder land use patterns by separating residential from productive spaces, by planning for public facilities, and by reducing the amount of land occupied by buildings.

Several chapters explore the degree to which old building sites are being used for new construction in villages or new areas are being developed to facilitate village expansion. In some cases, as is shown in the chapters by Shan Deqi, Joseph Wang, and Liu Baozhong, there is an enthusiasm for preservation and restoration, an effort to reclaim the magnificence of past architecture before forces destroy it. However, many unnoticed and unheralded traditional village landscapes in China face modification and destruction because their residents regard them as too ordinary, outdated, and dysfunctional to preserve. Still, the recent rediscovery of China's rich vernacular heritage of craft and symbolism offers at least some promise that more landscapes will be considered before they are summarily destroyed (see Lung 1991).

Each author's own experience in a village has been used as the starting point for observation, description, and analysis, with only implicit comparisons made between most villages. Neither individual authors nor the editor harbors any illusion that Chinese villages are treated exhaustively in this volume. Furthermore, it must be underscored that although villages in Hong Kong and Taiwan share many patterns with those on the mainland, the political, social, and economic environments within which rural settlements there developed over the past half century have been decidedly different from those of villages in the PRC. The placement of Sheung Wo Hang, Hong Kong, at the beginning of the "Tradition" section and Hsin Hsing, Taiwan, at the end of the "Transition" section suggests a degree of convergence with other Chinese villages, yet it also reveals the extent of divergence that accompanies change.

Each chapter focuses on the comprehension of known villages as *places,* emphasizing that which is visible, what one can look at and see. As readers will discover, not all of these villages resonate the China of the popular imagination, yet each village discussed is undeniably Chinese. Although each author attempts "to read" a Chinese village and use a vocabulary to describe its elements, the results should not be seen as a mere cataloging of the built environment. And although each author was asked to consider a specific array of village elements, no attempt was made to force each author to describe his or her village with a checklist through a common prism. Indeed, as a reading of the chapters will show, the voices and emphases of the various disciplinary perspectives vary yet complement one another as each village reveals its own order, its own complex of natural and human elements. While focusing on the physical appearance of individual villages, as these villages taken together begin to fill in the constellation that forms the Chinese countryside, *Chinese Landscapes* also documents more general social, economic, and political patterns.

CHAPTER 2

China's Rural Settlement Patterns

JIN QIMING AND LI WEI

CHINA, the most populous country in the world, is also the country with the largest rural population. More than 80 percent of China's population of over 1.13 billion people still live in a broad array of rural communities that range from relatively large compact villages rivaling towns in size to isolated farmsteads. Most of these settlements have a long history and definite regional patterns that reflect the physical and social diversity of China. Recent decades have witnessed dramatic improvements in China's rural sector, accompanied in many cases by the spatial reconstruction of rural landscapes.

Chinese villages differ, first, in terms of economic function, most depending on agricultural activities but some having a nonagricultural economic base. Agriculturally based villages include not only traditional grain-based farming villages, but also villages in which other primary economic activities such as herding, fishing, forestry, hunting, and pomiculture dominate. Grain-based farming villages are found throughout China, growing not only rice and wheat but a broad range of hardy grains. Herding villages are widely dispersed in the semiarid and arid areas of the country. Some of these villages are sedentary, whereas others are mobile. Not only are fishing villages found in the coastal and riverine areas of the country; some are found as well along natural and man-made lakes, where fish breeding and freshwater fishing play important roles. Over the past decade, especially, China has become one of the world's major freshwater fish breeding countries. Villages in many parts of the country specialize in the harvesting of timber products from nearby forests, and still others grow bamboo, mulberry bushes, tea, tung oil, and specialized fruit. In some marginal areas, such as those occupied by ethnic minorities like the Orogen (Elunchon), hunting is still the principal economic activity. Although villages purely engaged in sideline activities are rare, some villages specialize in the production of goods from the local area to supplement farming. The manufacture of millstones, stone tablets, and umbrellas (using bamboo and local paper coated with tung oil) are important sideline activities in some mountain villages. Silk and paper manufacture are carried out in many lowland rural areas.

In some rural areas of the country, nonagricultural activities play important roles in the formation of settlements. The highest-order rural settlement is the market town *(jizhen),* a settlement form that is essentially a village with a dominant farm-based economy but also a substantial—and today often growing—commercial sector. Commerce is usually concentrated along both sides of a street. Shops are usually open daily, and periodic fairs are characteristic. Many such settlements are transitional forms between true villages and designated towns (*jianzhi zhen*), the lowest-level settlement form in China's urban hierarchy. Small mining and industrial villages, taking advantage of pockets of natural resources excavated from the earth, are located in many areas of the country. Other nonagricultural village types include a variety of distinct forms such as border sentry villages, ferry villages, and villages focused on temples.

Village Shape

The shape or layout of Chinese villages ranges from tight discernible clusters to isolated dwellings that lack a formal nomenclature. Two basic morphological forms can be identified: nucleated villages and dispersed villages.

Within *nucleated villages (jicun),* houses and other associated buildings are built close together to form a compact settlement cluster. Spencer noted the "sheer compactness" of villages of this type, the general absence of green spaces and even space between dwellings (1971, 69). The population of Chinese nucleated villages varies from several thousand to fewer than a hundred residents. According to village layout, several subtypes of nucleated villages can be identified.

Compact villages (tuanzhuang) have a generally circular shape that may appear as an irregular polygon. Usually the east-west and the north-south axes vary little in length. Compact villages are usually located in or near the center of cropland where level land is easily accessible for village construction. Settlements throughout China's plains and basins are often of this type. Compact villages are the most common rural settlement pattern in China.

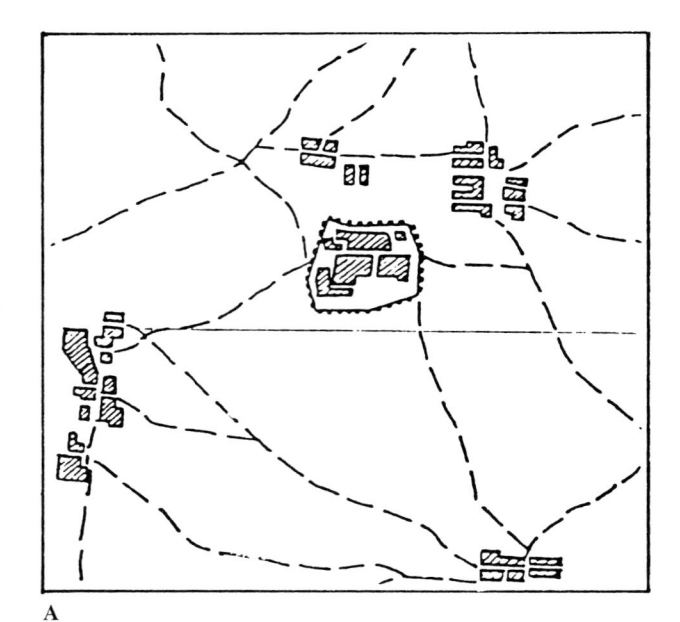

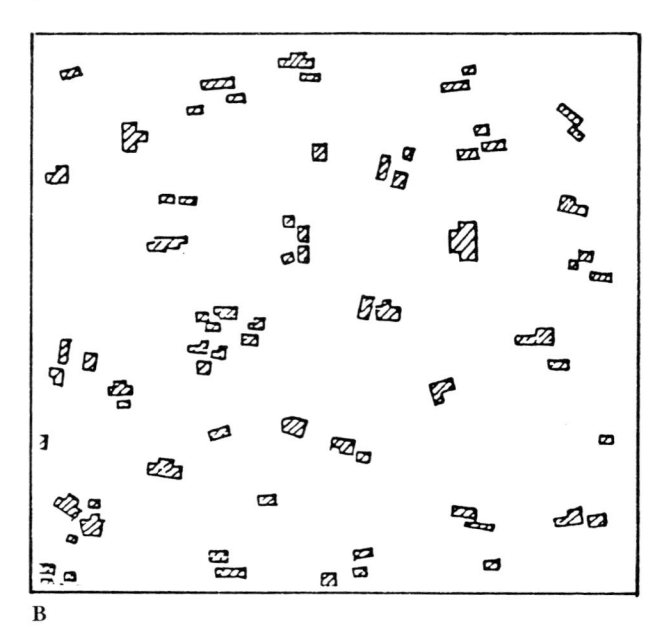

Figure 2.1. Common nucleated village plans: **(A)** Compact villages on the North China Plain; **(B)** compact villages in the lower Yangzi River region.

Among the advantages of compact villages are that people live close to each other, houses and roads are compactly laid out, and the space between buildings can serve community uses. This type of village, in addition to saving land, facilitates, in the modern period, the provision of public utilities such as sewage and communications systems. Disadvantages, especially if the village is large, include overcrowding and distance from farmland. Since most compact villages grew over time without planning, their internal arrangement is often one of disorder. There frequently are problems of ventilation, sunshine, and drainage, among others, which have led to disputes between neighbors.

Elongated or *linear villages (daizhuang)* are usually found along canals, rivers, or roads, sites that promote attenuated settlement forms. Following a Chinese preference for south-facing dwellings for enhanced sunlight and ventilation, elongated villages are more likely to extend from east to west than from north to south. Elongated settlements are usually built so as to avoid using farmland and are frequently found on natural or man-made levees with easy access to water. Though such a village may extend for a distance over 5 kilometers and contain several thousand people, most are only several hundred meters long. The distance between dwellings and farmland, the farming radius, is usually short. Chinese administrators generally believe that elongated villages are difficult to manage, especially with regard to the provision of public facilities such as schools, the propensity for traffic accidents, and, in the case of levees, the competing interests of habitation, on the one hand, and levee maintenance and flood protection, on the other.

Elongated villages found along river levees are principally located in the plains areas of the lower reaches of rivers in eastern China. Here, in generally sandy areas with water shortage problems, people usually live along the levees to ensure access to water year round. Smaller rivers may be dry during periods of drought, and a good deal of land cannot be used for agricultural purposes because of the needed irrigation canals. Thus, people build their houses on the broad levees to save farmland. In those plains areas with frequent floods, living on the levees allows residents to reduce or even avoid flood damage. Rivers, moreover, provide the convenience of water transportation. Shops in areas with networks of waterways sometimes have their fronts facing a street while their backs face the stream to facilitate the loading and unloading of goods.

Elongated villages are built along lake levees as well and on the naturally elevated areas that surround lakes or marshlands. Such villages are found throughout the middle and lower reaches of the Yangzi River (Changjiang) in eastern China, the eastern part of the North China Plain, and the northern part of the Northeast China Plain. During periods of extremely heavy precipitation, as the waters rise to flood, lake and marsh levee settlements are a safe haven.

Elongated villages along roads are widely scattered throughout the country and can be seen in every province. In the hilly areas of the Yunnan-Guizhou plateau, elongated settlements built along roads or streets are called "road villages" *(lucun)* or "street villages" *(jiecun)*. With good transportation, they are often convenient for commercial activities. Some "road villages" follow natural routes along the foot of a mountain or a river terrace and are thus topographically derived. In all types of elongated villages, dwellings may be found single or double file.

Another type of linear settlement looks like a string of beads: Several small compact villages in series may be found along a ridge, a river valley, or a lake, situated several hundred meters apart from each other.

Ring villages (huanzhuang) are not common in China but are sometimes found around a small

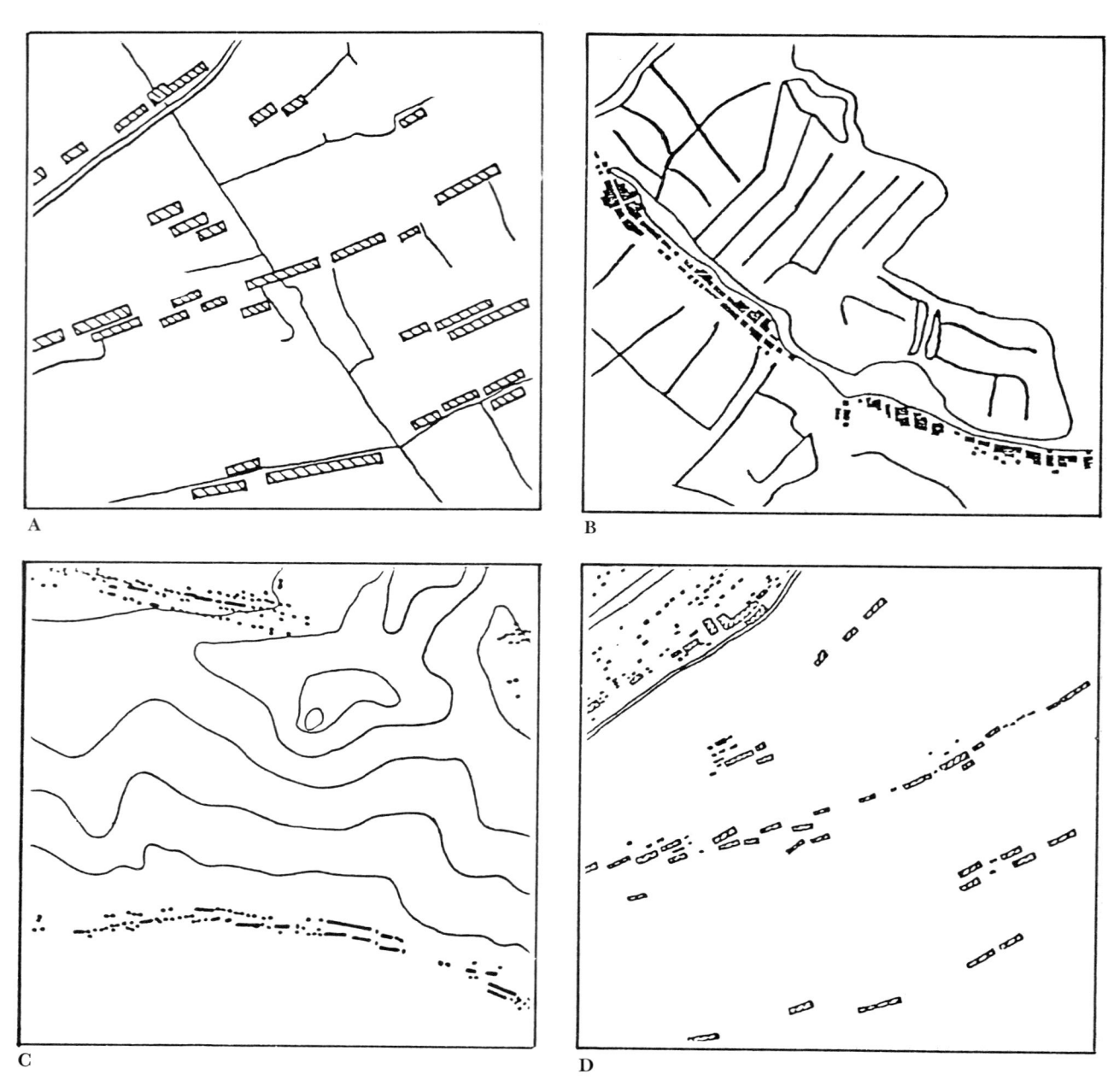

Figure 2.2. Common elongated or linear village plans: **(A)** Linear village on the sandy-soil plains; **(B)** linear village along a lake levee; **(C)** linear village at the base of a mountain; **(D)** linear village along a river levee.

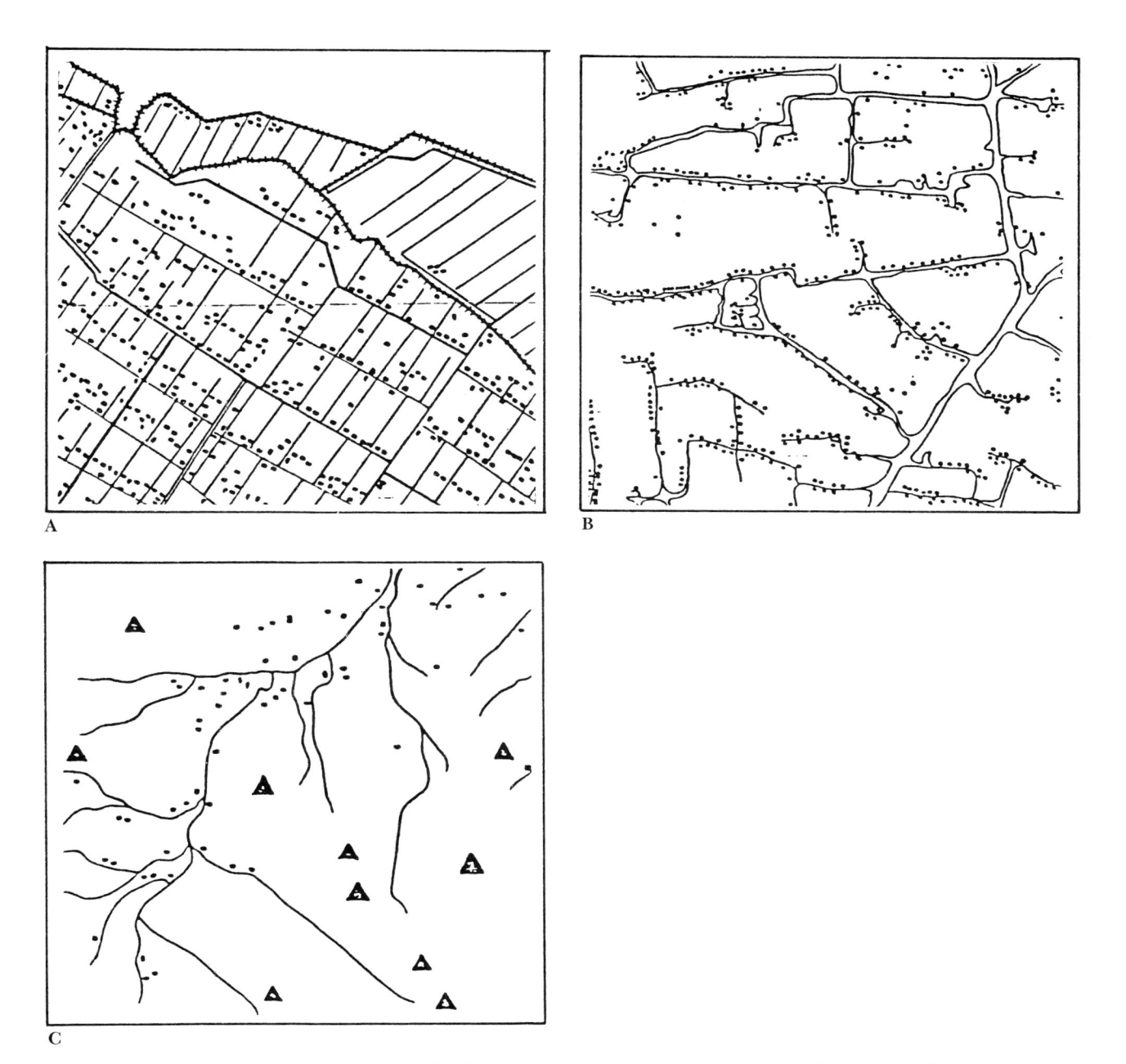

Figure 2.3. Common dispersed village plans: **(A)** Dispersed village along the coastal plain; **(B)** dispersed village in the lower Yangzi region, an area of canals; **(C)** dispersed village in mountainous area.

lake or hillock, or fitted to a river meander. In the level plains, if there is an isolated hillock, the village may be located in the upslope areas in order to preserve farmland and provide good drainage. In such piedmont areas, common sources of water are springs and shallow wells.

Dispersed villages (sancun) are communities in which dwellings are generally not contiguous but are distributed throughout the landscape. Although many dwellings may be single-family, some may be multiple-household extended family complexes. No clear boundaries identify such villages. In general, the "village" is defined by custom and administrative concurrence. Dispersed villages are not especially common in China but are found nonetheless in many areas of the country, including coastal as well as mountain areas. The two subtypes of dispersed settlement may be termed the "regular" or "standard" type *(guizexing)* and the "irregular" type *(buguizexing)*.

Where the distance between dwellings is fairly uniform, a regular dispersed village form exists. Such homesteads may be situated along a piedmont, river terrace, or road. Called "lala streets" *(lalajie)* in northeast China, villages of this type are found where individual houses, generally less than 100 meters apart, stretch along a road for 2 to 3 kilometers. In some coastal areas, such as at the mouth of the Yangzi River and along the Bohai Sea, new farmland reclamation in the twentieth century has brought with it such a pattern. Here farmlands are divided by irrigation canals into a grid system with 25 *mu* (15 *mu* equals 1 hectare) of land in a single cell farmed by one household, which has its dwelling built along a road bordering the cell.

Irregular dispersed villages are principally found in heavily dissected mountain areas, in both south and north China. In these areas, individual homesteads are dispersed without any recognizable pattern because of the scattered croplands. Settlement in such areas often was characterized by the displacement of aboriginal groups, who withdrew southward beyond Han control. Han Chinese settlers, finding the terrain inhospitable to compact settlement, then dispersed themselves throughout these rugged regions to better exploit the fragmented portions of valley and hillslope land available.

Dispersed settlement patterns have a number of advantages, including the ability to choose optimal locations with good ventilation and more natural light, avoidance of disputes with neighbors, and immediate accessibility to farmland. Disadvantages are numerous. For the most part, dispersed villagers have not had available to them basic services and amenities taken for granted by villagers living in compact villages. Even today, the costs of providing education, health, running water, cable radio service, electricity, and other services cannot be accomplished reasonably. Assistance of neighbors is not easy to obtain, nor is there much social interaction for isolated villagers. From the point of view of land use, individual dispersed households require more land than is needed for a comparable nucleated village, since each household demands its own threshing area and pond. However, dispersed villages are often found in areas where population densities are not great.

Special Rural Settlement Forms

The vast western plateaus of China are largely occupied by nomadic and seminomadic pastoralists, most of whom traditionally have lived in various types of tents (see Lung 1991, 57–60). The tents of Tibetan herdsmen are usually square and made of fur; those of Mongols and Kazakhs are round and made of felt. Mongolian yurts are relatively easy to pitch or strike and move. Nomadic households may live in a single yurt, or two if the household is large. The nomadic Mongols move at least four times and as often as ten times each year. Thus, this residential form is actually a mobile rural settlement.

Throughout the coastal zones of China, including the middle and lower reaches of the Yangzi River and the lower reaches of the Zhujiang, or Pearl River, many fishing households live on boats. Some vessels are transient; others are anchored in harbors, where they constitute a special settlement form. Throughout southern China, where boatmen are engaged in transport services, their residences are like those of herdsmen, a mobile rural settlement form.

Two unique settlement forms, the imposing tamped earth villages of southwestern Fujian and the subterranean habitats of the loessial plateau in northern China, will be discussed later in this chapter and in detail in subsequent chapters.

Village Size

Some 800 million people live in more than 5 million rural settlements in China. On average, then, each settlement provides a habitat for 160 persons, which by general Chinese standards would be a relatively small village of some twenty-five to thirty households. As a convenient but rough generalization for China as a whole, small villages have populations less than 200, medium-size villages between 200 and 1,000, and large villages in excess of 1,000. Village settlements of different sizes and types are usually found in most areas of the country, although certain types predominate in some regions. A variety of patterns is discernible even within a single province. Villages of different scales in general differ in their administrative and commercial characteristics.

Whether at the national level or by province, there is a clear relationship between topography and village size. However, although larger villages are characteristic of the broad plains of China and smaller villages of the more rugged areas, small villages are also distributed widely in the plains. Fragmented parcels of arable land, taking advantage of microclimates, are generally associated with small villages.

Large villages, exceeding 1,000 in population, are most common in areas of the country where arable land is concentrated and population densities are high. They are found in greatest numbers on the North China Plain, in northeast China, along the lower Yangzi River, and at the mouths of rivers along the southeast coast. Villages in these areas usually have household sizes ranging between 200 and 300 per village; they sometimes exceed 500 households, each household averaging five to six people. Today such large villages generally are designated as seats of township government *(xiang zhengfu suozaidi),* the successor of commune headquarters, established in 1958 to organize rural development. Where such a natural village *(ziran cun)* conforms to an administrative unit, either a township or an administrative village, there is an ease of administration not generally encountered with smaller villages. With such large villages, one normally finds a degree of commercialization with a limited variety of shops and services provided. Usually an elementary school is present in a large village. Although an overwhelming majority of the village population is engaged in primary economic activities, such villages have the appearance of proto-market towns. Market towns *(jizhen),* however, are by Chinese definitions clearly distinct from villages with more limited commercial activities.

In a 1937 survey of villages in Dingxian county, Hebei province, in north China, the largest village had approximately 800 households and the smallest 50 households, with an average of about 200 households. Nearby in Luanxian county, 81.9 percent of the villages had populations that exceeded 1,000 people. In the south-central areas of the North China Plain and in the central plain of northeast China, where large villages are most characteristic, some 30 to 80 large villages may be located in an area of 100 square kilometers. Many large villages are found within sight of each other throughout these regions. In the Hai River plain, there are some 50 natural villages per 100 square kilometers, whereas in the northern sections of the northeast plain this density is reduced to 10 to 20 per 100 square kilometers. Some coastal fishing villages in south China also exceed 1,000 in population.

Medium-size villages, those with populations between 200 and 1,000, are widespread throughout China. In most cases, several medium-size natural villages are combined to form a single administrative village, with the larger or better-established settlement becoming the site for the administration of the "village." Commerce is extremely limited in such villages. Perhaps a barber shop or a commission shop *(daixiaodian)* selling daily needs articles may operate, but little other business is transacted. An elementary school usually operates in the administrative center for the village. Throughout the country in recent years, the middle-sized villages have been most active in village planning and reconstruction.

Medium-scale villages, with populations somewhat above 200, are numerous in the densely populated and intensively cultivated lower Yangzi River valley. On average in this region, some 100 medium-size villages are found in an area of 100 square kilometers. However, along the shores of Lake Tai in southern Jiangsu province, the number of medium-size villages per l00 square kilometers ranges between 400 and 700.

Small villages, although numerous in China, have a smaller total farming population than the two larger village types. Such villages are usually without a defined street, shops, or an elementary school. Often the residents live in separate hamlets or isolated dwellings in which the amount of land given over to residential uses is comparatively large. This type is most common in hilly and mountainous areas in which arable land is fragmented and in which access to water is limited. However, small villages are found as well in the plains areas of south China, where such conditions do not limit occupance.

In the rugged areas of the Daxinganling, Yinshan, Helanshan, and Hengduanshan mountain ranges, the size of villages is especially small, often with only 3 to 5 households. Moreover, they are sparsely distributed, averaging 2 to 10 villages per 100 square kilometers. Even in the river valleys associated with these areas, villages often do not exceed 20 or so households.

Within Sichuan, the most populous of China's provinces with a total of more than 100 million people, few villages exceed 100 people, whereas the number of villages in any area is large. In western Sichuan, throughout the fertile and productive Chengdu plain, for example, there are more than 1,000 villages per 100 square kilometers. Small villages are found in hilly areas throughout the country: eastern and central Sichuan, the Jiangnan region, the coastal ranges of Zhejiang and Fujian, and in the more rugged areas of both north and northeastern China.

Major Rural Settlement Systems and Regions

Using a set of general criteria, it is possible to divide Chinese rural settlement into three major systems with eleven relatively discrete regional patterns. These criteria include (1) elements of settlement structure: settlement patterns, scale, density, housing forms, and general sociocultural characteristics; (2) the relationship between settlement and natural environment; and (3) economic functions of the village settlements, especially their relationships to land use and agricultural production. Using these criteria, three general rural settlement systems incorporating eleven regions, as shown in Figure 2.4, can be delimited. The major differences among the settlement sys-

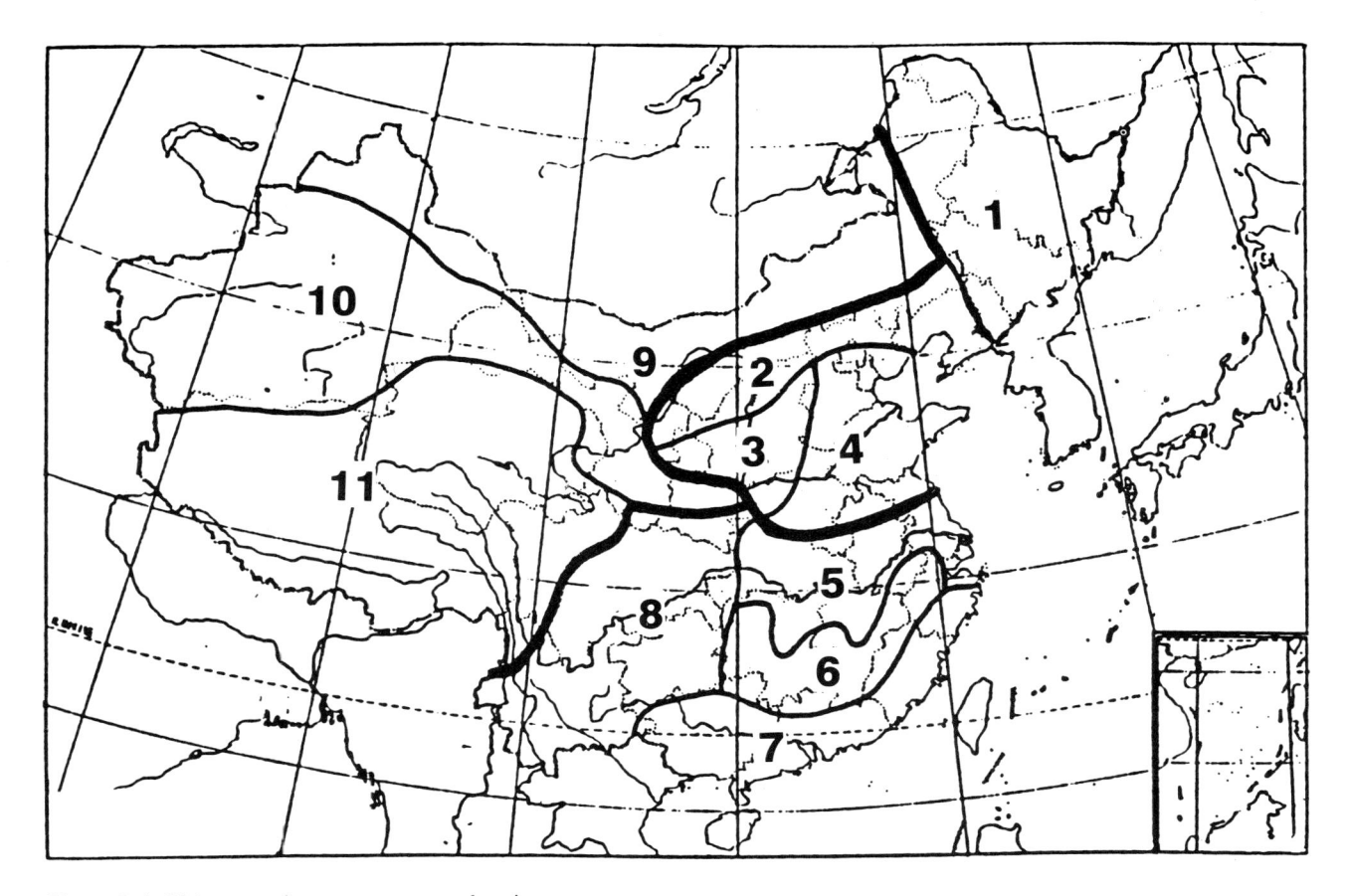

Figure 2.4. Chinese settlement systems and regions:

I. Northern Settlement System
    (1) Northeast China Rural Settlement Region
    (2) Great Wall Rural Settlement Region
    (3) Loess Plateau Rural Settlement Region
    (4) North China Plain Rural Settlement Region

II. Southern Settlement System
    (5) Middle-Lower Yangzi River Rural Settlement Region
    (6) South Yangzi River Hill Areas Rural Settlement Region
    (7) Southeast Coastal Rural Settlement Region
    (8) Southwest Rural Settlement Region

III. Western Settlement System
    (9) Northern Rural Settlement Region
    (10) Northwestern Rural Settlement Region
    (11) Qinghai-Xizang (Tibet) Rural Settlement Region

Table 1. Characteristics of Settlement Systems

	Northern System	Southern System	Western System
Major house types	houses with flat roofs and courtyards, *kang*	more storied dwellings, slope roofs	variety of types, tents
Scale	small, medium, large	small, medium, large	small
Density	generally dense	scattered	most scattered
Major form	compact	compact and elongated	dispersed, mobile
Environment	continental	tropical and subtropical	arid, semiarid
Agriculture	wheat and hardy grains	rice	stock raising

Table 2. Comparisons of Settlement Scale and Density

Township/County/Province	Settlement Region	Landform	Number of Villages Total	Small	Medium	Large	Villages per 100 km²	Average Village Population
Mishan/Heilongjiang	1	plain	837				18.5	278
Daozi/Qianan/Heilongjiang	1	plain	17	0	15	2		501
Shangyi/Hebei	2	plateau	641				24.0	264
Shahe/Anshan/Liaoning	2	plain	24	1	7	16		994
Xiji/Ningxia	3	loess	1825				58.0	156
Yijing/Yongshou/Shaanxi	3	loess	42	25	15	2		257
Anxin/Hebei	4	plain	185				25.5	1708
Shitun/Tongshan/Jiangsu	4	plain	57	4	40	13		772
Wujin/Jiangsu	5	plain	8303				471.0	149
Yingfang/Jiangning/Jiangsu	5	plain	129	113	16	0		140
Shuangxi/Chenggu/Shaanxi	6	low mountain	55				48.9	55
Dongshang/Yifeng/Jiangxi	6	hilly	116	114	2	0		56
Xiangtan/Hunan	6	hilly area	9512				349.3	110
Zhenhai/Zhejiang	7	coastal	1335				173.8	315
Yuhong/Lingyun/Guangxi	8	mountain	191	180	11	0	105.4	81
Gele/Huaning/Yunnan	8	mountain	83	64	19	0		140
Weibin/Xianyang/Shaanxi	10	valley	22				67.7	980

SOURCE: Compiled by Jin Qiming.

tems are shown in Table 1. Some comparisons of settlement scale and density within the regions are presented in Table 2.

Northern Settlement System

Northeast China Rural Settlement Region

All of the provinces of Heilongjiang and Jilin, part of eastern Liaoning province, and the northeastern portion of the Inner Mongolia Autonomous Region belong to this region, one of substantial physical and settlement diversity. With an extensive territory, abundant cropland, a development history of Han Chinese settlement that goes back only to the mid-nineteenth century, numerous draught animals and dryland crops, village settlements here usually have broad hinterlands with a great deal of unused arable land between the villages. Settlements are generally located on gently sloping sites or in river valleys, and building lots are comparatively large, although they vary from place to place within the region. A 1980 survey of building lots in Jilin province showed an average per capita building lot of 318 square meters, at least 1½ to 2 times the size of lots in north China and in the Yangzi basin. Dwellings commonly have a courtyard or garden with a low surrounding wall. There are limited settlements in the mountains, but these too have relatively large building lots.

Settlement sizes vary and include small, middle, and large villages, with a majority of villages being large. There are more than 47,000 villages in Heilongjiang province, each averaging 382 persons per village. Of the 971 villages that are seats of township governments and also market towns, each has an average population of more than 2,600. Overall the density of villages is low, with between 10 and 20 villages per 100 square kilometers.

The methods of construction and internal structure of dwellings in northeast China meet the needs of a climate of long, cold, snowy winters and short, warm, rainy summers. Winter averages six months of the year, with a winter period of as many as 230 days in the northern sections of the region. It is not surprising, then, that the *kang*, or heated bed, is a common fixture of most dwellings. In addition, *huoqiang*, or heated walls, built like *kang* with flues between the bricks, are used in some places to create a heat radiating surface to provide warmth in the winter period. Dwellings throughout the region generally have steep double-sloped roofs, with the exception of the dwellings of the Korean ethnic minority, which generally have four slopes (see Zhang 1985).

Great Wall Rural Settlement Region

This narrow region stretches along the Great Wall from the coast in southern Manchuria inland into the semiarid areas of the country. It includes the central and western sections of Liaoning, northern Hebei, eastern Shanxi, the Yellow River meander areas in Inner Mongolia, and the Yinchuan plain of the Ningxia Hui Autonomous Region. Farming is the major agricultural activity throughout the region, with dryland grains as the main crops. Limited rainfall generally restricts agricultural development and settlement. Available arable land is also limited.

Villages here are relatively large and sparsely located. For the most part, two natural villages form a single administrative village, although in some cases a single natural village constitutes an administrative village. In the Liaoning and Shanxi province portions of this region, villages with populations exceeding 1,000 are common, whereas those with populations below 200 are comparatively rare. Farther west in the meander areas of the Yellow River, where crop yields are low, about half the villages have populations around 200. Distances between villages average 3 to 5 kilometers, significantly greater than distances on the North China Plain. In more remote areas, especially in the hills, single dwellings, small hamlets, and villages with fewer than 100 people are found.

Except for the mountainous areas of northern Hebei and western Liaodong provinces, where stone is used for house construction, the walls of dwellings throughout the Great Wall Rural Settlement Region are commonly made of tamped earth or adobe bricks. Houses are often rather large and low with both front and back yards for vegetable growing. In areas of about 400 to 600 millimeters annual precipitation, flat or slightly arched roofs are common. These roofs can be used to dry grain in the sun and have become a characteristic house form here. Because of the cold winter, with a January average temperature of -8°C to -16°C, the windows facing north are small or absent, whereas windows facing south are quite large. Houses with huge southern glass windows occupying half the facade can be seen throughout the region. Although the Han nationality predominates in villages in the region, pastoral Mongols living in yurts are found as well in the central sections.

Loess Plateau Rural Settlement Region

Subterranean dwellings, unique to this region, are a settlement form with a long history. Throughout the loessial plateau in extensive portions of the provinces of Henan, Shanxi, Shaanxi, Ningxia, and Gansu, people have dug into the thickly layered loess to fashion subterranean dwellings. The loessial plateau is mantled with between 20 and 200 meters of fine silt, *huangtu* or "yellow earth," which has been blown in over millennia from the interior. Much of the loessial plateau, moreover, has been dramatically dissected into ravines by summer downpours, with perhaps only 10 percent remaining as a broad and level plateau. Since subterranean dwellings require only the living earth, they cost little, are easy to build, and provide a reasonably weatherproof house that is warm in winter and cool in summer. A shortcoming is that they are often badly ventilated and some are too damp. New types of cave dwelling have been designed to improve on the living environment.

As will be discussed in greater detail in Chapter 11, such dwellings comprise two types, cliffside dwellings and pit-type dwellings. Cliffside type subterranean settlements are excavated horizontally into the face of a loess bank or bluff *(kaoshan yaodong)*; nearby level land is left for tillage. Such settlement sites are often elongated, with linear groupings of residences along a gully face. In the front of each dwelling, the excavated soil is usually spread and pounded to create a forecourt.

In some areas of the loessial plateau that are less dissected and more mesa-like, peasants still dig square pits into the soil to form a "sunken courtyard." Off to the sides dwelling rooms that have the form of arch-shaped caves are excavated to form a *diyao* or *dikengyaodong*. Some adjacent chambers are interconnected and form a dwelling complex to house a large household.

Wherever possible, cliffside dwellings and the principal residential rooms of pit-type dwellings are oriented toward the south, as is the general case with surface dwellings elsewhere in China. Individual units of the cave dwellings are approximately 4 meters wide and 6 meters in depth. A door fits into the excavated opening and is surrounded with framed windows to admit air and light. Both the opening, often filled in with wood or cut stone, and the ceiling inside are arch-shaped. Cliff-type dwellings usually occupy marginal lands and thus do not compete for farmland, whereas pit-type villages destroy potential farmland as they are constructed. Above-ground dwellings are encountered in the region as well (see Hou et al. 1989; Golany 1992).

Settlement throughout this region is sparse, reflecting the overall low densities of population.

In the Yan'an area of Shaanxi province, the overall density is only 40 people per square kilometer, only a tenth of the densities found in the North China Plain and the Wei River valley to the south. Here, one can often walk half a day without encountering a village. Access to drinking water is a major problem throughout the region, and villagers often walk long distances to small streams in the valley bottoms to obtain water that they then carry back to their dwellings higher up. Subterranean villages are generally loosely structured, built to take advantage of terrain and microclimate characteristics.

Although one can encounter villages that exceed 1,000 or have fewer than 100 people, most settlements in this region range between 100 and 200. Three to five natural villages are generally organized into a single administrative village. Liangzi township, Yongshou county, in Shaanxi province, for example, has thirty-two natural villages with an average population of 243. Fourteen villages have populations below 100, five between 100 and 200, eleven between 200 and 500, and one between 500 and 1,000. The largest village has a population of 1,073; the smallest only 6 people.

Major efforts have been made in recent years not only to improve the quality of subterranean dwellings but also to improve these villages themselves. The importance of this task is suggested by the fact that even today some 40 million Chinese live in subterranean villages.

North China Plain Rural Settlement Region

The North China Plain Rural Settlement Region is one of the oldest occupied regions of the country. It includes all of Shandong province, the central and southern portions of Hebei, all except the western parts of Henan, the portions of northern Jiangsu along the Longhai railway line, and the Suxian area of northern Anhui. This is a region of hot summers and cold winters, with precipitation about 800 millimeters. Dryland crops, principally wheat and hardy grains, as well as cotton are dominant.

For the most part, villages throughout this region are large and compact. Indeed, large villages are more widely distributed here than elsewhere in China. At the least, the number of households in a village exceeds one hundred; some have more than one thousand households (Table 3). Villages on the North China Plain are fairly evenly distributed, owing to the long history of cultivation in this region. That the dry crops grown here require less attention from farmers than the rice cultivated farther south helps explain why fields are often at a greater distance from settlements. On average, the distance between villages on the North China Plain is 1 to 2 kilometers, with 35 to 70 large villages within a 100-

Table 3. Village Size: Qixian County, Henan Province

Township	Number of Villages	Average Village Population	Under 100	100–200	200–500	500–1000	Over 1000	Largest Village
Zhuanji	64	635	1	9	15	33	6	4400
Xingkou	53	649	1	3	17	28	4	3450
Yanggu	47	715	0	5	13	22	7	6400

SOURCE: Compiled by Jin Qiming.

square-kilometer area. As a result, agricultural densities are substantial, generally exceeding 500 people per square kilometer. By comparison, in the densely settled Yangzi region to the south, on average 200 to 400 smaller villages are located within an area of 100 square kilometers. In Luancheng county of Hebei province on the North China Plain, for example, nearly 46 percent of the 180 villages have populations less than 1,000, 28 percent between 1,000 and 2,000, 18 percent between 2,001 and 3,000, 6 percent between 3,001 and 4,500, nearly 2 percent between 4,501 and 10,000, and one village has 12,587 people. Even in these large villages, 80 to 90 percent of the population is engaged in agriculture. Villages generally are smaller in the areas to the south of the Yellow River than they are to the north of the river, with more villages of between 200 and 500 people.

Market towns historically have been well developed throughout this region. According to early-twentieth-century statistics for Hebei province, there were on average 6 market towns in each county, even though at that time economic conditions were weak. Even after 1949, when there were only 10 designated towns in all of Hebei province and many county government seats were located in villages, market towns existed in large numbers. According to a 1953 survey, more than 2,000 market towns were found throughout Hebei, but, because of governmental policies, these weakened in the following decades. With the expansion of the commodity economy in the 1980s, many market towns have been revived. By the end of 1984, some 2,200 were found in Hebei alone, averaging 15.8 per county. Designated towns have also increased in Hebei to 420, averaging 3 per county.

Siheyuan are the characteristic dwelling form of this region. In overall composition, a *siheyuan* is a quadrangle with buildings on four sides surrounding a large courtyard (see Blaser 1979; Lung 1991, 22–26). Such dwelling complexes generally have an orientation toward the south, balanced side-to-side symmetry, and a clear axis. The principal building in the complex is in the rear and faces south. Each building is broader than it is deep and usually divided into three bays *(jian)*. *Siheyuan* are associated with the city of Beijing and are frequently called Beijing courtyard houses, but they are found in rural areas as well. However, because of economic conditions, many in the rural villages of the North China Plain live in less-developed dwellings. In many cases, the dwelling is a simple rectangle without the courtyard; in others the courtyard complex is incomplete.

Southern Settlement System

Middle-Lower Yangzi River Rural Settlement Region

This region has as its axis the middle and lower reaches of the Yangzi River, running from Yichang at the entrance to the Yangzi Gorges in the west to the sea in the east. It encompasses the broad and varied flood plains located between the Huai River in the north and the Jiangnan hills to the south. An area of temperate climate and fertile soil, this region is one of the most densely settled areas of China. Not only is rainfall sufficient, generally exceeding 1,000 millimeters per year, water for irrigation of paddy fields is well developed through a network of trunk and secondary canals.

The number of villages throughout the middle and lower reaches of the Yangzi River region is staggering, ranking first in the country. Within any given county, the number of villages may be somewhere between 4,000 and 8,000. With a dense settlement pattern of 200 to 500 villages per 100 square kilometers in some areas, there is a separate village every quarter or half kilometer. On both banks of the Yangzi River in this region, population densities reach 1,000 people per square kilometer.

Accordingly, villages here are relatively small, often with only 30 to 60 households each. Those with more than 100 households are not common (Table 4). Villages in the hills are generally smaller than those in the plains. For example, in the Dabie Mountains of Anhui province, Jinzhai county has 7,950 natural villages, which have an average of 66 people each. Here approximately 19 natural villages are combined to form a single administrative village. Market towns throughout the region are also small, often with a population of less than 1,000. Compared to those on the North China Plain, market towns in this region often have larger nonagricultural populations. The demands of rice cultivation in the region place most villagers only a short distance from their fields.

Table 4. Middle-Lower Yangzi River Settlement Region Village Populations

	Number of Natural Villages	Average Village Population	Villages per 100 km^2
Gaoyou county Jiangsu	5764	124	301
Wujin county Jiangsu	8303	149	471
Jiading county Shanghai	3427	128	691
Jiashan county Zhejiang	1772	195	351
Wangjiang county Anhui	2231	216	167
Tianmen county Hubei	5841	211	238

SOURCE: Compiled by Jin Qiming.

Three somewhat different settlement subregional patterns can be discerned within this region: the hilly areas located in the upper reaches of the Hanshui River and the hills to the south of the Yangzi River in southern Anhui and Jiangsu provinces, the lower reaches of the Yangzi River, and the central plains of the Yangzi River. Within the hilly areas, villages are rather dispersed, small in size, and located on lower hill slopes above the valley bottoms. Houses made of tamped earth and thatch are still found in these less developed areas of the region. The coalescing plains of the lower Yangzi River encompass a network of canals that cut between extensive rice paddy fields. Along the coast, the villages are relatively dispersed. In the sandy areas of the Yangzi Delta, village size is generally between 500 and 1,000. To the west of the delta, village size is smaller, and they are closer together and more densely located. Most villages within this region are located along canals and not roads.

Housing throughout this region is generally substantial, owing to the historically high level of agricultural productivity and commercialization. Even prior to 1949, brick and tile dwellings were common, although thatch dwellings also were found in great numbers. In Lin'an county, Zhejiang province, for example, a pre-1949 survey revealed that 49 percent of the dwellings were multistoried, 23 percent were single-story, and 28 percent were thatched. Dwellings here are not only generally higher than those in northern China, they also are deeper. Although houses in this region are often sited, as they are in north China, to face south or southeast, the need is less for passive solar heating in winter than for ventilation in summer by the relatively steady winds. Buildings here are generally constructed to foil the penetration of sun into them. Thus, they have few windows, and broad overhanging eaves are common. The walls of many dwellings are painted white with a lime plaster to reflect the sun's rays. Heavy rainfall is shed from steeply pitched roofs.

Dwellings in the middle and lower Yangzi region are often two-story rectangles comprising three, five, or seven connected bays (see Zhongguo 1984). The larger rectangles are usually extensions of a three-bay base. Substantial work space, storage, and a kitchen are usually allocated to the first floor, as is some living space. Second floors are used for living as well as for grain storage. L-shaped, U-shaped, courtyard-type dwellings, as well as variants on these patterns are also found in the region. An important element in many of these dwellings is an open room to facilitate ventilation. Skywells *(tianjing)*, relatively narrow shafts built into a dwelling that resemble small courtyards, are also employed to evacuate hot air from many dwellings and lead light, cool air, and rainwater into the interiors.

South Yangzi River Hill Areas Rural Settlement Region

The region comprises southern Anhui, western Zhejiang, and most of Jiangxi and Hunan. While some peaks in this region exceed 1,000 meters, most of the area is rugged hills. Although this region shares the climatic characteristics of the Middle-Lower Yangzi River Region, the topographic differences are principally responsible for the differences in settlement patterns.

Villages are irregularly and sparsely distributed in this hilly region, occupying locations on sunny hillslopes and in small basins. Generally villages have fewer than 200 people in them, with most having around 50. Here five or six natural villages constitute a single administrative village. Some of the smallest villages in the country are found here (Table 5). For example, of the 116 natural villages in Dongshang township, Yifeng county, in northwestern Jiangxi province, only eight have populations in excess of 100 people; many are composed of only three to five households. Thus, the hinterlands of individual villages and market towns are comparatively extensive. The overall population density of this region is between 200 and 300 per square kilometer as compared to 600 to 1,000 in the Middle-Lower Yangzi River Region.

Dwellings throughout the hills of this region are often two-story and generally of tamped earth or adobe bricks, largely because of the absence of coal resources to fire bricks. Cut stone is used as well in some areas for wall construction up to window level, with tamped earth or adobe brick above to the roof line. The forms of dwellings differ greatly in the region, reflecting local customs. H-shaped patterns are common in the Huizhou area of Anhui province. Such dwellings have a skywell in the front and back of the dwelling; one of the two skywells usually contains a small pool lined with cut stone. Dwellings of this type in Hongcun village, Yixian county, Anhui, are discussed in Chapter 8. Wood is used to a much

Table 5. South Yangzi Hills Settlement Region Village Populations

	Number of Natural Villages	Average Village Population	Villages per 100 km²
Tongkou county Hunan	6010	104	273
Xiangtan county Hunan	9512	110	349
Xinchang county Zhejiang	1842	212	154
Wandai county Jiangxi	2967	129	174
Yifeng county Jiangxi	2310	103	119

SOURCE: Compiled by Jin Qiming.

greater extent in these dwellings than in other areas of the country.

Southeast Coastal Rural Settlement Region

Comprising southeastern Zhejiang, all of Fujian, Guangdong, Taiwan, and Hainan provinces, and the Guangxi Zhuang Autonomous Region, this portion of China has striking mountain ranges, narrow coastal plains, and short rivers that rush from the mountains to the sea. Ninety percent of Fujian is mountains; the other areas have a smaller percentage. Several prominent river basins, valleys, and deltas are found within this region—the Pearl River Delta, Hanjiang River Delta, West River Plain, and Minjiang River Valley, among others. The region has a subtropical climate that is both hot and humid. Marked differences of climate occur between coastal and inland areas as well as between the mountains and lowlands. Historically, this has been a region of substantial cultural and linguistic differentiation. This rich variety is clearly reflected in the diversity of settlement forms.

The scale and form of villages differ between the coastal and inland areas. Villages are rather small on Hainan Island, but in the more densely populated and productive Pearl River Delta and other productive areas, they are relatively large. In a 1980 survey carried out in Guangdong province, the 59,162 people of Lanbu township lived in 101 villages and the 95,002 people of Pingzhou township lived in 140 villages, with villages averaging 600 to 700 people. Most of these villages comprised a large central village *(zhongxin cun)* with several satellite hamlets. The large central village typically exceeded 1,000 in population, about four times the population of the related hamlets. The largest villages in southeastern China are found in the Chaoyang-Shantou plain area of northeastern Guangdong province. Here, where the population is large but arable land limited, average village size exceeds 1,000 and small villages are not common. The 65,601 residents living in Chengjiao township of Chaoyang county inhabit 21 natural villages with an average population of more than 3,000. The same pattern appears in neighboring townships, and there are several villages with populations that exceed 6,000.

Throughout the mountainous areas, however, where arable land is limited, transportation inconvenient, and population densities low, smaller villages are widely dispersed, with villages size averaging about 200 people. An example is found in Tunchang township, Tunchang county, on Hainan Island, where 14,974 people live in 78 villages, each with a population less than 200. Throughout the ethnic minority areas of Guangxi, similar small villages are numerous. In general, the dispersed nature of arable land and availability of water have led to a dispersed form of small villages that take form according to local topographic and social conditions.

A particularly unique settlement form of imposing castlelike buildings is found scattered throughout Longyan, Nanjing, Shanhang, and Yongding counties of southwestern Fujian as well as in northeastern Guangdong province. Multistoried tamped-earth-walled villages *(tulou,* or "earth buildings") have been built here over the centuries by Hakka (Kejia) people, a Han Chinese ethnic subgroup who migrated into the region from central China. Having migrated into these rugged areas rather late and finding themselves unwelcomed by earlier settlers, the Hakka expropriated marginal land and built substantial fortified building complexes with meter-thick walls of tamped earth. Two main shapes—circles and squares—dominate. Circular complexes have diameters that may exceed 70 meters and may have as many as three hundred rooms to house an extended family or clan, all of whom share a common surname. A village in Nanjing county is discussed in Chapter 12.

Southwest Rural Settlement Region

Southwestern China is framed by mountains and includes the Red Basin of Sichuan, most of the Yunnan and Guizhou plateaus, as well as the upland areas of southern Shaanxi and southwest Hubei provinces. Throughout the region, rivers cut deeply into the hillslopes before opening into intermontane plains of various sizes. The relative physical isolation imposed on the region by the encircling mountains has played a major role in ameliorating climate. Instead of the considerable seasonal extremes of temperature one normally would expect in the interior of Asia and at high elevations, in the basins and valleys of Sichuan and Yunnan especially, the differences in summer and winter temperatures are far smaller than those found along the coastal areas of China. Except in the high mountains themselves, snow and freezing temperatures are rare in the region. Together with adequate rainfall year round, the overall climatic conditions make possible a growing season that lasts eleven months in most parts of the region. Such a growing season is common in Sichuan province, which alone supports some 100 million people, a tenth of China's population, on some of the most intensively farmed areas in the country. To the south of Sichuan, the Yunnan plateau is strikingly temperate for its latitude. In Yunnan as well as Guizhou, heavily leached or eroded soils set limits on agriculture and have helped guide settlement.

Because this region is not only large but physiographically complex, it should not be surprising that there is great variety in settlement and housing forms. Furthermore, this region is ethnically diverse, peopled by some fifty of China's non-Han ethnic minorities, contributing further to the mosaic of habitat found here. The region can be divided into four settlement subregions: the western Sichuan plain subregion; the eastern Sichuan, western Hubei, and southern Shaanxi subregion; the Yunnan-Guizhou subregion; and the southern Yunnan subregion.

The western Sichuan subregion has the most striking and longest history of Chinese settlement in southwestern China. Especially noteworthy is the intricate Dujiang weir on the Chengdu plain, which has been in continuous use for some 2,200 years to regulate the flow of river water into and across one of China's most fertile plains. This engineering achievement has been an important factor in the ability of the plain to support a very dense farming population of between 500 and 800 in some twenty dispersed villages per square kilometer. Dispersed hamlets, here called *yuanzi* or courtyards, each traditionally contained about 10 households. Several of these *yuanzi* are discussed in Chapter 19. The houses found in *yuanzi* traditionally have been built of adobe bricks, arranged into an L- or U-shaped dwelling that frames a courtyard. Similar dwellings have always been found in the adjacent uplands, but there only some five or six *yuanzi* per square kilometer are found. Throughout this region, the principal concern in house construction has been to keep the dwelling cool and dry in spite of the high summer temperature and humidity levels outside. Substantial eaves typically shade the facade of most dwellings, and attention is given to enhancing ventilation.

In the hilly areas of eastern Sichuan, western Hubei, and southern Shaanxi, villages are small, dispersed, and not evenly distributed. For example, in the 8.7 square kilometers of Shaheying township in the upper reaches of the Hanshui River of southern Shaanxi, there are only 17 natural villages, averaging only 2 per square kilometer. More striking is that of Yanjing township, with 81 small villages averaging only 76 people per village spread over 42.8 square kilometers. In the rugged portions of Yichang county in Hubei, there is less than one village per square kilometer. For the most part, the degree of dispersion and the size of these villages are a function of degree of hillslope, quality of available soils, and microclimates. Throughout this region, the shape of dwellings evidences a high degree of flexibility in accommodating to the terrain. Front courtyards are rare, largely because of the scarcity of level land on which to spread them; land adjacent to a dwelling that is suitable for farming is used for that purpose rather than to accommodate the kind of courtyard so commonly found elsewhere in China. Nonetheless, at the rear of the dwelling, where it abuts the hillslope, a small "courtyard" might be marked out for storage and the stabling of animals. The dwellings themselves are frequently built of wooden frames constructed in a steplike fashion on the hillslopes, with the back higher than the front. Construction materials have always been drawn from the immediate environs. Thus bamboo, wood, and soil predominate.

Although, as elsewhere in this large region, the villages of the Yunnan-Guizhou plateau are small in scale, there are differences in the distributions of those in the plains and those in the hills. Table 6 shows these differences for two townships in Huaning county of Yunnan province. In the better developed lowland areas around Kunming, the capital of Yunnan, however, villages are relatively large and evenly distributed. Here, dwellings are usually rectangular, with flanking projections that define a small courtyard. The villages and dwellings of the non-Han ethnic minorities in the Yunnan-Guizhou region vary, although many elements of their settlements and habitats echo those found elsewhere in China (see Jin 1989, 302–310; Yunnan 1986).

The rugged topography of southern Yunnan has set limits on settlement, but here also villages vary in scale from small hamlets to those exceeding 2,000 in size. Villages in this subregion average about 200 people, or some forty to fifty households.

Throughout all of the subregions of southwest China, complex elements contribute to the choice of settlement sites: elevation, topography, rainfall, wind, soil type and thickness, possibility of floods, economic conditions, and transportation, among other factors. In general, village densities are lower than those found elsewhere in the southern regions of China.

Western Settlement System

The Western Settlement System emcompasses more than a third of the territory of China, representing most of the country that lies outside of

Table 6. Scale of Villages in the Yunnan-Guizhou Plateau

Township	Terrain	Number of Villages	Average Village Population	Under 100	100–200	200–500	500–1000	Over 1000	Largest Village
Gele	hills, valleys	83	140	33	31	19	0	0	308
Panxi	mixed: plains, hills	95	284	19	21	34	10	3	1740

SOURCE: Compiled by Jin Qiming.

what traditionally has been called China proper. An extensive region of substantial physical contrasts, it comprises much of the broad semiarid and arid area to the north and west of China's Great Wall as well as the high Qinghai-Xizang plateau. Although much of the region is uninhabitable because of aridity and remains empty, Figure 2.4 reveals that a portion of the region penetrates deep into the heart of China and serves as a transitional settlement zone between the Northern Settlement System and the Southern Settlement System. Non-Han minority groups, sharing ethnic affinities with groups across China's borders, are numerous. Inner Mongolia, Xinjiang, and Xizang (Tibet) were accorded the status of autonomous regions to acknowledge the distinct cultural patterns that separate them from the dominant Han culture in China. However, the in-migration of Han Chinese in recent decades, especially into the cities of the region, has contributed to significant changes in population structure.

The Western Settlement System is subdivided into three regions: Northern, Northwestern, and Qinghai-Xizang. Rural settlement in all three regions is based less on agriculture than on herding, an economic and ecological fact that has guided settlement patterns that differ significantly from elsewhere in the country.

The Northern Rural Settlement Region

The Northern Region stretches westward from the Daxinganling Mountains, which frame western Manchuria, through Inner Mongolia and includes the northern portions of the Xinjiang Uygur Autonomous Region. Here the settlement pattern is dominated by the pastoral requirements of the herding population. Although settlement traditionally was nomadic throughout much of the region, in recent decades more settlements have become fixed not only as Han Chinese have migrated into the region but also as a result of new grassland management experiments. Overgrazing has underscored the fragility of the physical environment and the limits on settlement. Settlement densities remain sparse, with from two to fifteen clusters of households per hundred square miles, the lowest in China. In this grassland region, characterized by nomadism and some dry farming, the yurt, made of a wooden lattice frame and covered with felt, continues to serve Mongols and Kazakhs as a distinctive habitat, an easily dismantled mobile dwelling.

The Northwestern Rural Settlement Region

The Northwestern Region ranges from south-central Shaanxi within the Great Wall, westward through Gansu, and includes adjacent portions of Qinghai and most of Xinjiang. The principal constraint on settlement here is water. Precipitation is generally less than 250 millimeters per year, often significantly less, with unreliable surface and ground water. Villages are sited where water is available—along irrigation canals, intermittent streams, and around wells in oasislike environments—and decrease in number and size from east to west. Overall densities in the region do not exceed 20 people per square kilometer, rarely exceeding 100 even in the settled river valleys.

Although most of the Northwestern Region is found in Xinjiang and Gansu provinces, relatively remote from the heart of Han Chinese culture, the Guanzhong area of south-central Shaanxi forms an important eastern salient of the region. Guanzhong, as one of the cradles of Chinese civilization, has a well-developed settlement history that reaches back more than seven thousand years to the new stone age. The neolithic site at Banpo, near today's city of Xi'an on the Wei River tributary of the Yellow River, was a nucleated village of some forty-five dwellings built on a river terrace. Most contemporary villages in the Guanzhong subregion share with Banpo and other neolithic villages similar river terrace sites. In size, however, contemporary villages range from 500 to 1,000 people, being much larger than early villages and nearly three times larger than villages found in the loessial plateau to the north, which is part of the Northern Settlement System (Table 7). Today, there are some sixty to eighty villages per hundred square kilometers within the Guanzhong subregion, a distribution that reflects the long history of intensive settlement by Chinese rather than a hospitable environment; virtually all arable land within the subregion has been brought under the plow. Many villages in this region have traditionally been surrounded by sun-baked tamped earth walls, which weather into irregular shapes. Village dwellings in the Guanzhong subregion are distinct. Most are rectangular in shape with a single sloping, shedlike roof, high in the back and lower in the front. Walls are usually of tamped earth or adobe brick, and a soil composition is frequently employed to seal the roof. Although formal courtyards are not commonly part of the design of dwellings in the Guanzhong subregion, the construction of earthen walls between nearby dwellings nonetheless usually creates a courtyardlike space.

The Northwestern Region continues west from Guanzhong for more than 2,000 kilometers through Gansu and Xinjiang to the border of the Soviet Union. As villages decrease in size from east to west, those with fifty or so households and a population of 250 are considered large anywhere in Gansu or Xinjiang. Villages are generally loosely structured with irregular spacing between dwellings and without consistency in orientation to the cardinal directions. As climatic conditions become drier toward the interior, settlements become increasingly dispersed, guided principally by access to water. Deserts make up nearly a quarter of Xinjiang's area. Were it not for the presence of snow-capped mountain ranges from which intermittent streams reach to the lower hillslopes, settlements would be extremely few.

Where seasonal herding forces the movement of a herd from one pasture to another along the lower hillslopes of the mountain ranges of northern Xinjiang, yurts are used. Along the margins of the extremely arid portions of southern Xinjiang, oasis settlements reflect adaptations made by non-Han ethnic minority groups over centuries of residence and resemble patterns found throughout the Middle East. Large walled courtyards, frequently shaded with arbors, are common. As in the Guanzhong subregion, tamped earth and adobe construction also dominate. Both flat and double-sloped roofs are found, but the characteristic high-pitched single-sloped roofs of Guanzhong are not common.

The Qinghai-Xizang Rural Settlement Region

With an area exceeding 2 million square kilometers and an elevation generally higher than 4,000 meters, the Qinghai-Xizang Region is ringed by high mountain ranges that generally isolate it. Much of the region is barren with thin soil and a harsh highland climate. However, the lake area of northeastern Qinghai and the valleys of southern Tibet provide environments suitable for farming and pastoral activities. Even here, however, pop-

Table 7. Villages of the Guanzhong Subregion

Township, Xianyang County	Number of Natural Villages	Average Village Population	Villages Per 100 km²
Weibin	22	980	67.7
Diaotai	18	904	78.3
Pingling	21	667	65.6
Weicheng	20	472	60.6

SOURCE: Compiled by Jin Qiming.

ulation densities are low with small rural settlements that are unevenly dispersed to take advantage of microclimates. Where local conditions elsewhere on the plateau allow, yaks, goats, and sheep are grazed, supporting only a small number of households, many of whom live in large rectangular or square tents.

Dwellings built by Tibetans are generally single-storied and square in shape, with a courtyard at the center. The exterior walls are of cut stone and built without windows to the outside. Because the soil is unsuitable for tamping into walls and there is insufficient fuel to fire bricks, local stone is depended on for building.

Village builders throughout the country have used whatever local materials and technologies were available to construct their habitats. Although common materials and craft are employed widely in China and reflect the pervasiveness of a common culture over millennia, unique village forms are found in some regions and are absent in others. Chinese village construction has been dominated by the use of earth, common soil, available wherever Chinese settled. The use of adobe and fired brick, the tamping of earth walls, and the excavation of subterranean dwellings are examples of common uses of materials in giving form to Chinese villages. Chinese village landscapes do have a broad regional character that reflects the patterns of natural environments across the country. Little, however, is exclusive to one region or another. Much more observation is necessary before one can speak with confidence of boundaries, hearths, and patterns of diffusion. It is too early for synthesis, however rudimentary, because of the continuing comparative dearth of local studies.

We acknowledge with a deep sense of gratitude the general assistance, keen interest, and constructive suggestions of Zhang Xiaolin.

CHAPTER 3

Village *Fengshui* Principles

FAN WEI

He was fishing up a stream in his boat, heedless of how far he had gone, when suddenly he came upon a forest of peach trees. On both banks for several meters there were no other kinds of trees. The fragrant grass was delicious and beautiful to look at, all patterned with fallen blossoms. The fisherman was extremely surprised and went on farther, determined to get to the end of the wood.

He found the end of the wood and the source of the stream together, at the foot of a cliff, and in this cliff a small cave in which there seemed to be a faint light. He left his boat and went in through the mouth of the cave. At first it was very narrow, only just wide enough for a man, but after forty or fifty meters he suddenly found himself in the open.

The place he had come to was level and spacious. There were houses and cottages arranged in a planned order. There were fine fields and beautiful pools. There were mulberry trees, bamboo groves, and many other kinds of trees as well. There were raised pathways round the fields. And he heard the sounds of chickens and of dogs. Going to and fro in all this, and busied in working and planting, were people, both men and women. Their dress was unlike that of people outside, but all of them, whether old people with white hair or children with their hair tied in a knot, all were happy and content with themselves.

In this way, the pastoral poet Tao Yuanming (356–427) vividly portrayed the type of village Chinese have aspired to for thousands of years. Such an ideal traditional village was a secluded village, one in which peasants could live and work in peace and contentment. Chinese traditionally have believed not only that certain locales are more favorable than others for settlement and that such locations can be discerned, but also that the auspiciousness of such selected places redounds to those occupying them as well as their descendants.

Fengshui, an esoteric set of theories and practices grounded in indigenous philosophies and human experiences (often translated into English as "geomancy") has been used in China to probe the landscape and to discern from the irregularity and asymmetry of mountains and waters appropriate locations for specific human occupancy. This chapter will explore the fundamental ideas and structure of *fengshui* as they specifically have affected the organization of space in Chinese villages. Later chapters will reveal specific applications of these general principles. *Fengshui* has also been important in site selection for individual dwellings and graves as well as in the selection of

Figure 3.1. This village landscape illustrates the components that contribute to good *fengshui*. [Source: Markert 1986, 237]

Figure 3.2. Mirroring the landscape shown in Figure 3.1, Matou village in Fujian province is nestled beneath a rising hill. The village is located in the Wuyi Mountains and is to the south of Chong'an. [Photograph, 1988]

imperial capitals, but these will not be examined in this volume (see Steinhardt 1990; Lee 1986; Wright 1977).

From earliest times, siting in China has revealed profound concern for harmony with nature, "a concern for cosmic pattern and the symbolism of the directions, the seasons, winds and constellations" (Needham 1971, 61). *Fengshui,* literally "wind and water," encompasses a constellation of patterns and symbols that reflect "the notion that human alterations of the landscape do not simply occupy empty space. Rather, building sites are viewed as manifesting certain properties which influence, even control, the fortunes of those who intrude upon the site" (Knapp 1986, 108–109). *Fengshui,* even to the present, enjoys enduring credibility within China.

The ancient Chinese classics, such as the *Shijing* [Book of songs] and the *Shujing* [Book of documents], which reach back to the Zhou period (1100–770 B.C.), indicate fundamental cosmo-symbolic practices relevant to the siting of imperial capitals: attention to the cardinal directions and the use of divination. Even though these and other books do not elaborate systematic theories or present detailed prescriptions, they contain general patterns that have fascinated and guided countless Chinese through the centuries. During the fourth century B.C., the book *Guanzi* suggested topographic factors that also should be considered, further systematizing thinking concerning the planned siting of settlements. *Fengshui* itself was mentioned in the *Zangjing* [Book of burial] during the Qin-Han period (221 B.C.–A.D. 220) and again in the *Zangjing* by Guo Pu in the Jin dynasty (A.D. 265–420). Guo Pu included such phrases as *cangfeng*, indicating a site that takes shelter from the northwest wind, and *deshui*, noting that water is at hand.

Figure 3.3. The selection of a building site by a *fengshui* practitioner and his assistants, using a "compass." The mountain to the back and the stream to the front are canonical elements of a good site. [Source: Sun 1905, n.p.]

Although the term *fengshui* adumbrates the pattern of the sites to be chosen, two additional terms —*kanyu* and *dili*—often used synonymously with *fengshui*, extend and embroider the range of meanings tied to the word *fengshui*. *Kanyu*, "the canopy of heaven and the chariot of the earth," suggests the linkage between heaven and earth as well as the connection to broader issues of Chinese cosmology. *Dili* implies an examination of the surface features of the earth. Both *kanyu* and *dili* are generally employed as descriptors in classical Chinese literature, whereas *fengshui* is a more colloquial usage. In English-language literature on this subject, the term "geomancy" is generally used, but many fault the use of this term, suggesting instead "topomancy" (Feuchtwang 1974, 4); "astro-ecology," "topographical siting," and "siting" (Bennett 1978, 2); and "mystical ecology" (Knapp 1986, 108–109). Throughout this essay, as elsewhere in this volume, the term *fengshui* will be used in its untranslated form to express the multiple meanings of the word. Needham, indicating the degree to which *fengshui* is rooted in China stated: "Purely superstitious though in many respects they became, the system of ideas as a whole undoubtedly contributed to the exceptional beauty of positioning of farmhouses, manors, villages and cities throughout the realm of Chinese culture" (1962, 240).

From the dawn of Chinese civilization, peasants have based their existence on agriculture and have thus attached great importance to their physical landscape. The Chinese prize *tu*, or "earth," and thus when building a dwelling speak of *antu* or *anzhai*, "settling the earth," the first and most important aspect of siting. In Liu Xi's *Shiming* [Chinese word explanations], published during the Eastern Han dynasty (c. A.D. 25–220), *zhai* (dwelling) is annotated as *ze*, "to select," which had the same pronunciation in ancient times. In the *Preface to the Yellow Emperor's Book of*

Housing, it is stated: "Man takes *'zhai'* as his home. If he lives in peace, his family will prosper and fare well." Ji Cheng, a famous landscape architect circa 1582, remarked: "Although artifacts can be preserved for thousands of years, who can outlive one hundred years? Creating a pleasant, serene, and comfortable place and dwelling in a selected house is all we can hope for." The dwelling and the village, thus, may be viewed as a refuge, a secluded place to escape from the affairs of the world. It has been stated that one is a Confucian in one's home and in the city—formal, dutiful, and restrained—but a Daoist in the countryside—carefree, primitive, and romantic.

Aesthetic values regarding nature were expressed in antiquity and filtered through *fengshui*. Laozi stated: "The excellence of a residence is in the suitability of the place. That of the mind is in abysmal stillness. That of association is in their being with the virtuous. That of the government is in its securing good order." Zhuangzi added: "Heaven and earth have their great beauties but do not speak of them; the four seasons have their clear marked regularity but do not discuss it; the sage seeks out the beauties of heaven and earth

Figure 3.5. A *fengshui* diagram of Huo village in Jiangxi province showing an embracing pattern of encircling ranges. [Source: Hong 1789–1796, n.p.]

and masters the principles of all things." Confucius said: "The wise take pleasure in rivers and lakes, the virtuous in mountains." For Chinese, these thoughts have helped to illustrate nature as a realm of reality. Man is at the center, and the site of his dwelling is the place that gathers the simple oneness of existence.

The architecture and layout of Chinese villages evolved over thousands of years of practice, a physical expression of numerous, often nebulous, sets of theories, notions, and traditions. Two major approaches to *fengshui*, however, are relatively evident: a Forms, sometimes called Configurations, School *(xingshizong)* and an Analytical, sometimes called Compass, School *(liqizong)*. The Forms School flourished first and has emphasized the comprehension of the physical configuration of terrestrial forms—mountains and watercourses—that define sites. The Analytical or Compass

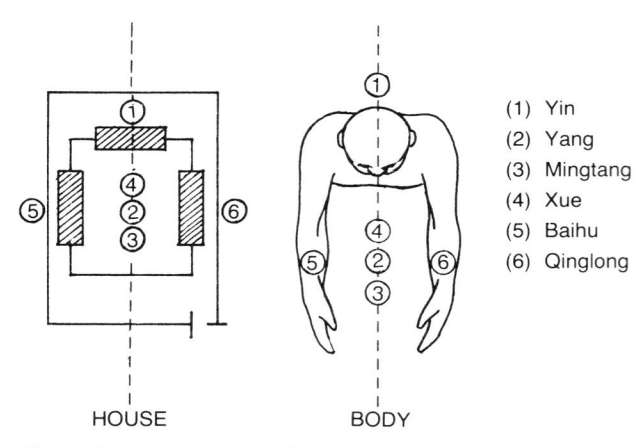

(1) Yin
(2) Yang
(3) Mingtang
(4) Xue
(5) Baihu
(6) Qinglong

HOUSE   BODY

Figure 3.4. *Fengshui* texts frequently present analogies that relate residences to the human body.

School, which is younger than the Forms School, emphasizes the directional components of a given site, especially the relationships among, inter alia, the Five Phases (Agents), the Eight Trigrams, the duodenary and sexagenary cycles, and the twenty-eight constellations.

Bennett distinguishes the two schools as "the intuitive and analytical approaches" (1978, 3). Both schools attempt to determine the patterns of cosmic energy flow, the ethereal property known as *qi,* which although invisible is considered closely related to visible things. The Forms School, on the one hand, has sought this understanding through comprehending terrestrial configurations, depending upon insight and without the intrusion of rational processes. On the other hand, the Analytical School addresses more abstract spatial and temporal dimensions of sites in an effort to "interpret" a whole from its constituent parts. Unlike the Forms School, the Analytical School utilizes an interpretative instrument, a *fengshui* "compass" *(luopan).* This compass is a saucerlike block of wood with a south-pointing compass at its center, surrounded by more than a dozen concentric rings representing the ordering of Chinese metaphysics. Over the centuries, the distinctions between the two schools have become blurred in actual practice and emphasis, reflecting in some measure the differences in Chinese landscapes from region to region. In southern China, where hilly terrain clearly evokes the components of the Forms School, emphasis is on such features. Where plains open broadly, as in much of northern China, emphasis is on directions according to the *luopan.* The context of landscape configurations is the critical element.

Life-force, it was believed, flowed from heaven and from the earth, "heavenly *qi*" and "earthly *qi*," forming together a unity associated with *yang* and *yin* that are causal to everything. As described by de Groot: "In every part of the ground, in every chain of mountains, in every bluff or rock, Nature has laid down a certain quantity of Yin or Terrestrial Breath. But according to the above doctrines, it cannot exert any life-producing influences unless it be at the same time imbued with some Yang or Celestial Breath. Geomancers alone are capable of deciding whether this latter be represented in an adequate proportion, and whether the ground has any value for building purposes and grave making" (1897, 949). The ability of geomancers to discern the natural qualities of the complementary opposites of *yin* and *yang* led to their being called *yinyang xiansheng* ("*yinyang* expert" or "*yinyang* interpreter"). In general, *yin* expresses the female aspect—the shade, the south bank of a stream, or the north slope of a mountain—and is associated with burial. *Yang* is a male characteristic—bright and active, the north bank of a stream, the south side of a mountain—and especially suitable for habitation, whether an individual house, village, or city.

Utilizing these fundamental concepts of *yin* and *yang* as well as other associated concepts, the practitioners of both the Forms School and the Analytical School attempt to discern *xue,* the site or location where vital life-force *(shengqi)* is modulated. The metaphorical name *xue,* meaning "lair," "cave," or "hole," is also used for acupuncture points of the human body. As a "central point," *xue* expresses Chinese concern for determining the middle, the place where *qi* collects. In the *Book of Songs,* the capital, "the city of Shang" (c. 16–11 centuries B.C.), is described as "carefully laid out at the center of four quarters." *Mingtang* ("the bright or cosmic court"), the palace for a king to meet the Five Emperors, or his sacrificial altar, is the name used to designate the meaning of being in the middle. Although it was believed that *qi* flowed naturally and according to phases, the flow was guided by "the wind and the water," *fengshui.* Thus, it is necessary to comprehend the tangible

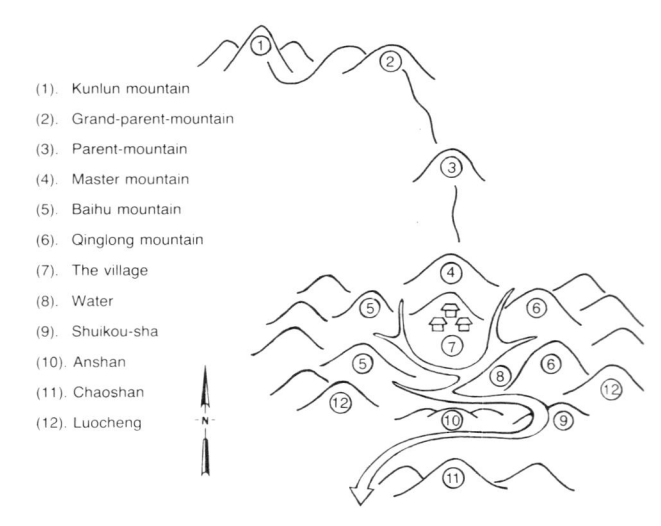

(1). Kunlun mountain
(2). Grand-parent-mountain
(3). Parent-mountain
(4). Master mountain
(5). Baihu mountain
(6). Qinglong mountain
(7). The village
(8). Water
(9). Shuikou-sha
(10). Anshan
(11). Chaoshan
(12). Luocheng

Figure 3.6. Serpentine mountains *(long)*, suggesting the undulations of a dragon, serve as the first-order elements of this village's *fengshui*. Prominent eminences *sha* and water *sha* complete the picture. The village is located at the *xue*.

land and water features, which themselves modulated the elusive and intangible *qi*. This comprehension is as necessary for the *qi* associated with *yinzhai,* the "dwellings of the dead," as it is for *yangzhai,* the "dwellings of the living." If a proper location is chosen, tapping life-force, then advantage and general good fortune will redound to those who occupy the site.

The lair, or *xue,* is generally located at the converging nucleus of a very long, clear, and winding chain or vein of mountains or hills located to the north or northwest of a chosen site. There are three general types of converging patterns for settlements: capitals must be at a large converging place, cities at middle-sized converging places, and villages at small converging places. With a village or at the level of an individual dwelling, the shape of the converging pattern often incorporates a main body with two embracing wings facing each other and having the appearance of a three-sided enclosure. At the scale of a grave, the residence of the dead, the shape is frequently that of an encircling armchair. *Fengshui* texts warn of establishing a settlement form on an inappropriately large or small site.

Of most importance in detecting a site are *long,* or dragons, which metaphorically describe the mountains or hill chains embracing an auspicious *fengshui* site. The Chinese conception of a dragon is more serpentlike, more sinuous than the Western conception of a dragon. Its form is perceived as undulating and interconnecting like veins in the human body, serving as circulation conduits through which *qi* courses. The phrase *lailong qumai,* which today means "origin and development, cause and effect," has long been a term used in *fengshui.* When talking of the beginning of a chain, *fengshui* practitioners name hills "parent hills" or "grandparent hills" to express the origin and development of the ridge. There may be many branches, to the degree that the *long* may be likened to a tree with its complex yet ramified structure; the farther the mountain chain stretches, the better the *fengshui* pattern. Hills must rise and fall, undulating in repeating patterns that mimic those of a dragon's anatomy.

The shape of hills is a key to siting: *xingfeng peitian,* "the earthly configurations are in agreement with the celestial order." The Five Phases *(wuxing)* here match the Five Planets' *wuxing:* wood, fire, earth, metal, and water. "Care is usually taken so that no part of the dwelling is shaded by hills on the east, south, or west, thus providing early sunrise and late sunset. This appearance heightens the appearance of *yang,* the life presence of the sun. Hills at the rear are thought necessary not only because they do not block the sun but because they also guard the rear flank" (Knapp 1986, 111–112). As summarized in the *Yangzhai shishu* [Ten books on *yang* dwellings]: "To have the front high and the rear low is to be cut off with no family. With the rear high and front low is to have

Figure 3.7. Representations of hill shapes related to the Five Phases (from top to bottom, wood, fire, earth, metal, and water). On the right, the land of a successful degree candidate is presented. Prominent mountains flank the back; those on the side are lower and rim the site. The dotted line indicates a stream. Specific sites for individual dwellings or graves must be located within this general *fengshui* landscape. [Source: Adapted from *Dixue tanyuan* 1966, 2, 13]

oxen and horses." Chinese have always avoided commanding heights for dwellings and larger settlements.

Water *(shui)* has also always been a concern of *fengshui* practitioners: "There is no auspicious place without water" and "While prospecting an area, the first step is to examine water" are two expressions of this importance. It has been believed that "if water were to dissipate, *shengqi* would disperse, and if water comes in, *shengqi* will gather." Also: "Prosperous are people where water is plentiful, and poor are people where water is scarce. People will swarm where water converges, and people will desert the place where water disperses." *Fengshui* experts "examine earth and taste water" to probe the healthfulness of an environment and to protect settlements from the possibility of inundation. A good location was often seen as one in a bend of the river. Even the neolithic village of Banpo in Shaanxi province took such a location. *Fengshui* notions state that "if a river comes from far away . . . the place where it turns round may be where the dragon stops and gathers." A meandering stream forming a girdle in front of a settlement site was seen as optimal. Water was seen as an integrative element rather than a separative one. Mountains and water complement each other in myriad combinations: "The nature of mountains is tranquil, its excellence is in moving; the nature of water is moving, its excellence is calm." Water is important in creating an emotional element to landscape, a bright surface that is in sharp contrast to the intricate elements of mountains.

Genealogies provide examples of the ecological concerns of those settling an area. In the *Preface to the Family History of Shuangxi, Chun County,* Zhejiang province, it is written: "The place is secluded, surrounded by two streams, with mountains and water running around it. Plants are luxuriant. It is perhaps the most fertile place in the western part of Chun county" (*Chunyi* Qing, vol. 1:58). In the *Genealogy of the Hongs at Guanyuan,* Jiangxi province, is the description of their forbears "now pacing up and down in the Zhong Mountains, now walking along the banks of the Zi River. They found here and there that pines and bamboos grow exuberantly, and that river and sands wind around the place. They thought this place could be inhabited" (Hong 1789–1796, vol. 1:35).

An account in the *Genealogy of the Chens,* Sichuan province, states, "When building manors and mansions, the gentry will not fell trees." The *Genealogy of the Hus of Mingjing,* Anhui province, warns that "*kanyu* experts consider it a good practice to preserve vital life-force *(shengqi)* by piling up earth and planting trees. This practice must be observed and never violated." A similar warning

Figure 3.8. As shown in this map of Meixi village in Anhui province, the stream winds in front of the village while the mountains ring the settlement.

occurs in the *History of Shanhe Village,* Anhui province: "Every family must take care of the mountains and water around. Plant trees and bamboo as shelters. Anyone who acts contrary to this shall be punished. . . . Keep an eye on the environment and protect it from damage. This is a chore for people of one hundred generations (*Shan Qing*) to undertake." Still, "the smoothness of the soil and the lushness of the vegetation justify the siting of this village" (Li 1834, vol. 1).

According to Eugene and Marja Anderson, village siting in south China

is basically a very practical system whereby a village is situated such that it does not take up farmland or lay itself open to floods and typhoons. . . . A well-sited village is protected from the elements. Typhoons, heat waves, storms and the like are broken in their force by the hills, spurs and groves. Erosion is limited by trees and terraces. Floods do not affect the sites for they are on elevated spots. The flowing streams assure a constant water supply, and (with frequent rains) flush salt from the fields. . . . The village does not take up the best farmland, which lies below it in the valley. . . . Wealth flows into the villages as the streams do, according to popular belief, and grows there like the lush vegetation. (1973, 34, 50)

"Local eminences," or *sha*—terrain features apart from the dominating dragon, *long*—are distinguishable nearby terrain features, such as ridges and watercourses, that define the settlement site. It is believed that the term *sha*, which means "sand," was used because *fengshui* experts once illustrated their ideas to their clients by piling up sand to form ridges and valleys that modeled the local surroundings. In general, these eminences are named:

Figure 3.9. A village in western Hunan province illustrates a settlement site within the bend of a stream.

Qinglong ("azure dragon"): Nearby hills to the left and front of the *mingtang,* the central space.

Baihu ("white tiger"): Nearby hills on the right and in front of the master hill.

Anshan ("table mountain"): Hills on the southern axis of the *mingtang,* especially the closest hill opposite the master hill.

Chaoshan ("worshiping mountain"): The second, third, and even fourth *anshan* at the south of the *mingtang.*

shuikoushan ("mouth of the stream mountain"): The hills at the entrance and the exit of the *mingtang* along the stream. They are often named Lion Hill, Elephant Hill, Snake Hill, and so forth.

Where ridges and watercourses are present, *sha* focus on these physiographic forms, but in other cases roads, ponds, and even man-made structures may become the eminences. *Mingtang,* introduced briefly above, is important in siting, because it constitutes the open space immediately in front of the *xue* and that bounded by the eminences. With houses it takes the form of the front courtyard, with tombs the sacrificial space before the tablet. In a village, it often is the large open grain-drying area or a large pond at the front of the village.

The azure dragon and the white tiger are the beings identified with two of the four cardinal directions, respectively, east and west. Together with the vermilion bird and the black tortoise, they are synonymous with directions in Chinese correlative thinking: "To the east was the azure dragon and the element wood emblemizing spring

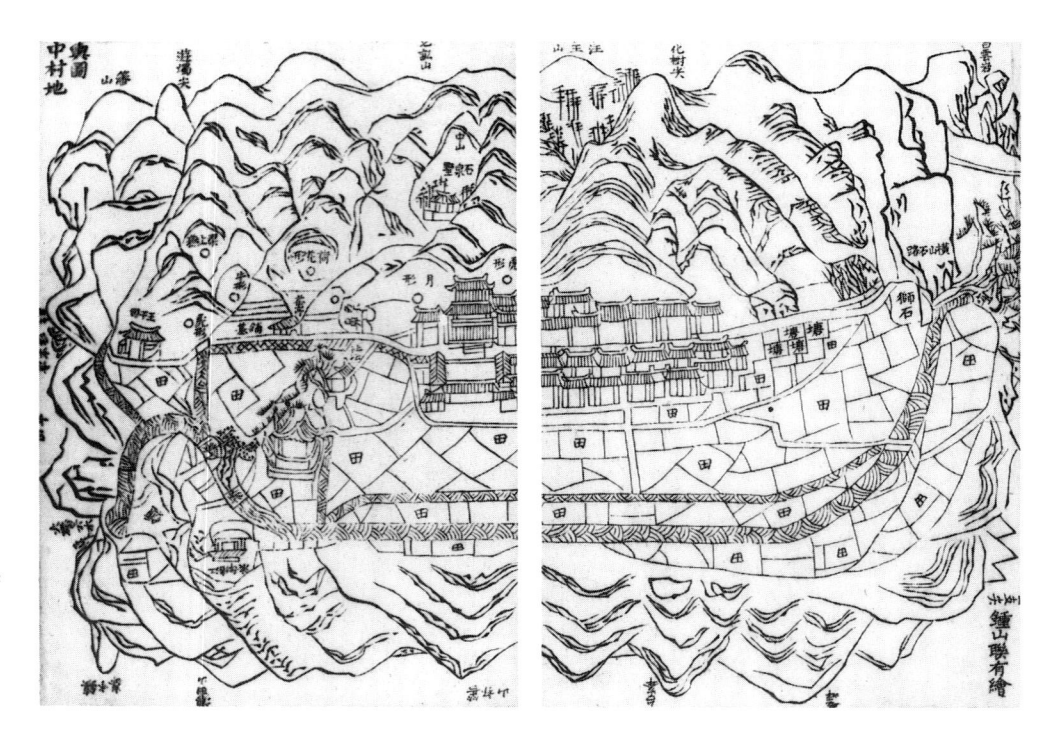

Figure 3.10. Zheng village in Anhui province reveals not only the "fit" of the village to the terrain but also orientation to the cardinal directions. [Source: Hong 1789–1796, n.p.]

and the rising sun. To the south was the vermilion phoenix and the element of fire indicating summer. To the west was the white tiger and the element of metal symbolizing autumn and harvest. Completing the cycle in the north was the black tortoise and the element water indicating winter. Man was anchored in the soil or earth, the fifth element, found in the center of the cosmic map" (Knapp 1986, 110). The azure dragon and the white tiger are also associated with *yang* and *yin* as well as their related topographical configurations.

Since these beings are associated with the four quadrants of heaven, their identification on earth is used to emphasize a harmony with heaven. Naming landmarks in terms of the azure dragon, vermilion bird, white tiger, and black tortoise has created a set of reference points that have clear spatial implications. When traveling even to an unknown Chinese village, town, or city, the use of these names immediately creates a familiar mental map. Although natural features such as boulders, ridges, ponds, and groves may be named in this way, bridges, pagodas, temples, and other man-made forms may also be placed within the cosmological map of the landscape.

Many Chinese villages were given form utilizing principles of *fengshui,* and villagers even today point out the prominence of *long, sha, xue,* and *shui* features, as discussed in several chapters in this book. From a practical point of view, however, it is often easier to see the defined components of *fengshui* as they are expressed at the scale of individual houses or imperial capitals than to identify them in villages. Chinese authors often wax poetic as they describe Chinese villages, pointing out the *fengshui* attributes, the creative yet structured ways in which humans over countless centuries have manipulated landscape in order to occupy it, creating places that express both folk culture and broader cosmology. Yet intuition, logic, and order have all helped give form to the picturesque patterns of many Chinese villages that appear in Chinese painting and in garden landscapes. Still, *fengshui* no doubt has helped restrain Chinese villagers from unwise ecological decisions, nurturing reasonably sound ecological practices and leading to "planned" settlements far ahead of their time.

I thank Professor Liu Zhuangchong of Tianjin University for his assistance with this manuscript and Professor Zang Erzhong of Beijing Institute of Civil Engineering for his constructive criticism.

Figure 3.11. This engraved tile (c. 200 B.C.) shows the Four Beings *(sishen)*. The azure dragon on the left faces east, the vermilion bird south, the white tiger west, and the black tortoise north in a clockwise direction. [Source: Wu 1963, 49]

CHAPTER 4

Changing Village Landscapes

RONALD G. KNAPP AND SHEN DONGQI

SIGNIFICANT efforts have been made throughout the China mainland in the four decades since 1949 to restructure rural settlement and to go beyond spontaneous settlement toward planned development and overall land-use planning. Central governmental policies, often expressed in active political movements whose avowed purposes were unrelated to settlement forms per se, have helped guide the restructuring of many Chinese villages. Broadly speaking, policies have promoted the spatial concentration of housing and subsidiary industrial production as well as the provision of a range of services not normally expected in farming areas (for an example of this in Zhejiang province, see Knapp and Shen 1991). There has been a "townization" of many villages with the creation of geometrically regular settlement forms that echo the spatial structures of Chinese urban places—axial symmetry, an intersecting grid system of paths and roads oriented to the cardinal directions, parallel rows of south-facing dwellings, centrally located administrative offices and services, and sometimes the enclosure of the settlement by a "wall."

The forty years since 1949 can be divided into five periods, each with its own attributes, governmental policies, and movements, providing a framework for examining their effects on rural settlement and housing:

1. the rehabilitation period (1949–1958)
2. the creation of the people's communes and the subsequent adjustments period (1958–1964)
3. the popularization of the Dazhai model of development and the Great Proletarian Cultural Revolution period (1964–1978)
4. the period since the Third Plenary Session of the Eleventh Central Committee of the Chinese Communist Party in December 1978, which led to the implementation of the responsibility system, the promotion of a commodity economy, and the dissolution of the commune structure itself (1978–1988)
5. the period since late 1988, representing a cooling off of "building fever"

Rehabilitation Period

After decades of turmoil, followed by the Japanese aggression after 1937, and then civil war, the ten years following the establishment of the People's Republic of China in 1949 was a period of national recovery. For the most part, this period was one of great enthusiasm and progress throughout urban and rural China. Not only was much accomplished toward correcting the ravages of the previous decades, but significant progress was made in agricultural and industrial production as well. Following the promulgation of the Land Reform Law in 1950 and the "differentiation of class status in rural areas," all rural residents were legally classed as either landlords, rich peasants, middle peasants, or poor peasants. Land, housing, and the tools of production were confiscated from landlords and redistributed to poor peasants. According to the law, ancestral shrines, temples, and landlords' houses "should not be damaged" and together with the "surplus houses of landlords . . . not suitable for the use of peasants" were to be transformed into facilities for "public use" by local governments (*Land Reform* 1950).

In general, the redistribution of the means of production allowed peasants to retain more of their output than formerly, an important factor in improving rural life. Because of the elimination of land rents, it is estimated that an additional 100 to 150 kilograms of grain per capita became available to improve nutrition. By 1952, commodities such as enamel washbasins and thermos bottles became common in Chinese villages, to some an important indicator of a bettering of rural life (Liu and Wu 1986, 92). Life continued to be difficult for many in the countryside. In general, it must be admitted, expectations were not very high. Significant differentials in income from one part of China to another as well as inherent difficulties in the way statistics were gathered and reported make it difficult to quantify countrywide comparisons (Vermeer 1982, 5–8).

From 1949 through 1957, little attention was given to altering or improving individual village sites or buildings as emphasis instead was placed on increasing agricultural production through a series of evolving agricultural organizational forms—mutual aid teams, agricultural producers' cooperatives, and finally communes in 1958. State investment in rural capital construction was limited and mainly focused on water conservancy and land reclamation rather than village structure itself. Most peasants continued to live in old houses, varying in type from region to region within the country. Where new housing was built, the materials continued to be tamped earth, adobe, or kiln-dried bricks for the walls, either load-bearing or with traditional wooden frameworks to support the roof. Thatched dwellings were still common in many areas of the country. Moreover, traditional patterns of housing design, size, and placement continued with very little attention paid to reducing land occupied by housing or improvement in the ventilation, lighting, and general sanitation of housing. Little concern throughout this period of rehabilitation was placed on anything beyond providing every villager with shelter, and only limited construction of public buildings in rural areas was carried out. By 1956, according to Chinese calculations, a socialist transformation of China's economy had been basically accomplished with both significant increases in agricultural output and living standards. Many villagers, even today, as they reflect on the 1950s recall quickly statistics that buttress for them the strides taken in living standards during these heady days.

During the rehabilitation period, the national Patriotic Sanitation Movement (*Aiguo weisheng yundong*), affected the quality of rural life. Begun in the early 1950s to eliminate "the four pests" and later expanded to embrace environmental sanitation, this countrywide movement came to focus later in the 1960s on improving health through the prevention of disease. The proper

Figure 4.1. Between 1952 and 1955 in Aiguo ("Patriotic") Village Agricultural Cooperative, Zhuxian county, in Shandong province, it was claimed that the incomes of some of the 125 households had increased four times—making possible the construction of new clay and wattle dwellings with thatched roofs to replace "tumbledown huts." Although a central radio was installed for the enjoyment of villagers after supper, most families continued to "sleep early to save oil." [Source: Chen 1955, 22]

maintenance of manure pits, the cleaning up of polluted ditches and ponds, and the elimination of pests such as rodents and mosquitoes were accompanied by attention to the quality of drinking water and the construction of public toilets.

Beginning in 1952, the press focused increasing attention on exemplary or model villages *(mofan cun)*, not only on their successes in environmental sanitation but also on changing land-use patterns that affected village form. No. 6 Village, Heshang *zhen,* Xiaoshan county, in Zhejiang, was one of these models, as was Taiyang village, Jishan county, Shanxi province (Yuan 1987, 78–79). In such villages that once were filthy, wells were capped and their aprons covered with cement to protect the cleanliness of drinking water. Latrines and animal manure pits were covered. Some improvement was made in the patterns and qual-

Figure 4.2. "To walk around Big Willows today is rather like making a visit to one of those neat little model villages seen in exhibitions," began an article describing one of China's "rural health models" in the mid-1950s. Nearly half of the 193 households in this village in Gansu province had met the standards of the "Five Haves and Eight Cleans" campaign. The "Five Haves" were a family latrine, a covered latrine, a pigsty, a chicken coop, and a cover on the well. The "Eight Cleans" included the house (inside and out), courtyard, lane, bedclothes, garments, kitchen, bowls, and chopsticks. Village lanes, as depicted in the photo, were swept on a rotating volunteer basis. [Source: Liu 1958, 15]

ity of local roads and the planting of trees in some villages began to reverse the long-term destruction of village vegetation that had made many village environments so stark. An especially significant advance in some villages was that space for humans and animals was clearly differentiated, a qualitative improvement that even in the early 1990s is not a universal fact in Chinese villages. In some cooperatives, facilities such as public toilets and small meeting halls were built. In summary, during this period villages throughout the country generally changed little in morphology, but made some improvement in the quality of their living environments.

The Commune Period and Adjustments

With the announcement of the "Great Leap Forward" in February 1958, a frenzied drive was begun in urban and rural areas of the country to propel China's economy forward. As part of this effort, as many as 600,000 "backyard furnaces" were constructed in China's villages to help speed rural efforts at industrialization. In the spring of 1958, some agricultural producers' cooperatives were amalgamated into larger entities that by July were being called people's communes *(renmin gongshe)*. Chairman Mao visited one of these communes, Qiliying, Xinxiang county, Henan province, in August 1958, proclaiming the value of this new institutional form in the pursuit of communism. By the end of the year, 26,425 people's communes had been organized, comprising more than 98 percent of the 122 million rural households in the country. On average during these early years, 28 agricultural producers' cooperatives were combined to form a people's commune, with each commune containing about 5,000 households or 25,000 people.

Communes not only preserved and enhanced collective ownership of the means of production, but also created a hierarchical structure of organization that imprinted the countryside with many patterns and forms that endure to the present. The three levels of organization (the commune, the production brigade, and the team) came both to provide a management scheme operating at different scales and to alter social organization. Enormous problems began to emerge in 1959, however, owing to overly ambitious planning,

Figure 4.3. The "high tide of socialist construction" is suggested by this *Shanxi ribao* [Shanxi daily] cartoon, which extols the transformation of sleepy villages via rural mechanization, the development of small-scale local industry, and bumper crops. [Source: Reprinted in Tang 1958, 2]

zealous cadres, and natural disasters that set back the gains of the early and mid-1950s. "Excessive egalitarianism as well as the indiscriminate transfer of natural resources" *(yi ping er diao)*, as they are termed today to underscore the errors of policy, had a major impact on reducing income levels and, as the Chinese say, "the enthusiasm of the masses" *(qunzhong jijixing)*. Many distinctive traditional houses were destroyed, and others were confiscated—as many homes of landlords had been during land reform—and used for administrative, storage, or productive purposes, or even subdivided to house large numbers of village households.

In the craze to "collectivize living" *(shenghuo jitihua)*, dispersed hamlets and villages in some cases were consolidated into single sites to increase the efficiency of agricultural production. From spring of 1958 to the end of the year in some areas, as military-style organization of village residents occurred, large dining halls and dormitories were built for villagers using bricks and stoves from their demolished houses. In some areas of the country, men and women—even married cou-

Figure 4.4. With more and more people "eating together in public dining rooms" as well as "children and old people . . . living under new communal conditions," increasing attention was paid in many villages to the elimination of diseases. The slogan on this village wall calls for the elimination of malaria. [Source: Ma 1959, 9]

Figure 4.5. Commonly built in people's communes in the late 1950s and throughout the 1960s and 1970s were community facilities such as assembly halls. Tangcun township, Jiande county, Zhejiang. [Photograph, 1990]

Figure 4.6. During the Great Leap Forward, which accompanied the rise of communes, emphasis was put on productive agricultural activities rather than on consumption. In this late 1958 cartoon, villagers are seen making do by meeting on the edge of a field (*ditou hui*) rather than in a building. The gable end of the house serves a surface for calling for increases in grain and pig production. [Source: *Renmin ribao* 12 December 1958, 8]

ples—the old, the very young, and adolescents were forced to live in separate quarters. Especially in some villages of north China, large multipurpose facilities that included space for assembly, recreation, lectures, and study were built. Drill grounds *(lianbing chang)* also appeared in many villages, providing space not only for martial purposes and athletics, but also for coordinated drying of grain. "Large in size and collective in nature" *(yi da er gong)*, a concept that proclaimed a higher degree of public ownership than that under the cooperatives in the mid-1950s, became the general slogan. Sometimes adjustments in these arrangements led to the construction of small apartment units of uniform size, with a single door and a single window, provided for each married couple. Common innovations in many villages during this period were public toilets and washrooms.

The excesses, regimentation, and overzealous efforts of the Great Leap Forward led to extraordinary waste and errors in countless villages. Plans made in a day or two, the faster the better, were often inadequate (not based on "concrete realities"). Many such "rapid plans" *(kuaisu guihua)* were also hurriedly implemented, so that they were only partially carried out without the full impact of their errors being felt.

As early as November 1958, even as excesses

were accelerating, a central government resolution set out to rectify some of the problems concerning people's communes. Central to the resolution was a call for the restoration of individual households and relaxation of the prohibition against using private kitchens. New house construction followed in some areas of the country, especially from the spring of 1959 on. Increasing also was the construction of facilities to provide commune welfare services—nursery schools, old folks homes, and public dining halls—usually advanced as a means to "liberate the labor power of women" and "increase overall labor efficiency." According to an October 25, 1958, *People's Daily* editorial, some 1,070,000 public dining halls were already operating to serve more than 80 percent of the villagers in nine provinces of north and northeastern China ("Banhao" 1958). The Chinese press continued to report favorably on public dining halls throughout 1959, with an emphasis on solving problems and making them more efficient. In 1960 and 1961, magazines and newspapers continued reporting on well-run dining halls, but such news did not appear in the following years ("Qunzhong" 1958; "Shenghuo" 1958; Jiang 1959; "Chaoyang" 1959; "Yige" 1960; Chen 1961). Most public dining halls were run by production brigades, that is, village-level organizations, utilizing kitchens and rooms in remodeled dwellings or larger spaces. Where funds were available, some dining halls were built that accommodated as many as 500 people at a single sitting.

In many places, the attempts to restructure living environments were accompanied by the alteration or destruction of temples, lineage halls, and other structures that expressed aspects of traditional sociocultural reality then in disrepute. The attack on structures was aimed not only at eliminating popular rituals deemed "feudal superstition" and inappropriate in a developing socialist state, but also at the power of local lineages who used the structures as venues for banquets and meetings (for brief discussions of some of these traditional activities in southern China, see Watson 1982; for north China, see Cohen 1990, 515–519). In the early 1950s, the landholdings that had financed many such village lineage halls and temples had been confiscated, weakening not only the ideology of common descent but also the exercise of local power without state intervention. The structures themselves often were converted to schools, offices, or workshops. With the rise of communes, however, temples and lineage halls in some areas were dismantled and their foundation stones and bricks recycled to support agriculture. Small shrines and large trees that gave identity to many villages similarly were destroyed in order to sever visible links with "superstitious practices." National debates about the preservation of China's cultural legacy intruded into local discussions of cultural preservation. In the early 1960s, it became increasingly clear: "Imperial tombs of long-dead emperors were safe; ancestral temples in living villages were something else again" (Croizier 1970, 47). In a critique of the efforts to repair some temples and lineage halls, using "money, materials, and manpower, and affecting agriculture," a call was made for "carrying out persuasion and explanations patiently among the masses" in order to break "old taboos and conventions" (Ding 1962, 20). During this period, the destruction and renovation of imposing multihalled structures altered the preexisting patterns in many villages. Some ritual practices, nonetheless, were transferred by villagers to their private quarters, as still-standing ritual buildings were transformed into cultural fragments, mere artifacts without content (Siu 1989, 125).

By 1962, after a devastating famine had struck many areas of rural China, recovery from the setbacks of the Great Leap Forward was on track,

Figure 4.7. A view of row-houses in one of China's first communes, Qiliying Brigade, in Xinxiang county, Henan province. The construction of residential areas here occupied much of the 1960s. Each two-story row-house faces south and has a courtyard to the front. [Source: Zhao 1983, 53]

and there was a weakening of emphasis on the construction and management of public or collective facilities. Recovery was accelerated under the influence of new policies that emphasized agricultural development. The "Eight-Point Charter for Agriculture," which served as the framework for agricultural development, had as its objective increases in grain yield as the index of prosperity. Throughout China, grain yields increased substantially and contributed to the amelioration of the difficulties villagers had faced in the years just passed.

In recent years, writers on Chinese rural development during the late 1950s and early 1960s have identified communes whose land-use plans during that time were "divorced from reality and lacking a scientific basis" *(tuoli shiji quefa kexue yiju)* without pointing out any successful plans. Among those criticized are the plans for Weixing People's Commune, Suiping county, Henan province; Suicheng People's Commune, Xushui county, Hebei province; and Hongqi People's Commune, Qingpu county, Shanghai Municipality (Yuan 1987, 88–91). Weixing ("Satellite") People's Commune was created in April 1958 as one of China's first communes with the amalgamation of five townships. Originally there were 238 individual villages with a total population of 43,252 people in 9,369 households. Plans were drawn up to restructure residential areas into three levels—a central residential area as part of the commune's headquarters, eight production brigade residential centers, and some production brigade satellite residential centers. According to the plans, the commune headquarters was to be reconstructed to house some 5,000 people on the site by 1962, with another 3,000 in an adjacent production brigade residential center. Critics have pointed out that from the point of view of capital and materials needed, the plans were impractical. What was

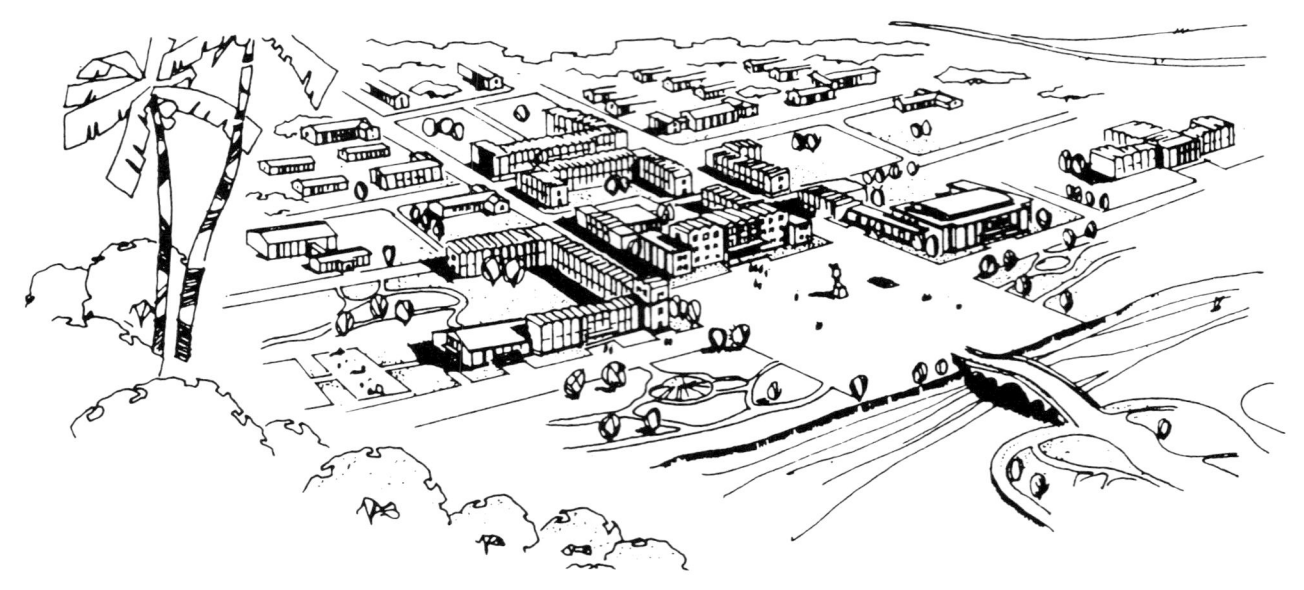

Figure 4.8. This bird's-eye view of the "village" center for Weixing People's Commune in Henan province reveals a quasi-urban appearance and suggests the scale of capital investment necessary to make it possible. The center was planned in 1962 to accommodate a population of 8,000, one-fifth of the commune's total. [Source: Yuan 1987, 89]

actually constructed is not known, but, as the figures indicate, the scale of construction planned would have created a small town in place of a village in a relatively short period of time.

The Architectural Society of China in 1963 convened a meeting of a number of specialists on rural construction, who warned that construction taking place in the countryside was consuming excessive amounts of valuable land. Looking to the future, the specialists recommended employing more rational site plans, reducing overall village size, setting aside land for development, and considering safety, economy, utility, and aesthetics in new rural housing construction. Later in the year, a national meeting in Beijing was convened to address these issues. Some attention was also given to the conservation of building materials and the need to innovate. One result was the development and popularization in house construction of prestressed concrete, a building material that twenty years later was to gain great popularity.

Popularization of the Dazhai Model

In 1964, Chairman Mao first mentioned Dazhai as a model of socialist development and set in train events that catapulted Dazhai into national prominence. The call "In Agriculture, learn from Dazhai" echoed throughout rural China until 1977, appearing as oversized vermilion characters on the walls of countless village houses throughout the country—a clarion call for future change.

Dazhai, as discussed in detail in Chapter 14, was a small village of eighty-two households farming some 80 hectares of rocky and hilly land in a semiarid area of the Taihang Mountains in Shanxi province of north China. The herculean efforts of the villagers of this vanguard brigade to overcome difficulty were used to inspire other villagers throughout the country in self-reliant rural construction. The Dazhai "spirit of self-reliance and hard struggle" contributed to the transformation of village landscapes, not only sculpted terraces that were synonymous with Dazhai, but habitats as well. Dazhai villagers overcame various natural disasters in the 1950s and 1960 to build terraces and water conservancy facilities, but it was the destruction of most of their below-ground cave dwellings and their surface dwellings in August 1963 that led to the complete refashioning of the village itself. Within three years, some two hundred stone-lined caves and more than five hundred dwelling rooms were constructed. The water and electricity supply was improved. Ownership of this new construction was held by the collective rather than privately as in the past, reflecting not only new social imperatives but also the fact that the village working as a collective had cut the stone, dug the caves, and carried out all the construction work.

Over the next four years, answering Chairman

Figure 4.9. The reconstruction of the settlement and fields of Dazhai in Shanxi province served the needs not only of villagers but also of the burgeoning phalanxes of visitors who came to learn from this vanguard brigade. [Source: *Tachai* 1972, n.p.]

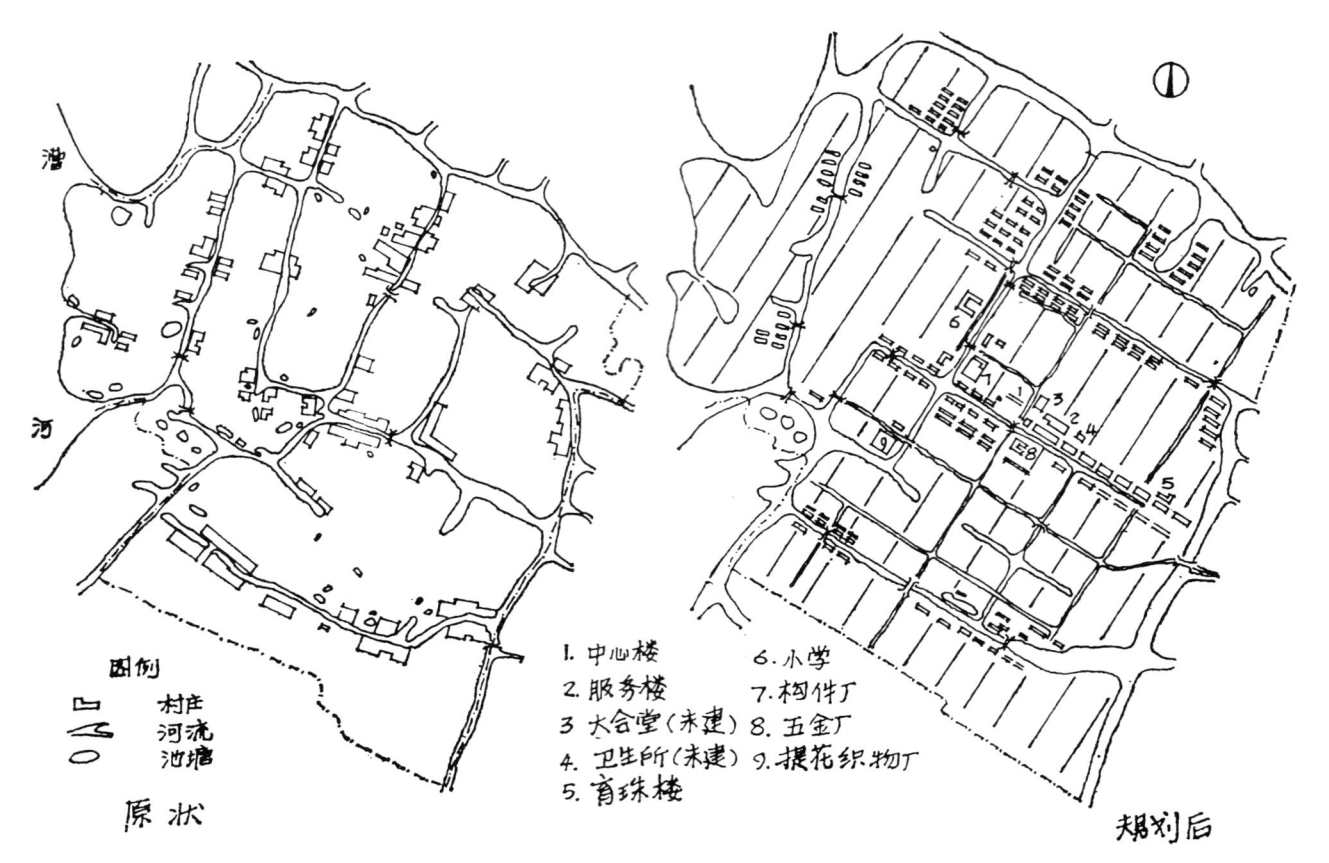

Figure 4.10. The transformation of many southern villages was carried out at the same time that articulated water conservancy systems were developed. This pattern is seen here in the original (**left**) and planning (**right**) maps for Weixing village, Wuxian county, Jiangsu. Planned for the village were the following: (1) central headquarters, (2) service building, (3) assembly hall (not built), (4) health station (not built), (5) sports building, (6) primary school, (7) components factory, (8) hardware factory, and (9) jacquard mill. [Source: Niu 1988, 29]

Mao's call to learn from Dazhai, many production brigades throughout the country attempted to emulate the Dazhai experience. In the years that followed, second- and third-generation efforts further spread the message of Dazhai. Ownership of all buildings in a Dazhai-type village was retained by the brigade. The occupants of new houses generally paid a monthly "rent," with the price of brick, tile, and wood salvaged from the residents' original homes calculated as an allowance to offset the monthly payment.

A common element of Dazhai-type villages was the row-house, usually placed in a geometrically regular pattern. A good example can be observed in the rebuilding of the village at Fenghuo Production Brigade, Fenghuo People's Commune, Liquan county, in Shaanxi province. The original village comprised three hamlets, with many of the dwellings carved into the face of the loessial hills. According to the plan spelled out in 1973, two of the original three hamlets were to be combined at a single site on the valley floor just below the cliff face. Eight pairs of two-story brick row-houses, totaling 176 units, were planned for this site. Each dwelling unit was fashioned with a courtyard and space for a pigpen, storage of firewood, a latrine, and a bathing area. On the east side of the dwelling area, an array of public facilities was built. These included a cultural center, assembly hall, brigade administrative headquarters, hostel, equipment repair station, grain mill, health center, and dining hall. On the south side of the village, a grain-drying area, a school, and collective pigsties were constructed.

Some new villages are strikingly regular, with patterns that mimic the symmetry, axiality, and enclosure of canonical urban plans. Houtun Brigade, Datun Commune, in Shen county, Hebei province, for example, was built anew after an earthquake decimated the original settlement in 1966. As seen in Figure 4.12, the village plan was oriented north-south with intersecting roads and ringed by a "wall" of trees. The three lanes running north-south, each 8 meters wide, served to separate the four teams, but a 12-meter-wide east-west road was built to link them. The plan was conceived to provide comparability in facilities for the brigade's four production teams; some facilities were duplicated within each residential compound and others, such as a meeting hall, the

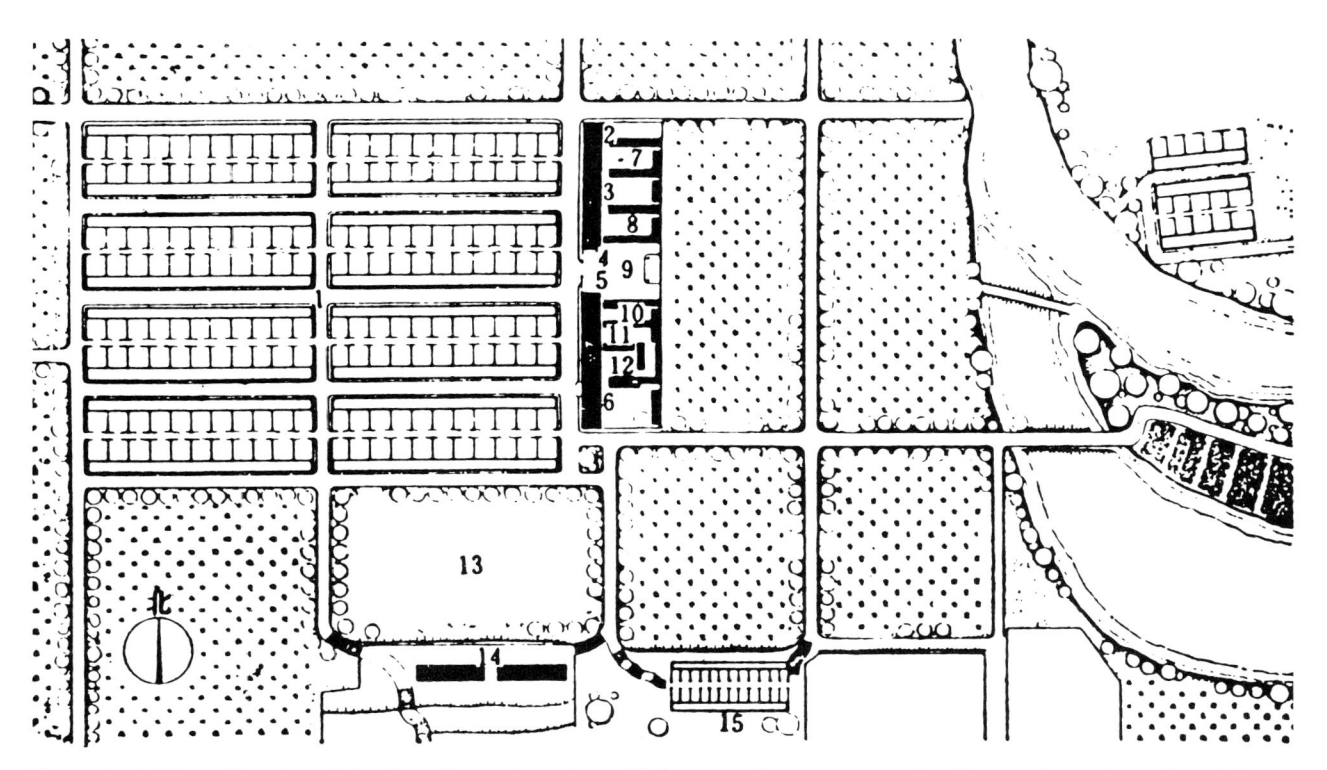

Figure 4.11. Plan of Fenghuo Brigade in Shaanxi province. Eight pairs of two-story row dwellings make up the residential area on the right (1). Shown in heavy black rectangles are the agricultural technical station (2), cultural center (3), assembly hall (4), administrative headquarters (5), hostel (6), equipment repair station (7), grain mill (8), open-air assembly area (9), health center (10), meeting room (11), dining hall (12), grain drying area (13), school (14), and pigsties (15). [Source: Gao and Zeng 1982, 85]

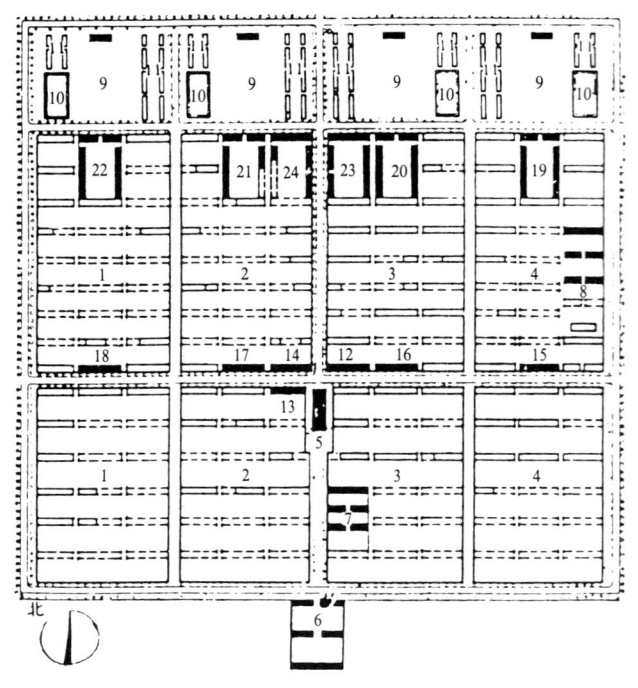

Figure 4.12. Plan of Houtun Brigade in Hebei province. The housing areas for each of the four production teams are numbered 1, 2, 3, and 4. At the center of each housing area is a team activity center (15, 16, 17, and 18). Each team has its own grain-drying area (9), water storage pond (10), and pigpens (11), as well as livestock pens (19, 20, 21, and 22). Shared facilities include a meeting hall (5), school (6), youth dormitory (7), reception center (8), headquarters (12), retail shop (13), health center (14), equipment service center (23), and sideline production center (24). [Source: Jiang 1984, 20]

vernacular architectural traditions of the regions in which they are found. Commenting on the leveling of old villages and the construction of new barracks-style housing in the Guanzhong area of China, one author has remarked that new villages of this type appear "peculiar" to foreign observers, since each looks much like "an urban industrial housing area of the nineteenth century—except that there's just one slice of it and in a rural setting" (Vermeer 1988, 177). The small front and back courtyards of houses in Dazhai-type villages such as Fenghuo and Houtun were usually too small for use as kitchen gardens, a clear indication of local political decisions calling for restrictions on private plots. Although private plots per se were officially permitted from 1962 onwards throughout China and provided many rural households with the land needed for the production of vegetables to supplement grain available from the collective, the political environment

Figure 4.13. One of the Dazhai-type villages constructed in the 1970s was the new village for Qinyong Brigade, Yinxian county, Zhejiang province. This barrackslike settlement nestled in the mountains consolidated numerous dispersed hamlets at a single location. Like Dazhai itself, this brigade attracted many visitors, who came to learn of the villagers' experiences in village transformation. [Photograph, 1988]

headquarters, a retail shop, and a health center, were to be shared.

To conserve materials and space, new dwelling units in Dazhai-type villages were usually built to minimal uniform standards, with the same low height, the same depth, and the same length, which reflected the then popular ideal of egalitarianism. Ventilation and light in many of these dwellings were unsatisfactory by either traditional or modern standards. In general, Dazhai-type row dwellings reflected in only limited ways the in some locales led to efforts to restrict or even eliminate such "vestiges of capitalism." The impetus for these efforts was the claim that "private plots were a remnant of the peasant small ownership system and a drag on the transition to higher stages of socialism" (Zweig 1989, 122). Rural settlement planning and the construction of new villages provided a vehicle for physically reducing such remnants of private property.

Some Chinese village construction went beyond the Dazhai model, adopting a mode the Chinese call "publicly funded, privately built" *(zijian gongzhu),* in which brigades or teams raised funds, purchased materials, designed development plans, and carried out the work. Ownership of individual apartments was held by each household and not the collective unit, as was the case in Dazhai. Over time, each household in turn repaid the collective for its contribution. One of the best known of this type of new village was Huaxi Production Brigade, Huashi Commune, Jiangyin county, in Jiangsu province. The brigade leadership drew up a fifteen-year plan in 1964 for the total rebuilding of the village. At the time, the brigade's 243 households lived in twelve small hamlets, the hamlet being a settlement form common in southern Jiangsu province. The plan called for the consolidation of these villages at a common site, and by 1972 the basic plan was in place. Accompanying the row dwellings were a school, a nursery, a kindergarten, a health station, shops, a dining hall, and a bathhouse. By the middle 1980s, Huaxi village had diversified its economy with workshops, factories, and services, even opening a hostel to accommodate foreign tourists wanting to experience rural life in China. By 1983, the village had been transformed, with 92 percent of the output value coming from industrial enterprises, 6 percent from agricultural sideline activities, and only 2 percent from agriculture (Huang and Lu 1988, 8–9; "A Visit" 1984, 36).

Per capita incomes increased only slightly in most of rural China in the 1960s, averaging about 140 *yuan,* an amount insufficient to enable most to

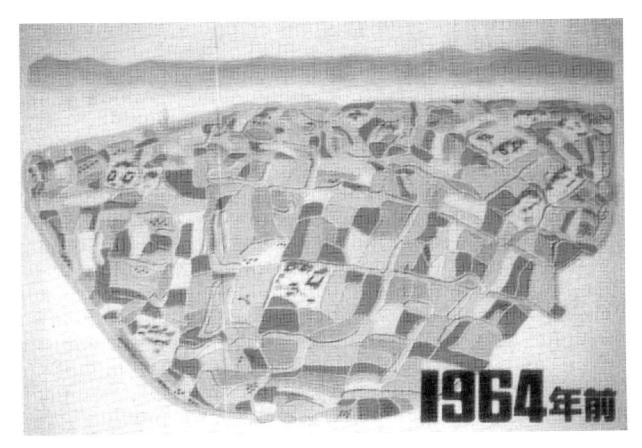

Figure 4.14. Comparative schematic maps of many Chinese villages have been drawn as part of the planning process. The 1964 rendering of Huaxi Brigade, Jiangsu province, shows twelve small dispersed hamlets with some 1,200 individual plots of land. The 1982 drawing reveals the consolidation of the fields and the planned concentration of the settlement. Generally oriented north-south, the residential areas of the village surround common village facilties, which include a number of industrial workshops. [Photograph, 1985]

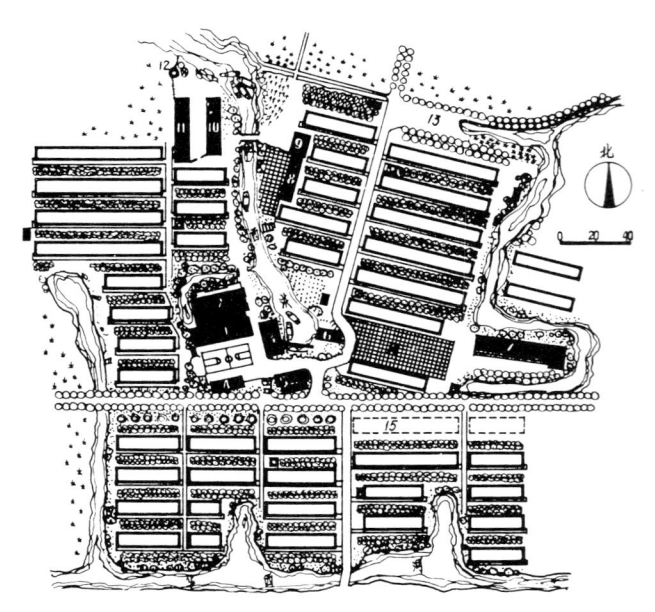

Figure 4.15. Developed in the mid-1980s, this revised plan for Huaxi shows an expansion of the village to accommodate the industrial developments underway and planned. [Source: Yuan 1987, 113]

under conditions where politics railed against such practices. Indeed, throughout the "Learn from Dazhai" era, some freestanding private dwellings were constructed in Chinese villages, but those who built them often were tagged with epithets that underscored their alleged bourgeois or capitalist tendencies and thus became targets of criticism during this period of tense political drama.

Campaigns to resettle urban middle-school graduates in the countryside, begun on a limited scale before the Great Leap Forward and accelerating in 1968 during the Cultural Revolution, also affected village morphology. Between 1966 and 1975 alone, some 12 million urban youths were transferred either long distances to China's frontier areas or to rural counties near their home cities as part of "up to the mountains, down to the villages" *(shang shan, xia xiang)* programs ("Twelve Million" 1976, 11–13). Motivated by ideological and developmental goals, these transfers were

invest on their own in housing improvement or new construction. Restraints on commerce and the production of agricultural crops other than grains set real limits on prosperity in the countryside. What cash income came to individual households from commerce, however, was further limited and, in many cases, brought to a standstill with the emergence of the Great Proletarian Cultural Revolution in 1966. Stressing local autarky and an emphasis on grain production, policies during this period constrained the economic base of most Chinese villages. Individual household incomes in Chinese villages during this time came principally from disbursements made by the collective and usually were in kind rather than in cash.

It is remarkable that some villagers did scrimp and save, accumulating small sums of money to renovate old dwellings or build new ones, even

Figure 4.16. The accommodations provided for "sent-down" youth in the late 1960s varied from village homes to barracks-style dormitories. This row structure was built to house some twenty or twenty-five youths from Hangzhou who were sent to live in Licun, an out-of-the-way village in Jiande county, Zhejiang province. [Photograph, 1990]

implemented to carry forward a utopian desire to create a "new socialist man," to relieve problems of urban unemployment, as well as to stimulate rural development (see also Bernstein 1977; Parish and Whyte 1978). The number of youths transferred to individual villages varied from place to place, putting different demands on existing housing. Sent-down youths sometimes were housed in vacant housing and a limited number lived with village families, but, in most cases, new structures were built to accommodate them. These ranged from clearly substandard huts, about which many complaints were issued in the press and in letters home, to substantial brick dormitory-style barracks, which stood in striking contrast to existing village housing stocks. Often the state settlement fee for urban youth was insufficient to build needed accommodations, and conflict arose in villages concerning using local resources to meet the demand (see Bernstein 1977, 134–135, 153–158).

The death of Chairman Mao in the fall of 1976 set in train a series of events that made it possible to explore new directions to overcome deficiencies in China's rural and urban economic and social system. While gross agricultural output value had nearly quadrupled between 1949 and 1980, rapid population increases during the same period resulted in only slight increases or actual decreases in per capita agricultural products. By the end of the 1970s, the Chinese government acknowledged not only a critical housing problem throughout the countryside, but a need to rebuild dilapidated villages.

Economic Reform Period

The watershed event that set significant new directions for China's economy was the Third Plenary Session of the Eleventh Central Committee of the Chinese Communist Party in December 1978. Policies were enacted during this session to correct "past mistakes," purging "leftist elements" and also creating conditions that would bring about an "upsurge" *(rechao)* in rural development. The principal elements of economic reform were "the responsibility system" *(ziren zhi)* and, subsequently, the promotion of a commodity economy *(shangpin jingji)*. The avowed purpose of these initiatives was the enrichment of China's economic structure by changing an economy based on grain to a pluralistic one. Throughout the countryside in the 1980s, industrialization drew many farm laborers from the fields, gradually helping to solve the continuing problem of underemployment of farm laborers—too many people on too little land. Net per capita incomes rose dramatically from 137 *yuan* in 1978 to 545 *yuan* in 1988 (Jianzhubu 1989, 2). Dramatic aggregate increases of this order, however, mask the significant variations from province to province, and indeed even the differences within provinces. New housing construction as well as the general improvement and reconstruction of village landscapes are but two indices of the success of the new economic policies.

As cash incomes increased, a housing boom began in the early 1980s and continued during the decade throughout most of China's countryside. Countrywide nearly one in three households was involved in the improvement of its dwellings by 1982. More housing was constructed between 1979 and 1985 in China than in the previous three decades, adding more than 5 square meters of housing stock per person (Li 1985, 18). This long-overdue renewal of rural housing stock included not only the building of housing of traditional designs using traditional materials, but also the introduction of designs and materials that broke with tradition. Fifty percent of new housing built countrywide in 1984, a particularly busy year, was of kiln-dried brick and wood frame construction, while only 15 percent was of earth and thatch (Xiao 1985, 1). By 1988, the percentage using modern materials had increased to 85 percent (Jianzhubu 1989, 3). Less wood and more concrete was being used in new houses than in the past. The change in materials stemmed not only from a shortage of timber and the high cost of wood, but also from governmental policies encouraging the substitution of other materials for wood in structural members and decorative elements. Use of prefabricated building components, such as prestressed panels used as floor and roof panels, increased dramatically. Other cement components, such as lintels, purlins, stairs, as well as window and door panels, also increased in use over the past decade.

Concern heightened during this period of great economic growth over the amount of land occupied by buildings and the need not only to limit newly occupied land but also to regain some of the land traditionally covered by housing. As in the "Learn from Dazhai" period, the consolidation of dispersed hamlets continued. Planners anticipated that in north China land-use planning for new villages could effect a 10 to 15 percent reduction in land occupied over old patterns. For south China, where dwellings traditionally have been more compact with smaller courtyards than those in the north, a 2 to 8 percent reduction was expected (Yuan 1987, 187–188). One innovative plan was the "plum blossom" plan for Baojian Production Brigade, Yangshi Commune, Wuxi county, Jiangsu province, which brought about the consolidation of nineteen natural villages into four hamlets surrounding a central residential and administrative area. About 100 *mu* of land was saved while overall residential space increased, because of the building of two-story rowhouses.

To accelerate the planning process, systematic efforts were effected throughout the country by 1985 to introduce land-use planning to village and town sites in order to curtail the random occupation of arable land and correct dysfunctional patterns of land use from the past. The Chinese press made much of the land-use plans and maps that were being drawn for most villages and towns. By the end of 1985, it was claimed that 98 percent of the villages and 85 percent of the towns had completed these planning exercises. The exercise involved two stages, the preparation of a "town and villages master plan" *(cunzhen zongti guihua)* and then the drawing-up of a "town and village construction plan" *(cunzhen jianshe guihua)*. The first was to be a township-wide exercise, treating the settlements as a system and involving not only the collection of township-level data but also consideration of the reasonableness of the inherited settlement pattern within the township. Reports and articles subsequently appeared detailing settlement hierarchies and ways of improving the geometry of settlement systems. The second stage was carried out on a village-by-village and town-by-town basis. Settlements were surveyed and mapped, facilities were inventoried, building quality was assessed, and recommendations were

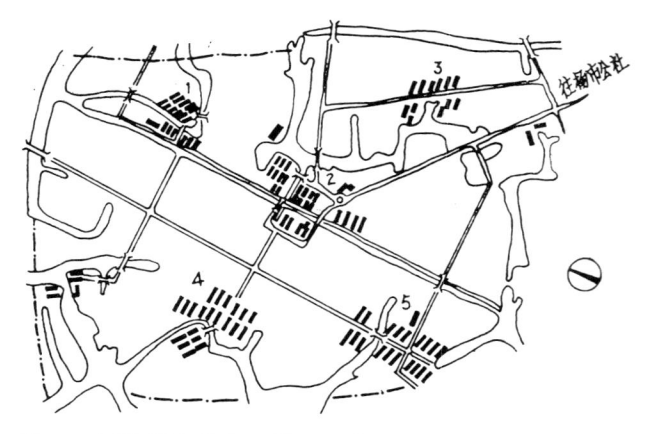

Figure 4.17. This "plum blossom" plan for Baojian Brigade, Jiangsu province, reduced land occupied by housing by 100 *mu*. [Source: Yuan 1987, 188]

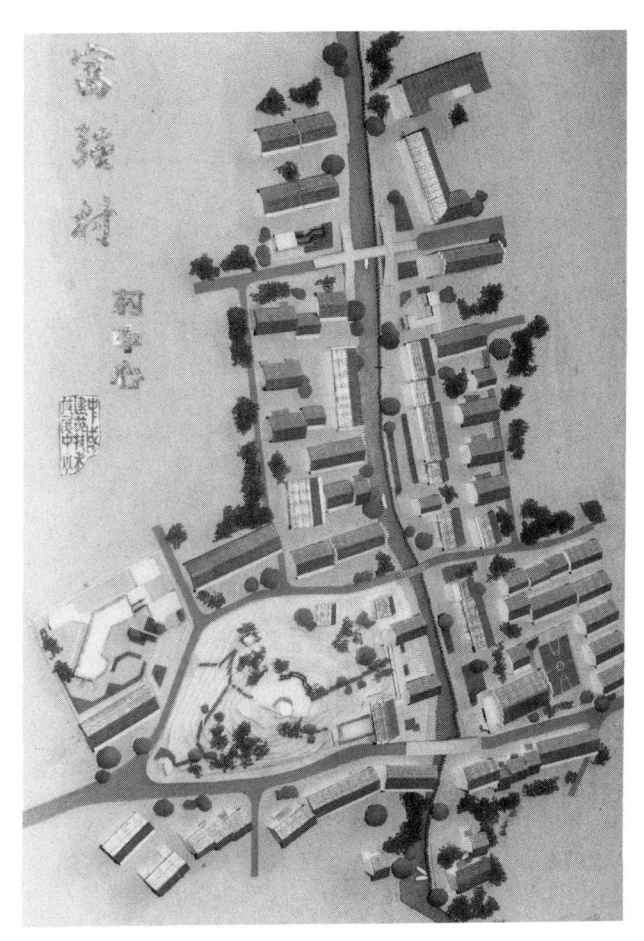

Figure 4.18. In the canal region of the lower Yangzi River, many villages are being rebuilt to preserve traditional patterns of orientation and access to the canal system. Fuqiang village, Shaoxing county, Zhejiang. [Photograph, 1988]

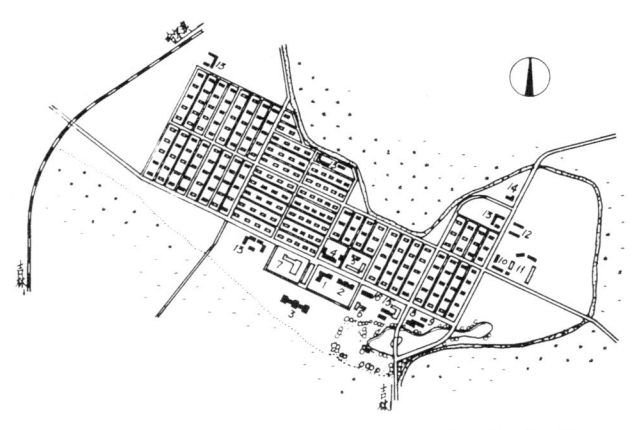

Figure 4.19. The townlike order planned for Aladi village, Yongji county, Jilin province, is apparent in this map. [Source: Yuan 1987, 107]

made for planned development. For most villages, a current map *(xianzhuang tu)* and a planning map *(guihua tu)* were drawn at a scale of 1:1,000, the first time in Chinese history that so many villages were mapped at a common, large scale with substantial detail. Planning maps and accompanying text generally indicated a target of the year 2000 for completion of plans. Although many of these maps and written plans are useful baselines for studying Chinese villages, a great many of them, it must be acknowledged, were completed by inexperienced novices with little training. As a result, the maps often neither accurately document current conditions nor adequately address future plans. A great many imitate the plans existing in Chinese cities with neat patterns of similar multistory dwellings built side by side.

Representative of the planning exercise was that carried out for Qiangaokan village in Liaoning province, a village with a population of some 2,217. Here as elsewhere, a current land-use map at a scale of 1:1,000 was prepared. This map revealed a relatively ordered housing plan, but one reflecting many individual decisions taken in the late 1970s when most housing was constructed. That some land had been wasted and that there were inefficiencies in land use was indeed likely. To resolve these problems, however, the planning map and accompanying written planning document recommended the regularization of lanes and housing and suggested more public facilities. The map clearly presupposed the renewal, that is, reconstruction, of even the re-

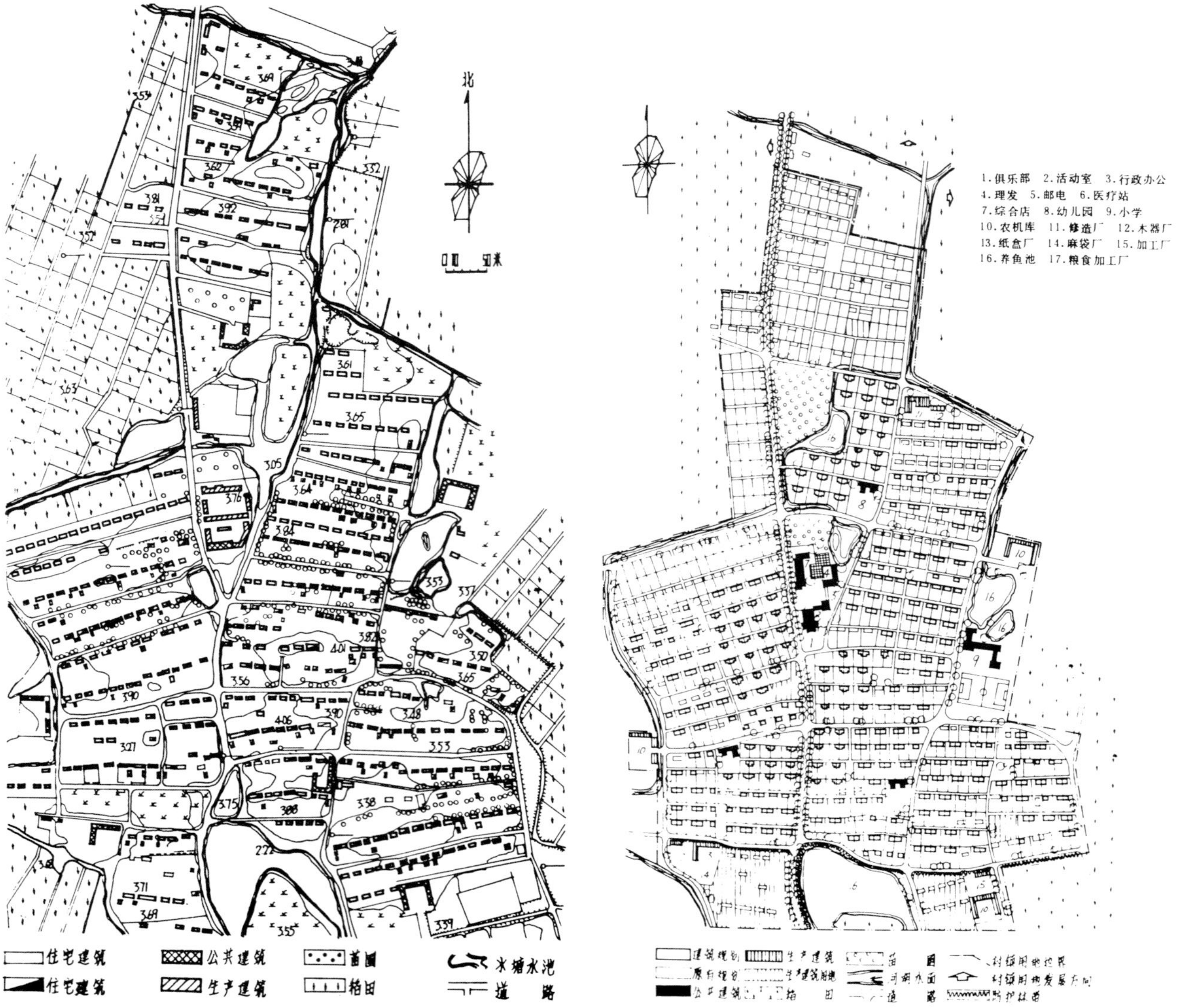

Figure 4.20. A comparison of the mid-1980s village map and the planning map for the year 2000 for Qiangaokan village, Liaoning province. [Source: Yuan 1987, 205–206]

cently built housing stock as the village grows to accommodate 2,600 people by the year 2000.

In order to go beyond the traditional "new dwellings in old style" (xin fangzi, lao yangzi), new design criteria have been drafted by architects and planners throughout the 1980s. A principal impetus has been the need to reduce building lot size, conserve materials, and improve the use of space. Designs have been solicited via provincial and national competitions and popularized in countless plan books and manuals. The pace and quality of planning, however, have generally been inadequate to meet the varied demands in the countryside, and the indiscriminate occupation of farmland continues to be a problem as village and town sites expand in an unplanned manner. Concern for such irrational use of land in a country where per capita arable land is currently only 0.1 hectare (about two-thirds the size of an olympic swimming pool), having decreased by about 11 percent since 1957, has led also to legislation to halt the assault on arable land and a redoubling of the efforts to plan village development. Although the implementation of a land management statute on January 1, 1987, has had some immediate effect on the problem, in many places where planning has been weak or dilatory, individual villagers nonetheless continued to build as they always had, expanding the size of their houses or building new dwellings on adjacent farmland with no attention to "a plan."

Throughout the country in the 1980s, much emphasis was placed on the construction of multistoried dwellings. In 1980, only 3 percent of new housing countrywide was multistoried, but by 1986 this figure had reached 36 percent (Jianzhubu 1989, 3). In southern China, more than half of new housing has been multistoried, and the trend is observable elsewhere in the country as well, especially in the prosperous periurban areas of China's major cities. There is in general a preoccupation with bigness in many new Chinese dwellings; newly constructed space often goes beyond a household's immediate needs for residential and work space. Some space is given over to actual or planned productive use in activities that can contribute cash incomes to the household. Thus, assembly work on a contractual basis for a factory or even traditional activities such as the processing of tea leaves or the raising of silkworms transform dwellings also into places of nonfarm and part-time employment. Taking advantage of increased incomes and relaxed policies, villagers throughout the country sometimes

Figure 4.21. The planned development of Yiduhe village, a prosperous settlement of 232 households in Huairou county to the north of Beijing, presents the appearance of a small town. [Photograph, 1987]

—兒子剛週歲，就蓋好結婚新房

Our son is just a year old, so we've just built him a new marriage house.

Figure 4.22. Drastic changes in policy relating to consumption spurred the building boom of the 1980s, including the building of homes for the next generation, a trend pointedly criticized in this cartoon. [Source: Drawing by Li Jinqun, in *Renmin ribao—haiwaiban* 10 September 1987, 1]

built new homes for young unmarried sons, at once "storing" wealth and meeting an inescapable future need ("Occupation" 1990, 1).

Most rural housing in the 1980s was built without blueprints—simply as imitations or copies of nearby houses—because of the severe shortage of skilled laborers and skilled instruction. The substantially identical structures and confusing mixture of styles give an impression either of monotony or of extreme chaos without originality. Many newly constructed rural dwellings preserve old floor plans, failing to be either practical or comfortable. Often materials were wasted in their construction, owing to poor skill levels or overbuilding.

Although efforts have been made to separate people and animals in new construction, the standards for indoor toilet facilities continue to be comparatively poor in China's countryside. In a 1990 survey of ten rural counties, including some surrounding Beijing and Shanghai and others in generally prosperous areas of Zhejiang province, no more than 30 percent achieved state standards for the disposal of human waste. Even in Jiading county within Shanghai Municipality only 11.72 percent of night soil was treated. The "Year 2000" plan for improving health care seeks the improvement of sanitary facilities in villages through publicity, education, and demonstration projects. It is claimed that intestinal diseases have been reduced by more than 70 percent in villages with improved toilets ("Drive for" 1991, 3). Sanitary conditions leave much to be desired in most villages in China's countryside, a problem that will require continuing attention in the years ahead.

Accompanying the construction of housing in many villages throughout the country in the 1980s was the creation of space for small workshops, restaurants, and retail shops—all evidence of the increasing commercialization of the rural economy at the village level and an increasing pluralism in village form and function. Furthermore, the reappearance of itinerant peddlers following circuits set in centuries past brought with it the reemergence of periodic markets in villages throughout the country. Most such morning markets did not require the construction of buildings per se, since peddlers simply set out their baskets and carts at a conveniently located open space, such as the junction of two roads or a bridgehead, as had traditionally been done. However, as marketing increased in many villages, simple fixed outdoor stalls have been built to isolate and control a growing activity that facilitates horizontal exchange among producers and, as reported for a village 40 kilometers southwest of Beijing, the sale of *yang huo* ("foreign things") such as Madonna tapes and Marlboro cigarettes (Wang, 1990, 25).

Based on welfare services initiated under the commune system, nursery schools and kindergar-

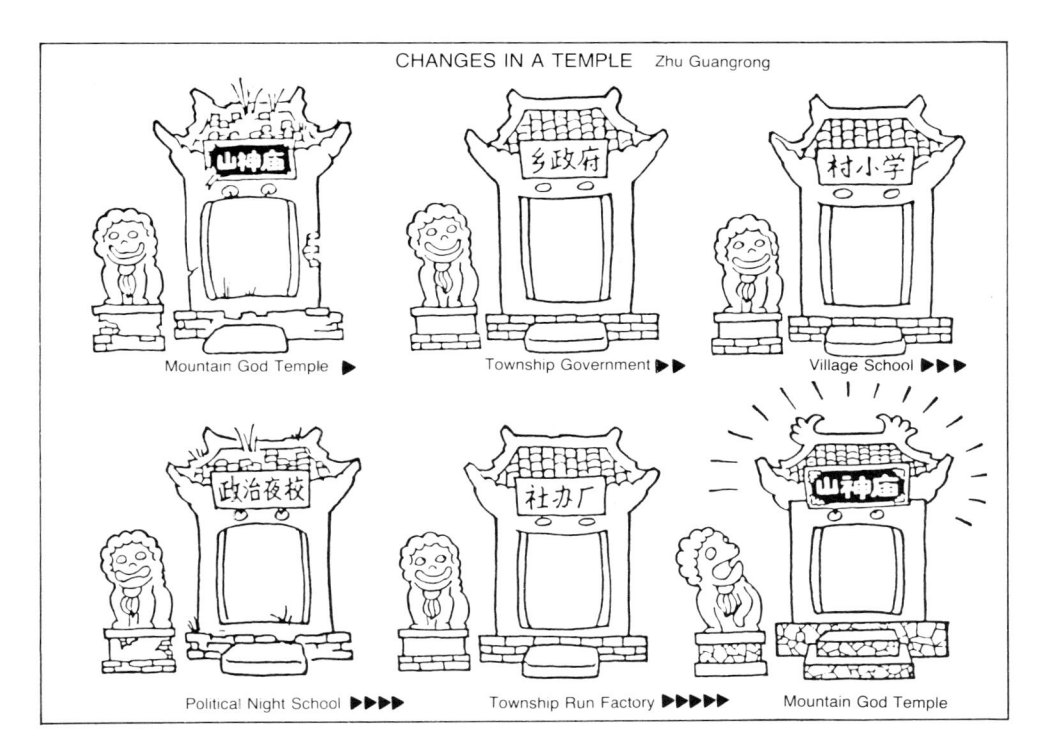

Figure 4.23. While many traditional structures such as temples, lineage halls, and large dwellings of landlords were razed in the 1950s and 1960s, others were recycled as the winds of politics blew. [Source: Redrawn from Zhu Guangrong, in *Beijing Review,* May 15–21, 1989, 40]

tens *(youeryuan)*, primary schools *(xiaoxue)*, homes for the aged *(jinglaoyuan)*, cultural centers *(wenhua zhongxin)*, as well as general recreational facilities were expanded and improved in countless villages during the decade. In cases where village prosperity made it possible, the construction of new facilities to support these welfare services introduced structures to rural China whose scale and design was unprecedented. During this period of reform, many large dwellings, lineage halls, and temples confiscated in the 1950s and 1960s and put to collective uses were returned to their individual or corporate owners. As shown in Figure 4.23, the recycling of temples in alternative guises reflects the ebb and flow of Chinese politics. Some newspapers reported "a craze" for the rebuilding of temples razed in the 1950s and 1960s, stating that in some villages "the temple is the best building while the school is the worst" ("Building Temples" 1987). Dilapidated and hazardous school buildings were reported in rural and urban areas throughout the country (Zhang 1990, 3).

Recent Adjustments

Even with the concern for land-use planning, the amount of arable land consumed because of housing and other construction continued to be an inescapable reality throughout much of China as the decade ended, although by 1990 "the drastic shrinkage" was reported to be under control (Liang 1990, 1). However, neither spatial nor temporal consistency characterizes the policy initiatives on rural settlement in China to address this complicated problem. Indeed, there is a significant amount of variation in the degree to which public policy differs in its articulation and implementation from one county to another even within a single province. Throughout most of the 1980s, neither policy nor planners seemed able to keep abreast of the rapid pace of overall construction that had been changing the face of China's rural landscapes. Even as China approached its eighth five-year plan (1991–1995), China's minister of construction pointed to the continuing shortages of trained planning personnel in the countryside. His target for each county in 1995 was but one college graduate and two secondary school graduates with overall responsibility for planning rural housing, promoting quality construction, and promoting appropriate vernacular styles ("Plans" 1991, 3). The tasks of village planners are complicated by the increasing pollution of ground water and the air by effluents discharged from village factories and workshops. Often using old equipment and obsolete technologies, rural enterprises pursuing short-term profits have introduced a conspicuous deteriorating element into many Chinese villages. Environmental issues in and around Chinese villages demand continuing attention if habitats are to be improved (Smil 1984, 143–148; Chang 1990, 7).

Architects, planners, and villagers themselves continue to be confronted with contradictions between traditional patterns and current needs. A common theme in discussions and in print is the need not only to acknowledge China's rich building and planning traditions, but also to go beyond them. For the most part, what appears in print concerning *fengshui* belittles its practice and its practitioners together with other "superstitious practices" that must be uprooted. Yet professional planners and villagers together generally continue to order new and old settlements in ways that reflect an understanding of traditional *fengshui* elements. Some architects and planners have attempted in limited ways to examine systematically the principles of *fengshui* in order to determine what is worth preserving. However, only rarely do such examinations find their way into print (Li and Wang 1989; Xue 1990). One cannot purchase in Chinese bookstores or even find easily in libraries copies of traditional *fengshui* manuals, readily available in Taiwan, Hong Kong, or Singapore, where the efficacy of the practices is popularly acknowledged. In late 1989, *fengshui* practitioners and "others profiting from superstition" became the focus of a nationwide crackdown on "six social vices," a campaign that also targeted drug dealers, gambling, prostitution, pornography, and the sale of women and children (Chang 1989). Throughout 1988 and 1989, much space in the press was given over to criticisms of excessive expenditures by many villagers in southeastern China in building large and ostentatious graves, draining resources that might be better invested in agriculture, rural industry, or even housing.

As the tenth anniversary of the 1979 First

Generous with death, stingy with life.

Figure 4.24. This *Nongmin ribao* [Farmer's daily] cartoon cynically points out that some farmers invest too heavily in ostentatious grave construction ("residences for the dead") at the expense of the maintenance of their dwellings ("residences of the living"), indirectly criticizing the neglect of investment in productive agriculture. [Source: Reprinted in *Zhejiang ribao* 12 February 1989, 4]

National Conference on Rural Housing Construction approached, Chinese development journals frequently reflected on the strides made during the decade and the challenges that lay ahead. It is now acknowledged that village planning did not move forward to the degree earlier statistics had suggested. Revised figures show that nationwide by 1989, 93.5 percent of towns had carried out preliminary land-use planning as had 76.8 percent of villages. Although the number of villages is less than indicated at the middle of the decade, when the effort was first initiated on a national scale, it is still a significant achievement that more than three-quarters of Chinese villages had begun to confront land-use issues (Zheng 1989), and fully 45 percent of rural households had completed the construction of new dwellings (*Nongcun* 1990, 1).

Throughout the 1980s, income disparities became increasingly apparent in rural China, whether viewed within a single village, from village to village, or from region to region (Vermeer 1982; Selden 1985). The reasons for these spatial inequalities are beyond the scope of this volume, but they have generally been stimulated as the collective has receded and as contract farming and sideline enterprises have increased. In many villages where there was once a substantial financial base derived from the collective that paid for needed public facilities and services, today there is no such fund. In some cases, as reported for a village in Yunnan province, a natural water supply system was installed some twenty years ago. Yet today local cadres are unable to raise sufficient public funds or even voluntary contributions to repair the leaking pipes. As a result, villagers now must carry buckets of drinking water from a distant spring as they once did in poorer, pre-Liberation days. "According to the village head, real incomes have increased substantially since decollectivization. The crisis . . . is not so much economic as organizational: a weakness of leadership and a loss of community cohesion" (Unger and Xiong 1990, 14).

The neglect of community facilities built during the 1950–1980 period is observable in villages throughout the country as economic institutions have undergone a transition from a redistributive to a market-oriented economy which has accompanied the expansion of the production responsibility system. In a study of villages in Fujian, Nee and Su, moreover, found a correlation between the level of economic development and the range of services and facilities provided for villagers (1990, 18–23). Affluent villages, utilizing resources from the public accumulation fund, the public welfare fund, and income from village collective enterprises, increasingly continue to support and build schools, health care and recreational facilities, to expand tap water and electric service and less visible village improvements, as well as invest in agricultural and industrial improvements. Poorer villages, however, clearly lag, letting the fruits of past collective actions deteriorate and failing to initiate new community-wide village improvements.

Recent national policy adjustments implemented to cool down an overheated economy and restrain consumption have had an effect on rural habitats. Government policies from 1988 onward have attempted to uproot structural defects in China's mixed economy, which has elements of both central planning and market orientation. As a result, many inefficient rural sideline enterprises have closed and others have suffered from the austerity policies, immediately affecting income levels of villagers and their propensity to build. This loss of income has been exacerbated by the rising costs of agricultural inputs such as seeds, fertilizers, and water, as well as a reduction in the above-quota price for grain paid by the government (Zweig 1990, 28). Together these changes have slowed the pace at which rural families could amass cash to levels far below the rates common in the early and mid-1980s that had fueled earlier "building fever." Furthermore, increases in the price of building materials as well as the more vigorous enforcement of land-use regulations than in the past have contributed to the "cooling off" (Li 1990, 1). Indeed, according to incomplete national statistics compiled from a survey by the State Statistical Bureau, "the house-building craze has abated." Housebuilding costs increased at an annual rate of nearly 22 percent between 1985 and 1988, eventually leading to a major reduction in houses built as the decade ended. Compared to 1989 figures, purchases of building materials by farmers were expected to drop by one-fifth in 1990 alone ("Farmers" 1990, 39–40). Most observers expect this trend to continue for the immediate future. This slowdown may provide an opportunity for planners and others concerned with issues of land-use planning and architecture to guide the refashioning of Chinese village landscapes that not only echo the past but also catch up with the requirements of a population long starved for decent habitation and services. Political movements since 1949 have acted to guide the appearance of Chinese rural landscapes, all too often divorcing them from their historical antecedents. Quite uniform and somewhat monotonic villages appear all over China, elements of which will be seen in many of the chapters that follow. The blurring, even obliteration, of local, regional, and historical differences in village form underscores the pervasive power of ideas and policies emanating from the center that far exceed those of earlier times.

We thank Mr. Yang Binhui of the Zhejiang Provincial Urban and Rural Construction Bureau and Mr. Deng Zhu of the Zhejiang Provincial Urban and Rural Planning and Design Research Institute for their assistance.

Tradition

Tradition
Introductory Perspectives

ALTHOUGH all of the contemporary villages presented in *Chinese Landscapes* have been "handed down" and thus in a literal sense are "traditional," some are more suggestive of their antecedents than others. The use of the term "tradition" for this section does not imply that any of the villages discussed within it are stagnant or unchanged, but that they reveal less of the comparative metamorphosis characteristic of so many other rural settlements. In these "traditional" villages, therefore, much of the cultural landscape persists in its original form, relatively unaltered, facilitating the emphasis on origins and continuities that characterizes the chapters in this section. What change has occurred generally has been more incremental than radical. Over the years, some village characteristics certainly disappeared without replacement, while others were superseded by elements "new" at the time but later "handed down" as traditional. The villages presented as case studies in this "Tradition" section generally preserve forms and activities that would have been familiar to a nineteenth-century visitor, who no doubt would have written of enduring patterns and the constancy of life in rural China from dynasty to dynasty.

Yet it is a fallacy to speak of China as "the country of 'eternal standstill'" (Eastman 1988, 241). From the seventeenth through nineteenth centuries especially, the forces of population growth and commercialization contributed to the fluidity of China's many landscapes. With increases in population, Chinese peasants not only moved into remote areas of the country to establish new settlements; they also filled in more settled areas with new villages not too distant from old ones. Feuds and uprisings brought destruction to many settlements, contributing eventually to village renewal. The commercialization of China's rural economy led to the transformation of many villages into market towns, with an increase in their functions and changes in their form.

In describing a village as traditional, neither approval nor criticism is suggested. The ambiguity of the term "tradition" indeed prompted Yi-fu Tuan to ask, "Why is it that the word 'traditional' can evoke, on the one hand, a feeling of the real and the authentic and hence some quality to be desired, but, on the other hand, a sense of limitation—of deficiency in boldness and originality?" (1989, 27). Tuan's question is a philosophical inquiry into choice versus constraint. He associates constraint with tradition, emphasizing that "the form and arrangement of dwellings . . . are constrained by the availability of local materials, the nature of the local climate and the socioeconomic facts of life" (p. 28). While small changes can be accommodated by tradition, "radical innovation," Tuan tells us, is not possible without material plenty (pp. 27–34).

The maintenance of past forms, the restraint on change characteristic of many villages presented in this section, reflects generally a continuing lack of opportunity, frustrated by limited resources. Relative isolation, at a distance from modern transport and expanding markets—as is characteristic of Hekeng, Dangjia, Yachuan, Shimadao, Hongcun, and Cangpo villages—clearly has constrained village development and helped conserve the traditional forms of the settlements. Even in recent times, only tentative progress has been made to free them from the constraints imposed by relative isolation. By comparison, villages such as Sheung Wo Hang, Xiqi, and Chawan, as well as Zhouzhuang market town, although not far from the vigorous economies of Hong Kong and Guangzhou in the Pearl River Delta or Shanghai in the lower Yangzi River Delta, preserve most of their traditional form. In the case of Sheung Wo Hang, only a short ride by car from modern Hong Kong, the traditional agricultural base of the village evaporated in the past, yet the village remains the residence for elderly women living out their days and others who find its bucolic atmosphere sufficient inducement to maintain a modern home there while commuting by car beyond the village. Here many old village structures are locked up, no longer used, but few have been condemned to oblivion by purposeful abandonment. Xiqi, Chawan, and Zhouzhuang are likely to be reintegrated into the economies of their nearby metropolises and in the future undergo substantial change. Here, as with other similar villages, the building of modern roads and bridges as well as the extension of bus and ferry systems portend future changes.

The inherited village landscapes described in this section are clearly utilitarian, with the business of living guiding their shape and the use of space. Environmental adaptation has helped structure the differences observed in the subterranean villages in the loessial uplands of Shaanxi and Gansu, the fishing villages of the southeast coast, the distinctive fortresslike villages of the Hakka in Fujian, and common farming villages throughout the country. Some traditional layouts —village plans—are tight rectangular grids that take full advantage of the natural landscape, such as in Xiqi and Chawan; most others are rather loosely structured.

As sketched in Chapter 3, however, even villages with what appears to be free spatial organization often emerged from a "site plan." The employment of the principles of *fengshui* in both site selection and the creation of internal village structure is described for Sheung Wo Hang, Cangpo, Hongcun, and Dangjia villages in this section. Each chapter reveals the high degree of environmental awareness of villagers and their knowledge of recurring patterns of nature. The ongoing impact of *fengshui* decision making on village layout is especially well described for Sheung Wo Hang. Continuing attention to *fengshui* is apparent even in villages, such as Lincun, presented in the later "Transition" section.

The known settlement history of villages in the "Tradition" section is generally richer than that of villages to be discussed in the "Transition" section. In some cases it is the emphasis of the authors on origins and developments rather than presentday circumstances that places their chapters in this section.

Although none of these "traditional" villages is a fossil, untouched by progress, enough of the past has been maintained to evoke in any visitor a respect for and an understanding of "old China." The authors of the chapters on Hongcun, Dangjia, Zhouzhuang, and Cangpo note calls for the preservation of these settlements, whose historical designation arises more from relatively intact "survival" than from any important and specific historical significance of the settlements. The intent in surveying traditional spatial aspects of Chinese villages is not to nurture a nostalgic, romantic view of the past but to document forms before they disappear or are corrupted beyond recognition.

In Taiwan and Hong Kong, whose transformation predates that being carried out on the mainland, only fragments of past rural environments have been preserved, usually without a sense of the settlement ensemble of which they were once part. An example is the Antai Lin mansion, which was moved brick by brick from its original location in eastern Taipei and reconstructed in a park in the northern part of the city in order to accommodate modern road building and the transformation of farmland to prime real estate. All over the island, preservationists have photographed and documented with drawings a large number of dwellings about to be razed, often salvaging mere lifeless two-dimensional representations of vernacular life. The efforts have been heroic, but it is a melancholy fact that much of value has been lost and what can now be saved are only "representative" fragments (Han and Hung 1973; Han 1983; Yu 1983; Lee 1984). At a larger scale, the surveying, mapping, and photographing of groups of village houses that lie in Yangmingshan National Park amidst the suburban sprawl of Taipei is an attempt to spur the preservation of extensive portions of Taiwan's cultural landscape in situ (Lee 1988). In late 1990, portions of a traditional village were recreated in a 3-hectare "World of Yesteryear" in Taipei to help afford youth in Taiwan a sense of their past. "Today's World" and "Tomorrow's World" are still under construction.

In the shadow of Hong Kong's high-rise apartment blocks, just a short walk from the Tsuen Wan MRT underground station, is found Sam Tung Uk, an eighteenth-century rectangular-walled Hakka village. Converted into a museum in 1987, this complex is no longer anchored to the environs that gave it birth, even though through its multimedia exhibits, visitors are able to glimpse Hong Kong's past village life. Weekend hikers are able to visit a smaller and less wealthy dwelling complex, the Sheung Yiu Folk Museum in Sai Kung. Here, in a less rich rural hamlet, the life of common peasants is well preserved and effectively presented. Yet, it is striking that even beyond these two museums there are countless other settlements and rural houses within Hong Kong that are worthy of preservation.

On the mainland, there are relatively few who call for the protection, preservation, and restoration of common rural buildings, pathscapes, trees, temples, lineage halls, and other vernacular forms. Destruction of the old continues to be rampant throughout the countryside, sometimes even surpassing the purposeful ruin of the 1950s and 1960s. All too many village buildings that once epitomized Chinese vernacular architectural traditions over the years have deteriorated or been vandalized to the degree that they are no longer safe to use. Through the heroic intervention of some architects and historians, however, some attempts are being made to stave off destruction. In several cases, wholesale preservation is demanded of what are called "living fossils" *(huo huashi)*, with the intent of creating "museum villages," frozen in time ("Renlei wenming" 1989, 1; "Shaanxi Hancheng" 1989, 1). Sometimes such demands are made without apparent consideration for the changing patterns of life of the current residents, but in other cases the villagers see a historical designation as a source of cash income from domestic as well as foreign tourists. For example, at Xidi village in Anhui and Zhaojiabao village in Fujian, efforts are being made to lure Chinese and foreign tourists to enjoy distinctive Song, Ming, and Qing village environments. Villages have been tidied up, parking lots constructed, and colorful tickets printed. Even villages without historical significance or truly ancient architecture offer opportunities "to taste rural life" (Tan 1987; Zhang 1991).

It is an inescapable fact that most of the villages described in this "Tradition" section will not be preserved intact into the future but will in time undergo an apparent "transition." In China as elsewhere in the world, as Shils pointed out in his book *Tradition,* "there are very few voices accredited among the educated which speak of 'going back'; practically none for 'standing still' " (1981, 2). In China's countryside, there is generally little fascination for aged objects. Inherited village landscapes, that which has been "handed down," are all too often seen as a burden to be disposed of.

CHAPTER 5

Sheung Wo Hang Village, Hong Kong
A Village Shaped by Fengshui

PATRICK H. HASE AND LEE MAN-YIP

MOST of the land of the northeastern part of the New Territories of Hong Kong is very rugged, occupied by steep granitic hills covered only with grass and scrub interspersed with patches of forest. Up to forty years ago, this was tiger country; today wild boar, deer, and porcupine are still common. The mountains in the area are broken up by narrow valleys, occupied now by arms of the sea. These drowned valleys link together to form a network, eventually broadening out into Mirs Bay and then on to the South China Sea. The northernmost of these Mirs Bay drowned valleys is Wo Hang—the name simply means "Valley of Rice"—some 11 kilometers long and from a few meters to nearly a kilometer wide. Originally the sea reached to within a kilometer of the end of the valley, but reclamation to increase the available farmland, probably completed in phases at various dates in the nineteenth century, has now pushed the coast nearly a kilometer farther out.

This area was settled relatively late. Not only did the area have little good farmland—mostly small patches at the heads of the little bays where one of the mountain streams reaches the sea—but the network of inlets and islands was attractive to pirates. Probably some farming and possibly even some tiny villages existed in the area by the Ming dynasty, but it was peripheral to the major lineages that dominated the Hong Kong region then. After the rescission of the Coastal Evacuation Order in 1669, these major lineages found it convenient to open the marginal eastern lands to newcomers, Hakkas from the northeast, while they concentrated themselves in the western river valleys (Faure 1986, 26–27, 156–158).

Wo Hang valley was settled in the late seventeenth century by a number of Hakka groups. One such group consisted of Lee Tak-wah and his son Lee Kuen-lam, who, according to the old Clan Record, came to the village site near the head of the valley in 1688. Their descendants now occupy the villages of Sheung Wo Hang ("Upper Wo Hang"), Ha Wo Hang ("Lower Wo Hang") and Tai Long within the valley, Tsiu Hang a little farther along the coast, and possibly Ma Yau Tong in Kwun Tong on the edge of the city. Since Lee Tak-wah was an only son, he

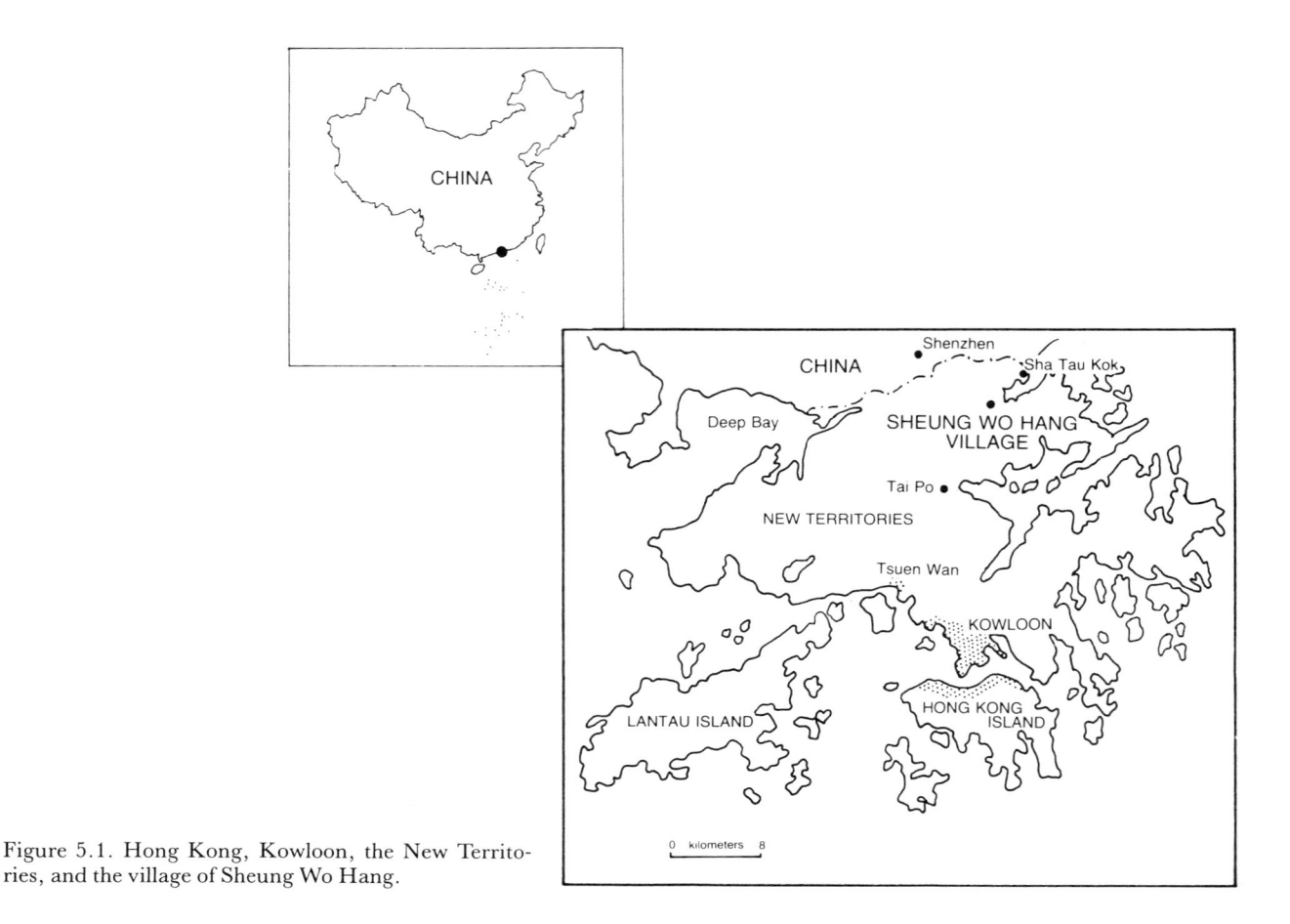

Figure 5.1. Hong Kong, Kowloon, the New Territories, and the village of Sheung Wo Hang.

brought the bones of his parents with him for reburial in his new home to signify, according to Hakka custom, his firm break with his old village, Wang Lung Tsai village in Pok Lo county to the west.

Historically, most of the villages in the Hong Kong region were villages of rice subsistence farmers, who grew no cash crops of any sort. Sheung Wo Hang was no exception. There was no silk produced anywhere in the region, and although some villages in the mountains grew tea for their own consumption and a surplus for sale in the local market towns, Sheung Wo Hang grew none. The villagers wore clothing of hemp cloth, from hemp plants they grew themselves. Sugar was produced for local sale in some villages of the Hong Kong region, but the great, heavy, ox-driven stone presses were very expensive. There were none in Sheung Wo Hang nor in any of the nearby villages. Two crops of rice and, in most cases, a third crop of winter sweet potatoes were grown in the small fields.

In Sheung Wo Hang, as in many villages of the region, the individual households owned the houses they occupied as well as the fields they had bought or opened up with their own labor. How-

Figure 5.2. The Wo Hang valley from the air (1964). [Reproduced courtesy of the Mapping and Survey Office, Hong Kong]

Figure 5.3. Perspective view of Sheung Wo Hang from the southwest, circa 1958.

ever, the great bulk of the agricultural land—especially the higher-quality double-crop paddy land—was owned by the communal and ancestral trusts. In Sheung Wo Hang, 89 percent of the double-crop paddy land was owned by village trusts in 1905, although only 31 percent of the dry cultivated areas high on the hillsides, much of which would have been opened by individuals, was owned by the trusts.

The lowland villages of the Hong Kong region rarely had any "cottage industries." Rather, the poor mountain villages were the home of the local stonecutters, carpenters, rice-grinder makers, rattan makers, weavers, and animal breeders. Upland villages were almost always short of the rice land needed for their basic subsistence. They usually sold their skills not for cash but for rice, and usually only within the circle of their immediately adjacent lowland villages. There seems to have been an almost complete lack of cottage industries in Sheung Wo Hang. Only a carpenter and a rice-grinder maker worked outside of agriculture, and they only sold their wares within the village. For their other needs, Sheung Wo Hang villagers either got a craftsman from a mountainside village to perform the task or went to the market town to purchase what was needed. However, as in other villages in the Hong Kong region, the women of Sheung Wo Hang cut grass and wood on the hills, and some of the men made charcoal for sale in the market town.

There was no traditional objection to villagers trading or making things, so long as this was done outside the village. Some villagers always seem to have worked in the market town. During the late nineteenth and early twentieth centuries, one village family had run a lime-kiln about a kilometer from the village, using coral as the raw material. Willingness to trade outside the village led to a willingness to send villagers abroad to earn more money than could be earned in the village. In recent generations, therefore, Sheung Wo Hang has depended less and less on agriculture and more and more on remittances sent back from the two-thirds of the villagers who are now resident abroad as well as on income earned by villagers

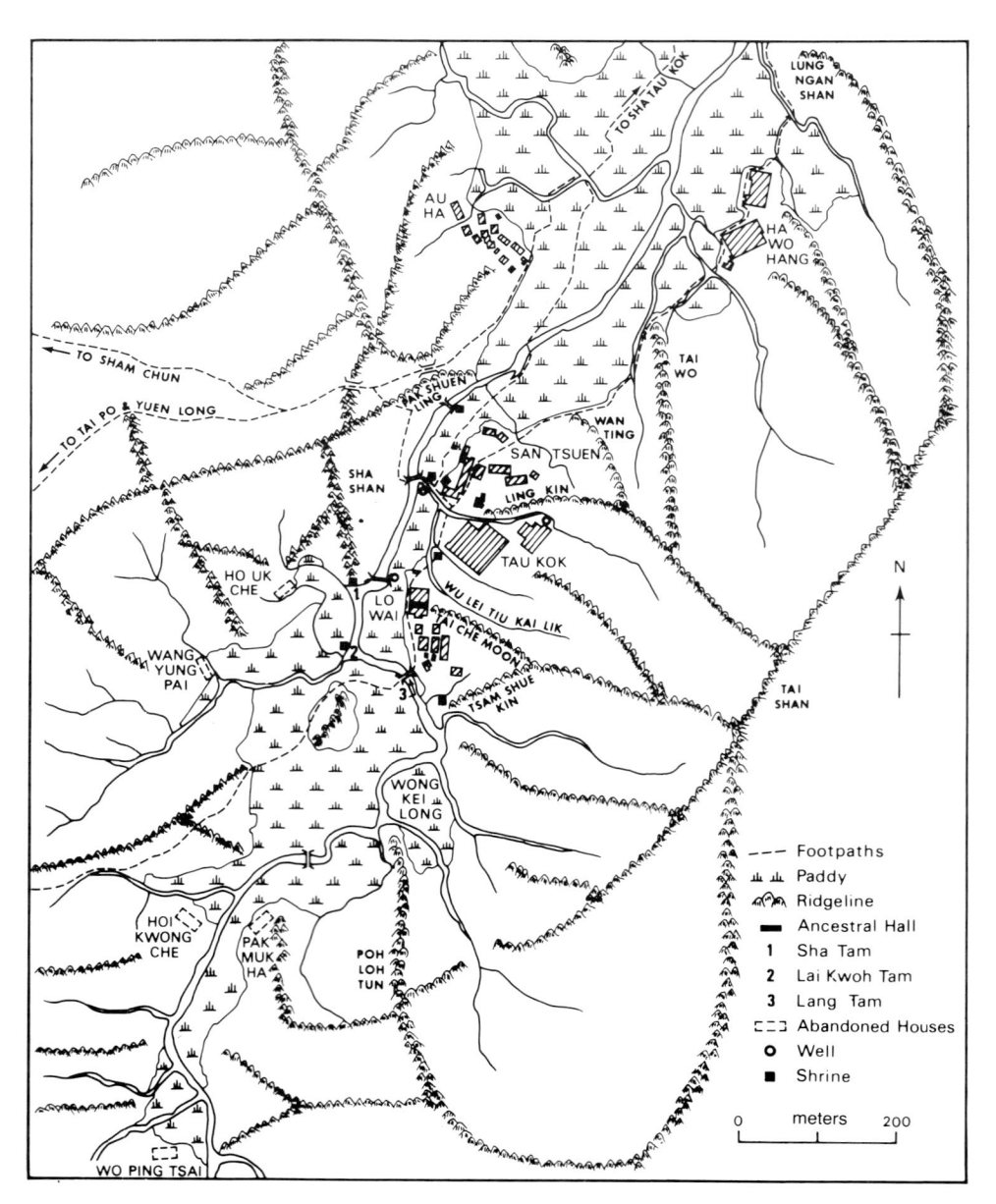

Figure 5.4. The Sheung Wo Hang village area.

still resident from nontraditional jobs in the city or New Towns of Hong Kong. From about 1970, agriculture has ceased to be practical here and in other New Territory villages because of the flood of cheap fresh food from China and the ever-increasing opportunities for better-paid work in the city. The last fields in Sheung Wo Hang went out of production in about 1975.

As elsewhere in the Hong Kong region at the end of the nineteenth century, the villagers of Sheung Wo Hang were a proud and independent people who spent little time on the affairs of the world outside the village. Classic gentry influence was conspicuously absent. Villagers revered learning—most of the substantial lowland villages had schools, run by villagers, and at least a third of the men in these villages were functionally literate—but the villagers did not identify learning solely with success in the examinations.

The village of Sheung Wo Hang, built where the Wo Hang valley narrows to a width of about 15 meters, looks across a very narrow strip of farmland at the steep and wooded hill marking the northern edge of the valley. It is backed by an almost equally steep and very much higher hill, which forms the southern edge. In short, the village acts rather like a cork in a bottle: the upper basin of the stream can only be reached by passing through the village. This position has allowed the villagers to maintain very tight control of ownership and use of the fields there.

In the period from 1900 to 1905, Sheung Wo Hang comprised 85 to 100 households with a total population of about 700. In 1947, the village had 117 households with a population of 507 males. Throughout this area, about a third of a hectare of good land or half a hectare of poorer land was required for subsistence for an average-size household (Faure 1989, 46–57, 212–214; Hase 1981). The 75 or so hectares of land owned by Sheung Wo Hang, taking into account those lands owned by the village but too far away from it to have been farmed directly, should have been sufficient to provide subsistence for perhaps 135 households, so the village was not poor and had spare income needed for ritual and other needs.

Early in the century, the most important lines of communication within the Wo Hang area were footpaths that connected the various market towns of the area; the most important of these crossed the pass immediately to the north of the village. The only footpath of significance within Sheung Wo Hang village itself crossed the river by one of the main irrigation dams and then zig-zagged up the northern hill to join the main path at the summit of the pass. A small number of

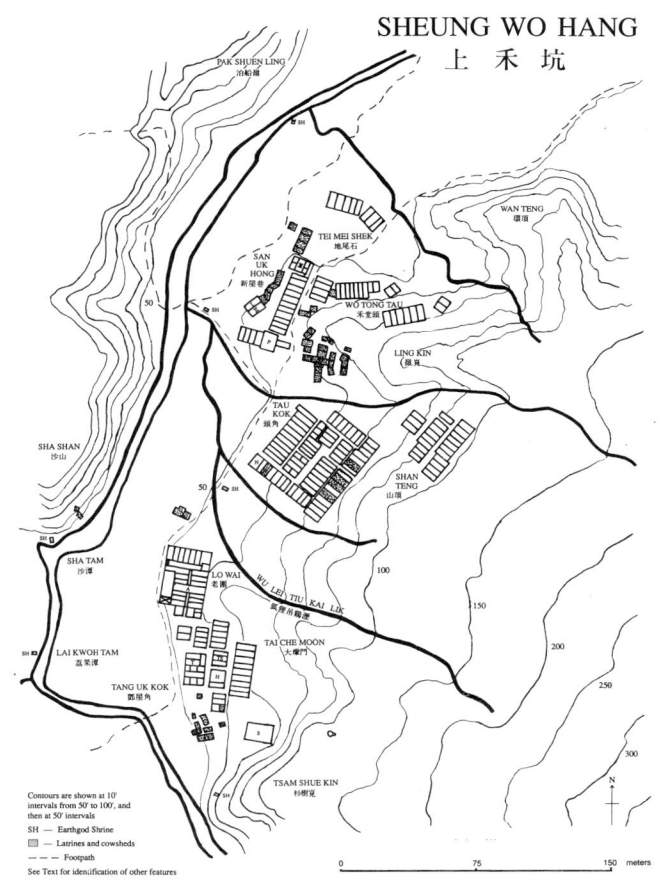

Figure 5.5. The component parts of Sheung Wo Hang.

other footpaths were supplemented by grasscutters' paths leading into the hills as well as narrow lanes separating the terraces of houses. Even today, the pattern remains more or less the same, although the access path over the northern hill is now a steep and narrow but motorable road. This road ends at the irrigation dam, from which access remains solely by the old footpaths.

Sheung Wo Hang village in 1905 comprised, as now, three built-up areas. The oldest part of the village lay to the south, just south of the narrowest part of the valley. This is Lo Wai, the "Old Walled Village," and its extensions. To the northeast and separated from Lo Wai by a strip of *fengshui (fung shui)* woodland, is the section known as Tau Kok, the "Square Block," again with its extension. Tau Kok is built in the narrowest part of the valley on a sloping site immediately facing the northern hill. Farther northeast, separated from Tau Kok by another strip of land left undisturbed for *fengshui* reasons, is an area with a number of scattered blocks of buildings. This area may have been known as "San Tsuen" ("the New Village") in the nineteenth century. In 1905, there was a total of 185 housing units in the settlement, about two for each household: some 47 housing units plus an ancestral hall and school in Lo Wai, 89 housing units and a meeting hall in Tau Kok, and 49 housing units and a meeting hall in "San Tsuen."

Almost all old village houses in the Hong Kong area are single-story, built on brick foundations of burnt blue brick with roofs of tile laid on pine rafters. Such sturdy construction was necessitated by

Figure 5.6. Lo Wai, the "Old Walled Village," from the southwest.

the typhoons that sweep the area every few years. Because construction was expensive, villagers cut costs by building to standard plans based on terraces or rows of several adjacent houses rather than to the courtyard plans found elsewhere in China.

The size of a house was determined by the length of the roof timber. Timber, cut and finished to standard lengths of about 4 meters and diameters of about 20 centimeters, was supplied from villages near Guangzhou (Canton) and shipped to local market towns for sale to carpenters. Houses were built as rectangles, usually about three or four times as long as they were wide. The width of each house was the length of the roof timber, which rested directly on the gables of the walls. In this area, the use of wooden frameworks to support the roof was traditionally found only in major temples and ancestral halls. Long walls were shared as party walls with adjacent houses in rows of from two to about fifteen houses in length. It should be pointed out that villages of indigenous Hakka families in the Hong Kong region cannot easily be distinguished from Punti (non-Hakka) villages—there is little in their layout and construction that can be called typically Hakka (see Knapp 1986, 45–49, 93–97; Lung 1991, 70–83).

Since providing openings in the walls was expensive, village houses usually had a door only in one of the short walls and perhaps a tiny window in the back. The door normally opened into a 2- or 3-meter-square *tianjing (tin tseng)*, or skywell, which was edged by a lean-to roof or completely covered over. If left open to the sky, the *tianjing* was sunk about 15 centimeters to catch rainwater, which passed through a buried drain to the outside. It normally contained a brick stove and a brick water container that was filled each morning

Figure 5.7. Three small traditional houses arranged along a terrace, Wo Tong Tau, Sheung Wo Hang. The left-hand and center houses were built before 1900; the right-hand house was added about 1920. The houses were built in standard *tianjing* or *tin tseng* and *xia tang* or *ha tong* format, but the *tianjing* has been roofed over.

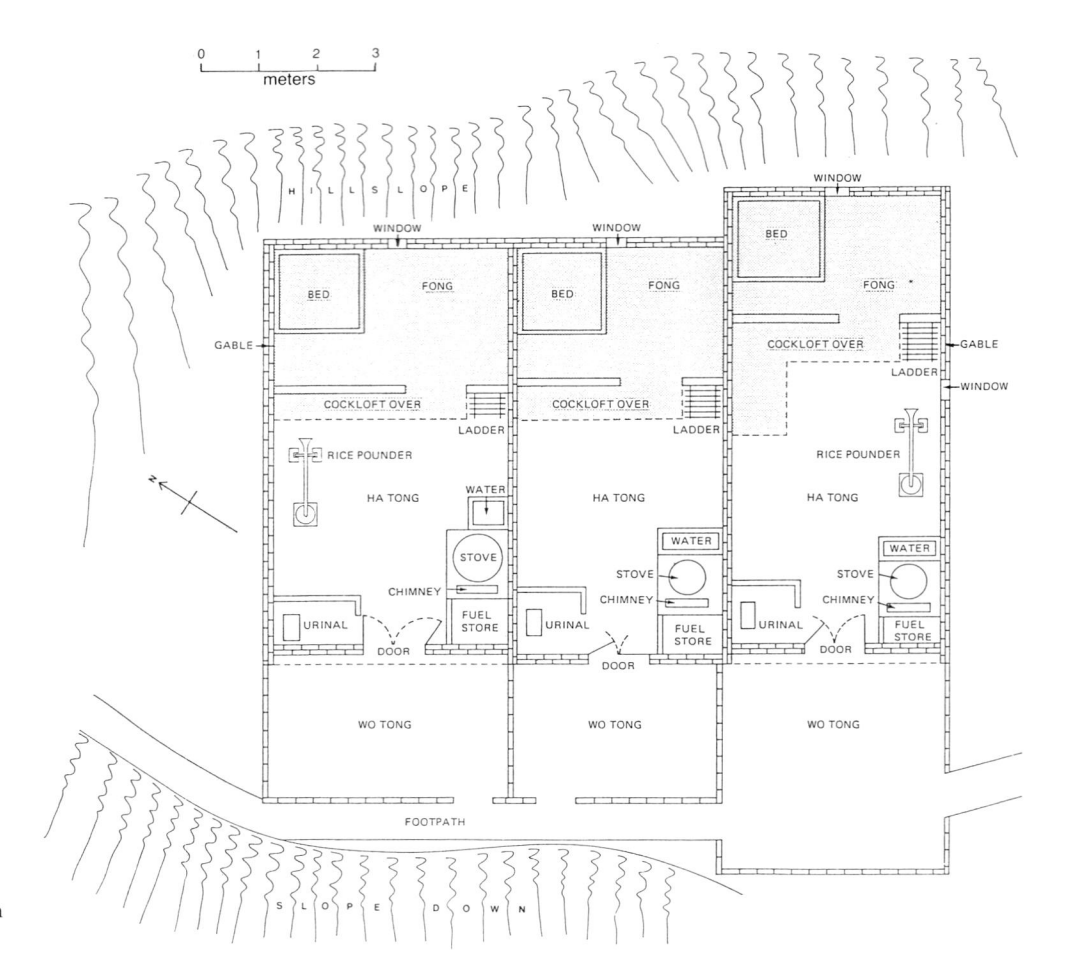

Figure 5.8. The plan of the three small traditional houses pictured in Figure 5.7.

from the village well or stream. Opposite the stove was a corner walled off with a nearly 2-meter-high screen wall, which contained the family urine bucket. Urine collected here was periodically poured into a big jar outside the house, where it would be kept until it could be used as fertilizer. Next to the urinal was a stone slab table under which the rice ready for use was stored in a large unglazed earthenware pot. The slab itself was used daily for cooking preparation. Farm implements, including the plow and harrow, were also kept here, slung on hooks from the rafters.

On the side of the *tianjing* opposite the street door was the real front wall of the house with the main door. During the day, this door was always left open to allow light into the house. At night, when this door was closed, the house was rather dark and airless. To allow the residents to know when dawn had broken and to let in some air, the custom in the Sheung Wo Hang area was to build the main door frame with two lintels. Thus, the door did not reach the head of the opening, leaving a gap between the two lintels similar to a skylight. Although not glazed, this "skylight" was protected with stout wooden bars against robbers.

The house proper consisted of a single room,

open to the rafters. The back third was cut off with a screen wall about 2 meters high to form the master bedroom *(fang* or *fong)*. This area was ceiled with planks to form a cockloft between the ceiling and the rafters. Accessible by a ladder in one corner of the house, the cockloft was used for the secure storage of grain in baskets and served as the "bedroom" for the unmarried sons of the family. The main room *(xia tang* or *ha tong)* in front of the cockloft served a variety of household needs. In most houses in the past, for example, a stone rice pounder was set in the floor along one wall (rice pounders have been superseded by more modern types of milling and have by now been removed from houses that are still inhabited). According to elderly villagers, a single house of this sort cost about 60 silver dollars to build in the early years of this century, using bricks from the brickworks near the pass just north of Sheung Wo Hang.

Where a family owned more than one house unit, one of the units would be used as a barn or to allow two brothers to live together without splitting the family. If the house units were adjacent, a door might be opened between adjacent *tianjing* to interconnect the dwellings. A superfluous street door might then be bricked up or left locked. Where a family owned only one house unit, the skywell would often be roofed over and the cockloft extended over one side of the main room to expand the usable space. However, in making more room the house would become darker and more airless. Ideally, houses consisted of three interconnecting house units, but this ideal home was not commonly found. Three-unit houses usually indicated an extended family that had not divided its inherited property.

Since houses were small and constricted, villagers owning pigs or cattle could not usually keep them inside the house. Small sheds of mud brick or bamboo for domestic animals were, therefore, built on the periphery of the village. Latrines, grounds for drying manure, and bonfire sites for rubbish were provided nearby. Latrines were privately owned, often by ancestral trusts. Individual villagers contracted with a latrine owner to use his facility in return for a number of baskets of prepared manure at the end of the year (Hase 1983, 1988). Sheung Wo Hang had thirty latrines in 1905, about one to every three households. Latrines and cowsheds had little *fengshui* significance. Although they were not built in the most sensitive *fengshui* areas, they were permitted in areas where houses would not be allowed. Today in Sheung Wo Hang, most of the old latrines and cowsheds are in ruins, because the poor materials of which they were built have not stood up well to the weather. They are no longer needed, because modern sewerage has reached the village and agriculture has been given up.

Few traditional houses have survived in Sheung Wo Hang without change. Many have been rebuilt as two- or three-story buildings with windows on each floor. Rebuilt houses generally are on the old building lots within the old rows. Although these newly rebuilt houses still cannot have windows in the side walls or in the back walls for *fengshui* reasons, they are much brighter and airier than the old houses. Elderly villagers remember that the old houses were almost unbearable in the tropical summer. Many houses survive from the 1960s and 1970s with the old layout intact, locked up by villagers who have left to work abroad. Only a few houses have been built on new sites in Sheung Wo Hang since 1905, and the village layout is still almost the same as then.

All three types of nucleated village plans common to the Hong Kong area can be seen in Sheung Wo Hang. No dispersed village layouts exist in the area, however. The first village type found is the walled village, or *wai,* composed of rows of houses arranged in a regular square or rectangular block. Each *wai* is either surrounded by a wall or enveloped by the unbroken face made up of the rear walls of each row of houses. In the latter case, the front face of the block is broken by the doors of the front row of houses as well as by the gateway leading to the other rows. If a separate wall is built in front of the front row of houses, only one gateway is provided in the center of the wall. In a *wai*, the rows of houses are built to similar lengths, parallel to each other, and separated by lanes often only a meter wide. One row of buildings is built at right angles at each "open" end of the parallel rows of houses. This row is sometimes composed of houses, sometimes of cowsheds and latrines. Access is essentially only at the front of the block, although narrow and undemonstrative doorways may also be provided toward the back. Usually a *wai* is fronted by a wide communal rice-drying ground or *hetang (wo tong)*. With regard to the *fengshui* of a *wai*, the "direction" of a *wai* is the direction of the front entrance, and all houses within the *wai* are assumed to share that direction. At Sheung Wo Hang, Lo Wai and Tau Kok are both *wai*. Ha Wo Hang is built as two *wai*. Within a *wai*, space is always very restricted and houses are usually small. Open space is found only outside the *wai*, where the *hetang* serves also as the normal play space for children and as a meeting area for adults except when needed at harvest time.

The two other major village layouts are the two subtypes of unwalled village, or *cun (tsuen)*. The regular *cun* has its rows of houses built parallel to each other, separated by narrow lanes. Although these rows of houses may be of different lengths, with no regular shape to the whole, all the houses of such a *cun* share a single direction and *fengshui* characteristic. The Shan Teng extension to Tau Kok is of this type.

In irregular *cun*, rows of houses are not parallel to each other. Usually such *cun* have their rows of houses arranged along the line of a hill. Since the hill bends, these rows all face slightly different directions and have slightly different *fengshui* characteristics. The "San Tsuen" part of Wo Hang is of this type, with its rows of houses facing in eight different directions, almost all related to the line of Ling Kin hill. Au Ha village is also of this type.

The *Fengshui* of Sheung Wo Hang

The early history of the Lees in Wo Hang is not completely clear. The Lees, according to village tradition, were but one of four Hakka families who occupied the valley—the others being the Hos, the Tsangs, and the Tangs—and the last of the four to arrive. In fact, it seems more likely that the four groups entered Wo Hang at more or less at the same time, close to the date of the rescission of the Coastal Evacuation Order. It seems probable, however, that the other three families built their permanent homes before the Lees. Hakka tradition in the New Territories suggests that when a family settled an area, they invariably lived first in matsheds (*maoliao* or *mau liu*) and only built permanent brick houses some time later.

Village tradition states that the Lees lived in *maoliao* for a full generation and built their permanent houses only after they had become wealthy enough to employ a *fengshui* expert to choose the optimum site. The site was selected at the very end of Lee Kuen-lam's life; the houses were completed by his sons between 1720 and 1730. The Lees are insistent that their site was chosen by a genuine *fengshui* expert, whereas the other settling families had chosen their sites without so high a level of professional advice. The Lees have worshiped the *fengshui* expert Lee Sam-yau, who is no relation to them, in their ancestral hall ever since. The history of the valley between 1720 and 1911 shows a *fengshui* struggle between the Lees and the other families, which gradually led to the other families being forced out and the Lees' eventual monopoly of the valley.

The *fengshui* specifications given by Lee Sam-

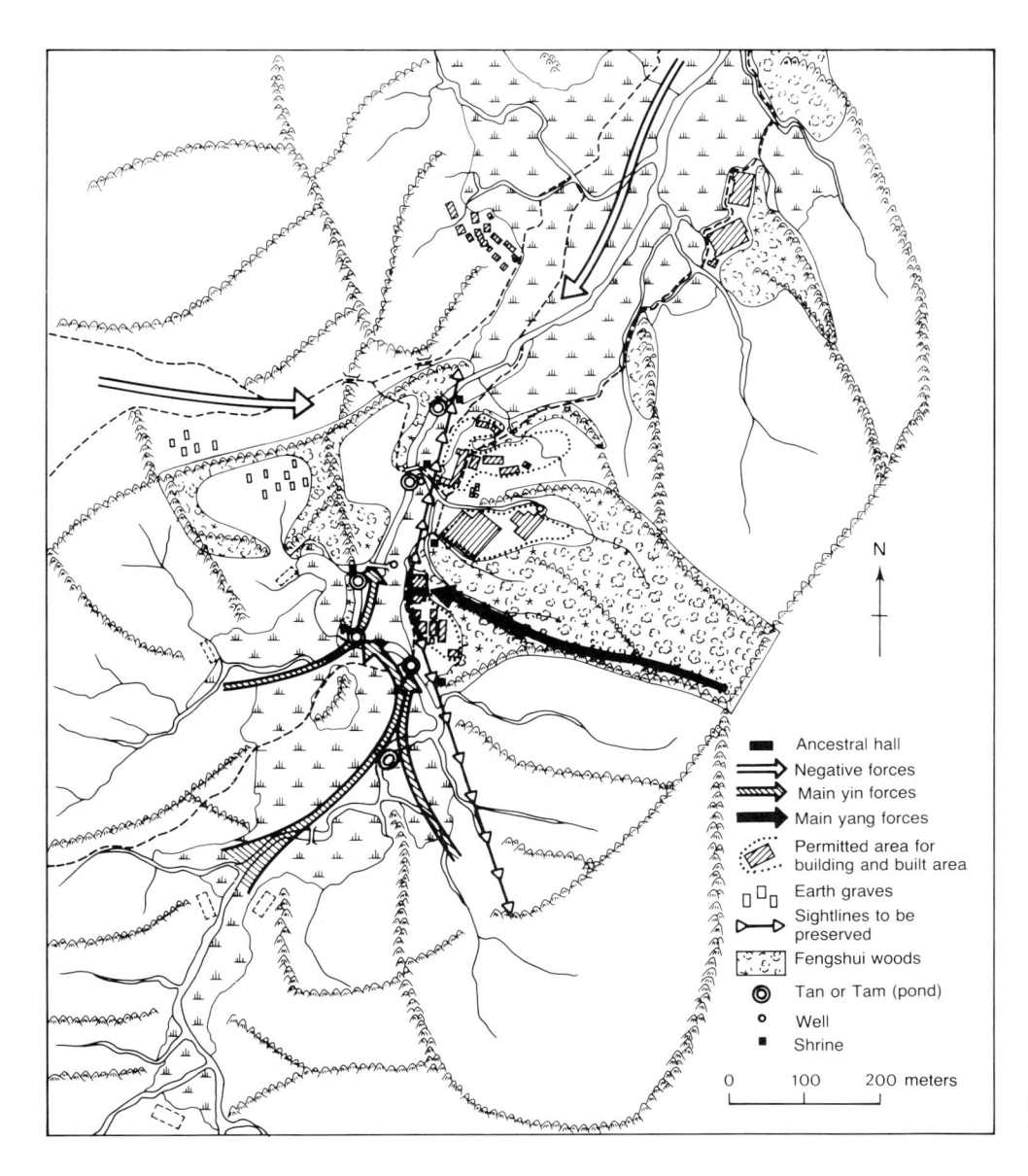

Figure 5.9. The *fengshui* of Sheung Wo Hang.

yau have not survived. However, they can be reconstructed by looking at the shape of the village and its relationship to the watercourses and ridges in the vicinity, and by questioning elderly villagers about the regulations the village used to protect its *fengshui*.

The dominant mountain in the area is the 260-meter-high peak of the ridge that runs along the southern side of the valley. This peak is called by the villagers Tai Shan, grandiloquently reminiscent of China's most eminent mountain in Shandong province. Lee Sam-yau identified this peak and the Tai Che Moon ridge that runs straight down from it as "the dragon's pulse," the main *yang* force in the area. Tai Che Moon is suitably guarded by protective ridges on either side—Ling Kin to the north and Cham Shue Kin to the south. The main *yin* forces were identified along the courses of the streams flowing in three broad curves across the valley. Where the three curves met at the foot of the Tai Che Moon—where the *yin* and the *yang* forces were in balance—was therefore the *xue (yuet)*, the best *fengshui* site in the valley.

Two major negative forces were identified in the area, one running along the excessively open sea channel to the north and one running through the Wo Hang Pass, where the breach in the mountain wall allowed undesirable forces, or *shaqi (shat hei)*, free passage. In addition, two minor *fengshui* problems were noted. First, Tai Shan was extremely precipitous, and therefore the *yang* force in the area was likely to flow excessively swiftly—perhaps *past* rather than *into* the "marriage" site of the *yin* and *yang*. Also, the ridge that blocked off from the valley the dangerous forces flowing through the pass has a spur, called Sha Shan, that pointed straight at the "marriage" site of the *yin* and *yang*; it had the force of "a spear pointed at the heart."

Taking all of the *fengshui* factors into consideration, the siting and layout of the permanent houses of the Lees in 1720 and all subsequent developments within the village have followed the thirteen rules outlined below:

Figure 5.10. The Ancestral Hall and adjacent buildings were built immediately in front of the tip of Tai Che Moon, Lo Wai.

1. The Ancestral Hall was built immediately in front of the tip of Tai Che Moon, parallel to the line of the ridge and as close to the bank of the river as possible while remaining safely above the worst flood level. Thus, the Ancestral Hall faces approximately northwest, immediately facing Sha Shan. To avoid the Sha Shan "spear," a courtyard with a high wall (taller than an adult male) was built in front of the Ancestral Hall, whose sole entrance was a gateway facing southwest, i.e., looking straight down the major *yin* flow line.

2. The slopes behind the Ancestral Hall—from Tai Che Moon and the whole area between Cham Shue Kin and Ling Kin right to the ridge line of Tai Shan—were kept as heavily wooded as possible to slow down the flow of the *yang* forces. No agriculture, fuel cutting, or excavation, including the digging of graves, was permitted. The area between Ling Kin and the next ridge, Wan Teng, could be used for growing fruit trees and vegetables, but the field banks, at least, were to be kept covered by trees.

3. All streams running down from Tai Shan within the protected area were preserved. The stream known as Wu Lei Tiu Kai Lik, which runs from the peak of Tai Shan, parallel to Tai Che Moon, was preserved with a broad band of untouched woodland on either side, all through the village area down to the flood plain. It seems likely that the course of this stream was altered in the area immediately above the flood plain to optimize its *fengshui* effect.

4. The major ridges north of Wan Teng—those that impeded the flow of negative forces down the open sea channel as seen

from the northern edge of the village—were left wooded, or at least the seaward ends of them were. A major example is Lung Ngan Shan, north of Ha Wo Hang.

5. The ridge protecting the village from the forces flowing through the pass was left heavily wooded. Sha Shan, the ridge line itself, and the northernmost section—Pak Shuen Ling—were to be left untouched with no agriculture, cutting, or excavation permitted. Only one footpath was allowed to cross this ridge. It was laid out at the far northern edge of the village, as far away from the Ancestral Hall as was practical, and screened from the village by a band of trees and had two sharply angled bends in it to discourage the flow of *shaqi*.

6. The Ancestral Hall was to have an unrestricted view of the whole of the *yin* curves, the whole of the ridge protecting the village from the forces flowing through the pass, and the forward edges of the two protective ridges north and south of the site, Ling Kin and Cham Shue Kin. No cutting or construction work was to impede these sightlines. Most important were the sightline down the major *yin* flow line to its source in the area called Wong Kei Long, and on to the mountain known as Poh Loh Tun immediately behind it, as well as the sightline between the Ancestral Hall and Pak Shuen Ling.

7. Six Earth God shrines were built at strategic *fengshui* sites on the periphery of the village. The superior shrine, the Tai Wong Ye, was built at the very tip of Sha Shan in front of a huge boulder towering over the river. It faced straight down the maximum *yin* flow line to guard the area from the Sha Shan "spearpoint" and to protect the *yin* force. Of the ordinary or lower-level Earth God shrines, known as Pak Kung shrines, the second in importance was the Lai Kwoh shrine, built on the banks of the river opposite the Ancestral Hall for the spirit of the river. The third was oriented

Figure 5.11. The view from the Ancestral Hall along the main *yin* flow line toward Poh Loh Tun.

Figure 5.12. The Pak Kung Earth God shrine at Wu Lei Tiu Kai Lik, looking toward Lo Wai.

toward Sha Shan. The fourth was built on the line of Ling Kin, immediately facing the entrance to the path up to the pass, to reinforce the effects of the double bend and the protective effect of Ling Kin. The fifth and sixth were at the northern and southern extremities of the village area. These spots were the least important and were not marked by stone shrines like the other four —worship was conducted at the foot of spirit trees.

8. In the part of the village lying between Wu Lei Tiu Kai Lik and Ling Kin, no construction was to take place forward of the Pak Kung shrine at Wu Lei Tiu Kai Lik, to avoid any interference with the *fengshui* effect of this shrine and to ensure that the sightline from the Ancestral Hall to the Ling Kin ridge was not impeded.

9. At Pak Shuen Ling, a band of trees was planted on both banks of the river to ensure that the sea channel could not be seen from the village site, and in particular not from the Ancestral Hall. Other bands of trees were planted to extend the line of the Wan Teng ridge down to the flood plain.

10. Irrigation water for the main rice fields of the village was drawn from six or seven dams that were carefully sited to ensure that water flow slowed down or became still at critical nodes of the *yin* flow lines. The most important of the resulting pools or *tan (tam)* were the Shek Pa Tam and the Lang Tam, at the confluence points on the main river, and the Sha Tam and Lai Kwoh Tam immediately in front of the Tai Wong Ye and river spirit shrines. Drinking water was drawn from these pools during most of the village's history. Wells, dug immediately adjacent to the pools, have only existed here for some fifty years.

11. Houses in the northernmost part of the village (the "San Tsuen" area) were to be built only beyond the riverside end of the Ling Kin ridge (but not sufficiently forward to interfere with the sightline from the Ancestral Hall to Pak Shuen Ling) or sufficiently far over the Ling Kin ridge line that their rooflines could not be seen from the Tau Kok and Lo Wai areas, in order to preserve the *fengshui* value of Ling Kin. The houses had also to be built so that they lay below the ridge line of Wan Teng and its riverward extension of woods.

12. All other things being equal, houses were to be built parallel to the *yang* flow line and at right angles to the *yin* flow line. No houses were to be built so that their shared roofline was higher than the roofline of the houses immediately behind.

13. Earth graves were only to be permitted out of the line of sight of the Ancestral Hall— either over the northern hill ridge line or in the Chung Yan Tei Woh area behind the Sha Shan spur, which was to be left untouched for this purpose and rimmed with *fengshui* woods. Double burial is common in the Hong Kong region, as it is in neighboring areas of Guangdong, Fujian, and Taiwan. In rural Hong Kong, the dead are buried in an earth grave for seven years until the flesh has decayed, then exhumed and the bones cleaned and placed in an urn, which in turn is either placed on the hillside or reburied in an underground chamber. The urn is often a positive *fengshui* feature, but the earth grave is always, as a place connected with dangerous ghosts and evil spirits, feared and avoided. Urns are placed carefully to maximize their positive effect, whereas earth graves are always concentrated in just one or two areas to minimize their negative *fengshui* impact.

These *fengshui* rules have had major effects on the layout of the village. The isolation of Lo Wai from Tau Kok by the Wu Lei Tiu Kai Lik *fengshui* area and its distance from the access road at the northern end of the village have caused the Lo Wai area to become rather empty. Here only about half a dozen houses are still inhabited, as villagers prefer to live in the more cheerful and bustling Tau Kok area. There is evidence that even in 1905 this part of the village was decaying. Since the local school closed in the mid-1970s, the area's decay has been even more evident.

In Tau Kok, the rule that nothing could be built forward of the Pak Kung shrine has meant that the reasonably flat land just above the cultivable area could not be used for building. Instead, rows of houses have been constructed on the steep land at the foot of the slope, requiring expensive platforming as well as awkward and expensive stone-paved flights of steps to link the rows.

It is to the north of the village, however, that the influence of *fengshui* on the layout of the village is most marked. Here, the space available for house building was very restricted, with only a narrow strip suitable, crammed in between the three constraints of the sightline from the Ancestral Hall to Pak Shuen Ling, the ridge line of Ling Kin, and the ridge line of Wan Teng. Much of this land, although suitable on *fengshui* grounds, was steep and difficult to use. Houses tended, therefore, to be built wherever sites big enough for a row of houses could be formed, with small rows of houses built at several different levels separated by narrow, steep pathways in a rather formless layout.

Only at the riverside end of Ling Kin was there any land that could be developed more coherently —but this area was forward of the protection of the Wan Teng ridge and open to the negative influences coming down the sea channel. To cope with this problem, the row of houses closest to the Ling Kin stream (probably the oldest construction in this part of the village) was built facing southwest. The solid back wall of this row—built without windows—would face squarely into this dangerous direction. When the houses of San Uk Hong came to be built, they could not be built parallel to the older block, because the land above the floodplain is too restricted here. Therefore, they were built as a single row of houses at right angles to the older block, despite the exposure to the dangerous direction. To counter this exposure, the builders built the northernmost house at a right angle to the rest, so that at least *some* protection was provided. The villagers believe that this house has never been lived in because of its *fengshui* dangers. Owned by the ancestral trust to which all the San Uk Hong people belong, the building has been used as a barn for the other houses in the row, although it is large and well built. Likewise, the row of two houses lying in front of San Uk Hong could not be built parallel to the houses of San Uk Hong unless the San Uk Hong *hetang* were sacrificed for them—which clearly the San Uk Hong people would not agree to—or they were allowed to intrude into the sightline from the Ancestral Hall to Pak Shuen Ling—which was out of the question. Therefore, one house had to be built at a most curious and awkward angle, explicable only on *fengshui* grounds.

It is clear that the houses in the poorest *fengshui* situation are those at Tei Mei Shek, painfully exposed to the north. The easternmost row of these houses is built so that it faces directly into the Wan Teng slope and away, in part, from the danger. The other row is too far out to be protected. A screen of trees was planted immediately in front of the houses—these trees are one of the most sensitive *fengshui* features in the village and one the Tei Mei Shek people will fight to preserve —but it can have only a limited effect. The second house from the east—almost as a gesture of

Figure 5.13. Almost as a gesture of despair, one house was built with its doorway at an angle to the side walls to improve its *fengshui*.

despair—built its doorway at an angle to the side walls so that it faces into Wan Teng. This feature is almost unique in the New Territories.

Today, Sheung Wo Hang village still endeavors to protect its *fengshui,* although perhaps not quite so strenuously as before. A house has been allowed to intrude a little into the Wu Lei Tiu Kai Lik area. Rebuilding in the "San Tsuen" area has brought some rooflines over the two sensitive ridge lines. Some windows have appeared in *fengshui*-sensitive back walls. However, the widening of the Sha Tau Kok road through the pass—giving greater scope for the movement of *shaqi*—was viewed with considerable disquiet by the village. When the access path was made motorable, the village insisted that it be kept as narrow as possible and that the two sharply angled bends in it be preserved, making driving to the village awkward.

The villagers of Sheung Wo Hang have always been aware that their food, if coarse, was abundant; their houses, if dark and airless were still weather-proof and sturdy; their clothing, if rough, was tough and long-wearing. They have been proud of their well-built and large school, their adequate—if not particularly large—Ancestral Hall, and the two or three meeting halls maintained by sections of the clan for communal purposes. They have been aware of their political significance, at least within the surrounding mountains and valleys, and have been very proud of it. Their tradition of learning, their scholars and teachers, their excellent *fengshui* and fine graves, and their self-dependence and strength all were things to be proud of.

Sheung Wo Hang is interesting precisely because nothing about the place is atypical of the region as a whole. It is larger in size than the average village but still within the normal range. It is certainly richer than some other villages; yet there are many more prosperous ones. Socially, economically, politically, and historically, Sheung Wo Hang is entirely typical of hundreds of other villages throughout the New Territories of Hong Kong.

CHAPTER 6

Xiqi Village, Guangdong
Compact with Ecological Planning

JONATHAN HAMMOND

XIQI village is nestled into a low, forested hillside in Taishan county, Guangdong province. The village, approximately 2 kilometers off the main road, can be seen clearly from it across a vista of rice paddies. Most of the small lanes that appear to run from the road to the village actually dead-end at small clusters of houses, canals, or flooded fields. One path, however, does reach the village after passing through a bamboo grove, a gently sloping bank with several green funeral jars strewn about, and a small sugarcane field that forces one to tiptoe along the 15-centimeter-wide elevated embankments between rice paddy fields.

Each of the paddy fields surrounding Xiqi village is planted at a slightly different time so that the fields ripen in succession, creating a patchwork of iridescent jade and golden greens. As one nears the village, it is necessary to walk along an irrigation canal for several hundred meters to a bridge of stone slabs. After crossing the bridge, the path leading into the village passes an abandoned temple at the flank of the hill and a village altar to the God of Earth and Grain set at the edge of a majestic stand of trees. Finally, the path leads to the open threshing floor that sits at the front of the village.

Taishan county, located just to the west of the Pearl River Delta some 100 kilometers southwest of Guangzhou, shares with much of Guangdong province a varied topography of mountains, hills, and flat valleys. It straddles the Tropic of Cancer, enjoying a semitropical climate with cool, relatively dry winters and a warm, moist summer monsoon season that allows for the planting of at least two rice crops per year. Other crops often intermixed with the rice paddy fields on a rotating basis include water plants such as lotus, water chestnuts, and arrowroot, as well as patches of taro, green beans, squash, tomatoes, melons, cucumbers, and bitter melon. There are also orchards of lichee, oranges, tangerines, mangoes, and bananas. The hilly areas of the county, which had been completely deforested, have since 1950 been replanted, primarily with pine and eucalyptus trees. Under these trees grow a profusion of ferns, vines, and shrubs, which are cut on a regular basis to fuel cooking stoves and the local brick kilns.

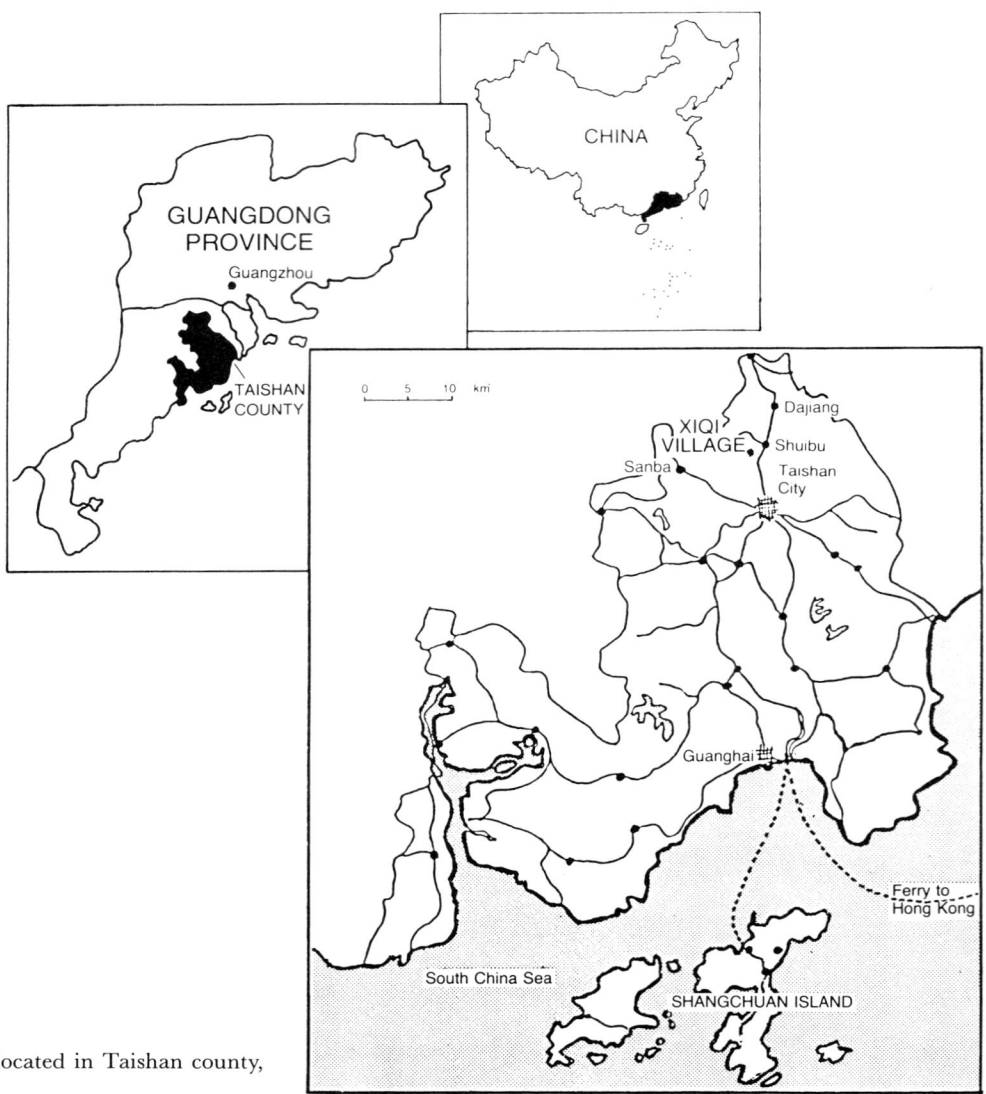

Figure 6.1. Xiqi village is located in Taishan county, Guangdong province.

Taishan county has long been a major center for the migration of Chinese people to the United States. Soon after gold was discovered in California in the nineteenth century, Chinese from Taishan began to stream into California. By 1854, as many as a thousand Chinese per month were coming into the ports on the west coast of the United States, mostly from Taishan and the three neighboring counties, known collectively as the Sze-Yap district (Gillenkirk and Motlow, 1987). Taishan people typically explain that out-migration was stimulated by the poverty of the area.

The proximity of the ports of Hong Kong, Guangzhou, and Macau further encouraged many Taishanese people to travel overseas to seek their fortunes. However, unlike European migrants, who after leaving the old country often cut their ties with home and family, the Chinese migrants usually kept in contact with their home villages, sending money to support wives and other family members left behind. In Xiqi village, as in virtually any village in Taishan county, the majority of the houses have pictures of relatives standing in front of Christmas trees in San Francisco, Chicago, Seattle, Vancouver, and various other North American cities.

Mr. Xi, a seventy-eight-year-old resident of Xiqi, stated: "There are one hundred people in this village nowadays. I can't be sure how many people have been to San Francisco from our village, but I think it is about a thousand. Most of them live in San Francisco and a few in other cities." In fact, a number of houses in the village are empty because their former occupants have moved overseas. Several large houses at the rear of the village were built by "rich" overseas Chi-

Figure 6.2. View of Xiqi village across the rice paddy fields.

Figure 6.3. Section view of Xiqi village.

nese from the village in the 1930s. In addition, there are several new or remodeled homes that were built by people returning from overseas who plan some day to retire in the village. It is fascinating to contemplate that this tiny village is the ancestral home of so many American citizens.

A walk around the perimeter of Xiqi village reveals that it is an excellent example of siting according to the principles of *fengshui*. Nestled within an azure dragon/white tiger configuration, the village faces more-or-less due south. The village site has been set into the south-facing slope of a hill in such a way that prominent arms of the hill flank the east and west sides of the village. Moreover, the apparent height of the hill is greatly increased by a grove of trees that has been allowed to grow up on three sides of the village—east, north, and west—leaving the south side open to the sun.

Speaking about the trees around the back of the village, one villager recalled that "there used to be many more trees in the old days." He continued, "These big trees were planted by our ancestors, and they are blessed with good *fengshui*." When asked why the trees enhanced the *fengshui*, he responded: "*Fengshui* is just superstition, but this village has a good orientation. When winter comes, the trees block the north wind, so the vil-

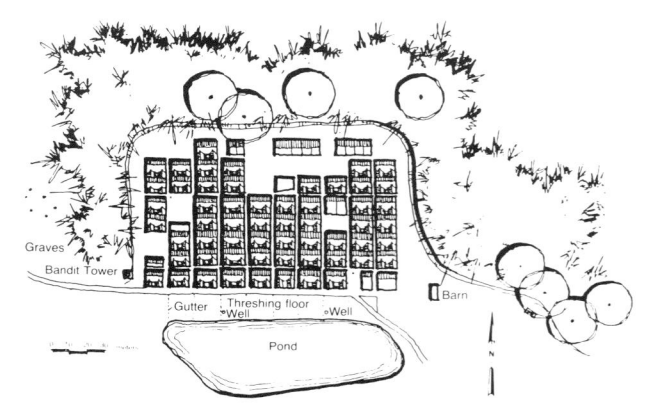

Figure 6.4 Plan of Xiqi village.

Figure 6.5. The "front" of Xiqi village with the pond, threshing floor, "bandit tower," and lanes reaching into the village itself.

Xiqi Village, Guangdong

lage stays warm. In the summer, the trees create a lot of shade, so it's cooler. So, many people like to live here."

Xiqi village consists of seventy houses set in a tight rectangular grid, with a density of approximately 60 houses per hectare. This high density can in part be explained in terms of the kinship structure of the village. Not only is everyone in the village a member of the Xi clan, but it is typical in such villages for the people most closely related to one another to live in the same part of the village (Baker 1968, 126–128).

Although the placement and orientation of the village in the landscape can be understood in terms of the principles of *fengshui,* the actual layout of the village and its component parts are better understood by looking at other factors, especially cultural, social, and physical factors. Villages throughout Taishan county consist of essentially the same component parts that are present in Xiqi village.

A tight rectilinear grid with a definite front and back, displaying functional distinctions depending on location, is characteristic of Taishan village settlements. The front of such villages opens onto a broad landscape of rice paddies, and the back is sheltered by a hillslope and a grove of trees. At the front of the village on the south side are public-use areas, including, perhaps, a threshing floor, a well, a banyan tree, and a village altar or shrine.

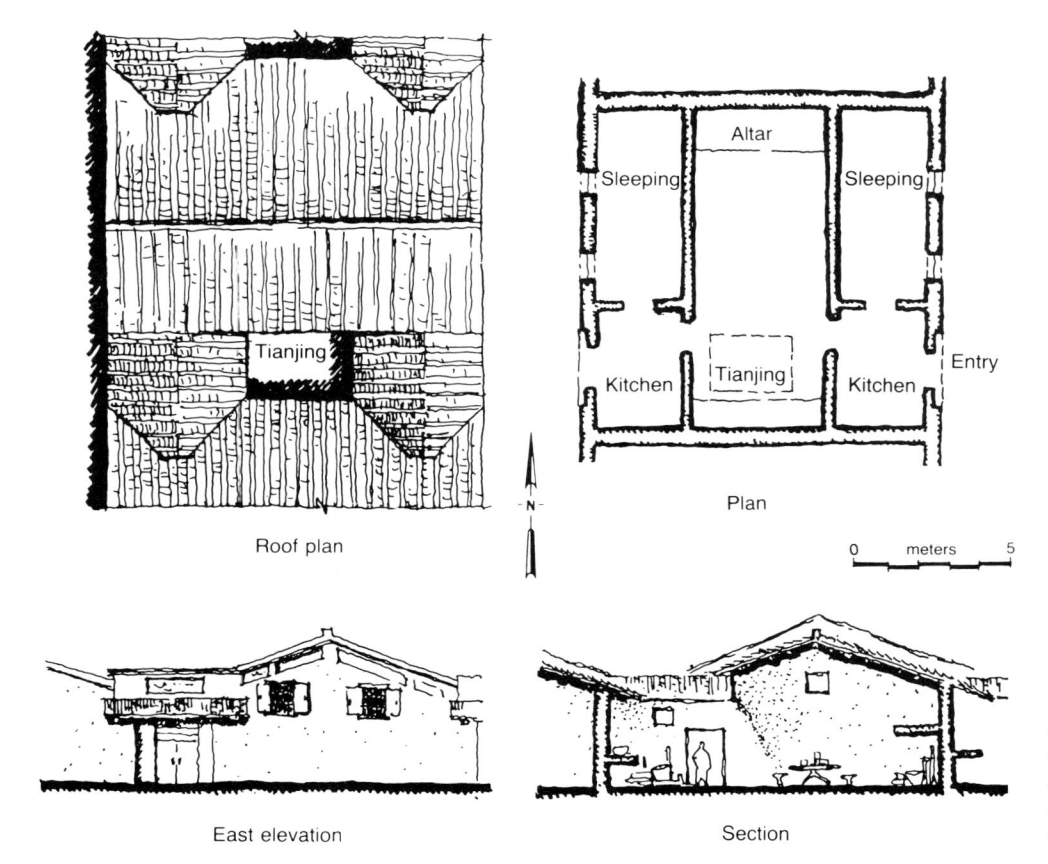

Figure 6.6. Plan and section of a typical house. All older houses within Xiqi village follow this general plan.

Somewhat hidden to the rear are facilities such as makeshift latrines, night soil storage pots, and pigpens.

Throughout the central part of Xiqi village, virtually all of the houses are identical. Each dwelling is approximately 10 meters by 12 meters with a 1.6-meter-wide lane on the east and west sides and abutting walls on the north and south sides. Even the houses that face out onto the threshing floor have no windows penetrating the south wall. The size and floor plan of these houses are typical of the vast majority of pre-1949 Taishan county houses. In Xiqi village the houses are one-story *tianjing,* or skywell, style houses,

Figure 6.8. Interior open room looking toward the *tianjing,* which lets in light and air. Xiqi village.

Figure 6.7. View of the intersecting portions of a Xiqi dwelling unit, showing the skywell *(tianjing)*.

found in one form or another in most of the southeastern provinces of China. A *tianjing*-style house is a modification of the traditional Chinese courtyard house, modified specifically for southern Chinese conditions. In effect, the individual buildings typical of traditional courtyard houses have been pushed together and fused into a single building that encircles the skywell. The more compact house plan is a necessity in southern China, where arable land is more limited, productive, and expensive than in the north. The *tianjing* itself is a sunken space open to the sky, usually only several square meters in size, with an open shaft providing natural light and ventilation. The interiors of *tianjing*-style houses generally have excellent natural light that is filtered through the *tianjing* and enhanced by additional skylights. *Tianjing* in Xiqi village are all located on the south side of the house so that the low-angle winter sun will penetrate deep into the central room. In addition, since there is more rain in the south than in the northern areas, a higher proportion of roofed-over area is desirable (see also Knapp 1989, 38–40).

Facing the *tianjing* on the north wall is the family altar—placed in a small loft in the open central room. To the sides of the central room are the sleeping rooms and either one or two kitchens. Sleeping rooms usually also contain a 2-meter-wide loft used for storage. Entry doors on the east and west sides look out onto the street and directly into the neighbor's kitchen door. These doors are kept open when people are home during the day, and women neighbors can visit with one another while they do their cooking.

Figure 6.10. A modern two-story addition to an older dwelling in Xiqi.

At the rear of the village are six very tall towerlike houses. Built in the 1930s, they are all owned by overseas Chinese and are all unoccupied. Although it was not possible to visit any of these, each appears to be well built. Three and four stories high, they were built on smaller lots than the older houses. The exteriors of these houses are decorated in what is locally called "Western style," an amalgam of European and Chinese motifs that features sculpted stucco work and bright decorative paintings. At the end of the 1980s, several two-story houses were built in a rather boxy style typical of "modern" rural houses found in many other Chinese villages. Most are decorated with fanciful tile work and have painted decorative motifs.

Within the grid of 10 meter by 12 meter houses, the only open spaces are empty lots that have never been built on or on which houses have been abandoned and fallen into ruin. Nine 1.6-meter-wide lanes run north-south through the village. Only two 50-centimeter-wide alleys run east to west. Until modern times, few wheeled vehicles and few horses were used in this area, so the streets needed only to be wide enough to accom-

Figure 6.9. "Tower house" at the rear of Xiqi village, built by overseas Chinese.

modate a person carrying a load on a shoulder pole. The minimal widths have had three important advantages: little potential productive land is lost, the lanes are very deep in relation to their width so they are usually shaded, and they are easy to defend. In fact, the lanes are so narrow that entering them from the bright openness of the threshing floor feels like entering a private space. In a sense one has, because the village consists of a single family line; everyone outside the clan is an outsider unless related by marriage.

The lanes are paved with slabs of granite and concrete. Each lane slopes down to the south, with a narrow gutter incised into it to lead water to the village pond. People use the lane to carry out kitchen chores such as plucking chickens and preparing vegetables. Any kitchen waste that is not used for pig food is washed into the gutters and eventually flows into the pond, where it provides nutrients for fish. People frequently bring chairs and benches into the street, where they sit and socialize with their backs against the walls of their dwellings. It is necessary for them to stand up in order to let a person pass. Young women can be seen in the lanes working at their sewing frames. Stretched across such a frame might be an evening dress, on which they patiently sew sequins for the elegant ladies of the West. Piecework on these dresses is commissioned by contractors from Hong Kong.

At the front of the settlement is the village threshing floor. Located on the south side of the village, the threshing floor gets full sun virtually all day in both summer and winter. It is protected from the cold winds that come out of the north in the wintertime and takes advantage of the breezes that typically come out of the south in the summertime. When it is first harvested, rice is brought here to be threshed; later it is spread and dried. From a functional perspective, the threshing floor is actually a multipurpose workspace, the primary "public open space" for the village.

Figure 6.11. Grain being dried on the threshing floor on the southern side of Xiqi village. In the background is the "bandit tower."

Consider for a moment the function of the threshing floor as a solar dryer. Grain, firewood, herbs, vegetables, and clothes are all dried on the flat, clean, concrete surface of the threshing floor or on temporary bamboo drying racks. With an area of some 2,400 square meters, the floor is seldom fully used except at harvest time, although in sunny weather there is always something being dried. During the year, assuming only 50 percent of days are sunny, approximately 232 million BTUs of solar energy (ASHRAE 1982) falls on its surface (the energy equivalent of 2,540 gallons of propane). If, for example, one assumed that the floor was on the average only 10 percent covered with agricultural products being dried, the energy equivalent of 254 gallons of propane would have been provided by the sun. (Propane is used in this comparison because it is typically used by farmers in the United States for drying grain.) Based on this simple analysis, it is obvious that the threshing floor makes a major contribution to the Chinese energy economy.

Access to water also contributes to the variety of functions performed on the threshing floor. Not only is it adjacent to the pond, the village's two wells have been sunk within the bounds of the threshing floor. A few days before Chinese New Year, for example, it is traditional to wash the family bed. All of the village women on a common day transport their wooden beds to the threshing floor, disassemble them, scrub them down, and then spread the wooden parts on the threshing floor to dry. As they work, they talk back and forth across the floor.

The work activities on the floor provide many opportunities for social interaction among the villagers. Many functions require that people come to the floor at the same time. For example, the grain to be dried has to be spread on the threshing floor each morning and then taken in each evening before the dew falls. Water must be carried from the well or the pond before meals are prepared, and young girls often gather at the well in the afternoon to wash their hair. On warm summer evenings, people gather on the threshing floor after dinner, taking in the night air, watching the children play, and talking about what they had for dinner. These congregations of people reinforce the utility of the threshing floor as a meeting and socializing space.

Just beyond the threshing floor is the village pond. The pond has many uses in addition to being a drainage catchment pool and a home to fish. It is a convenient place to fetch wash water, a

Figure 6.12. A typical 1.6-meter-wide lane being used as a work space. Xiqi village.

place to wash clothes, and a place to rinse chamber pots. The pond also provides a place where water buffaloes can immerse themselves, wallowing with just their noses above water on warm summer afternoons.

The gutters that run down the village lanes all drain into the pond, so that the village itself forms a watershed that helps keep the pond full. Nutrients that accumulate in the village, including chicken droppings and food waste, are washed into the pond via these gutters, enriching the pond and ultimately making their way back to the village in the form of fish. The fish and invertebrates from the pond are important sources of protein for the villagers. The arrangement of the pond, the well, the threshing floor, and the village drainage system is remarkably efficient. It serves socially, it serves climatically, providing a sunny, protected place to work in the winter, and in addition it works ecologically in terms of the recycling of nutrients.

A typical characteristic of Taishan villages is the presence of a large tree, usually a banyan (*ficus religiosa*), at the entrance to the village or at some prominent place with a good view. Usually equipped with a few stone benches, such trees serve as meeting places, particularly during the heat of the late afternoon. Xiqi village differs somewhat in that there is a grove of giant old trees on a knoll above a lane that runs into the village. There is a cleared space under the trees but no benches, perhaps because the site is a bit too isolated from the daily activities of the village to serve as a regular meeting place. There is instead a bench by the pond under a small tree where the lane enters the village.

Although Xiqi's grove may not be a regular meeting place, the importance of the trees to the image of the village is clear. As discussed earlier, villagers consider the grove of trees as part of the beneficial *fengshui* of the village. Mr. Xi believes that the trees were planted by the ancestors of the residents of the village, but some say they may be a remnant of the original monsoon forest that blanketed the area.

Approaching Xiqi village, one frequently sees on the knoll above the path an old woman, enveloped in incense, bowing to an outdoor altar. Located near the grove of large trees is the altar to the God of Earth and Grain (She Ji zhi Shen). During my first visit to Taishan in 1980, altars of this sort were nonexistent, as most had been destroyed during the Cultural Revolution. Now

Figure 6.13. Altar to the God of Earth and Grain, Xiqi village.

virtually every village has rebuilt its altar with fresh new bricks. All the Xi families contributed to rebuild their village shrine in 1989. Next to the altar in Xiqi village is a lanternlike furnace where spirit money is burned. In the past, most women of the village worshiped at this altar on the first day of the first month, the second day of the second month, the third day of the third month, and so on, of the traditional lunar calendar, burning incense and providing offerings of rice, wine, vegetables, chicken, and pork. Now these observances are conducted primarily by a few old women.

The Xiqi village "bandit tower" or "watch tower" was built with contributions from all of the families in the village in the early 1920s as protection from bandits during the warlord period. The tower is a reinforced concrete structure approximately 12 meters high, built on a 4 meter by 4 meter base. By Taishan standards, it is a small bandit tower; many are over twice as tall (see Lu and Wei 1990, 135–143; Lung 1991, 64–67). Apparently the tower served its purpose as a deterrent to bandits, because Xiqi village was never attacked and the tower never had to be used.

Taishan villages are remarkable for their ecological, aesthetic, and functional attributes. Each village is a distinct compact unit nestled into the landscape, embraced by its hills and/or grove of trees, with carefully tended rice and vegetable plots spreading before it. The compactness of the layout of Xiqi village reinforces the sense that the village represents a single clan unit. One has a sense of entering a private space, a domain, when entering the tiny lanes. Contrasting with the intimacy of the street is the openness of the threshing floor. From a designer's perspective, Xiqi village is remarkably efficient, providing both living and working space in a very small area.

Architects and planners can learn from the elegant physical form of villages like Xiqi, where attentiveness to *fengshui* principles has created a visually harmonious rural environment despite the density of human settlement by siting villages against hills and surrounding them with screening vegetation. The compact layout used in Xiqi village forms a rich environment of single-family houses, efficiently serving the inhabitants with relatively comfortable environments and heightened social interaction.

This chapter was written with support from the University of Illinois Research Board. I thank my graduate assistants Qu Ying and Paul Fuesel as well as my friend and colleague Jim Warfield for their assistance.

CHAPTER 7

Chawan Village, Guangdong
Fishing and Farming Along the South China Sea

JAMES P. WARFIELD

LOCATED just 20 kilometers off the southeast coast, Shangchuan Island is a subtropical landscape some 140 square kilometers in size. The island, like other areas of Taishan county, mainland Guangdong province, of which it is part, is blessed with high temperatures, heavy precipitation, as well as luxurious and varied flora. Running north to south, Shangchuan is a long, narrow island pinched at the center. Its sinuous eastern shoreline is exposed to Nanhai, the South China Sea, whose waters provide a livelihood for many villagers along China's coastal rim. Three long, sandy beaches grace this eastern shoreline, and the Feisha resort at the central bay attracts Chinese vacationers from all over the country as well as Sunday travelers from elsewhere in Guangdong province. Shangchuan is served twice daily by hour-long ferry service originating in the "Ever Waveless Sea" at Guanghai, a busy town of perhaps 20,000, which has long relied on junk and fishing-boat building as a major industry.

The village of Chawan, or "Tea Bay," begins just a few hundred meters from the sweeping line of sand dunes that separates beach from farmland in the northernmost inlet of the island. Nestled in a natural nook at the base of the island's mountain spine, Chawan is backed on the west and the south by rocky slopes and low, dense tropical vegetation. Though farmed wherever possible, this land is generally conceded to the water buffalo and cattle on the lower slopes, while the goats and wild monkeys claim the higher levels. Chawan's major rice paddies lie to the north, beginning at the village edge and extending to a mountain range that turns east into the sea. The minor strip of land between the village and the dunes is irrigated and farmed where soil quality permits; grassy land in the area is used for grazing.

Chawan's village layout is clearly related to its natural environment, ordered as is customary by a rigid rectangular grid. The village plan is skewed slightly southeast to follow the coastline, however. Attitudes of urban closure are apparent in the plan of the village, as layers of landscape and built architecture have been consciously placed between the village's major open spaces and the sea. The southeastern half of Chawan follows a strict grid and seems to be conceived as a

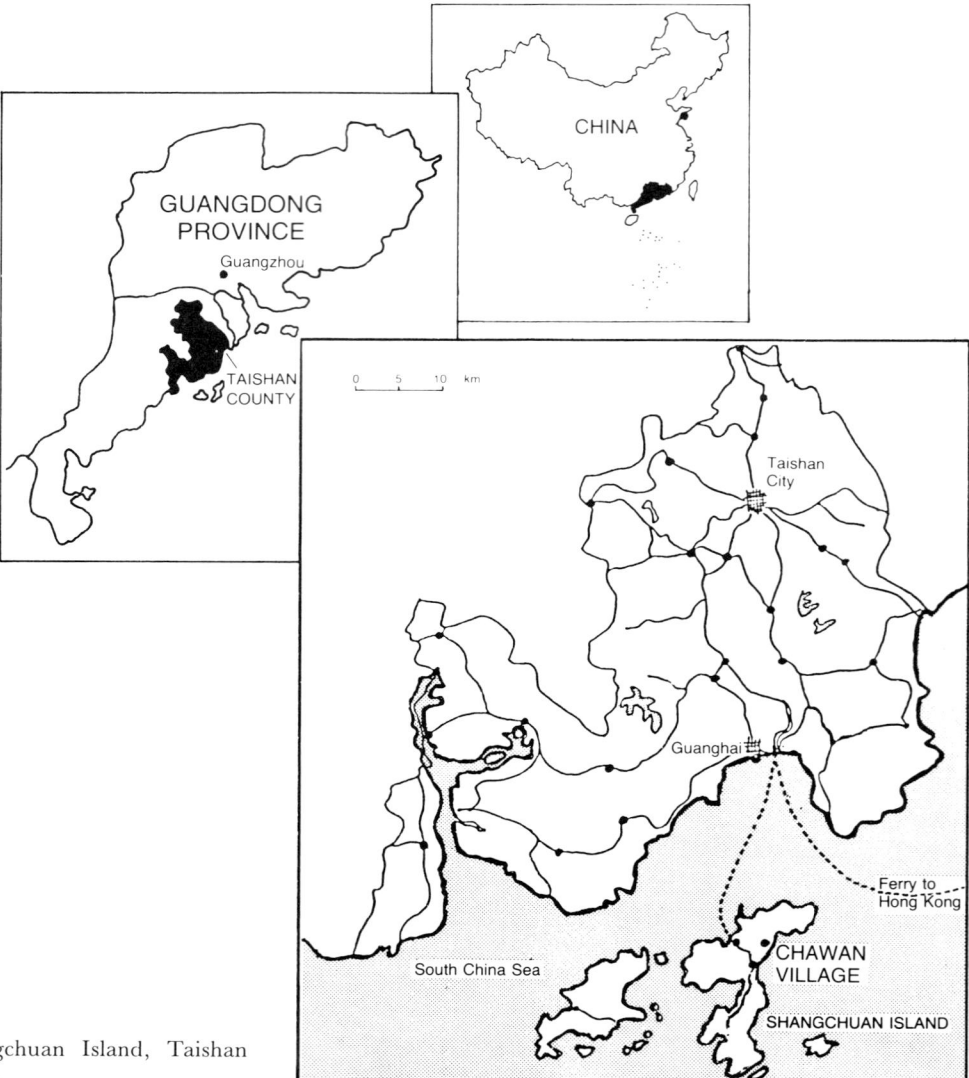

Figure 7.1. Map of Shangchuan Island, Taishan county, Guangdong province.

vertical man-made barrier against the natural forces of the South China Sea. One- and two-story residences are lined in blocks approximately parallel to the dunes and the coastline in obvious anticipation of typhoon winds. A cultivated line of both palm and coniferous trees just southeast of the village reinforces this barrier between human civilization and the sea. A rigid architectural edge characterizes the northeast face of the village, as the end block buildings terminate in a nearly straight line. The strict vertical face of the village is reinforced at ground level by a working plaza, a hard architectural surface some 10 meters wide. Used for threshing and drying grass, this linear

Chawan Village, Guangdong 109

Figure 7.2. Chawan, held in a nook of encircling mountains, is located some several hundred meters from the sand dunes.

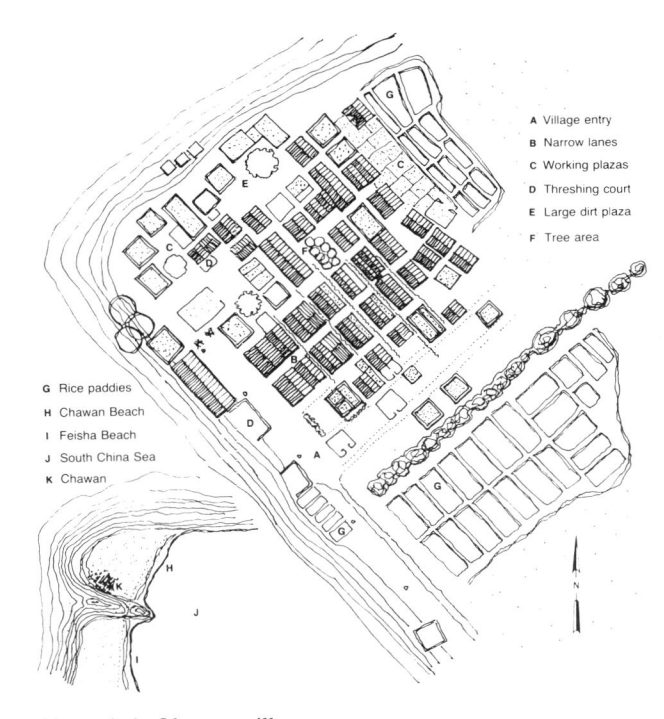

A Village entry
B Narrow lanes
C Working plazas
D Threshing court
E Large dirt plaza
F Tree area

G Rice paddies
H Chawan Beach
I Feisha Beach
J South China Sea
K Chawan

Figure 7.3. Chawan village map.

space, one of the most significant places in Chawan, is framed by residences on the southwest and rice fields on the northeast. As a major workplace, it symbolically ties home to livelihood in a manner as personal as a garden plot off one's back patio in the West.

The rigidity of the village plan breaks down in the northwest and southwest portions of the village. There, residences are less dense, and streets at times widen into forecourts or threshing surfaces and at times even open into plazas or treed spaces. Structures at this edge of the village—including homes and storage buildings—are clearly the product of past village sprawl, which now has reached the foot of the mountains. More recent new growth is to be found on all edges of the village, as more modern flat-roofed homes, often larger in area and sporting colored tiles, have been added. Nearly every new structure in the village, whether street infill or detached, remains true in orientation to the original grid.

Figure 7.4. New and old dwellings define the expanding perimeter of Chawan village.

Figure 7.5. A working plaza some 10 meters wide used for threshing and drying grain is found in the northeast section of Chawan village.

Major access to the village is from the southeast on an unimproved road from Feisha. Trucks and buses and motor vehicles stop at the town's edge, as only bicycles and pedestrians are able to negotiate the narrow streets of the village. This point of entry connects to the recently constructed road that has been cut over the mountain and parallels the long-established narrow mountain trails cut through tropical vegetation along the coast. The village entry is a place of both planned and casual meeting, as it leads to the beach and fishing and to many rice fields as well. Villagers often rush to the entry to greet fishermen as they return laden with baskets full—or perhaps disappointingly sparse—with the latest catch.

The village entry provides access to the narrow lanes of the eastern part of the village, corridors

Figure 7.6. The unimproved road from Feisha in the southeast leads to the edge of Chawan village, a place of both planned and casual meeting.

Figure 7.7. Narrow lanes in Chawan form corridors that reach through the village, intersecting other lanes to reach every dwelling.

flanked by bright white walls and undulating tile rooflines. These major lanes are crossed by minor ones that lead to the less formal west side of the village and that carry an open stone-lined trench for water drainage.

The lanes of Chawan are sites of activity from dawn until long after dusk. The narrow lanes are unpaved except for the placement of large stone pavers at certain key areas, before entry doors or at the water pump. Because the narrow lanes are seldom in full sunlight, they afford cool, breezy, shady places for work, socialization, or relaxation. A woman may be seen sitting on the door stoop preparing food, or a fisherman may use the street to repair his net. Transactions between neighbors or relatives next door or directly opposite are common, as neighbors are often relatives and some families may even occupy adjacent homes or buildings across the lane. One could speculate that such street activities are perhaps as important as access or circulation, as crowds in the street seldom give way to those passing through on bicycle or on foot, who can easily take an alternative route in this small village.

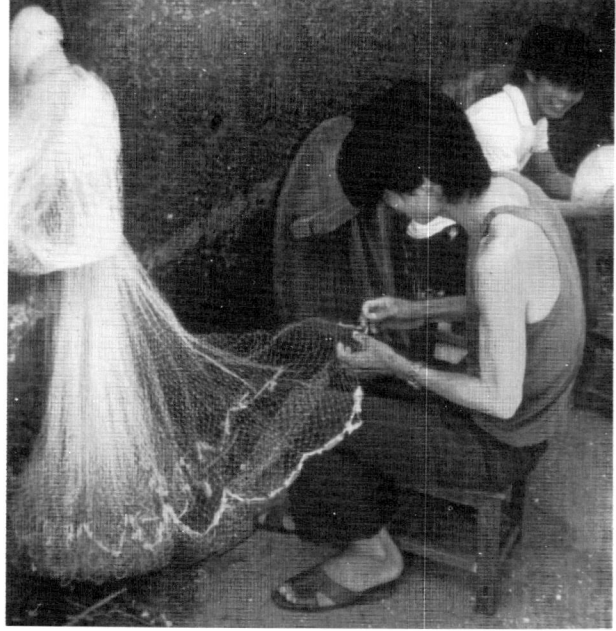

Figure 7.8. Space in front of dwellings in Chawan's narrow lanes is used for having a meal or repairing nets. Unlike the dark and separated interiors of the older dwellings, the lanes afford a cool and breezy place as well as contact with neighbors.

The straight, narrow urban character of the lanes of the east part of town contrasts with the looseness of the ones to the west, which are often spatially relieved by open courts defined by low walls or by the simple absence of buildings. In these sections of the village, most open spaces serve some type of work activity—drying clothes, threshing rice, drying fish or bacon, housing chickens, or hanging nets. Occasionally, the architectural austerity is broken by a tree in the space. Such a spot becomes a focus. Small child-size chairs may be brought outside and individuals may sit leisurely sipping tea or rice water or eating watermelon, or a group may form to complete a task or gossip, or both. Similarly, at mealtime, portable folding tables may be brought from the kitchen into these treed shady areas for full meals to be served.

One corner near the center of village has a public space in place of a corner structure. This unique place in the village has a collection of trees and is a favorite locale for many families of the area to set up tables and eat and socialize, especially during the mid-day meal, when field workers and fishermen alike return to the village. At such times, the multigenerational makeup of the community becomes apparent. Grandparents tending to children and the young and middle-aged working people join in family or community activities in which age is no limiting factor.

With two forms of outdoor livelihood, fishing and farming, Chawan residents accept a lifestyle that exposes them to the elements for long hours. Thus, it is not surprising that both small and large outdoor places take on special significance in daily life. These places include the streets, courts, and plazas as well as working places in and adjacent to the village, and in no insignificant way include Chawan beach as well. Portable hand-cranked rice threshers are set up in these spaces and fed freshly cut rice stalks from piles brought from the

Figure 7.9. The western portion of Chawan has a looser spatial structure with small open spaces for drying clothes, fish, or grain, as well as for threshing.

fields. Separated grain is spread out to dry on large concrete threshing floors, while the stalks stripped of their grain are spread out to dry on less significant areas of the plaza floor. Peanuts and small fish are dried here as well, spread in shallow baskets or laid on wooden racks. Such harvesting activities are performed in Chawan mainly by women. Normal male-female ratios are upset here because the fishing techniques of the South China Sea fishermen require two crews of twelve able-bodied men for three or four hours per event, and the fishermen of Chawan often go out twice daily. The absence of two dozen of the hardiest men from a village with a population of only 200 leaves a heavy harvesting burden for the women and the young.

Perhaps the largest open space within Chawan is the least utilized. A large dirt plaza on the north is dominated by a single large deciduous tree. The lack of a significant structure opening onto it, however, relegates the space to a mere stopping off point before preceding into town from the mountain or the fields. Cows are often tethered to the tree, and playing children or occasional individuals visiting a small food and supply store constitute the major plaza activity. A description of this store and a second one in the east district suggests the relative commercial sophistication of Chawan: The store on the dirt plaza is run by a single old man, who tends his grandchild simultaneously. Children are his most common customers, as they are sent by elders to purchase three or four biscuits—which he removes one-by-one from an airtight paper drum—or a measure of flour or salt. Farmers or fishermen drop by occasionally to purchase a single cigarette from an open package. By comparison, the store on the east side is more sophisticated. Two women run this operation, which occupies a large single room. Canned foods, paper and dry goods, and boxed soap products adorn the shelf on the back wall, while candies and stationery products are featured in a single glass case on the floor. The plastered walls are adorned with calendar photos of Western women.

No discussion of the "places" of Chawan would be complete without the inclusion of the fish harvesting spot on the beach. Though not defined architecturally, this is a place as real in the minds of the fishermen as any street or court inside the village. Although unidentifiable to an outsider viewing the length of the Chawan beach when fishermen are not present, the fishermen know and understand this work place as one where livelihood, teamwork, and camaraderie are shared twice daily. The exact place of the fish harvesting is not fixed, but moves linearly up and down Chawan beach. When fishermen are present, it is clearly defined as the space some 50 to 75 meters wide between two fishing boats pointed to the sea. After the fishermen roll out and drop their long single U-shaped net, they return to shore and ritually pull the net back to land. At this time, the area constantly narrows and is defined by the closing ends of the net. Within this place, the group leader and cashier sell the larger fish to buyers and then stack the catch of small fish and squid into equally divided shares. Once the net is collected and stored and the two heavy boats are lugged beyond tideline, the two dozen fishermen meet in a circle to collect their take and establish the time and place of their next effort. Because the limits of Chawan beach are so clearly defined by the mountains at either end and because it begins so near the southeast entry of the village of Cha-

Figure 7.10. The Chawan beach, though not defined architecturally, is a work place for the harvesting of fish.

Figure 7.11. Along the shore adjacent to the village of Chawan, fishermen roll out their U-shaped net in the water and then pull the net back to land.

wan, this section of the beach and sea is clearly thought of as territory linked and belonging to the village. The fishermen are possessive and even shout at or chase off trolling or anchored junks that come too close to shore.

The architectural character of Chawan and some other villages of Shangchuan Island is strikingly different from other villages in Taishan county. Chawan is a "white village" reminiscent in many ways of what one might see along the coastal Mediterranean. As in other villages in Guangdong province, the walls of houses are constructed of load-bearing stone cut from the mountain or black brick common to the region. Most wall surfaces are white-painted stucco, brilliant in the tropical sun when new. But they are soon blasted gray by harsh salt and sand winds and mottled by green and black molds that thrive in the humid tropics. Pitched gray-tile roofs, gable end to the sea, predominate and yield the distinctive architectural form of Chawan. Some 30 to 40 percent of the rooftops are flat.

The houses of Chawan are basic in plan organization and building construction, whether the dwellings are old or new. For the most part, walls are laid out forthrightly in a simple rectangular grid, as shown in the illustrations, with only slight variations. In both old and newer homes, interior and exterior walls are load-bearing, usually about 0.4 meters thick. Older homes are of tamped earth construction with earth, concrete, or tile floors frequently arranged into a six-bay compact plan. Newer houses are usually built of rubble stone taken from the hills above the village and typically occupy a smaller building lot with four rooms at ground level. In older homes, a partial second level, generally of light wood construction, is sometimes added in rooms with higher ceilings. The resulting loft space is accessible by a steep wooden stairway or a ladder and is used for sleep-

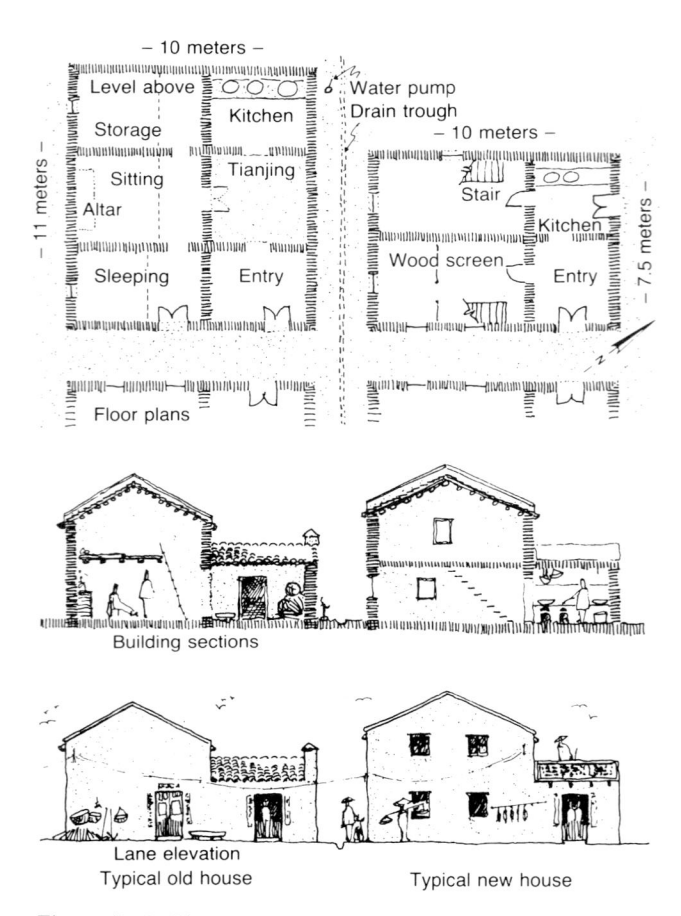

Figure 7.12. Plans, sections, and elevations of a typical old and new dwelling, Chawan.

minimal light and ventilation. With unpainted interior walls of earth or gray-blue brick, the interiors become quite dark. However, the presence of a *tianjing,* a skywell or small open court, in many of the older dwellings not only affords a small personal space within the house, but also leads some air and natural light into what would otherwise be windowless space. Architect and Taishan specialist Jonathan Hammond speculates that this minimalist attitude toward fenestration may have been the architectural result of a fear of marauding bandits, who repeatedly through history, especially early in this century, preyed upon Taishan villagers. Certainly, other villages and towns of the region have powerful architectural manifestations of this concern for defense and protection in the form of "bandit towers," fortified multistory structures that dominate their skylines (Lu and Wei 1990, 135–143).

Hand pumps in the lanes provide water for the residents of Chawan. Public toilet facilities are located outside the homes and are arranged by neighborhood. Although electricity is available in all dwellings, power supply is minimal and is used primarily for lighting at night as well as for radios and electric fans at all times. Multispeed floor model electric fans are a major product of factories throughout Taishan county. The shiny surfaces and slick manufactured lines of these electric fans stand in stark contrast to the otherwise earthy interiors and furnishings of the older homes.

Today Chawan is a village rooted in the past but on the verge of imminent change. Although most villagers continue to rely on farming and fishing for their livelihood, not strikingly unlike that of generations before, the lives of their children may be markedly changed by a number of new forces. Electricity is bringing technology and communications heretofore unavailable to the people of Chawan and neighboring villages. A few television sets have appeared in nearby Feisha

ing or storage to supplement the space on the ground level. Most newer homes are built with preplanned second-floor rooms, two rooms equal in size to those of the ground level as well as a long outdoor rooftop second-floor terrace. The presence of this terrace as well as windows on the second level enhance the livability of these elevated spaces when compared to traditional homes. Both old and new houses employ wood beam and tile roof construction.

Windows in older dwellings are extremely limited and quite small, if present, allowing only and are already a mainstay in the military base on the island. Construction has begun to improve the road that links Chawan to Feisha and ultimately Shangchuan town and the ferry landing on the other side of the island. The completion of this project will improve Chawan's access to Guanghai on the mainland, a city many believe destined to take on new importance with its direct ferry link to Hong Kong and Macau. As elsewhere in China, the nature of change in Chawan will no doubt be tempered by the central government's policies. Openness to the West should greatly affect Chawan, but more conservative policies combined with strong traditional values may well delay change and turn the next generation of villagers back to the dependable ways of fishing and farming that have supported Chawan for generations.

I would like to thank Jonathan Hammond, Dan Hamburg, and Steve Liu for their assistance. Thanks also to Jim Chen and his family on Shangchuan Island. Research for this chapter was supported in part by the University of Illinois at Urbana-Champaign Research Board and the UIUC-Tongji University China Program.

CHAPTER 8

Hongcun Village, Anhui
A Place of Rivers and Lakes

SHAN DEQI

HONGCUN village is located in Jilian township, less than 11 kilometers northeast of the county seat of Yixian, southern Anhui province. Yixian is one of a dozen counties that make up Huizhou prefecture, famous in China as the home of the "Huizhou merchants," a powerful group of businessmen whose wealth came from the sale of salt, tea, timber, bamboo, and other products.

The area's cultural history dates to the Song dynasty (960–1279), when scholars from the north swarmed into the region. In combination with the local population, the overall culture and economy developed apace in subsequent centuries. Huizhou became especially prosperous during the Ming dynasty (1368–1644), when, under the pressure of a large population and limited cultivable land, many merchants of Huizhou left the region in search of opportunity. Their numbers increased to such a level that Chinese all over the country claimed: "Where there is no merchant from Huizhou, there is no town." Transplanted businessmen from Huizhou then used considerable parts of their riches to build up their home villages and towns in the Huizhou region, leaving a legacy of luxurious houses, ancestral temples, schools, paved roads, bridges, memorial halls, and stone archways that imbue the region with fine examples of vernacular architectural forms. Vernacular housing is well developed, marked especially by the quality of its brick, stone, and wood carving (Zhang et al. 1957). Huizhou, moreover, is the home of the famous "four treasures of the study" (writing brush, ink stick, ink slab, and paper), as well as distinctive opera, cuisine, painting, and literary traditions.

Under the influence of Confucian ethics—especially the Lixue school—a well-developed economy and culture, population growth, and a need for protection, certain village patterns developed here during the Ming period. Hongcun village is a fine example of this Huizhou heritage. The village is dominated by a patriarchal clan—the Wang family—that has lived in the village for some eight hundred years. Overall building density is high. It is apparent that the village site was chosen carefully with an overall plan in mind.

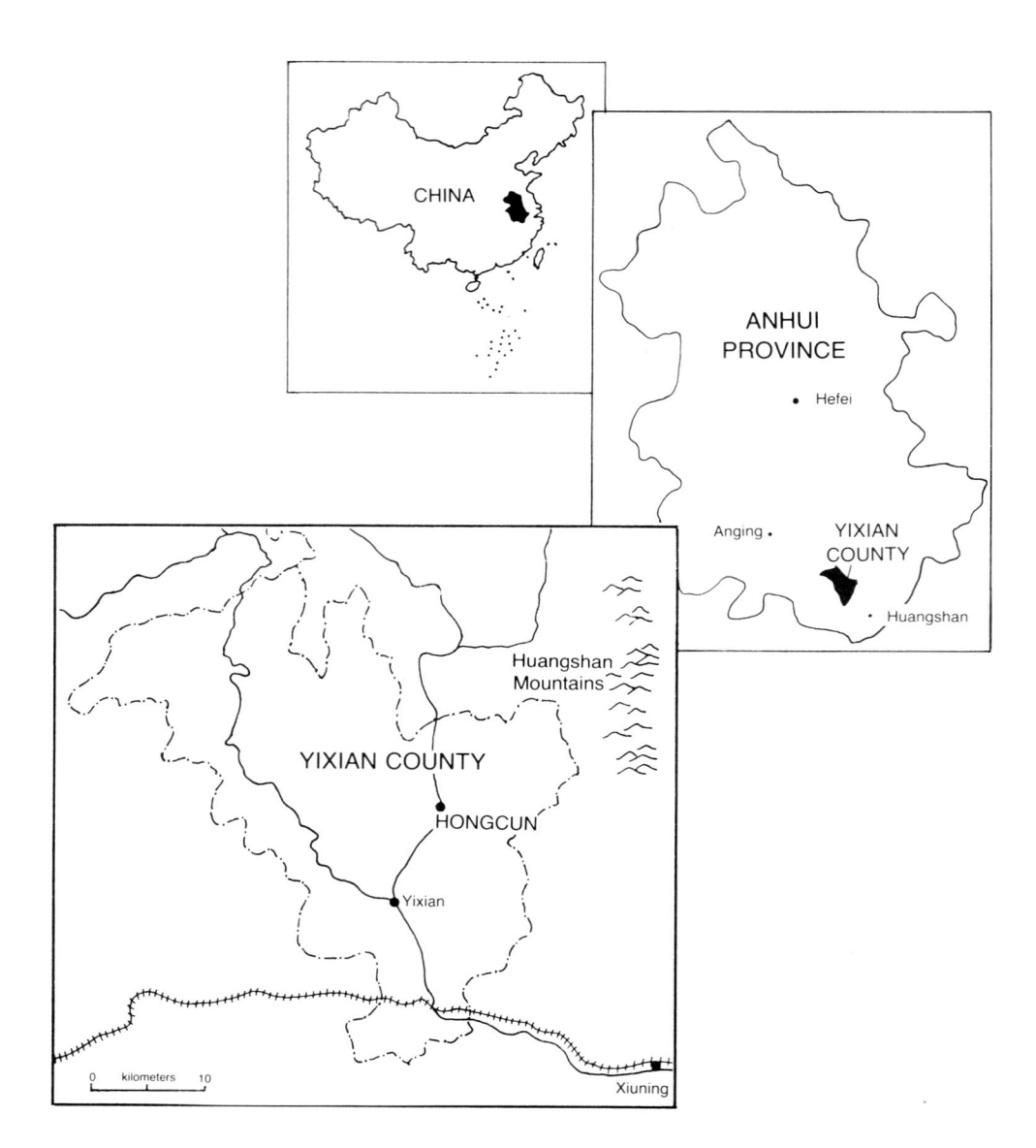

Figure 8.1. Hongcun village is located in Yixian county in southern Anhui province.

The use of inside and outside space is consistent with the notion "void inside, substance outside." Decorative adornment is simple yet elegant.

Hongcun village is situated at the southern foot of Leigang hill in the northern portion of a basin. Shady at the back, the village has a southern exposure with a wide field of vision before it. The site of Hongcun village, with water and hillocks in its environs, according to the dictates of *fengshui*, is supposed to have had a positive influence on the fortune of its residents.

Records indicate that there was no sign of

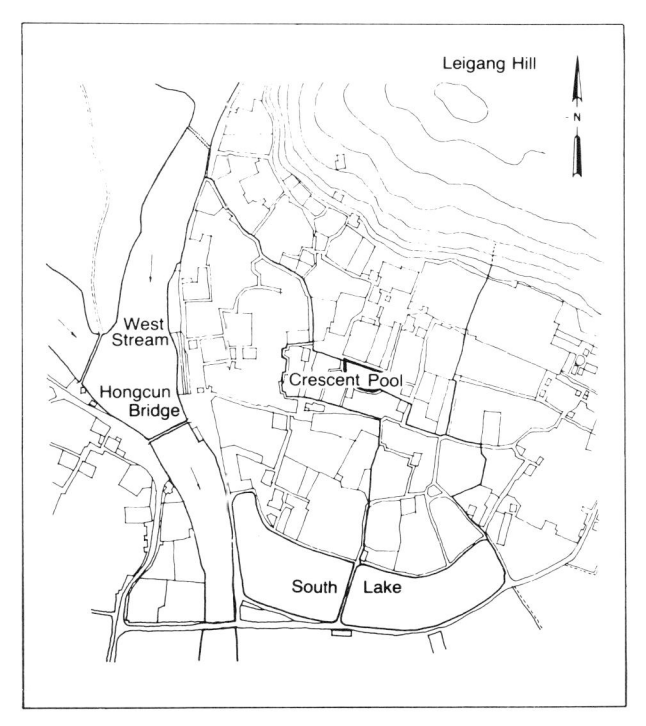

Figure 8.2. Map of Hongcun village.

human habitation on the site of Hongcun village before it was first settled by migrants from the north during the Song dynasty. During the Ming dynasty, as the settlement took its contemporary form, water was directed into the village through man-made canals, and a crescent-shaped pond, about 3,000 square meters in area, was excavated. With a straight edge along its northern side and an arcuate southern rim, several important houses and ancestral shrines were situated around it. The open area in the east has always been used for village public activities. The ancestral temple of the Wang family, which unfortunately no longer exists, was situated at the center of the north bank of the pond.

There is no doubt that the crescent-shaped pool has always been viewed as the spiritual center of the village. It has served also as a central location for women to do laundry, as a ready source of water to fight fires, and as a component in the regulation of water flow through the village. Its central location affects the microclimate of the vil-

Figure 8.3. Perspective view of Hongcun village looking toward the west. South Lake appears on the left.

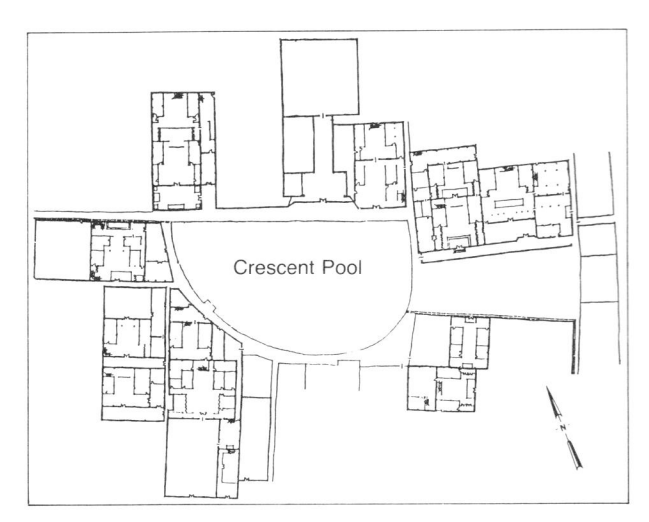

Figure 8.4. The arrangement of dwellings around the crescent pool in Hongcun village.

Figure 8.5. The crescent pool, located in the center of Hongcun village, serves multiple uses, including as a site for the washing of clothes.

Figure 8.6. A view from the south of the Hongcun village perimeter facing South Lake.

lage, and, as the coolest and most scenic portion of the village, it has served as a public place for villagers to stroll, socialize, and relieve boredom.

A great event in Hongcun's history was the construction of South Lake about 150 years after the initial excavation of the crescent pool. About 18,000 square meters in size, the lake is sunny and enchanting in spring, filled with lotuses in summer, surrounded by red leaves in fall, and often touched with snow in winter. As the village became more prosperous, overall planning and development to beautify the village included the planting of willows and poplars around the lake, the paving of roads and paths, the construction of large dwellings, ancestral shrines, and academies of classical learning, and also the raising of an enclosing wall around the lake itself. Construction of the wall was completed about four hundred years ago, and it has been preserved to the present with little change.

The *shuikou,* "the mouth of the waterway," is an important component of traditional villages throughout the Huizhou region. Although it represents the gateway into the village, it does not necessarily take a gate form. It may be a memorial archway, a pavilion, a bridge, a pagoda, or even trees such as a Chinese hawthorn and a ginkgo. As boundary between interior and exterior spaces, the *shuikou* helped define the extent of control or the domain of the patriarchal clan controlling a village.

All parts of Hongcun village are connected with well laid out slabstone lanes, each paralleled with a narrow canal that brings clean water to every family. Utilization of water in Hongcun, however, goes far beyond common domestic needs. Many families have built water gardens or pools within their dwellings, not only for washing, bathing, and fire safety, but also to beautify the internal environment. The water garden of the Wu house, for example, serves as the focus for a reading "room." With a corridor trimmed with window tracery, the space is one of calmness. At one of the Wang dwellings, the water garden constitutes a pool behind the gate of the house. In another village house, the water garden is only a small goldfish pool. Elsewhere in Huizhou, canals often cut across villages and towns, and waterside lanes are a distinctive feature. However, they rarely have a crescent pool to serve as the center of activity. Hongcun's South Lake as well not only has ecological significance, but also contributes to the aesthetic quality of the settlement. Its surrounding trees, slabstone pavements, buildings, and carved stone walls beautify the exterior environment of the village.

Typical vernacular dwelling plans throughout the Huizhou region are square and squat, without emphasizing the horizontal as is done in much of

Figure 8.7. Narrow lanes paved with cut stone are lined with narrow channels that lead water into the individual dwellings in Hongcun village.

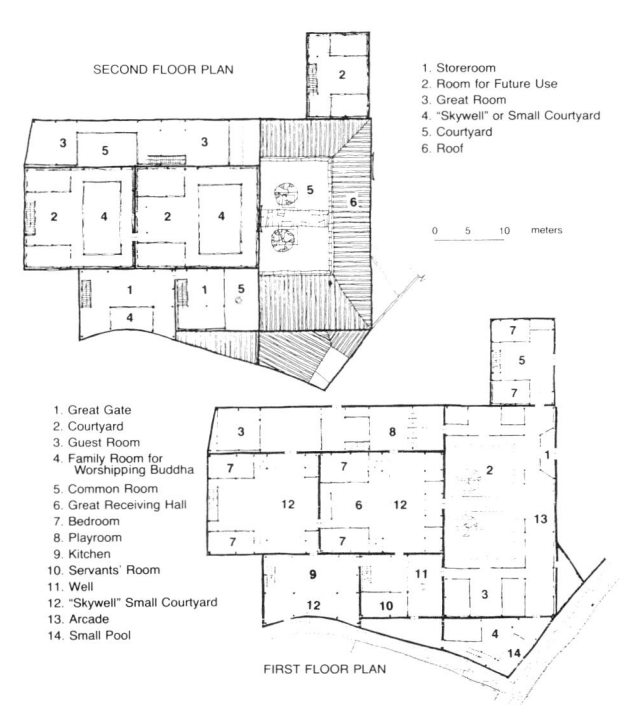

Figure 8.8. Completed at the end of the Qing dynasty, the Wang Dinggui residence in Hongcun village comprises two stories with many rooms and open spaces for special uses.

Chinese architecture. Most are two stories, with storage and rooms for possible future use on the upper floor; the common room, bedrooms, and kitchen are on the ground floor. Exteriors are plain; neither windows nor doors generally are found on the south facade. On the east and the west side of the north facade, there usually are two small openings leading to the back hall and back courtyard. The hall or living room for the family is close to the small front courtyard. It is a "murky gray" space, neither interior nor exterior. The central hall is used for receiving guests, for meetings and rituals, as well as for household sideline production. Bedrooms that border on the left and right sides of the central hall are usually very small.

During the Ming and Qing dynasties, formal sumptuary regulations fixed the external appearance of a dwelling by defining scale and limiting decoration and colors according to the rank and status of the owner. Following these dictates, the exteriors of traditional houses in Huizhou were constructed to appear simple and frugal. However, interiors were often elaborately decorated. In the interior of many dwellings, the "three unique skills of the Huizhou region"—exquisite wood, brick, and stone carving—are abundant. An outstanding example in Hongcun is the great house of the Wang family, completed at the end of the Qing dynasty, where the beams, ledges, partition boards, doors, and windows are all elaborately carved, in striking contrast with the exterior. Following local customs and conditions, the designs not only include abstract ornamental flowers, birds, and other animals, but also represent historical figures, folk tales, and landscapes. Auspicious decorative elements abound (see Knapp 1989, 140–178; Song and Ma 1990).

Furniture—a long narrow table, a square table, and matching chairs—as a rule has always been

Figure 8.9. The central hall of most dwellings in Hongcun village contains elaborately carved wood and stone. Furniture is arranged according to a symmetrical pattern. Calligraphy and paintings are prominently displayed.

arranged according to the axial symmetry of the central hall of each dwelling. In the center of the wall would hang fine examples of calligraphy and paintings in association with the memorial tablets of ancestors. In the old days, active spaces for women and children were restricted to the areas behind the central hall. The staircase to the second floor was usually found in this private back space.

A degree of privacy was required at the entrance of Huizhou dwellings, and thus a two-gate system was adopted. The external gate takes many forms. It is often massive yet simply decorated with patterns evoking good fortune or luck. The space within the external gate leads to a small courtyard decorated with plants, and then on to the inside door, which is usually of wood.

The principles of *yin* and *yang* are evident in the design of the interior and exterior environment of Hongcun village. For example, complementary patterns are seen in dark interiors and bright exteriors; white walls and dark eaves and roofs; the great void of bright sky and the real volume of buildings *(xu* and *shi); and hard, irregular rocks, buildings, and paths contrasting with soft, smooth water and curved edges of pools.

Walls provide protection and privacy, but they also have aesthetic functions. Throughout Hongcun, there are house walls, garden walls, and courtyard walls used as white "screens" for displaying rocks, bonsai, flowers, and trees. Alleys throughout the village are narrow but harmonious in scale with the sense of sight formed by

Figure 8.10. Massive entryways lead to most large village dwellings in Hongcun. Shown here is the entryway to the Wang Dinggui residence.

Figure 8.11 A view from the arcade across the courtyard to the second entryway of Wang Dinggui's dwelling, Hongcun village.

Figure 8.12. Black ridge lines of the steeped gables contrast with the white walls of the Wang Dinggui residence and other dwellings in the Huizhou region.

Figure 8.13. Behind the walls of most Hongcun dwellings, open "courtyards" of water are important elements of the design. Overhanging benches offer places to contemplate. The lattice doors framing rooms adjacent to the water "courtyard" are removable and make possible the direct linkage of interior and exterior space.

Figure 8.14. On the western side of Hongcun village, several large trees provide space for community activities and recreation.

archways, arched doors, and small carved windows.

Efforts are being made to preserve Hongcun village, to bequeath its atmosphere of age and tranquility to generations not yet born. Perhaps more residences dating from the Ming dynasty remain in the Huizhou region than anywhere else in China. Solid foundations, firm building materials, and relative isolation have contributed to the maintenance of whole villages. In the lingering solitude of Hongcun and other preserved villages, a glimpse can be had of treasures of China's vernacular past that are only today being sought out by photographers, painters, and casual visitors.

My thanks to the officials in Anhui province and Yixian county who offered assistance during my field work. This project is part of the "Man and Dwelling Environment" research project of the Chinese National Natural Science Research Foundation.

CHAPTER 9

Dangjia Village, Shaanxi
A Brilliant Pearl

LIU BAOZHONG

SITUATED about 9 kilometers northeast of the Hancheng county seat and near the border of neighboring Shanxi province, Dangjia village is nearly 5 kilometers from the south-flowing flank of the great bend of the Huanghe (Yellow River). In this sector, the Huanghe receives from the short but rapidly moving rivers of Shaanxi the easily eroded and wind-blown loessial soil (*huangtu*, or "yellow earth") that gives the river its name. The region is one of great historical significance. At the Dragon Gate (Longmen), the first emperor of the Xia dynasty (c. 2100–1600 B.C.) pursued the great task of harnessing "China's sorrow," as the Huanghe has traditionally been called.

Dangjia ("Dang family") village itself sits on two slightly elevated platforms that fill a calabash-shaped ravine. Ascending the Dangjia knoll, some 400 meters high, one is able to see on the horizon the Huanghe meeting the sky. In the region below are found some of China's richest reserves of coal, easily accessible to villagers for firing pottery utensils, heating homes, and cooking. Nearby waterways have facilitated access to the fine stone of Jiangzhou in neighboring Shanxi province.

Records tell us that in the year 1331, there was just one inhabitant in this barren spot, a man by the name of Dang Shuxuan. Escaping famine in Chaoyi, several kilometers away, Dang Shuxuan wandered the hills until settling on the southeastern hillslopes of this ravine, at a site called East Solar Bend. Here he leased a parcel of land from a nearby Buddhist temple, dug a cave home into the earth, and became the forefather of subsequent members of the Dang clan. Settlement increased slowly over the next century and a half, with little change in fortune for the village residents. However, in 1495, the son of a merchant who was a fifth-generation descendent of the Jia family of Shanxi province married into the village.

Prosperity came and with it the establishment of family schools and the education of promising young men in the village. According to village records of the Ming and Qing dynasties, four persons passed the provincial civil service examination and were granted the *juren* degree, an

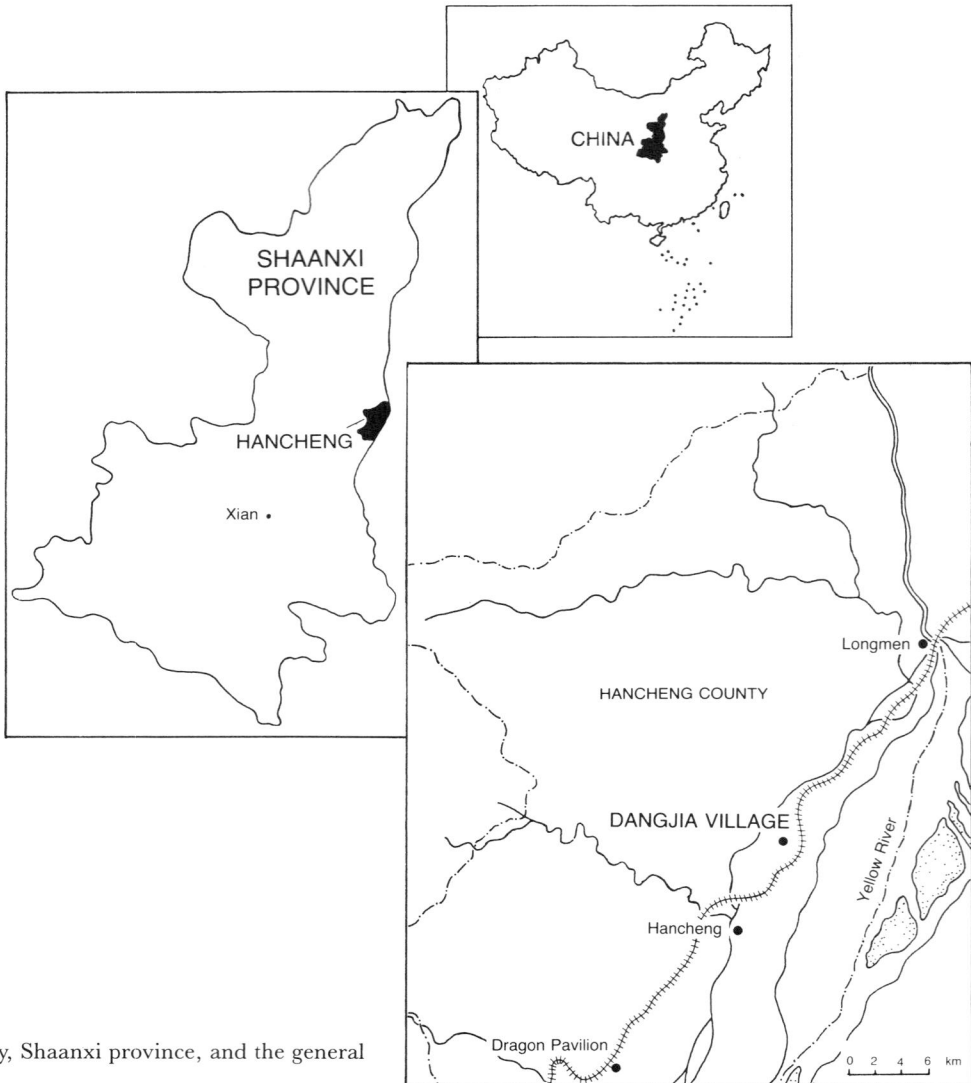

Figure 9.1. Hancheng county, Shaanxi province, and the general location of Dangjia village.

extraordinary achievement for a remote village. One other person from Dangjia became a successful candidate in the imperial examination in Beijing and was granted the *jinshi* degree; subsequently he was appointed to posts in the Imperial Academy, and the Ministry of Justice, and later he was installed as prefectural magistrate. In the waning years of the Qing dynasty, in the late nineteenth century, forty-four pupils passed the county-level examination, earning the *xiucai* degree. Generation after generation, the accomplishments of the Dang family and the commercial acumen of the Jia family brought prosperity to this remote location. The village took form

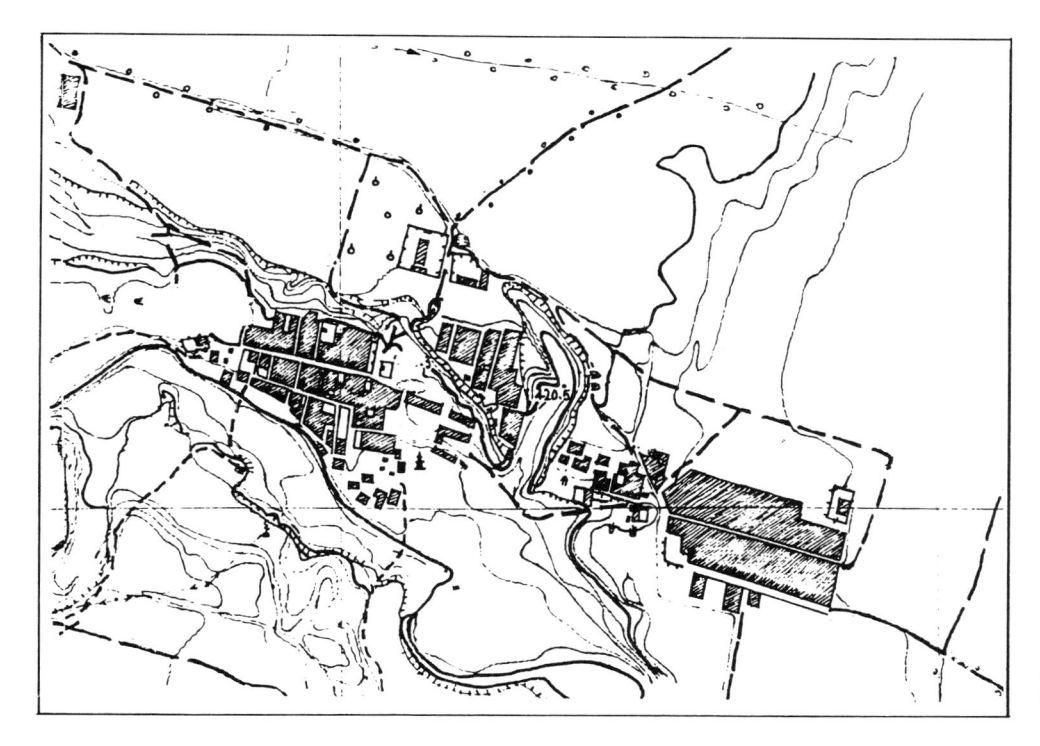

Figure 9.2. Map of Dangjia village.

Figure 9.3. Vertical aerial photograph of Dangjia village.

Figure 9.4. Panoramic view of Dangjia village.

Figure 9.5. The Wenxing Pagoda, said to be fitted with an "antispectral pearl," is believed by many villagers to have protected Dangjia from dust storms that plague the region.

especially during the seventy-year period from 1796 to 1861, as imposing new dwellings were built. Most of these are extant, bequeathing an architecturally noteworthy rural settlement rivaled by only a handful of others in China.

The grandeur of the village and the prosperity of its families is attributed by many villagers today not simply to the status of some of their descendants, but to the especially favorable *fengshui* circumstances of the village itself. In spite of its location in a region swept regularly by winds that blow the easily lifted silt of the plateau into the air, Dangjia village has been remarkably free of dust and, according to villagers, "winds that sweep away riches." The 40-meter-high ridges that frame the village environment both to the north and to the south and the village location in a slender ravine together help reduce the impact and intensity of seasonal winds. Villagers believe that Bi Stream, which flows alongside the village, also acts to purify the air. Village lore, moreover, tells that early residents perceived a gap in their embracing ridges and to remedy this defect constructed a pagoda. Named after the deity charged with protecting literary genius, the Wenxing Pagoda had fitted into its summit "an antidust pearl," an effort that villagers still believe has insured through the years a relatively clean environment.

Streets and alleys in the village crisscross, with irregularity only where the settlement brushes up against the hillslopes and the river. Throughout the interior of the village, the lanes are paved with cut stone.

Most residences were constructed around courtyards, both as *siheyuan* buildings arranged along the four lateral sides of the courtyard and as *sanheyuan* buildings on only three sides. In most residences the buildings meet at right angles, as has been traditional elsewhere in China, but in some cases here in Dangjia village dwellings take the form of a tetrahedron. Varying in height, elaborately decorated entryways of brick, stone, and wood grace most of the dwellings. Cut stone, again varying in pattern, is used in distinctive thresholds and pillar posts. Special steps for mounting and fastening horses are found in front of many gates. Roof ridges, screen walls, lateral walls, column bases, and window lattices are carved in forms that express good luck, high rank, long life, progeny, as well as propitiousness and satisfactory achievements (for an examination of these patterns elsewhere in China, see Knapp 1989, 140–178). Elaborately carved archways commemorate widows for their noble deeds.

The layout of dwelling complexes puts great

Figure 9.6. A perspective view of Dangjia village, suggesting the rectangular lattice design of the lanes. [Photo courtesy of Olivier Laude, 1989]

Figure 9.7. A lane separating residences in Dangjia village.

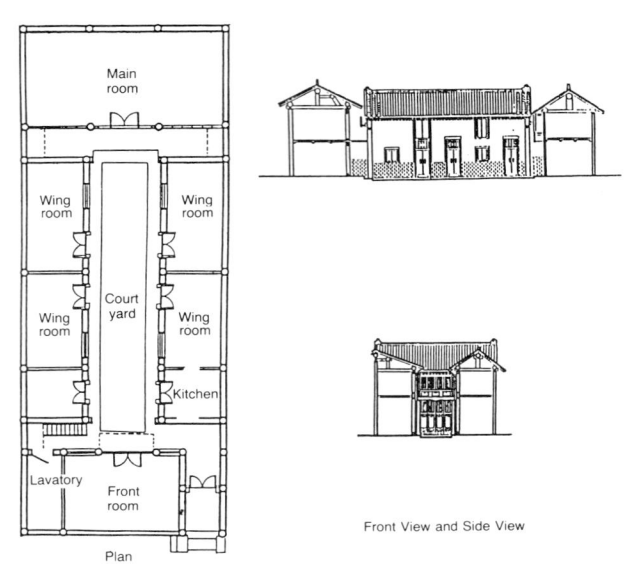

Figure 9.8. The plan and elevations of a typical Dangjia village residence.

emphasis on combining elements, differing in scale in accordance with the status and wealth of the owner. Some regard the typical pattern for each residential compound as a metaphor for a human body: the main room corresponds to the human head, the front room to the legs, and the left and right wing rooms to the arms. Together they constitute a complete dwelling unit. The ridges of the outer screen wall, the outermost building, and the inner building generally rise in succession from front to back. According to tradition, this style of construction acted as a charm "exalting three ranks in rapid succession" and indicated that the Dang family wished for their offspring to become successful candidates for the *xiucai, juren,* and *jinshi* civil service degrees.

Measurements of space in Dangjia conform to general Chinese beliefs in which odd numbers, considered positive and masculine, are emphasized. Structures throughout the village generally consist of odd numbers of *jian,* the basic Chinese building module, sometimes translated "bay," which often forms a room. Front structures, which include the entryway, usually are of five narrow bays; the main rear structure comprises three wider bays. Wing structures perpendicular to these complete the circuit around the courtyard. They usually contain three or five compartments; occasionally out of necessity these less important side structures are divided into even multiples. Windows and doors were not allowed

Figure 9.9. The carved entryway to a Dangjia village residence. [Photo courtesy of Olivier Laude, 1989]

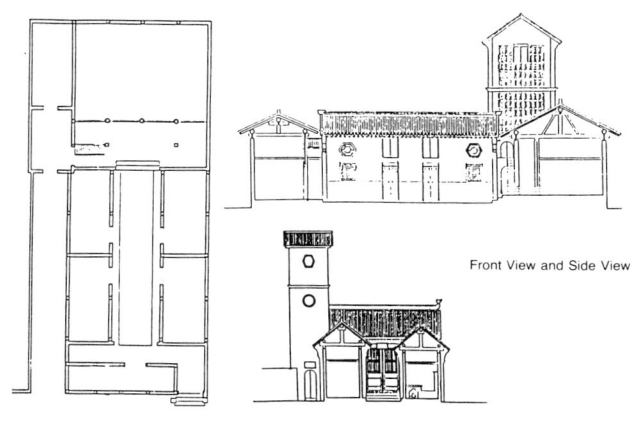

Figure 9.10. Plan and elevations of a large Dangjia village residence with a tower.

to be set directly opposite each other, a position considered especially inauspicious.

There is evidence that the Yellow River Diagram was used in setting the height of each of the four structures around a courtyard. Figure 9.12 indicates the prescribed elements. Measurements within the village confirm the application of these principles: the height of the structure on the west was fixed using digits that incorporated three or eight, such as 1.38, 1.038, or 0.938 *zhang* (1 *zhang* = 3.333 meters); that of the structure on the east used four or nine, e.g., 1.49, 1.049, or 0.949 *zhang;* the front of the house on the south used two or seven; and the north, one or six.

Usually the orientation of every compound was determined by the orientation of the street or alley. Dwelling compounds along north-south alleys or streets were aligned with eastern or western exposures; those along east-west lanes had northern or southern exposures. Main entrances centrally placed along the front wall were called principal gates; those at the sides, corner doors. The location of each entrance followed the notation of the *bagua,* the Eight Trigrams or Octadiagram.

The best design for a compound follows a south-facing layout with a north hall and a gate placed at a southeastern location. A pair of wings for subsidiary rooms symmetrically stretches out to both sides. Redbud (*cercis Chinensis*) might be planted so as to bloom within the courtyard. The wafting fragrance, it was believed, brought good fortune to an entire family.

Architects today believe that the fine level of preservation of Dangjia village may be ascribed to

Figure 9.11. A view down a Dangjia village lane with a tower in the background. [Photo courtesy of Olivier Laude, 1989]

五行	FIVE ELEMENTS	Wood	Fire	Earth	Metal	Water
方向	DIRECTION	East	South	Center	West	North
季節	SEASON	Spring	Summer	Midsummer	Autumn	Winter
顏色	COLOR	Blue	Red	Yellow	White	Black
四神	FOUR BEINGS	Azure Dragon	Vermilion Bird	Palace	White Tiger	Snake & Tortoise

Figure 9.12. The Eight Trigrams and the Five Elements.

the overall design and high quality of materials used in the village's construction. Another important factor that has contributed to the village's survival was its protection by imperial authorities. It is said that the Qing emperor Xianfeng (1851–1862), appreciating the honesty and abilities of the residents of Hancheng county, granted an imperial edict permitting local residents to build their excellent houses. The population responded, elaborately decorating the facades of all dwellings, including not only those of the rich but also the more humble shelters of those with less means. The decorations included not only screen walls and mounting steps, but also antithetical couplets hung symmetrically on both sides of entryways. Subject matter for decoration extended to various realms, including music, chess, calligraphy and painting, pine, bamboo, flowering plum, and orchids. Whatever the subject matter, the themes evoked auspiciousness and good fortune, high rank, long life, and progeny, among others (see Li 1988; Knapp 1989, 149–175; Wang

1990; and Pan 1990 for an elaboration of these themes).

The spacious central main room served as a memorial hall to honor the ancestors. Here, portraits of ancestors were hung on the wall above an altar that faced the main entryway. On ceremonial occasions, such as those accompanying mourning or wedding rites, and during festivals, the wooden partitions that separated the rooms were removed to enlarge the space, opening the room to the gallery in front. The rooms that flanked the main room on the east and west served traditionally as bedrooms for brothers. Tradition prescribed that the elder brother resided in the east room and younger brothers in the west. For convenient inspection of their children and as a precaution against strangers and burglars, parents of the household occupied front rooms, a pattern that differs from elsewhere in China. Kitchens were placed in the eastern wing room to signify a good omen—following the sun rising from the east, the family itself was to grow.

The layout of Dangjia village was well designed. Graveyards were located on the northern slopes to conform to the saying, "Houses with a southern exposure shelter the living, tombs with a northern exposure house the dead." Stone slabs, inscribed with the words "stone of Mount Tai dares to resist evil," were erected at the foot of walls that marked the turning points of lanes.

Nowadays Dangjia village is home to some three hundred households with 1,300 inhabitants. The village has been enlarged and reformed in response to population increases and advances in the collective economy. Nonetheless, the village retains its traditional flavor with many original features preserved. Recently built multistory buildings are concentrated in the northern quarter of the village, where they do no harm to the preservation of the village's original form. For the future, efforts must be made to adopt further measures to safeguard the village, and to preserve, utilize, and improve it. It is necessary to improve the water supply and sewage drainage to ameliorate daily life in the older sections of the village. To improve the economic structure of the village by diversifying the economy, farming, forestation, stock breeding, fishing, and orchards all need to be promoted. In carrying forward changes that will improve the lives of the village's inhabitants, it is imperative that planners not only preserve the splendid architectural achievements of the past but learn from the traditional village planning principles that gave the village form.

I would like to thank Olivier Laude and Ronald G. Knapp as well as drafting students Jiao Liuquan, Wu Maode, Zhou Ruoqi, and Shao Xiaoguang.

CHAPTER 10

Zhouzhuang, Jiangsu
A Historic Market Town

JOSEPH C. WANG

The quiet market town of Zhouzhuang lies in the midst of the Taihu lake district of southeastern Jiangsu province. Interwoven and carved by waterways, which have played a role in keeping the settlement a step back in time, this rural community was designated in 1986 as the "last frontier" of historically preservable townships of its type by the Planning Department of Tongji University in Shanghai. Having just recently celebrated the nine hundredth anniversary of its founding, the community leaders of Zhouzhuang were equally enthusiastic about proposals for a joint effort with the university to preserve one of the few remaining traditional settlements of the lower Yangzi region.

Zhouzhuang is one of countless settlements scattered throughout this "water country," which also encompasses the northern section of Zhejiang province and a portion of southeastern Anhui province. Bounded on the north by the Yangzi River and on the west by Taihu (Lake Tai), the region lies between the two metropolises of Shanghai and Nanjing. The Grand Canal, which historically served as the strategic shipping route between Beijing in the north and Hangzhou in the south, flows north and south through the region midway between Lake Tai and Zhouzhuang.

Although the climate of this portion of China may be described as temperate, the area around Zhouzhuang experiences four distinct seasons with hot summers but relatively mild winters. With a frost-free period of some 230 days, the mean annual temperature reaches 16°C. Precipitation is a plentiful 1,100 millimeters. Favored with such climatic advantages and fertile soil, the lower reaches of the Yangzi River provide some of China's most productive farming areas, in terms of both products from the land and bounty harvested from the canals and lakes. The area has long been known as *yu mi zhi xiang* ("the land of fish and rice").

Zhouzhuang township sits amidst this region noteworthy for its hydrography: Not only is Zhouzhuang surrounded by four major lakes, but fully 24 percent of the township's 40 hectares is covered by water. Administratively and linguistically, Zhouzhuang has always been linked to

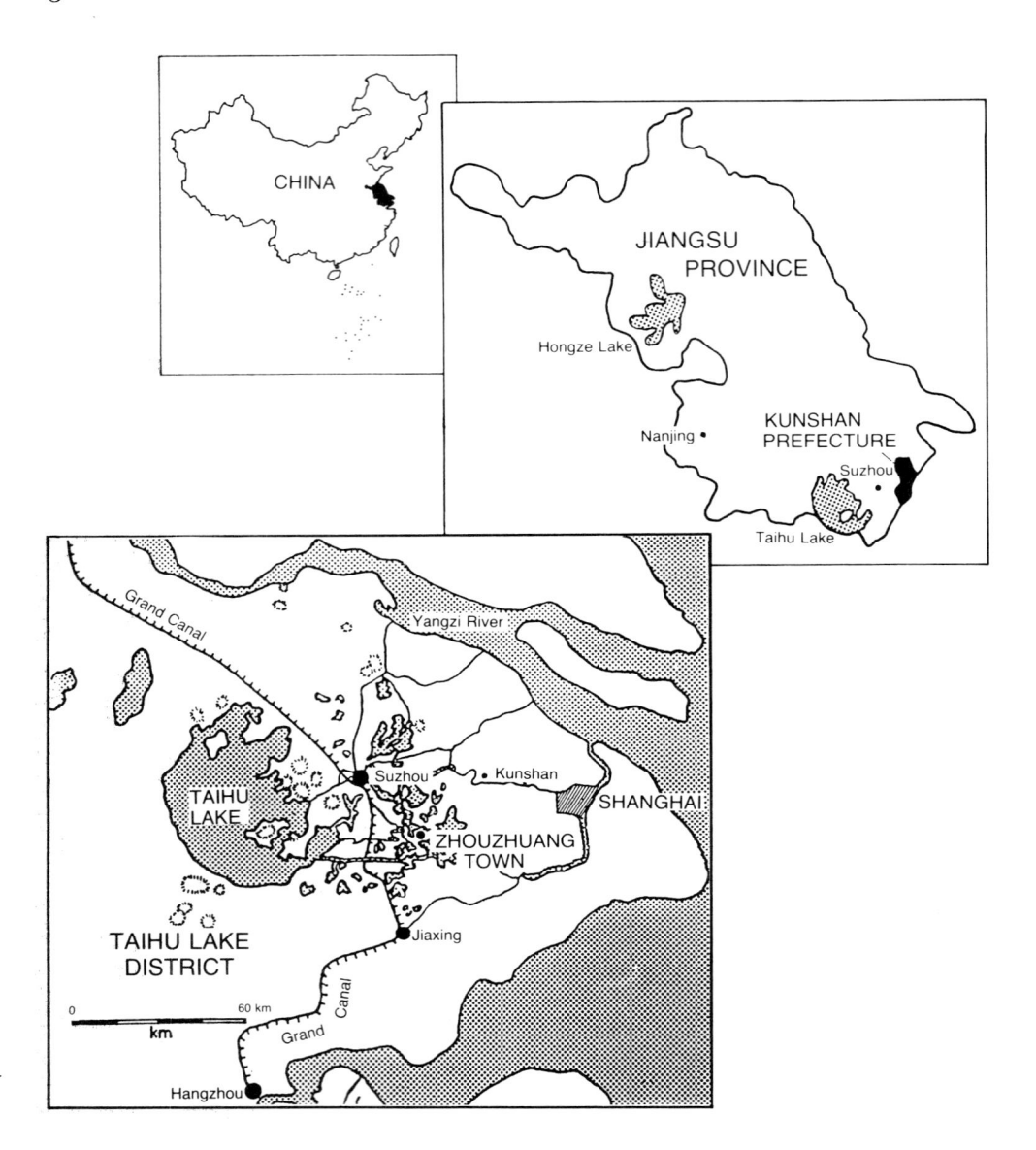

Figure 10.1. The Taihu lake region and the location of Zhouzhuang.

Suzhou, a city known for its high culture, gardens, canals, and soft-spoken language. Zhouzhuang has been for centuries an important market town, or *jizhen,* a village with substantial periodic trading activity for its agricultural hinterland. In 1986, Zhouzhuang's administrative status was elevated to that of a *jianzhi zhen,* or "designated town," within Kunshan county in recognition of its growing commercial importance. The new status linked it to China's urban hierarchy yet acknowledged its position as the principal market for the surrounding rural population.

Zhouzhuang can be reached either by bus or by

small packetboat from Shanghai. The bus journey takes about three hours. Travelers must get off at Jishuigang (literally "rough water harbor"), an important shipping junction to the north of Zhouzhuang, and take a ferry across a hundred-meter-wide waterway. Here on the edge of Zhouzhuang village proper, the traveler is confronted with a vast expanse of farmland dotted with low-rise farmhouses on the distant western horizon. As with much of the landscape of the lower Yangzi plain, the environs of Zhouzhuang are flat and featureless. However, close inspection of the orderly earth, which has been readied for planting, hints at the character of this rural community.

A straight, narrow road of pounded earth in the middle of an open field leads visitors from the bank of the stream to the village headquarters. A modern-looking, two-story structure of reinforced concrete construction, this administration building reflects the penetration of modernization into the community. Community leaders, however, assert that, unlike other enterprising townships in the area, Zhouzhuang has been able to boost its economy even while managing to maintain and improve many elements of the original Ming and Qing townscape and architecture. At a time of rapid economic growth, Zhouzhuang village is an oasis in an endangered region where "progress" is synonymous with social, cultural, and environmental erosion. The natural setting of the village contributes to its relatively uncontaminated state, according to some preservation specialists. Surrounded by water on all sides, Zhouzhuang owes its integrity as a well-preserved vernacular settlement to its physical isolation from the outside world. Tourism has not yet reached the village, and few foreign visitors have found their way to this remote rural community.

The region is endowed with a rich cultural heritage, which some claim is unparalleled by any other section of the country. Archaeological discoveries in the 1970s confirmed that the cultural history of the Taihu district began some seven thousand years ago and is as old as the better-known areas of the Huanghe (Yellow River) valley in north China. Ever since the Song dynasty (960–1279), the region has been an important economic and cultural center of China. Not only has it been the birthplace and breeding ground of numerous scholar laureates (those who placed first, second, and third in palace examinations), poets, statesmen, artists, and craftsmen, but the region also has attracted wealthy merchants and retired government officials who established their households here. A Chinese saying acknowledges these notable residents in calling the region the "land of brilliant mountains and graceful rivers, and also the homeland of exceptional people." Many residences built during the Ming and Qing periods in towns and villages of the region have survived the turmoil of the past and today are well maintained and actively used.

According to historical accounts, a wealthy landlord named Zhou Di first established a farming settlement on this site in 1086 during the Northern Song dynasty. He later donated his own house along with 200 *mu,* about 13 hectares, of farmland to build a temple complex for the community. In appreciation of his charitable deeds and in his honor, the villagers named the community Zhouzhuang, or Zhou village.

The village began to grow in 1127, when Emperor Gaozong moved his capital from Kaifeng to nearby Hangzhou in Zhejiang province and established there the capital of the Southern Song dynasty. But it was not until near the end of the Yuan dynasty (1271–1368), when the millionaire Shen Wansan founded his headquarters in Zhouzhuang, that the village enjoyed its major expansion. It was during the Yuan dynasty that the Nanshihe and the Beishihe, which together constitute the main north-south waterway, were

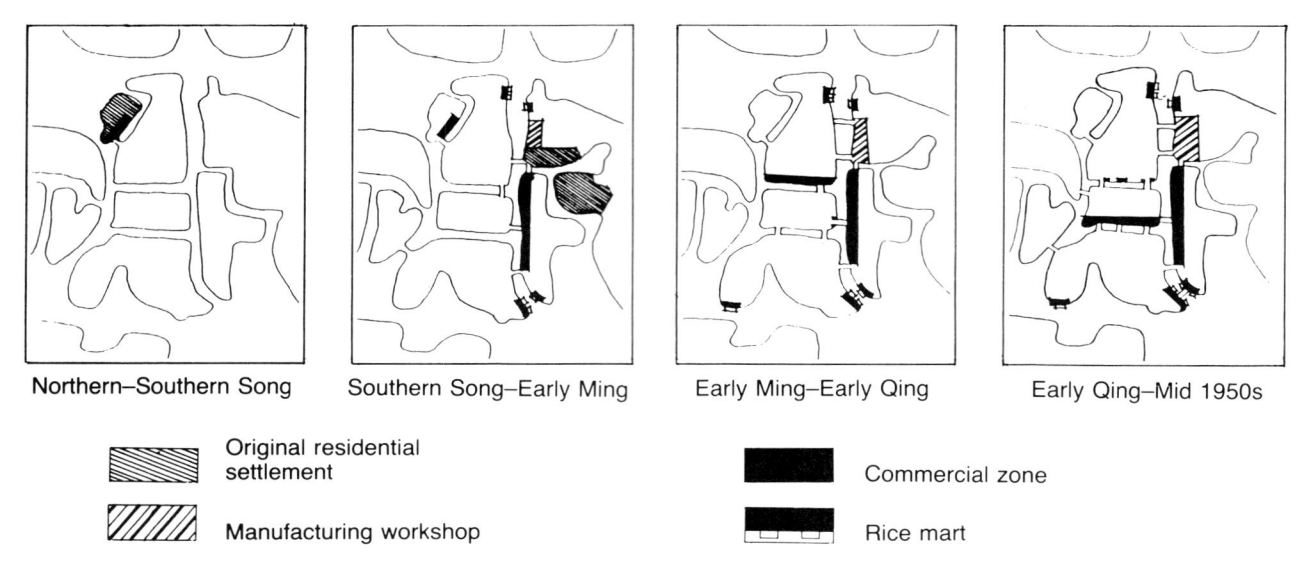

| Northern–Southern Song | Southern Song–Early Ming | Early Ming–Early Qing | Early Qing–Mid 1950s |

- Original residential settlement
- Manufacturing workshop
- Commercial zone
- Rice mart

Figure 10.2. The general evolution of Zhouzhuang's village form. [Source: Sketches taken from Tongji daxue 1986, *Zhouzhuang*, 1]

established as the central axis of the village. Fu'an Bridge, which was built in 1335, has since served as the focal point along this water axis. Near the end of the Ming dynasty (1368–1644), the commercial center of the village expanded westward toward Zhongshijie and Hegongjie. Zhouzhuang village reached its peak of growth and prosperity in the eighteenth century, during the Kangxi and Qianlong reigns of the Qing dynasty, when it claimed a population of over 3,000 residents. Besides the Yuan period Fu'an Bridge, six bridges survive from the Ming dynasty and three from the Qing dynasty.

In modern times, the village population has varied from nearly 4,000, as reported in the 1953 census, to a 1986 population of only 1,838 persons in 707 households, according to a Tongji University survey. Of the 1986 population, 802 were farmers, 720 students, 202 business personnel, and the rest teachers, medical personnel, factory workers, and local government employees. In addition, some 3,000 transient workers commuted daily to Zhouzhuang from nearby communities to fish in the surrounding lakes or to work in one of the village's fifteen factories. Of the villagers remaining in Zhouzhuang in 1986, the average age was sixty-one years. The older residents, who account for about one-quarter of the population, appear to be content with what they have and continue to "live in their past memories and old habits"; they are clearly a force in historic preservation in Zhouzhuang. Many in the younger generation, however, seem restless in Zhouzhuang, unhappy with the status quo and eager to seek new life-styles and employment elsewhere.

Walking along the waterways over arched stone bridges and through narrow alleys, one immediately recognizes the close resemblance between Zhouzhuang and Suzhou, the nearby historical city that serves as the model of all watertowns in the Lower Yangzi River Basin. Like Suzhou,

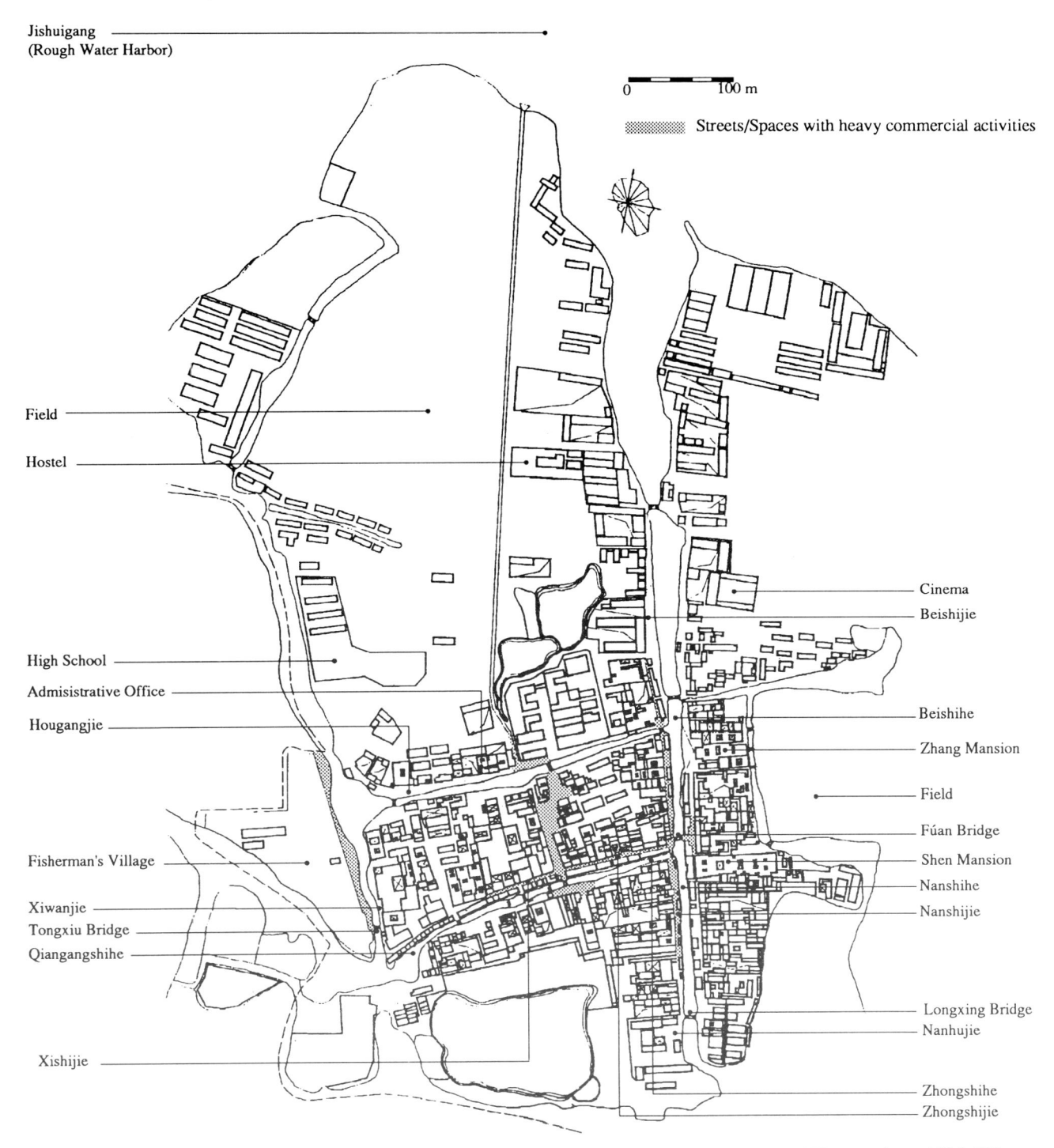

Figure 10.3. Zhouzhuang in 1986. [Source: Map redrawn by Men-chou Liu from Tongji daxue and Jiangsu sheng 1986, 21]

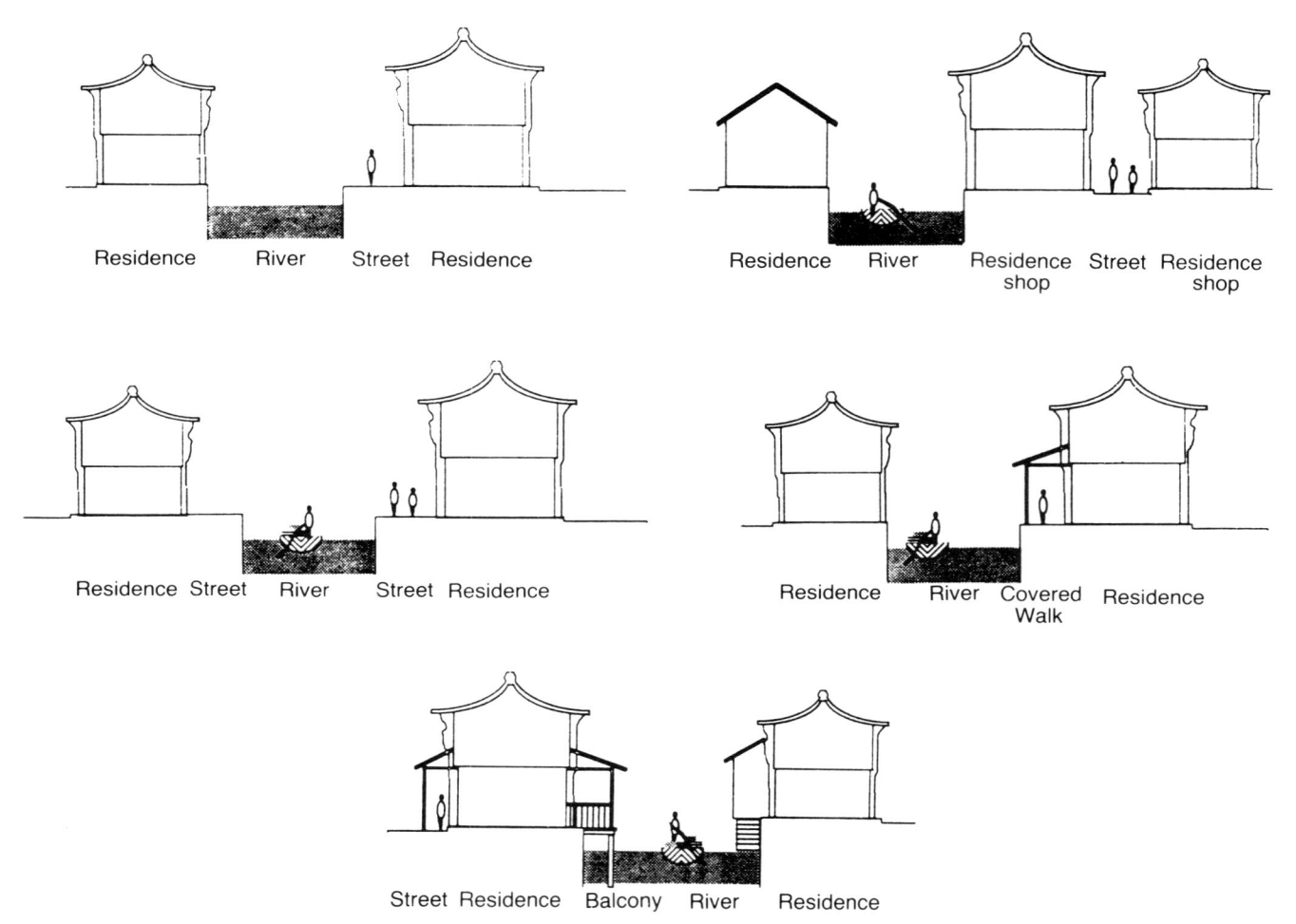

Figure 10.4. Typical river-street-building combinations found in Zhouzhuang. [Drawn by Men-chou Liu]

Zhouzhuang uses waterways as the backbone of its layout and planning. The main streets in the village were laid parallel to the rivers, and the majority of its buildings were designed to face streets in the front and water at the back. This model was traditional in watertowns, which at one time relied almost exclusively on water for transportation, trading, and domestic activities. Like Suzhou, also, the architectural elements in Zhouzhuang evolved from local conditions and on a scale appropriate to its character and setting. Most buildings in the village are one- or two-story timber-framed structures with gray tile roofs and white-washed exterior walls. This predominantly black-and-white scheme is highlighted in spots by dark brown woodwork and deep red window frames on the building facades. Local stones, found everywhere in the village, have been skill-

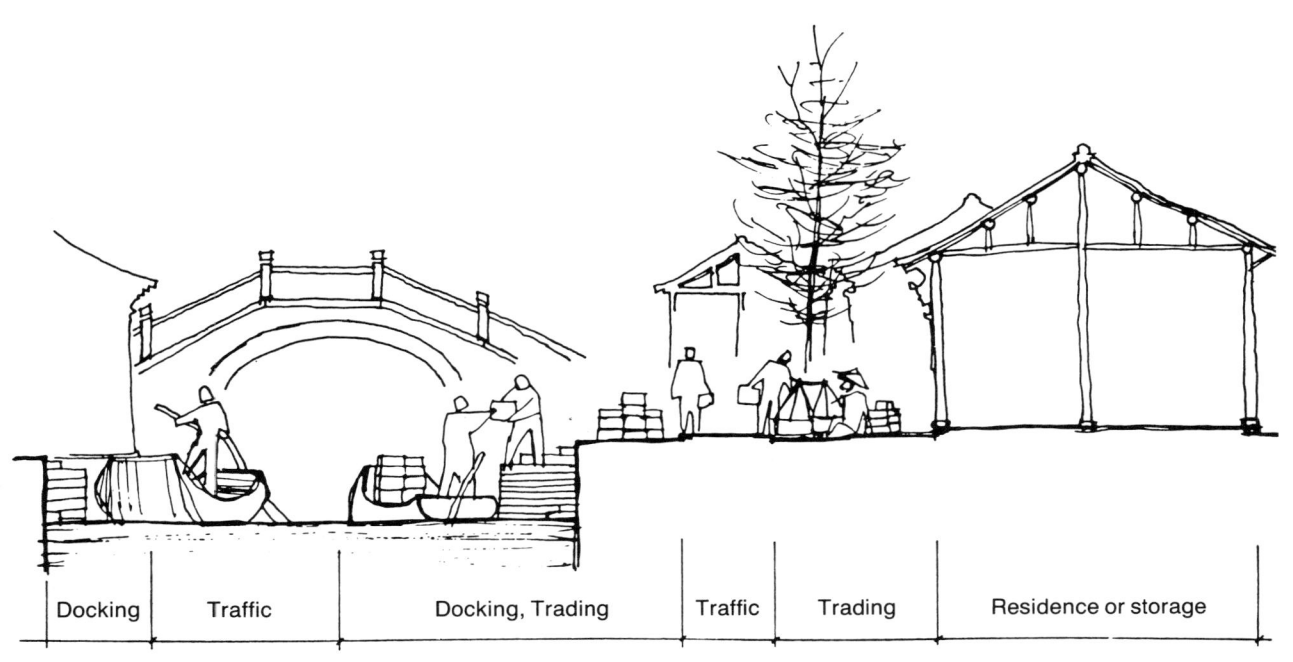

| Docking | Traffic | Docking, Trading | Traffic | Trading | Residence or storage |

Figure 10.5 The river, street, and buildings form multifunctional spaces for daily routines and spontaneous activities of Zhouzhuang's residents. [Drawn by Men-chou Liu]

fully used for bridges, street pavements, river banks, private and public wharves, and water squares along the waterways.

Unlike Suzhou's regular chessboardlike canal system, the waterways in Zhouzhuang are more natural in form, varying in width from 8 or 10 meters to between 10 and 20 meters. Overall, the network takes the shape of the Chinese character *jing* (well), carving the already small parcels of land—veritable islets—into even smaller and more intimate groupings of houses, shops, and bridges. Zhouzhuang village itself covers seven islands linked by nineteen stone bridges, many of which are arched. Bridges serve more than the utilitarian function as connectors of circulation. Historically, the placement of a bridge marked a focal point in the social, economic, and artistic life of the villagers.

Zhouzhuang is in many ways a self-contained community with facilities beyond those normally found in Chinese villages. In addition to a number of restaurants that serve breakfast and tea, there is a high school, a public library, a movie theater, a clinic, a bank, a post office, a housing bureau, and three small hotels. The presence of both a chamber of commerce and an office of taxation suggests the level of energy directed toward economic development. Although electricity is available throughout the settlement, served by power plants located in Shanghai, Zhouzhuang proper has no running water or sewage system. Traditional *matong,* wooden portable chamberpots, continue to be used in Zhouzhuang. An integral part of the early morning street scenes of Zhouzhuang are the *matong* set by the doorstep of each household for collection.

Figure 10.6. View of Zhouzhuang from its southwestern corner. To the left of Tongxiu Bridge in the background lies Fisherman's Village, which has some two hundred fishing boats. [Photo 1989, courtesy of Dan Redmond]

Figure 10.7. Fu'an Bridge, the focal point of Zhouzhuang, is viewed here from Longxing Bridge at the southern end of Nanshihe. In Zhouzhuang, as in other watertowns of the Taihu region, building facades facing the water are usually more open, delicate, and playful. They are treated with a greater variety of building materials than street-facing facades, which consist of rather bleak, thick walls punctured with simple doorways and small, high windows. [Photo 1989, courtesy of Janey Chan]

Zhouzhuang, Jiangsu

This quiet community is even quieter on work days, which span the period from Monday through Saturday. On a typical work day few people can be seen in the streets. "Everybody is at work—in factories, in the fields, and on nearby lakes," explains a local fisherman in his soft-spoken southern Wu dialect when approached at a juncture of Zhongshihe, an east-west stream river in the heart of Zhouzhuang. No dogs bark or cocks crow, the sounds usually heard in a traditional Chinese village. The only sound audible comes from motorboats that occasionally pass, loaded with farm products and building materials. Another fisherman explains the absence of automobiles and bicycles: "Cars are not allowed in this village, and it is not practical to ride a bike when you have so many arched bridges." Like a mind reader, he continues: "If you want to see a big crowd and hear noises, you should be here at about five o'clock each morning." The place he is speaking about is one of the sites of a daily farmers' market.

Figure 10.8. A view along a residential lane in Zhouzhuang in the early morning hours before the wooden *matong* are emptied. [Photo 1989, courtesy of Janey Chan]

Figure 10.9. Private access to dwellings along Zhouzhuang's Qiangangshihe is via stone steps and an overhanging wooden "porch." [Photo 1989, courtesy of Dan Redmond]

Zhouzhuang has reached a crossroads as China strives toward modernization. At issue is the controversy, the contradiction, between modernization and preservation. As Zhouzhuang stands today in a somewhat decayed form, uncertainties confront both the tradition-minded historians and architects as well as the utilitarian-minded economists and developers. Aside from the hustle and bustle each morning at several market places,

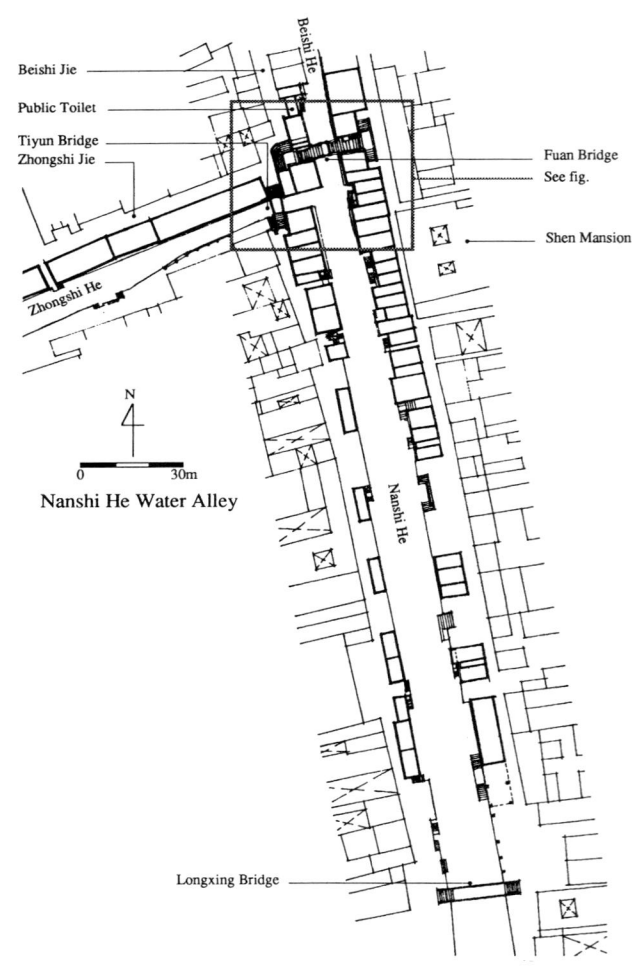

Figure 10.10. Public, semipublic, and private access to the water along Zhouzhuang's Nanshihe water alley exists in a variety of configurations. [Drawn by Men-chou Liu]

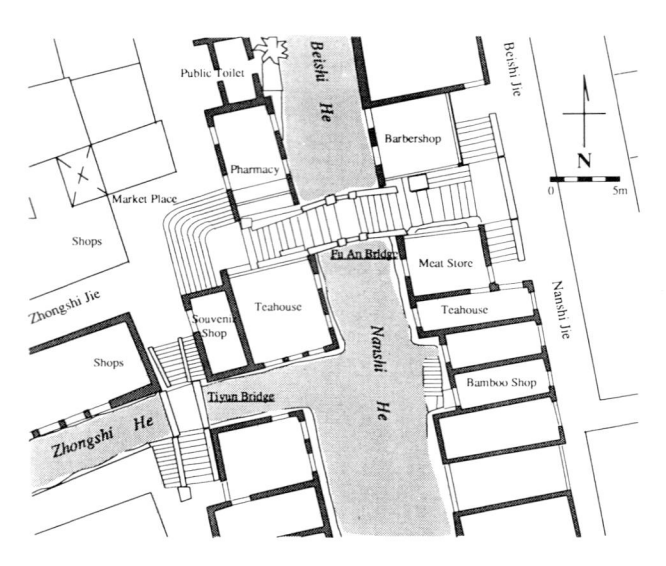

Figure 10.11. At the juncture of Beishihe, Nanshihe, and Zhongshihe is the physical and spiritual center of Zhouzhuang, all articulated around Fu'an Bridge, built in 1335 during the Yuan dynasty. [Source: Redrawn by Men-chou Liu from Ruan 1988, 111]

during most of the day the streets of Zhouzhuang are deserted, its waterways sparsely traveled, and its shops and restaurants poorly patronized. Like many historical settlements in China, Zhouzhuang has become a sleepy town, a once-splendid stage of human drama lying nearly vacant and largely underutilized.

In the autumn of 1985, a group of architecture and planning students from Tongji University conducted a series of extensive field studies in the village. As a result of the year-long study, a proposal for the conservation and redesign of Zhouzhuang was produced. The guiding principles of the proposal are the separation of developing industries from the old village center and the routing of regional highways away from the historical district, thus making the old village core a relatively pollution-free and pedestrian-only environment. Of particular interest to future tourism is the proposed redesign of the Beishihe-Nanshihe,

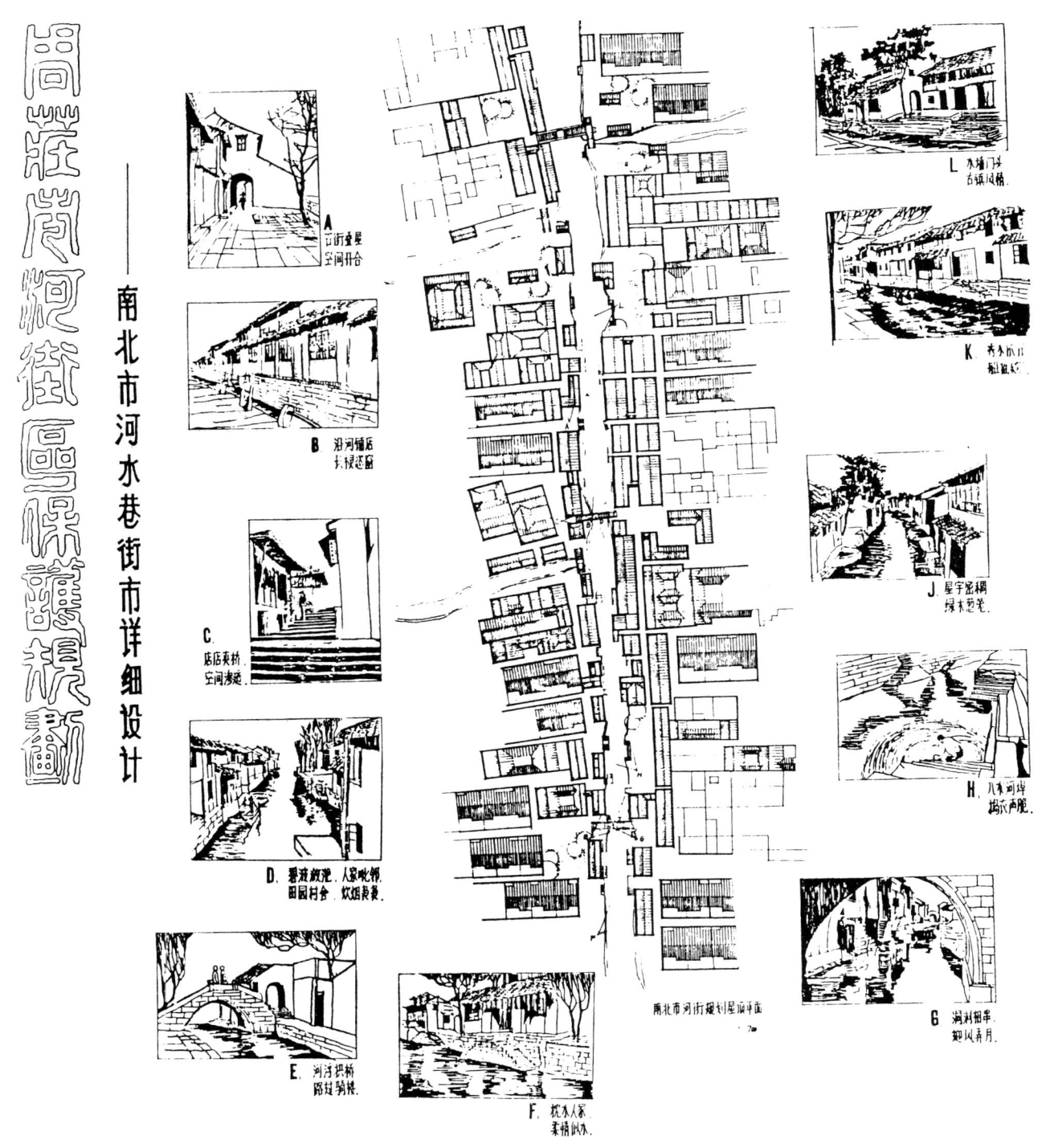

Figure 10.12. Detailed design completed by students of Tongji University in 1986 for Zhouzhuang's Nanshihe-Beishihe axis. [Source: Tongji daxue and Jiangsu sheng, 1986, 10]

the north-south canal strip, in the heart of Zhouzhuang. Included in the design scheme are several waterfront teahouses and restaurants, small shops, an art gallery, landscaped open spaces, and docks for oarsmen-operated pleasure boats, all creating a sequence of water-land touring experiences for future visitors. Significantly, the proposal attempts to preserve elements of Zhouzhuang's history while adding new elements that enhance and articulate the unique character of Zhou village.

I am grateful for the invaluable assistance of Professor Ruan Yisan of Tongji University, Shanghai, who introduced me to Zhouzhuang in the fall of 1986 and provided much of the information for this chapter. I extend my thanks also to Clara Cox, Information Director at the College of Architecture and Urban Studies, Virginia Polytechnic Institute, for her editorial assistance, and to Men-chou Li for his graphic work on Zhouzhuang. Janey Chan, James Doherty, Dan Redmond, Terry Stone, and David Sunkel kindly lent their photographs, some of which appear in this chapter.

CHAPTER 11

Yachuan Village, Gansu, and Shimadao Village, Shaanxi
Subterranean Villages

GIDEON GOLANY

SUBTERRANEAN or underground villages are scattered throughout a zone of loessial soil in north China that stretches approximately 3,000 kilometers west to east and 1,300 kilometers north to south. They are concentrated in the five provinces of Shanxi, Henan, Shaanxi, Gansu, and the Ningxia Autonomous Region. The Huanghe (Yellow River) forms the backbone of this loessial zone, a semiarid region that includes the cradle of Chinese civilization. Archaeological and textual findings provide evidence that subterranean dwellings have existed in these areas of China for more than four thousand years. Even today some thirty to forty million people, about 20 percent of the population of the five provinces, live in underground villages that vary in population from a few hundred to a few thousand.

A combination of environmental factors has supported the development of below-ground villages and contributed to their maintenance as an important settlement form to the present. Over many thousands of years, Chinese peasants learned how to treat the soil in designing space that is not confined by the availability of wood or stone but rather the ubiquity of a unique compacted earth.

Physiographically, the loessial region is a plateau ranging from 1,000 to 1,500 meters above sea level. The loessial soil that gives the plateau its character is a fine wind-borne silt that has been blown in over millennia from the Mongolian uplands. Loess deposits layer the region to depths that range between 100 and 200 meters. Called *huangtu* ("yellow earth") in Chinese, loess holds firm under conditions of low humidity, compacts well vertically, and forms a hard crust when it is dry. Under the impact of torrential summer thunderstorms, however, loessial soils erode easily into a dissected landscape composed of diverse and unique forms such as high tablelands, elongated or rounded mounds, narrow and steep valleys, cliffs, landslides, sinkholes, and funnels. This variety of landscape forms has led to great variation in settlement forms, clear evidence of thoughtful adjustment to local conditions. The erosion of this soil into numerous tributaries that feed into the major river of north China has loaded this mighty river with heavy silt and

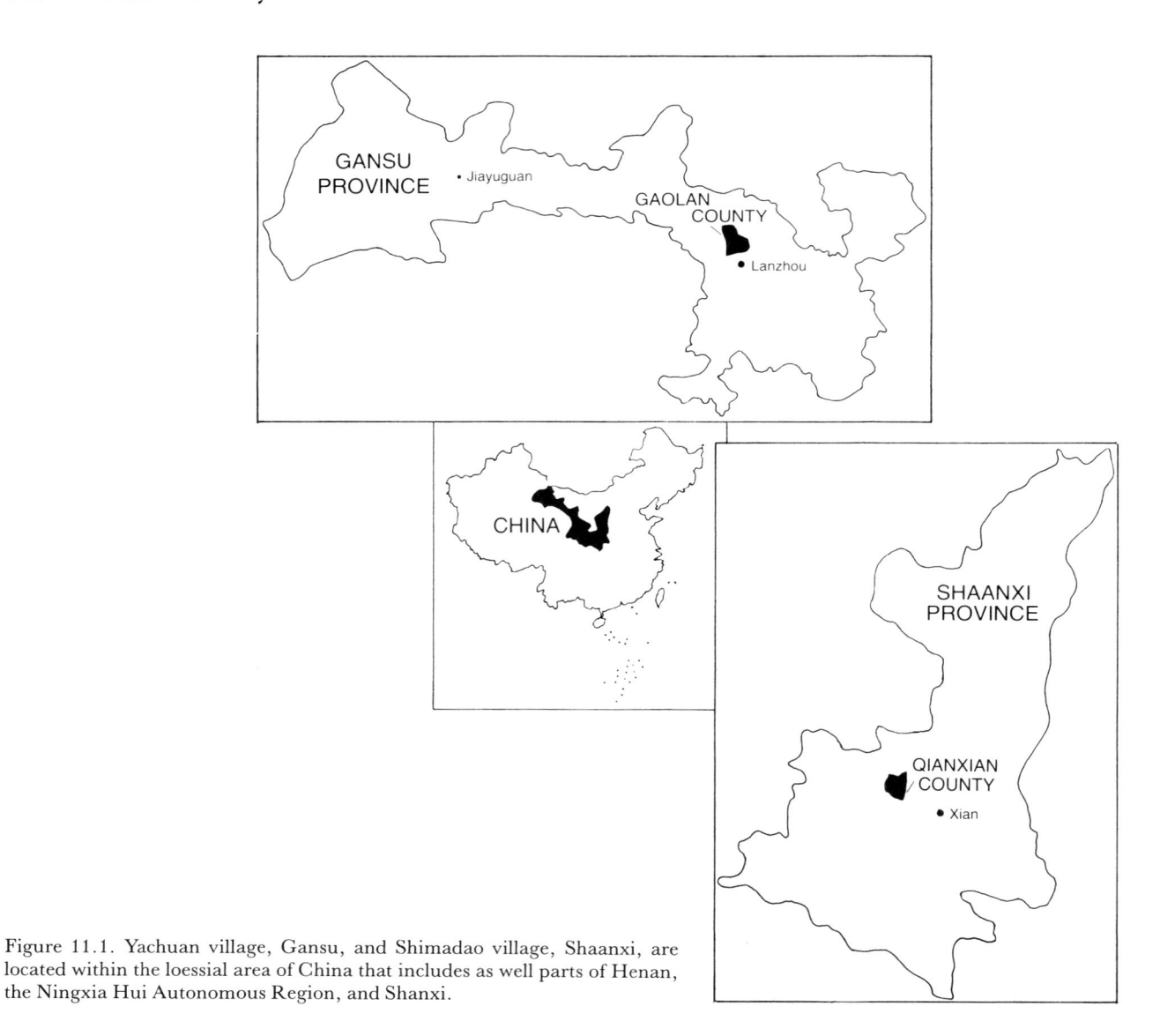

Figure 11.1. Yachuan village, Gansu, and Shimadao village, Shaanxi, are located within the loessial area of China that includes as well parts of Henan, the Ningxia Hui Autonomous Region, and Shanxi.

earned it the name "Yellow River" (Huanghe) to describe its ochre appearance.

Using an abundantly available resource, the soil, Chinese peasants have employed a "cut and use" method of construction without the need for building materials that has made it possible to construct dwellings relatively quickly. Such dwellings are not only comparatively inexpensive; they also are remarkably warm in winter and cool in summer, an important factor in a region with a stressful continental climate of very cold winters and hot summers. The heat gain and heat loss processes occur over the duration of a season, with the outdoor summer temperature reaching

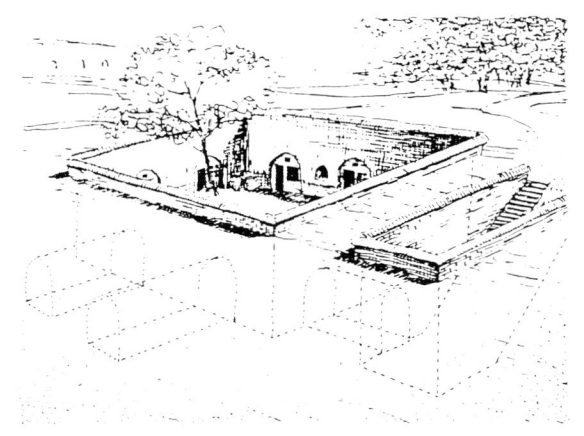

A. Pit cave dwelling type

B. Cliff cave dwelling type

C. Earth-sheltered (above-ground) dwelling constructed of stones, adobe, or bricks, similar in design to cave dwelling

D. Semi-below-ground dwelling on flat site

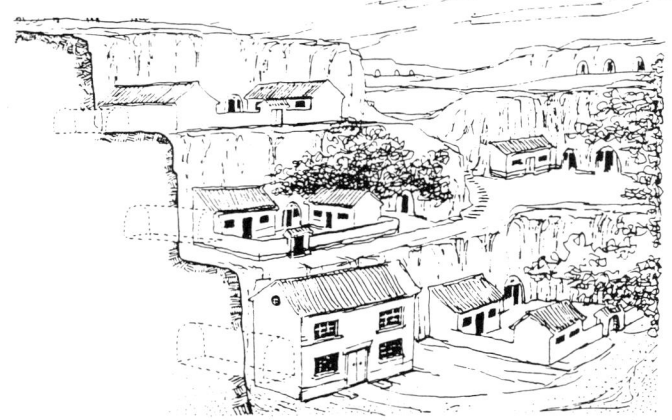

E. Combined below-and above-ground dwellings, cliff site

Figure 11.2. Cave dwelling types associated with the loessial plateau. [Source: Adapted from Golany 1992, 67]

Figure 11.3. View of Wang Jia Terrace and neighborhood, Yan'an, overlooking the valley. [Source: Golany 1990, 55]

the indoor, below-ground space in the winter and vice versa. The soil functions not only as an insulator but also as a heat retainer and processor, providing stable and comfortable living environments of approximately 25°C during the summer and 10° in winter.

Below-ground villages in China include two basic types of subterranean dwellings, cliffside cave dwellings and pit cave dwellings. Although both may be found in some villages, in varying relative proportions, more often a village has either one type or the other. Some villages offer variants along a continuum between the two types, for example, semi-below-ground dwellings on flat sites, combined below- and above-ground dwellings on a cliff site, and earth-sheltered dwellings constructed of stones, adobe, or bricks that are similar in design to cave dwellings but are completely above ground. The basic dwelling types are discussed below in general terms, with

Figure 11.4. An overall view of below-ground dwellings along the cliff at Fushan county, east of Linfen, Shanxi province, 1984. [Photograph, 1984]

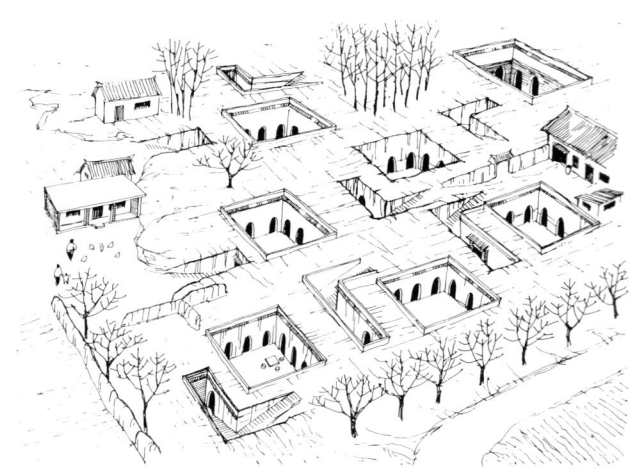

Figure 11.5. A Perspective view of Longtou village, Mangshan township, near Luoyang, Henan province. [Source: Golany, 1992]

Figure 11.6. A bird's-eye view of cave dwellings along the threshold of the plateau and cliffs in the Qingyang region, Gansu province. [Source: Golany 1992, 50]

two representative settlements introduced to present the spatial character of different village forms.

Cliff Villages

Cliff-type villages typically utilize a site that cannot be used for other purposes, yet leave the soil above for agricultural development. Here, dwellings and other associated built forms in the village are primarily dug into the vertical face of terraced cliffs. The excavated soil usually is spread before each dwelling to create a fronting terrace, which is frequently surrounded by a wall to form a courtyard. Usually found where the terrain is not suitable for agriculture, the dwelling and courtyard together consume only a minimum amount of level land. Such construction minimizes or, in some cases, eliminates the threat of vertical water penetration through cavities and reduces the risk of collapse due to the thick mass of soil above the dwelling.

A preference for southern orientation is usually characteristic of cliff-dwelling sites, availing the dwelling of optimal exposure to natural sunlight and minimal exposure to prevailing winds. Although lacking bi- or multidirectional ventilation, cliff dwellings are better ventilated than the pit types discussed below. In fact, both lack a ventilation system. Condensation levels are increased during the periods of high humidity that accompany the summer rains.

The design of many cliff-type villages represents a horizontal yet articulated terraced form spread out along a ravine. In general, terraces are cut into cliffs, establishing approximately a 95-degree angle between the cliff and the created terrace. Most cliff dwellings have a one-sided room facade, but it is not unusual to see a two- or three-sided cliff dwelling with perpendicular facades

Yachuan Village, Gansu, and Shimadao Village, Shaanxi

where the local topography permits. The excavated soil, which varies in amount depending on the extent of the dwelling complex, is used to reinforce and enlarge the terrace and to build access roads. Many cliff-dwelling villages combine above- and below-ground space usage. Above-ground kitchens and storage areas are frequently found on the terrace adjacent to the below-ground sleeping and general living quarters.

Yachuan village is located in Gaolan county, Gansu province, some 20 kilometers north of the city of Lanzhou. Located in the western portion of the loessial uplands in an area of undulating and dissected topography, the village has a population of 254 people. Of the 43 households, 10 families live in cliffside dwellings combined with above-ground houses and 4 or 5 families live only in below-ground dwellings.

Set into a rather barren environment is the dwelling complex for the Cao Yiren family, comprising the farmer-builder, his wife, and three

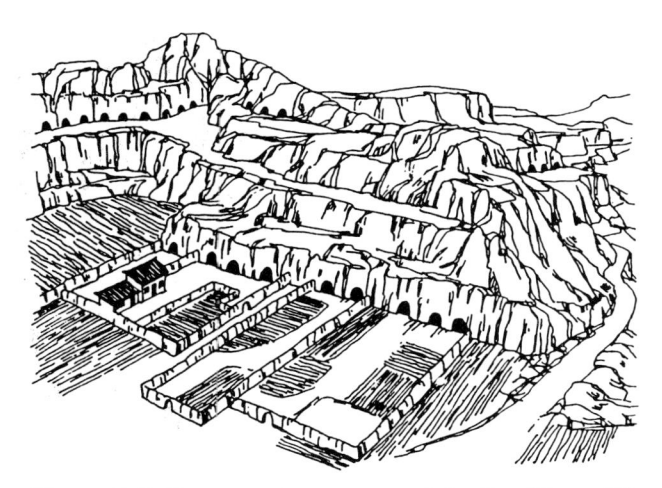

Figure 11.7. Barren environs surround the Cao Yiren cliffside dwelling, the unit on the left, in Yachuan village, Gansu province. [Source: Golany 1990, 67]

Figure 11.8. Perspective view of the Cao Yiren dwelling, Yachuan. [Source: Golany 1990, 67]

children. Arranged in a row fronting on an enclosed courtyard, the four cliffside units of the dwelling all face southward. The complex was excavated in 1978 over a one-month period, with the work done only in the evenings. The units were left unoccupied for two years while the interiors dried out.

The plan of the dwelling complex reveals that only three of the four excavated caves have entryways directly into the courtyard. One cave serves as a pigsty and pig run separate from the living area to the east. Nearby and separated from the outside by a curtain, a 5-meter-deep storage cave for grain and other dry foods opens onto an elevated patio raised somewhat above the courtyard fronting the residential area. In the southwest corner, there is a rectangular above-ground building that includes a bedroom, a storage area, and a kitchen. To the east is a large courtyard that contains a kitchen garden and provides entry into the dwelling.

Entry through a parabolic arch leads into a kitchen, which leads either to a deeper low-ceilinged storage room through a small opening or through a passageway into the principal bedroom for the household. Dominating the bedroom

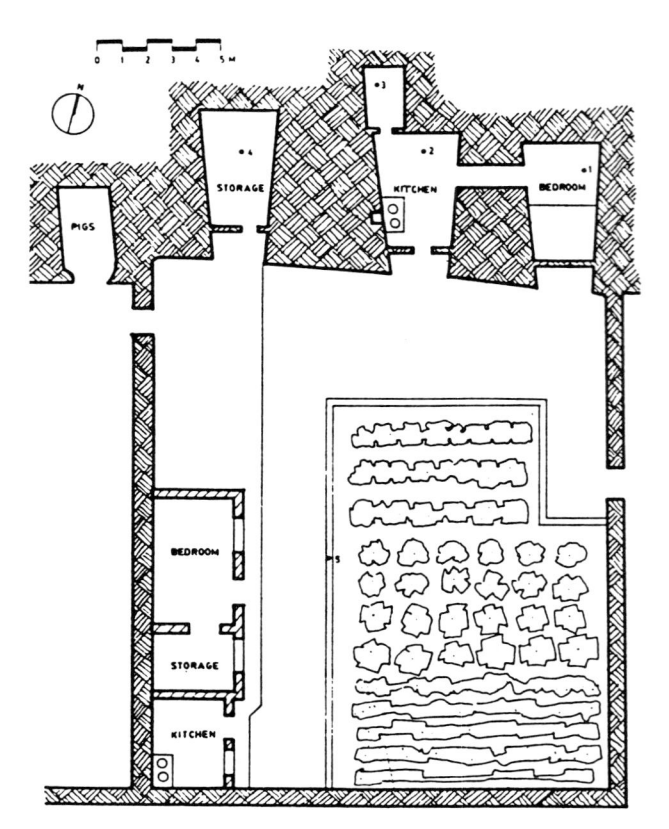

Figure 11.9. Plan view of the Cao Yiren dwelling, Yachuan. [Source: Golany 1990, 67]

Figure 11.10. The view from within the bedroom looking into the kitchen of the Cao Yiren family dwelling in Yachuan. On the left is the *kang* with bedding piled on top. [Source: Golany 1990, 68]

is a *kang,* the traditional heatable brick bed, which occupies almost half the room. A large window brings light into the room. This bedroom has no direct access to the outside.

An interesting aspect of the design of three of these excavated units is that the front of each unit is made narrower than the back, in an attempt to minimize the penetration of outside radiation. Still, the courtyard generates much heat during the afternoon period and consequently influences the temperatures within the four rooms. All indoor areas have dramatic temperature fluctuations during the day in summer, although there is more stability during the winter months. In this area of striking aridity, relative humidities are quite low.

In general, the view of and the view from a cliffside dwelling are both appealing. Cliff dwellers enjoy a direct view of the surrounding area, especially the nearby lowlands, and thus are able to overcome the feeling of confinement associated with living in below-ground spaces. Integrated as they are into their dissected surroundings, cliff villages usually provide an overall landscape that is attractive and picturesque.

Pit Villages

Villages of pit dwellings are predominant on the flat or rolling terrain of the loessial plateau, and their design is primarily influenced by such an environment. Here, with an absence of cliff faces in which to dig, villagers excavate large pits, generally 8 meters by 10 meters, to a depth of 7 to 9 meters. Rooms are then excavated into each of the four sides of the pit. Traditionally, it appears as if few preconceived notions of planning or design guided the choice of pit-dwelling sites. In more modern times, however, dwellings within pit-type villages have been built using a grid system. In some cases, a constant distance between dwellings is maintained, allowing for reasonable bordering zones between dwelling units.

Following tradition, extended family dwelling units include from four to eight or more subterranean rooms. Most such dwellings have two rooms on each of the four sides. With an orientation to compass directions, two rooms thus are oriented facing south, a preferred direction for residences throughout China. These rooms are reserved for the most important members of a family, usually the senior generation. The sides facing east and west are given to those second in the hierarchy of the family's members. Rooms facing north are used for storage, for housing farm animals, and for the sloped below-ground entrance into the pit dwelling. Some pit units have more rooms and accommodate more than one family. In general, rooms are not confined exclusively to one function. Most rooms have a large *kang* bed just inside, serving in the winter as an elevated radiator of heat.

In most cases, no fence surrounds the opening of the pit, so villagers as well as animals must learn to watch for the opening. Small toilet rooms are often located at the curve of the tunnel entrance. The waste, which is covered with shoveled soil, is taken occasionally and used for soil fertilization.

Pit dwellings satisfy in a unique design the traditional Chinese concept of enclosure and intimacy within the dwelling unit. In some cases, the common vernacular practice of constructing a series of two courtyards is followed, providing a transitional space through an entryway that is formed from a graded stairway constructed partly underground and partly open to the sky.

Similar to rooms in cliff-side dwellings, pit-dwelling rooms average 2.9 meters wide and 6 or more meters in length, and are designed in vaulted form, 2.5 or more meters in height. The facades for most rooms are parabolic in shape, although others are semicircular or elliptical. An advantage of the vault form is that it is expandable in depth and height. Width, however, is limited to a maximum of 3.5 meters, principally because of soil constraints. In some cases, the ceiling is slanted from the front of the room to the back in order to concentrate and intensify the

Figure 11.11. A general view from the west of the Bai Lesheng family dwelling in Shimadao village, Shaanxi province. Although located on a terrace overlooking a lowland, the dwellings are of the pit type. [Source: Golany 1990, 90]

penetration of the light that passes through the large facade. Rooms are usually entered through a single door with a large window beside it and above it.

Shimadao village, located at a high elevation above a terraced valley, includes many pit cave dwellings on flat sites, each with nearly square courtyards open to the sky. Here in the northern part of Qianxian county, some 75 kilometers northwest of Xi'an, the provincial capital of Shaanxi province, one finds adjacent to the village the impressive imperial tombs of the Tang dynasty (618–907). In this area, few villages are located in the lowlands; most have been excavated into the flat areas along the edge of the plateau.

The dwelling complex of the Bai Lesheng household, built some twenty years ago, represents the complex design of pit-cave-type dwellings common to the area. Two excavated sunken courtyards form the core of the dwelling. A relatively small one, transitional to the larger more private one, is used to store agricultural equipment and has storage caves off it in two directions. From this cluttered forecourtyard, a tunnel 3 meters long by 2 meters wide leads through the loess to the interior courtyard. This larger, more private courtyard is 9 by 9 meters in size, with three bedrooms, a kitchen, a storage room, and a cave in which to keep cattle dug into its sides. Three generations, including eleven people with five children, share the dwelling. The northern room that faces south is 6 meters deep, 3 meters

Figure 11.12. A perspective view of the the two courtyards of the Bai Lesheng dwelling, Shimadao village. [Source: Golany 1990, 90]

Figure 11.13. Facades providing entry into the walls of the pit. [Source: Golany 1990, 90]

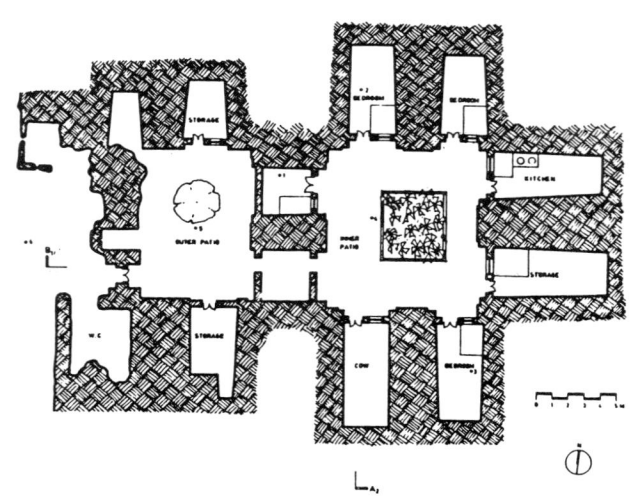

Figure 11.14. A plan of the Bai Lesheng dwelling, Shimadao village, emphasizing the double courtyard and associated excavations. [Source: Golany 1990, 90]

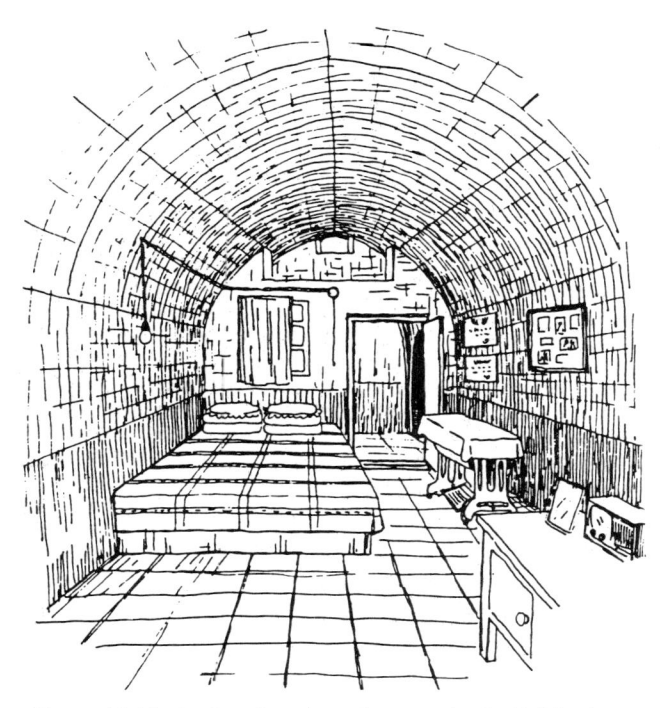

Figure 11.15. An interior view of a room in the Bai Lesheng dwelling, Shimadao village. [Source: Golany 1990, 90]

high, and 3 meters wide; it is occupied by the grandparents.

Traditionally, throughout the loessial regions of China, many villages and dispersed dwellings were totally subterranean. More recently, however, above-ground structures have been appearing in increasing numbers in many such villages. There are recognizable "pros and cons" in the use of subterranean versus above-ground space, which should be evaluated, like any other land use, in terms of trade-offs. My research concerning earth-sheltered housing throughout the world indicates that its pros outweigh its cons; this is particularly true in the case of China.

Chinese subterranean villages provide much intimacy and privacy for residents. From an economic point of view, they are less expensive by 50 percent than an equivalent above-ground space because of the dual use of the land, little use—if any—of building materials, and quick construction. Two laborers can dig one room unit with two days' work. The construction work itself can be done by farmers with their general knowledge, without special training. Tool requirements are few: a simple hoe, a shovel, and a basket for removing the soil. What results is a suitable environment for the stressful climate, providing stable, seasonal indoor ambient temperatures. Energy savings is an added feature.

Living below ground historically has had a negative image in China. Prior to 1949, subterranean dwellings were associated with poverty, inefficiency, and unhealthiness. More recently, the Chinese government and the Architectural Society of China have called for determining the strengths of this habitat form and eliminating its weaknesses. Because of their vast consumption of land, pit-type villages are being discouraged for new housing development in the loessial areas of China, but cliffside dwellings are being encouraged. Room size certainly is constrained by the character of the soil, often making it difficult for such dwellings to accommodate modern furniture and large electrical appliances. In recent decades, the supply of electricity and water to subterranean dwellings has improved, but serious deficiencies in handling sewage perpetuate unsatisfactory sanitary conditions. However, with good village location and innovative design it is possible to eliminate the weaknesses and provide a pleasing, healthy, well-lighted environment that reflects well on the heritage of the Chinese subterranean village.

CHAPTER 12

Hekeng Village, Fujian
Unique Habitats

OLIVIER LAUDE

AMONG the most distinctive landscapes in China are those found in the mountainous junction linking the provinces of Fujian, Guangdong, and Jiangxi. This region is dominated by a Han ethnic subgroup generally known as the Hakka, from a term meaning "guest families" *(kejia),* which is usually applied by local Chinese settlers to newcomers or strangers. The Hakka have sometimes been described as if they were a non-Han ethnic minority. In fact, they are Han, but Han with a sense of identity that clearly distinguishes them from other Han Chinese.

Between the fourth and seventeenth centuries, in at least three waves, Hakkas migrated from north central China in search of a new homeland. It is not clear how the Hakka were able to preserve their distinctiveness while inhabiting and passing through areas in which different Han groups dominated. It is also a curiosity that they left no traces along their migration routes of the patterns that subsequently came to characterize them in the many counties of the south where they became the majority population. However, general isolation in a relatively remote area of southern China together with the distinctive Hakka social and economic structure led over time to environmental adaptation, architecture, and village landscapes that are both creative and successful (see Huang 1984a, 189–194; 1984b, 182–187; "Fujian" 1989, 6–39).

Hekeng is a typical Hakka village that has grown along the axis of a gentle stream within a narrow valley flanked by low hills. Administratively, Hekeng comprises the major portion of the administrative village of Qujiang, Shuyang township, in the western part of Nanjing county. Hekeng itself is divided into two parts, an upper and a lower village, with a total population of 1,300. This chapter will focus on the upper village, a village in which all of the 700 residents have the single surname Zhang. The Zhang clan hall on the southern side of the village commemorates twenty-one generations of Zhangs, but it is a genealogical record with several gaps in it.

What makes Hekeng and other Hakka settlements so distinctive are the *tulou,* or "earthen buildings," which tower above the surrounding countryside. These multistoried fortlike struc-

Figure 12.1. General location of Hekeng village, Shuyang township, Nanjing county, Fujian province.

tures rise three and four stories, unlike most other traditional Chinese dwellings, organizing space vertically rather than horizontally in order to cluster people and livestock in rural tenements or dwelling complexes. Although the Hakka have been most identified with *tulou,* it is increasingly clear that non-Hakka may have built this dwelling type even before Hakka migrated to the region (Huang 1989, 28).

Tulou in Hekeng and other Hakka villages come in various shapes and sizes. There are both square and rectangular shapes, but clearly the most unique and distinctive habitats are the round ones. *Tulou* sometimes reach 75 meters in diameter and provide homes for twenty-five or thirty related families of 150 or more people. In many villages of Nanjing and neighboring Yongding counties, there are old *tulou* that villagers claim were built in the seventeenth century. Villagers in Hekeng, however, proudly point to a square edi-

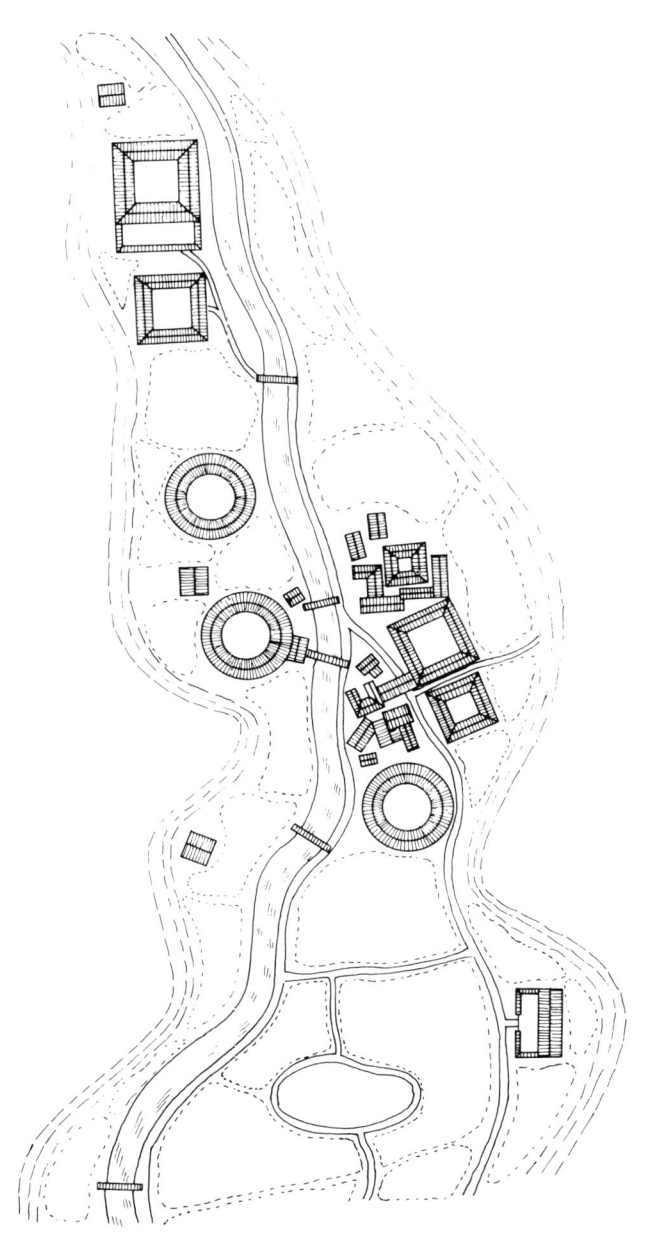

Figure 12.2. Schematic map of Hekeng village. [Drawing courtesy of Thorina Rose]

Hekeng Village, Fujian 165

fice that lore says is four hundred years old. Built during the Ming dynasty, it probably stood alone until joined by other shaped structures to eventually form the picturesque village seen today. Although many of the *tulou* in Hekeng appear old, most in fact have been erected since 1949, especially during the 1950s.

Hekeng's largest and most populated *tulou* was built in 1958. An imposing round structure, called a *yuanlou* or "round building," it serves as a visual gateway to the rest of the upper village. This important *yuanlou* is sandwiched between two paths. One path leads past an ancestral hall on the edge of the village up a steep slope to reach a highway and bus stop about a hundred meters above the valley. The other runs generally parallel to the stream that follows the valley and serves as the main artery linking the upper and lower villages. Three small bridges allow this path to weave its way downstream and tie the settlement together. The two paths converge in Hekeng's center, where two square *tulou* stand on the right stream bank and directly across the stream a *yuanlou* rises, surrounded by vegetable gardens, small rice paddies, and a pond. Within this loose triangular conglomeration of buildings where Hekeng spreads out most noticeably, four stores sell beer, peanuts, sugar, sweets, toothpaste, soap, and laundry detergent. Business is slow, and most stores close during much of the day as their owners leave to work the fields. Beyond the narrow stretch of flat land that is the left bank, cobblestone walkways, some veritable stairs, lead villagers into the hills to their fields, sometimes as much as forty-five minutes away.

All buildings in Hekeng have been built using traditional construction techniques and materials. Unlike so many villages elsewhere in China, Hekeng has no new structures of fired brick and concrete. However, placed among the five large

Figure 12.3. Perspective view of the upper village. [Photograph, 1990]

tulou are smaller one- and two-story rectangular dwellings housing a single or a few families, also built in the traditional manner using tamped earth. The tamped earth, or *hangtu,* method of wall construction has a long history in China, being found not only in the drier areas of north China but also throughout south China (see Shan 1981; Knapp 1986, 54–57; Knapp 1989, 70–72). Nowhere in the country, however, are the walls as thick or as high as they are in Hakka villages of southwestern Fujian province.

In building a tamped earth wall, the soil is piled into a rectangular caisson and then pounded with rammers until its bearing strength has been increased to carry another layer above it. The caisson is then raised and the process repeated until the wall reaches a desired height. The basic *hangtu* process can be observed in many areas of China today, but it is not possible to confirm the means by which large *tulou* are built. Villagers state that none has been built since the 1950s, principally because of strict adherence to policies that forbid the use of the raw material needed to construct them. Tamped earth walls for *tulou* require very fine and fertile silt washed from the hillsides, sorted by water, and deposited within the paddy fields in the valley bottoms. Unsorted soil found higher in the hills lacks the ability to be compacted to form high walls. The volume of paddy silt needed to construct a large *tulou* is enormous, providing a clear contradiction for villagers wanting both to farm rich soil and to have substantial dwellings. In recent decades, only small buildings with limited materials requirements have been built.

As seen in the illustrations, the walls of *tulou* are

Figure 12.4. Two of the larger round buildings *(yuanlou)* lie adjacent to a square building and several smaller dwellings. [Photograph, 1990]

Figure 12.5. Close-up of one of Hekeng's largest *tulou,* a three-story structure with windows only on the two upper floors. A single entry leads into the complex. [Photograph, 1990]

provided security, presenting a formidable challenge to enemies and bandits. Indeed, it is generally believed that it was the enmity of other settlers and the fear of bandits that influenced the Hakka to build such secure structures.

Beyond the intimidating facade and through the main gate and load-bearing walls of a *tulou*, one enters a large circular courtyard. Most such courtyards in neighboring villages are cluttered with privies, pigsties, and secondary kitchens, but in Hekeng village most are relatively tidy. Most are paved with rounded stones, although some are simply packed earth. Here children are permitted to play among chickens and ducks as well as hanging laundry. Sometimes rice is dried here also, and occasionally in the largest village *tulou* a movie is shown by a traveling projection crew. In the courtyard also is at least one well to supply water needs for the residents. It is easy to imagine that under difficult circumstances and once they had harvested their crops, villagers could live rather self-sufficiently within their *tulou*. In the

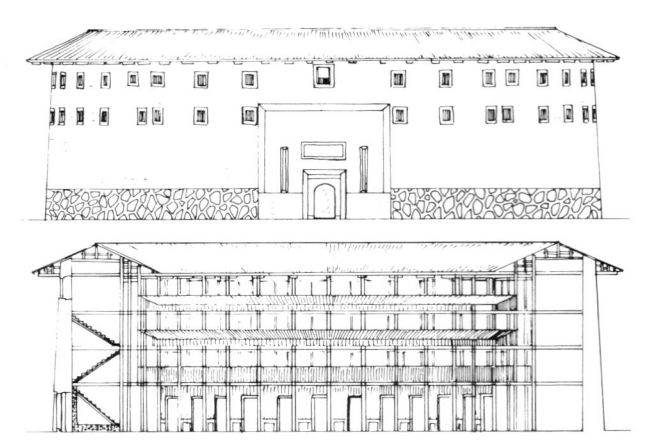

Figure 12.6. An elevation and section view of a Hekeng *tulou* showing its battered walls and interior wooden structure. [Drawing courtesy of Thorina Rose]

Figure 12.7. The entryway to a *yuanlou* reveals a tamped earth wall set upon a stone base. [Photograph, 1990]

Figure 12.8. The interior perimeter of each *tulou* is constructed of wood. Individual "apartments" run vertically with a kitchen on the first floor and bedrooms or storage above. [Photograph, 1990]

slightly battered and built upon substantial stone bases. No windows and only a single arcuate entryway break the first level of any *tulou*. Sometimes even the second floor is without windows. Small windows generally appear only on upper floors. With an outer shell of compacted paddy soil up to a meter and a half thick, these ramparts

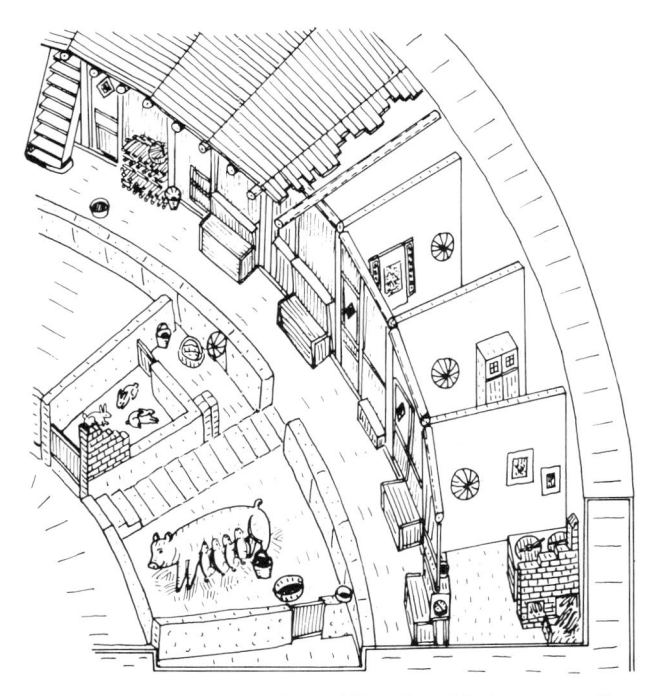

Figure 12.9. Cut-away view of first floor kitchens revealing stoves, cabinets, and storage areas. In some *tulou,* the courtyard is used for raising pigs, rabbits, and chickens, but in Hekeng most pigs are kept outside the building. [Drawing courtesy of Thorina Rose]

Figure 12.10. A view of Hekeng verandas and roof structures. Some small buildings, as shown here, are placed in the central courtyard. [Photograph, 1990]

decades since 1949, a time of relative peace in China's countryside, it has made sense to place pigsties and latrines outside the building for reasons of sanitation. Furthermore, beneath the wide overhanging eaves of the outer rim, abundant dry space exists to store firewood and further remove clutter from the courtyard inside. The ancestral hall of some *tulou* takes up about half of the courtyard, the building's core, and diminishes any sense of openness. In Hekeng, however, ancestral halls are not usually found in this open space but instead occupy a large space along the rim directly opposite the entryways.

The layout within each Hekeng village *tulou* is similar. The interior perimeter, whether the building is round or rectangular, is constructed of wood, locked into place by the secure placement of floor joists deep into the earthen walls. The wooden structures utilize the *chuandou* method of framing with tie beams mortised into or tenoned through the columns to form an interlocking matrix. The weight of the heavy tiled roof is carried by both the thick walls and the wooden framework to the ground. The double pitched roof leads water away from the walls on the exterior and into the courtyard in the interior, where much of it is collected for later use.

Depending upon the size of the structure and the number of families to be housed, the living areas are crafted of equal size along the interior walls. Space is divided into *jian,* or bays, the basic Chinese building module. Elsewhere in China, *jian* is the interval between four columns, but here beams are supported by only two columns and the wall. Instead of a *jian* being a true rectangle, *jian* within *tulou* are essentially trapezoidal in shape, narrower in the front with a broader rear. The equidistant spacing of pillars and beams helps standardize the building process, creating spaces that are essentially similar. The number of ground-floor *jian* ranges upward from forty.

Each family lives within a vertical apartment, usually two *jian* wide. If required, and where space is available, the family may have additional *jian*. Whatever space a family has at ground level is carried up into the upper stories in tenementlike fashion. At ground level, each family has a kitchen in one *jian*, equipped with a stove vented through the wall, storage space for wood, water containers, and cupboards. In an adjacent *jian* of equal size, there is a table with benches, shelves, and storage for eating utensils and condiments. The cutting of vegetables and meat as well as some summertime cooking frequently are carried out just outside the kitchen door, adjacent to the open courtyard. Both rooms are linked to the outside through simple latticework frames. Kitchens are small and cramped but are a place for social gatherings. Family members often do not eat at a table but instead gather at the entrance of their kitchen to chat with neighbors as they eat. Here also, many household chores—knitting, washing clothes, sewing, and preparing meals—are carried out.

Four wooden stairways lead to verandas that ring the upper floors of most *tulou*. The second floor is used principally for the dry storage of grain and other food, because it is not too far from the kitchen. Bedrooms are found on the third and fourth floors, depending on the size of the *tulou*. On these upper floors also are stored family valuables, including wooden coffins bought to give peace of mind to elderly members of the family.

Laundry is often hung to dry along the verandas of these upper floors. The individual rooms occupied by each family are all relatively small but grow in size as the building rises, making the sleeping quarters on the upper levels the most spacious, luminous, and comfortable.

The rhythm of life in Hekeng varies with the seasons, but with two rice harvests a year and a winter crop, villagers spend a good deal of each day tending their crops—weeding, tilling, pruning, and preparing new fields to continue the cycle. Hekeng and other Hakka villages are surrounded by vegetable gardens, orchards, and terraced rice paddies, which support these scattered communities. Besides the rice terraces, the hillslopes are covered with stands of camphor and pine trees, tea bushes, hemp and banana plants, as well as clusters of bamboo. Numerous paths lead to uncultivated hillsides and the firewood that villagers must gather. Also in the hills, villagers, according to the season, search for wildlife, mushrooms, fungi, and local medicinal herbs—commodities that over the years have been plundered with the result that villagers speak of the difficulty of finding that which once was relatively plentiful.

A typical day in Hekeng starts around 5:30 A.M. for women and 7:30 A.M. for men. Early in the day, small columns of dark smoke curl from small flues that protrude from the walls of each *tulou,* the number equaling the number of kitchen stoves inside as well as the number of families. The women get up early to cook breakfast, often making a rice porridge that must cook slowly. They also tend to the chickens and ducks, feed the pigs and rabbits, and begin to do laundry early in the morning. When the men get up, the family eats together, often sitting on benches outside the kitchen. No one rushes off to work. Instead, everyone takes time to stretch, stroll around, and digest their first meal of rice and vegetables sometimes supplemented by a little meat or fish. Sweet potatoes, a Hakka staple, often complement each meal. The diet is simple and plentiful but remains monotonously unvaried throughout the year, except during festivals, when minced squabs, wintermelon soups, meat-stuffed tofu, and salt-baked chicken replace the ordinary menu. Festivals are times of plenty, breaking the dietary pattern and repetition of everyday life.

Around 9:00 A.M., both men and women walk to the fields, leaving grandparents and children in the village. Throughout the day, the old and the young cluster at the front gate, sitting on stools to play and chat. Men and women and older children typically spend three or four hours in the fields over the course of a morning, returning home near noon for lunch. After lunch, some simply rest; others nap, eat, chat, or perform tasks around the family's living quarters. Around 3:00 P.M., men, women, and older children return to the fields for another three or four hours work.

Before dinner, honoring the long-standing tradition of daily washing, most men and older boys in the village gather to bathe at one of several spots along the stream that passes through Hekeng. Along the stream bank at these same spots earlier in the day, younger girls and married women did laundry on large flat stones put there for that purpose. Women bathe in the privacy of their own bedrooms instead of in the streams. After a late dinner, most everyone sits around chatting before heading off to bed. When most are asleep, the main gate is closed.

Ever since 1949 great efforts and sacrifices have been expended in connecting the Hakka hinterlands to their neighboring coastal plains. It is now relatively easy for Chinese and outsiders alike to reach these once isolated and almost forgotten hills, even though the routes of access consist mainly of dirt roads. A steady flow of buses and supply trucks connect the Hekeng Hakka to Hakka elsewhere in Fujian, Guangdong or Jiangxi, facilitating trade and travel and greatly improving the villagers' standard of living. Goods, people, and even livestock are ferried from one village to another on small motorized tricycles, three-wheeled "trucks" with room enough for a driver, some passengers, and boxes and baskets. Small, isolated hamlets are reached by foot via an extensive network of interconnecting mountain paths. On these roads and paths that connect villages and their markets, rice, honey, citrus fruits, pigs, ducks, chickens, tobacco, tea, rabbits, frogs, and snakes, as well as brides-to-be, local officials, and an occasional tourist also pass. As more and more sophisticated goods enter the local economy, Hekeng's shopkeepers keep abreast of new developments in foodstuffs and household goods. Domestic sodas have been introduced from Xiamen. Almost everyone wears plastic sandals, and school children sport colorful T-shirts reflecting contemporary Chinese trends.

Hakka villagers treat outsiders with a kind of friendly indifference, displaying a warmth and a genuine interest for that which is foreign, seemingly well aware of the socioeconomic forces that shape their communities as well as the immediate world that surrounds them. They recognize their uniqueness within China and are aware of successful emigrants who have resettled in Southeast Asia and the United States. Even though no one apparently has emigrated abroad since 1949, many of Hekeng's inhabitants continue to have contact with relatives abroad. Overseas Hakkas, during the past decade, have invested in villages throughout the region, providing the funds needed to build schools and factories—necessary investment that contributes to the region's relative economic prosperity.

To survive, families in Hekeng and other villages appear to have paid little attention to the government's one-child policy. Their traditional farming techniques still require numerous male children to work the fields, and females are all too often still looked down upon as unnecessary mouths to feed. Couples will, out of necessity, brave official wrath and conceive until boys are brought into their world. It is not unusual to see large families with up to six young children. Only two children are generally registered and thus officially noted. Some villagers comment that unregistered children may be forced to go without a formal education or other benefits to which their "official" siblings are entitled—a fact of life most villagers seem to accept. In general, Hakkas are keen on educating themselves and their children. Some Hekeng children walk up to 10 kilometers to reach the nearest middle school, where they board, returning home only on weekends to visit their family. A few of the best and brightest students enter technical colleges and universities but apparently rarely return to Hekeng. Although some villagers appear resigned or unconcerned about being tied to the land, others wish to escape the difficult lives they lead. Already one-fourth of Hekeng's population has found jobs outside the village, driving motorized tricycles or buses, running restaurants, working in brick or fertilizer factories, or working as coal miners in neighboring Yongding county's rich coal fields.

Hekeng's villagers are easygoing, ingenious, purposeful, and persistent, characteristics that can be felt immediately upon entering their village. Firewood is stacked neatly under the *tulou*'s eaves, pigpens are cleaned regularly, and alleyways are swept and kept clear of clutter. Hekeng strikes the visitor as a well-planned and organized village in which people lead disciplined lives that are tied to fixed rhythms. Despite the many hardships they must face every day, villagers rise above circumstances to stand out as remarkable people inhabiting some of the most distinctive village landscapes in China.

CHAPTER 13

Cangpo Village, Zhejiang
A Relict with a Future?

RONALD G. KNAPP

FEW settlements claiming to be as old as Cangpo village, Zhejiang province, still maintain so much of their original layout. However, Cangpo is no living fossil, no bequeathed landscape unspoiled by the passage of time. Still, after forty-one successive generations, villagers walk the same stone paths as their forebears, catch the cool breeze in the same pavilions, fetch water from the same wells and ditches, nourish nearby fields with wooden buckets of night soil collected from countless private latrines, search for brush in the surrounding hills to fuel their large cooking stoves, tend their free-ranging pigs, chickens, and ducks, and bury their dead on the flanking hillslopes. For nearly a thousand years, this remote settlement grew only slowly, little changed by forces from outside. Since 1949, however, the currents of successive political campaigns have brought hope and dashed it, one time after another, affecting village life in many ways. At the beginning of the 1990s, Cangpo presents a melancholy village landscape of contradictions.

Like many other settlements in the rugged areas of southern Zhejiang province, Cangpo sits on a rather level riverine terrace within walking distance of both streams and hillslopes. The Nanxijiang river runs north to south for some 145 kilometers through Yongjia county, eventually mixing its clear blue waters with those of the muddy Oujiang river near Wenzhou. The drainage basin that has the Nanxijiang as its axis is well defined, isolated from the north, east, and west by 500 to 700 meter high ranges, with easy access until recently only by water from the south. Relative isolation helps explain in part the persistence of village form and the preservation of a way of life that is only reluctantly being surrendered.

Like other nearby villages in Gangtou township, Cangpo is essentially a single-surname village, settled and subsequently developed by a population all claiming the surname Li. In just over two hundred years, successive Lis gave form to the village, which changed little for the next eight hundred years. During the last years of the Five Dynasties period in 955, a Mr. Li came to the middle Nanxijiang area from Fujian province, chose a wife from a nearby hamlet, and built a simple dwelling. Little has been passed down

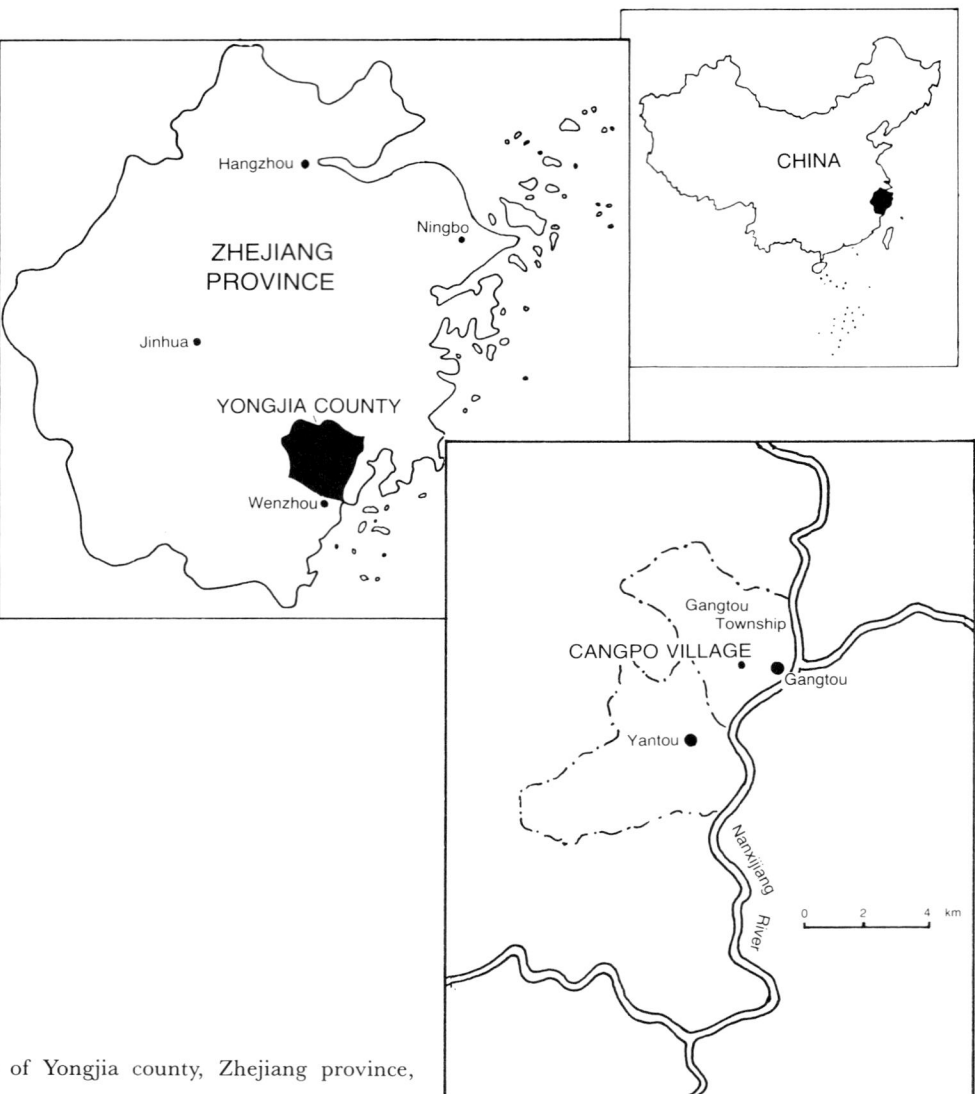

Figure 13.1. General map of Yongjia county, Zhejiang province, locating Cangpo village.

through history about this first generation, but remains of Mr. Li's grave still can be seen in the southwest quadrant of the village. By the fifth generation, about 1055, Cangpo had incorporated three nearby hamlets—Dongzhai, Xizhai, and Maxiyuan—each representing a branch (*fang*) of the Li clan with its own ancestral hall.

Two brothers of the sixth generation in 1128 built a pair of pavilions that survive to this day. Although the wooden pillars, benches, roof structure, and tiles of the pavilions no doubt have undergone repair and replacement many times, the stone bases in which the pillars rest, the steps, and the overall architectural form have been

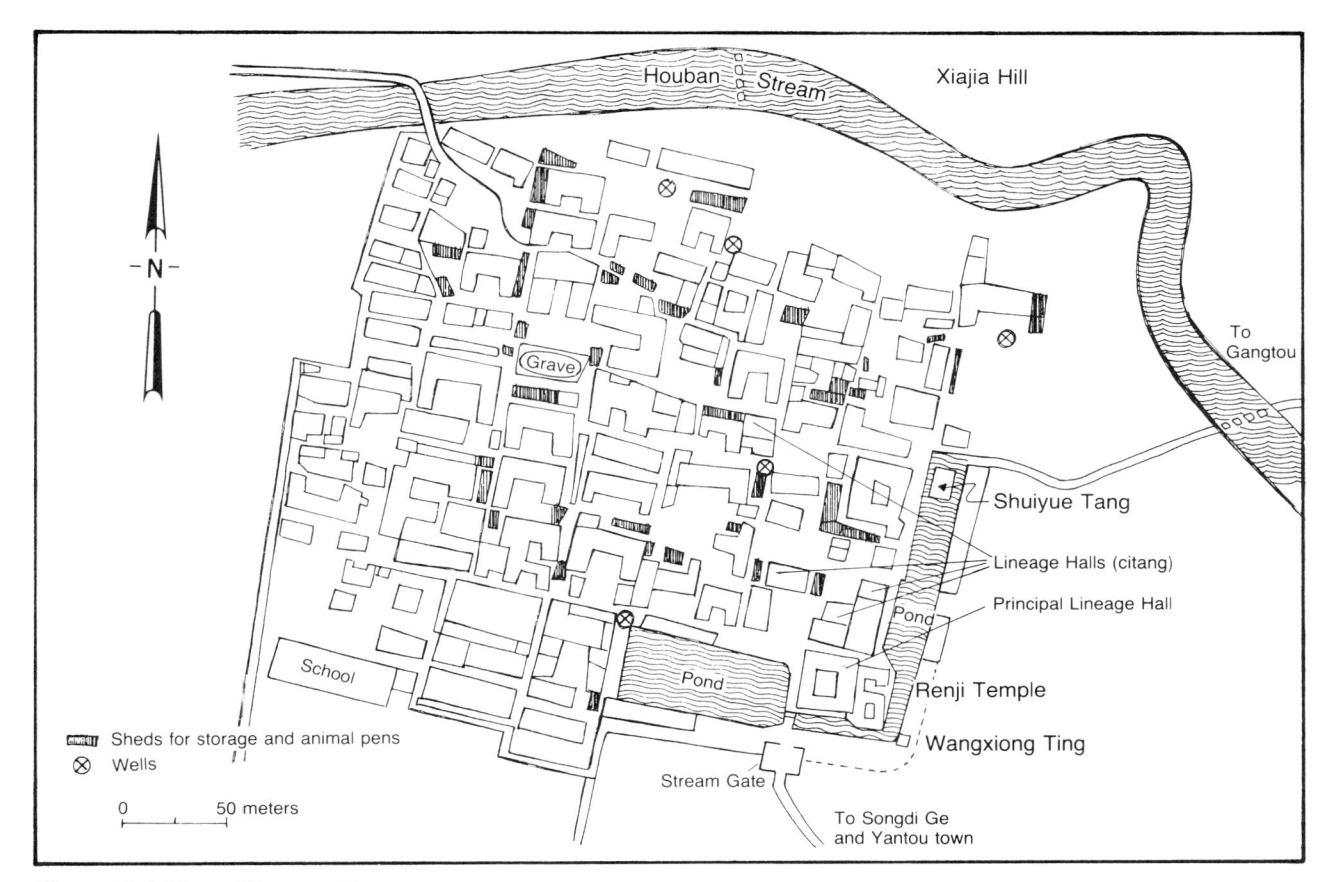

Figure 13.2. Map of Cangpo village.

maintained with little change for nearly nine hundred years. The elder brother, Li Qiushan, built his house some 300 meters to the south of the three adjacent hamlets of Cangpo at a place called Fangxiang. Here the elder brother also built a pavilion, called Songdi Ge ("the pavilion for seeing younger brother off"). Standing in this pavilion, the elder brother could bid good-bye to his younger brother, who would cross the path northward to Cangpo, where the younger brother, Li Jiamu, built a matching pavilion called Wangxiong Ting ("the pavilion for gazing at elder brother"). As recounted by villagers, the younger brother, on returning from a visit to his elder brother, would light a lamp in the pavilion to signal that he had returned home safely. Today Wangxiong Ting together with several other sites provide young and old men of the village with shelter from the sun and a place to catch a strong, cool breeze and chat as they move through the rhythm of a village day. According to village lore, the age and beauty of these pavilions are of no greater significance than the lesson of mutual love and caring between brothers that has been transmitted with the physical structures themselves.

Until the last quarter of the twelfth century,

Figure 13.3. The main gate of Cangpo faces south and serves as a cool spot for the sale of refreshments and for those wanting to idle away time. This gate, some believe, has the appearance of a fierce tiger. The remnants of the surrounding wall are visible. [Photograph, 1990]

Figure 13.4. The southeast corner of Cangpo, showing the Wangxiong Pavilion and Renji Temple. [Photograph, 1990]

Cangpo Village, Zhejiang   177

Figure 13.5. Close-up of Wangxiong Ting, "the pavilion for gazing at elder brother," which today is used as a place for Cangpo men to chat and enjoy the breeze during their mid-day break from working in the fields. [Photograph, 1990]

Cangpo village—as has been the case with so many Chinese villages before and after—by and large grew in an unplanned way, with new dwellings and other needed structures built adjacent to old ones to meet new needs and aligned according to individual prescriptions given by geomancers. What specifically prompted a coordinated design for the village in 1178 is unknown, but two centuries of experience with the immediate and surrounding environment led to the fashioning of a cultural landscape of significant utility and substantial beauty. By the twelfth century most of the dwellings and ancestral halls were sited to face south or slightly southwest, a pattern continued down to the present. The principal entryway to the village was from the south. Nearby, to the west, north, and east, lay the fields, among which were many of the graves of the Lis.

Those who planned the village layout appear to have applied elements of both the Forms and Analytical schools of *fengshui,* discussed in Chapter 3, adding several elements that go beyond the general concerns of *fengshui.* Cangpo took shape with alignments generally ordered to the cardinal directions. Furthermore, the topographical forms of the encircling ridges and the position or absence of flowing water were apparently well analyzed. It may be remembered that, in the regenerative cycle of the Five Phases *(wuxing),* east corresponds to wood, south to fire, west to metal, north to water, and the center to the earth. Each of these corresponds as well to a specific shape for hills. Ideally, as shown earlier in Figure 3.7, each direction should have an appropriate hill shape that corresponds to the cycle. In the case of Cangpo, the several western hills—to be discussed below in another context—have rather pointed peaks signifying fire and capable of destroying metal, the signature of the west; a broad and flat mountain peak would have been preferred in this direction. To the north, representing water, there in fact was no water sufficient to overcome the expected fire from the south or the intrusive fire signified by the western peaks. This abundance of fire obviously presented a danger to the wood on the east. To alleviate any danger from the abundance of fire, two relatively large rectangular ponds were dug in the southeast portion of the village, and stone-lined ditches to bring running water around and through the village also were built. Through such artifice, the village was protected from the geomantic fire.

Over a period of time, stones gathered from the nearby tributaries of the Nanxijiang river were used to build a 2.4-meter-high stone wall without mortar around the village. On the south side, Xi Men (Stream Gate) was constructed of wood and tile as the main entry to Cangpo; smaller gates on the west, north, and east led to the fields. Some say the complex structure of Xi Men had the appearance of a fierce tiger capable of keeping misfortune from the village. The slightly hump backed stone bridge just inside the gate was seen as the crouching body of the protective tiger. The four walls, it was further claimed, provided the mountain lair for the protective tiger of the west, and the two green pools of water, the habitat for the dragon of the east, together emblematic of completedness.

A further imaginative design effort is clearly

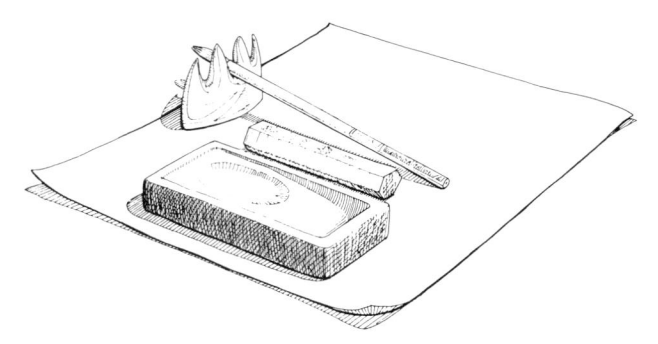

Figure 13.6. A unique design element for Cangpo was the "four treasures of the studio" *(wenfang sibao)* composition—ink slab, ink stick, writing brush, and paper. [Drawing courtesy of Camy Fischer]

Figure 13.7. Bi Jie, ("Writing Brush Lane"), which runs through Cangpo from east to west, was oriented so as to appear to rest in the crook of the mountain range observable in the background—which has a shape similar to that of a brush stand *(bijia)*. On the right foreground are oblong stones laid to represent ink sticks. [Photograph, 1990]

observable even today in a composition known as *wenfang sibao* ("four treasures of the studio"—writing brush, ink stick, ink slab, and paper), an invocation that no effort should be spared in learning and that the village might produce many scholars. The overall square village was seen as the first treasure, a sheet of blank paper. The larger rectangular pond was seen as the ink slab. Alongside the ink slab were placed two slender rectangular pieces of stone 4.5 by 0.5 by 0.3 meters to represent ink sticks. Each of these was beveled on the end to suggest that they had been ground down on the ink slab to make ink. Added to these three was the pivotal element of the calligrapher, a brush, represented by a long west to east paved lane—Bi Jie ("Writing Brush Lane")—aligned so that it would "rest" on the several fire-shaped hills bordering the village on the west. Even casual observation confirms that these rising and falling hills with their fixed peaks appear like a resting stand or brush holder used by calligraphers to hold their brushes as they work.

Several surviving structures bordering the ponds were built at the end of the twelfth century by the tenth generation of Lis, although they undoubtedly have been altered or rebuilt many times. Renji Miao ("Temple of Benevolence and Relief") includes both a front hall and a back hall, with a rectangular fish pool between them. Along the east, south, and west sides of the temple are overhanging wooden seats capable of seating perhaps a hundred people. Several unknown images appear to have been worshiped here; the structure served also as a school. To the north of Renji Temple, stands an earlier structure, built on a small island and called Shuiyue Tang ("Water and Moon Hall"). It is claimed that the two buildings were built to resemble a corner of the celebrated Lingyin Temple in Hangzhou, parts of which were built in the fourth century. The principal lineage hall for the Lis was built adjacent to the other two buildings. Together the three structures served as the community spaces for Cangpo. The lineage hall included a large stage for the periodic performance of local opera, a popular medium with plots that provided entertainment and also inculcated values.

The central and northern thirds of Cangpo have always constituted the residential area of the village, with private space defined by walls and gates. Mixed in with the dwellings are private grain-drying areas, vegetable plots, latrines, and sheds for animals. Here the only public spaces are the lanes and the immediate areas around wells.

Although on a map the lanes may at first glance appear to crisscross, to form a grid, actually only Bi Jie, Writing Brush Lane, runs the 300 meters from wall to wall. Most other lanes are less than 100 meters in length, with many ending at a side or end wall of a dwelling. At many of these intersections, an inscription is found—*Taishan zai ci* ("Mount Tai is here")—either painted on the wall or cut into the stone facing the oncoming lane as a sign to keep malevolence at bay. Most of the lanes are more than routes of access, serving as

Figure 13.8. The entryway to one of Cangpo's small shops, which once was a commission shop under the former commune system. Cangpo, like other settlements throughout China, has been given a zipcode, 325113, shown above the door. [Photograph, 1990]

Figure 13.9. A remnant of a former lineage hall is now used as a rice mill. Under the eaves can still be seen slogans of the 1970s: "In agriculture, learn from Dazhai" and "In industry, learn from Daqing." [Photograph, 1990]

well as linear public spaces. As in other villages discussed in this volume, villagers commonly bring a stool to the lane outside their gates to catch the breeze and chat with neighbors or passersby. Most of Cangpo's meter-or-so-wide lanes are paved with cobblestones, high toward the center and gently sloping to a stone-lined drainage ditch on both sides. Although water no longer flows freely through these drainage ditches, they still serve households as a convenient place over which to peel vegetables or let children urinate. The splash of an occasional bucket of water carries the debris down through the village.

At a number of locations, a lane may widen somewhat to accommodate a well, a node for village interaction. At one time, some thirty wells, each about 8 meters deep, were found in the village, but today there are only fifteen. The well closest to South Pond has always been considered the best well. Throughout the day, a steady stream of villagers comes to the wells to draw water to carry back to their homes in a pair of metal buckets suspended from a shoulder pole. Today, also serving as spaces for daily interaction, there are seven small daily needs shops and a stall at the front gate.

Clearly absent in Chinese villages like Cangpo are the fountains and assembly areas that are such a prominent part of contemporary Chinese town and city design. Once lineage halls, behind their high walls, provided an important venue for community life, but today those still standing have other uses. In recent decades, the largest hall, some 900 meters square, was converted to serve as the village's elementary school. With the opening of a new multistory school in 1989, the hall was cleaned out and today generally stands empty. With its broad spaces, given shape by massive pillars and beams, the hall serves temporarily in the summer months as a transit site for large baskets of watermelons on their way to market. The large stage that is the focal point of its central courtyard still suggests the grandeur of the carpentry that created it during the Ming dynasty in spite of the effects of weathering, gravity, decay, and abuse over the years. The long, high ceremonial table and the ancestral tablets that once occupied the hall are long gone, having fueled the passions of a number of past campaigns to weaken the village's clan structure and old habits. In their place is a small recessed cabinet in the wall holding a shallow ceramic vessel into which incense sticks are stuck and lit.

Throughout Cangpo, the cobblestone lanes are defined further by the stone outer walls of the residential compounds. Especially in the northwestern section of the village, where a serpentine lane leads to the north, the sense of definition is clear and particularly aesthetically pleasing. Such stone walls vary in height from 2 to 4 meters, are generally wider at the base than at the top, and are all constructed without mortar, using only stones graded by the nearby streams. The walls are most canyonlike where they are in fact the back walls of dwellings. Walls outlining courtyards are typically less substantial.

Residential units take many forms, from rather small triple-bay dwellings to large courtyard-style complexes several buildings deep. Since 1949, Cangpo village's population has more than doubled, from 945 to 2,137 in 1989, with nearly a tripling of the number of households. As a result, dwellings that might have served no more than a dozen people in the past today have been fragmented for four or more households with perhaps 20 to 25 individuals. The traditional hierarchical demarcation and use of space—the central hall, bedrooms arranged by generation, and kitchen—

Figure 13.10. In the northwestern quadrant of Cangpo, stones taken from nearby streams form the walls surrounding residences and lanes. [Photograph, 1990]

by and large have been negated, as each household today simply claims its own multifunctional limited space. Sleeping and eating space for many families commingle, with no special space available as a main hall to receive guests. The reality of limited resources, limited space, and population pressure has created contradictions that have forced adjustments. To the degree possible, each household maintains its own living space—far removed from the division or seclusion provided their wealthy forebears within their walled microcosms. Perhaps most critical in the maintenance of a household's own living space is having its own cooking stove. Where many households occupy a large old dwelling, there will be as many separate cooking stoves as there are households.

At the end of 1984, Cangpo was surveyed as part of a countywide effort to begin rural settlement planning. The 1:1,000-scale map completed in December 1984 has changed little in the years since. A small number of especially dilapidated dwellings were pulled down or fell down, and perhaps twenty new two-story brick and cement houses have been built along the periphery by those fortunate enough to have the resources and to have gained approval.

Of the 101 residential structures that were identified in the 1984 survey, 16 were clearly old and once magnificent dwellings. Villagers claim that most of these date to the Ming dynasty (1368–1644) or Qing dynasty (1644–1911), but unfortunately none has been dated precisely. Most of these large dwellings reveal a structure and layout that has its antecedents in the building forms of the Song dynasty (960–1279). From the Song dynasty onwards, *chuandou* (pillars and transverse tie beams) wooden frameworks became dominant in the prosperous areas of southeastern China. Unlike the massive *tailiang* (pillars and beams) structures common in north China in grand temples as well as common houses, *chuandou* structures utilize timber of smaller diameter and are often gracefully carved. Moreover, the pillars used in *chuandou* structures reach directly from the ground to support the roof purlins and carry the heavy weight of the roof tiles and rafters directly to the ground. The space between the pillars is filled in with brick or some other medium to form a non-load-bearing curtain wall and is often plastered with lime. These white curtain walls together with the natural irregularity of the pillars present a very pleasing appearance to many dwellings in Cangpo. In the best dwellings, an encircling box-bond wall of narrow gray bricks clearly indicates the wealth of the household. Perhaps fifty of Cangpo's older dwellings are rather modest, with rough stone or brick load-bearing walls that support the roof directly (see also Knapp 1986, 52–87; 1989, 68–87).

Over ninety percent of all dwellings remaining in Cangpo are two-storied, varying in length from a single to as many as seven bays. As elsewhere in China, even numbers of bays such as four or eight are avoided. Three-, five-, and seven-bay dwellings predominate. The largest old structure has seven bays along its longitudinal axis with a pair of perpendicular wings, each with three bays, for a total of thirteen bays.

Although only a quarter of the dwellings have a clearly defined courtyard, embraced by buildings on two, three, or four sides, nearly three-quarters of all dwellings in the village have open spaces of various configurations that serve as forecourts for the dwellings. In only one case, excluding the large lineage hall, is the courtyard of a true skywell *(tianjing)* type, surrounded on four sides by buildings. Twelve are U-shaped and fourteen are L-shaped. Most older dwellings are separated from each other by high walls that provided enclosure for the household.

Interior space and exterior space are linked by verandas, important transitional or intermediate spaces in larger dwellings in Zhejiang and elsewhere in southern China. Where ambient temperatures and rainfall are both high, wide verandas provide a protected location that keeps the hot rays of the sun from penetrating the dwelling and allows ventilation of the interior through open doors or lattice windows even during a downpour. Not only does much daily work take place along the veranda—preparation of vegetables for cooking, sewing, repairing tools, making handicrafted baskets and mats, for example—but it is also an area where children play, men smoke and relax, and women get together to chat. A meter or so deep, verandas are usually elevated a step or two above the stone courtyard where chickens and ducks roam freely.

In the courtyard or forecourt are a few plants for decoration, large cisterns to collect rainwater, and an area for storage. Bulky agricultural implements, baskets of various sizes, carts, and bicycles all compete for space, limited today by the pressure of many people living in a small space. A household today only has approximately one two-story bay available to it. It is no wonder that so much activity takes place adjacent to the dwelling.

Kitchen garden plots are scattered throughout the village. Some fifty in number, they vary in size and provide principally greens and other vegetables that are picked daily by the household. Exceeding these private gardens in number but not in size are sheds that house pigs; pigpens generally have an attached latrine. Many households use chamber pots at night and empty them in the morning into their latrine. Both the human and animal excrement are treated and carried to the rice fields or kitchen gardens to be used as a rich organic fertilizer.

As in most Chinese villages, men in Cangpo divide their time between the fields and the home. Several times each day, the number depending on

Figure 13.11. Several sets of stone steps carry villagers across the stream on the north side of Cangpo village to the fields and graves. [Photograph, 1990]

the season, men walk back and forth to the fields, where planting, fertilizing, weeding, and harvesting are among the most important activities. The phrase "go out to work each day, and each day return to rest" (*zi chu er zuo, zi ru er xiu*) describes well the rhythm of life for village men. Although much of the work in the fields is solitary, especially since the adoption of the contract system in about 1984, many men join together in the Wangxiong Pavilion or the Renji Temple to stretch out on the cool stone floors for a noontime or after-dinner smoke and nap. Women help in the nearby fields and orchards as needed, but their days are quite busy at home with food preparation, the washing of clothes, the drawing of water, the care of children or grandchildren, and countless other household chores. Neither radios nor TVs are common in Cangpo, unlike so many other Chinese villages. Thus, days are less punctuated by the unexpected than they are by the recurrent patterns of daily life that have defined Cangpo as a place for nearly a millennium.

Cangpo village had a past more glorious than its present. Today, it is a common village in one of Zhejiang's poorest counties ("Wo sheng" 1989, 1). Cangpo is not like so many other Chinese villages in China's peri-urban areas where rural affluence reveals itself in new multistoried dwellings and households vie for the latest electronic equipment, colorful decorations, and stylish furniture. Cangpo is more embedded in its past, where not only the outlines of its village layout were established, but the structure of village life itself took form. In Cangpo there are few of the indications of a village connected to the outside: no incipient local industries, no restaurants, no pool tables, no bus stop, no motorbikes. Villagers nonetheless feed themselves well from the meticulously tended paddy and dry fields and orchards surrounding the village.

A striking element of Cangpo's cultural landscape, however, is a Christian chapel set in the middle of contracted land on the northeastern corner of the village. Half a dozen similar chapels with crosses placed high above the gable end can be spotted during just an hour's walk from Cangpo in the open countryside—a frequency not found elsewhere in Zhejiang province. Most have been built since the mid-1980s by village Christians; the one in Cangpo was completed in the fall of 1987. Further research may determine whether Christianity in this relatively remote area had a pre-Liberation history and current patterns represent a reappearance of suppressed faith, or whether other forces at work have contributed to the appearance of Christian practices here in recent years. Although there is no evidence of Buddhist or Daoist religious facilities in Cangpo, some temples are being refurbished in nearby areas, and numerous images of popular deities appear in roadside pavilions in the immediate environs of Cangpo.

There is in Cangpo an abundance of surplus labor, with as many as 300 young men and

Figure 13.12. Set amidst the fields on the northern side of Cangpo is a Christian chapel, the only religious building in the village. [Photograph, 1990]

women away from the village at any time trying to earn some cash from carpentry, sewing, sales, and other opportunities. Unlike so many Chinese villages, Cangpo has no traditional cottage industries or modern workshops to offer employment. None of these young men or women has returned to the village with the financial wherewithal, knowledge, or connections to plant a significant seed for change in the village. Villagers speak proudly of their new three-story elementary school for 340 students, a community project completed in 1988. The school is sited adjacent to the "four treasures of the study," a tangible manifestation of the village's long-standing hope that Cangpo will someday bring forth scholars, who then through leadership or donation might enrich the whole village. Besides restoration of the clan halls and inclusion of the village in the provincial-level Nanxijiang Scenic Sites Regional Plan, village leaders speak of the construction of a public latrine as the next important community objective for Cangpo village.

Preliminary support for this project was provided by the Research Travel Awards Program of SUNY New Paltz. A grant from the National Geographic Society's Committee for Research and Exploration made possible field work in Cangpo and other villages in Zhejiang province in 1990. The collaboration of Shen Dongqi and the assistance of the Zhejiang Provincial Urban and Rural Planning and Design Research Institute have been critically important in my research.

Transition

Transition
Introductory Perspectives

Chapters in this "Transition" section focus on many of the striking and observable transformations of Chinese village landscapes in recent decades, which were discussed in a general way in Chapter 4. They contrast with those in the "Tradition" section, which emphasized the conservation of traditional rural settlements, focusing on origins and continuities and slow, often relatively imperceptible change rather than conspicuous transformation. Even villages in transition, however, as the following chapters reveal, continue to preserve many elements of traditional village form.

Whereas the trend in much of the developing world has been toward depopulation of villages because of out-migration to cities in search of opportunity, in China (excepting, of course, Taiwan and Hong Kong) rural out-migration to cities has been constrained by a rigid household registration system that binds villagers to their locality. In fact, there were increases in China's rural population in the decades after 1949—not only the number of individuals but also the number of separate households at least doubled in most villages—which strained traditional patterns of living. With the growth in population of Chinese villages over the past forty years, most residences that once housed a few households were subdivided to provide shelter for many more. Makeshift kitchens and other needed space frequently were added in courtyards and along lanes to meet immediate needs, giving many villages an unkempt appearance. Increasingly crowded conditions set the stage for the expansion of new village housing once households had resources to build.

As political campaigns swept over landscapes in the People's Republic of China in the decades after 1949, fine, large residences, temples, and lineage halls in many villages were torn down, abandoned, or vacated for other uses, leaving shells that merely echoed their past. Communization in MaGaoqiao village in Sichuan, for example, altered residential patterns as well as erased many prominent parts of the pre-Liberation village landscape. Even more drastic village transformation occurred in the 1960s and 1970s in Dazhai village—the well-known model village that served as the focus of a nationwide emulation campaign—whose barracks-style buildings hardly evoke traditional village homes.

During the 1980s, especially, the geometry and

morphology of much of the countryside on the China mainland underwent an unprecedented metamorphosis. As a result, some villages no longer occupy their original sites, having been demolished and rebuilt elsewhere in a style alien to tradition. Others, such as Lincun and Weigang villages, are made up of multistory buildings that are more urban in appearance and modern in materials than their antecedents. New housing continues to be built on the sites of former dwellings in many villages, as needs and resources permit. In mixing traditional and "modern" housing, many such villages have gained an appearance of disorder.

As the following chapters show, more and more village layouts—or at least some parts of villages—are revealing a high degree of geometric order that comes from the use of a plan. Yet major portions of prosperous villages, like Lincun in Fujian, continue to be crisscrossed by zigzaging unpaved alleys, with order apparent only along the newly paved thoroughfare and on the edge of the original village. The disorderly appearance arises also in Lincun and other villages because of the continued practice of *fengshui* by villagers in their attempt to insure good fortune. The presence of scattered pigpens and outhouses as well as mounds of discarded plastic, paper, and glass—the accouterments of progress—further contributes to clutter and provides evidence of villages undergoing transformation.

A great many villages are no longer simply ensembles of residences for local peasants but instead have become transitional settlement forms in which the residents are both farmers and factory workers. Such villages are generally found in close proximity to vibrant cities, such as Weigang near Nanjing and Lincun near Xiamen. Where villagers continue to be principally occupied in primary production, even when increasingly commercialized, the village plan itself may change little, as seen in Longlin village in Hainan. However, in most cases, as the economic base of the village becomes diverse, there is an observable impact on village morphology. The impact is seen in more than simply the addition of factory buildings or workshops—often large and out of scale with other village structures—such as the starch factory in Fengjiacun or the small steel rolling mill in MaGaoqiao. Small-scale cottage-based processing and manufacturing activities, often under contract to urban factories, have dispersed modern equipment and materials throughout China's countryside. With the decentralization of industry, the resulting environmental damage, air pollution, and water pollution reveal how undeveloped the infrastructure needed to sustain industrial production is. In the case of Dacaiyuan, in contrast, the wealth that has flowed into the village has come from villagers involved in circular migration, working outside the village but sending cash home. Here, although new housing has increased, it has done so in an environment in which modern industry has not intruded on the inherited residential character of the village.

In the villages discussed in this section, electricity and piped water are common in village homes. Primary as well as nursery schools are found in most villages, a positive legacy of the state's penetration of the countryside after 1949. Small private shops selling daily needs as well as food stalls and outdoor markets have increased in number in these settlements during the 1980s, adding an economic and social dimension more characteristic of towns than villages. Accompanying the demise of lineage-based ritual and the facilities that made it possible, there has been an increase in community meeting halls that serve political as well as social needs. Movies are shown periodically, and many villages have small reading rooms and other facilities to meet the emerging cultural needs of villagers. Rare are skating rinks, as found in suburban Weigang, but billiard tables became de rigueur in many villages throughout the China mainland in the late 1980s. For most villagers, social interaction beyond the courtyard and family continues to occur at bridgeheads, under large trees, at bus stops, and along the lanes where neighbors stand or sit and chat. The rebuilding of temples, such as in Lincun and Longlin on the mainland and in Hsin Hsing on Taiwan, has reintroduced a traditional element of community into many villages.

There generally is no explicit rejection of the past in the "modernization" of Chinese villages, and one can often observe the inherent durability of traditional patterns, the past in the present landscape. However, much that has been inherited is not adequate to meet new needs. Old village paths and roads usually are not wide enough or straight enough for the passage of modern vehicles, even the ubiquitous "walking tractor" trucks. The feeder roads and bridges leading to villages are themselves often inadequate. When improved roads skirt existing villages as they pass through the countryside from one city or town to another, fresh village construction frequently follows along the newly laid road. This new construction is usually accompanied by the relocation of the old village to the new site as well as a filling in of the space between the sites. Often a village made up of two parts—one new and one old—emerges.

As disposable incomes rise, villagers generally set new standards and pursue rising expectations —about water, electricity, sewage disposal, as well as leisure. Television antennas are observable all over China, and it is no longer out of the ordinary in especially prosperous villages in the periurban areas of large mainland cities to discover local cable TV systems, if perhaps only a step up from the cabled radio systems common in the past that brought the state's message directly into rural homes or dispersed it via loudspeakers to village neighborhoods. In what otherwise would appear to be remote parts of China's countryside, it remains jarring to encounter a satellite dish or fax machine, installed either by a private entrepreneur or a village enterprise. Electrification, making possible lighting and television at night, is undoubtedly affecting patterns of social interaction and the transmission of new ideas into the countryside.

Changes in village landscapes are often accelerated by new opportunities and desires. Much of the transformation has been accomplished anonymously, the actions of individuals and households. Much, however, has been and continues to be collective, the result of decisions by local authorities and village entrepreneurs. Chinese village landscapes are, for the most part, clearly *in transition*, "work in progress," patchworks whose final form is indeterminate. Although traditional Chinese villages are not likely to disappear in the foreseeable future, countless villages are undergoing a transition, a passage from one form to another with continuing and cumulative adaptations that meet changing social and economic needs.

CHAPTER 14

Dazhai Village, Shanxi
A Model Landscape

CHRISTOPHER L. SALTER

DAZHAI is China's largest diorama. Within an area of some 57 hectares in the mountains of eastern Shanxi province, each of 2,900 farm plots, 770 rooms, and numerous loess cave pigsties, shops, small factories, and roadways was laid out and maintained with the precision of a Chinese jade landscape. No portion of the design was left to chance; no raw edges of untended earth were allowed to detract from the overwhelming image of total modification and complete manipulation. To see the landscape of Dazhai Brigade (the village subdivision of Dazhai People's Commune) in the late 1970s was to see an embodiment of China's most ambitious hopes for land transformed. It was the future in miniature, the present in suspension. It was Mao's world manifest.

No one who has read of the People's Republic in any depth over the past several decades is ignorant of the frequency with which Dazhai was cited as "the standard bearer," "the beacon brigade" in China's agricultural battles. Throughout the 1970s, virtually all travelers to China interested in agriculture, rural development, or self-reliance found themselves winding their ways into the Taihang Mountains for the sake of a pilgrimage to this loessland village. Even visitors to villages elsewhere in China confronted the five large vermilion characters *Nongye xue Dazhai* ("In agriculture, learn from Dazhai") painted boldly on countless walls, visible reminders of the special place that Dazhai played in Chinese discussions of rural development. Dazhai was much more than a destination for foreigners, however. More than 6 million Chinese traveled to the small village, this model brigade, in the decade and a half following 1963 for on-the-spot observation, making pilgrimages to learn from its example.

This chapter focuses on several aspects of Dazhai as a place: the approaches, the terraces, the dwellings, and water control. In addition, it examines what can be learned from reading the Dazhai landscape and explores the lingering enigma of Dazhai, and what the Dazhai model has taught us. These elements are examined not only through images given form as lore by the Chinese press, but also from images gained during a one-day visit to Dazhai in August 1977.

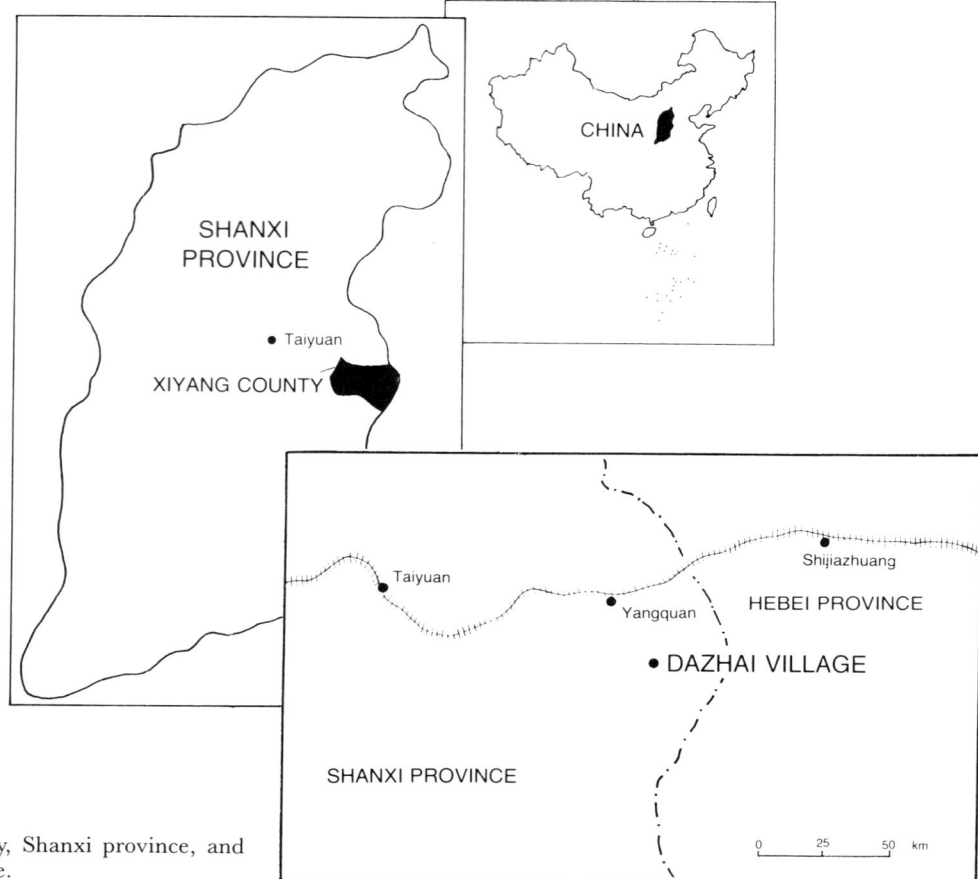

Figure 14.1. Xiyang county, Shanxi province, and the location of Dazhai village.

Approaches to the Village

The Lore

There have been a number of ways to approach Dazhai, to see the outlines of this mountain village from afar. Some first experienced the village by focused movement through *Peking Review,* a host of Foreign Languages Press publications, numerous references to the brigade in U.S. Consulate-General translations, and continuing coverage in the Chinese press. For many viewers, Dazhai's existential space and shape indeed had more mass than the barebones silhouette of the pitch-roofed dormitories and the clean-swept courtyards of the village itself. They arrived in Dazhai far before they first set foot in Xiyang county. For many geographers and others, reading of Dazhai in a text was to see it reflected in rural landscapes in the Wuyi Mountains of Fujian or in the shadows of the Qinling Mountains south of the Weihe river. This distant vision of Dazhai was one the Chinese sent forward with as much power as any image that emanated from the People's Republic of China in the decades after 1949.

The Landscape

My personal approach to Dazhai began with the dawning sun giving shape to the shadows of the

Figure 14.2. In a region plagued by drought, Dazhai is a linear village situated beneath sculpted fields that themselves control the flow of water across them. Many of the long buildings are dormitories built to accommodate those who come to learn from Dazhai. [Source: Tannenbaum 1971, 17]

Taihang Mountains as the train from Beijing climbed its way toward the city of Yangquan in Shanxi province, the last railroad link between Beijing and Dazhai. A heavy rain had been falling during the night, and the loesslands were deep brownish yellow, pouring themselves into muddy rivulets that cascaded toward the rail line and valley bottom. August vegetation was lush, captured mostly in the small maize plots etched in narrow, erratic step terraces spread along the slopes of the hills. There was in this countryside no reiteration of the southeast China dedication to manicured landscape and the consequent stretch of terraces from stream to ridgetop. This mountainous village landscape was a scene in need of a model, in need of an example. This was land ready for a Dazhai.

As graphic as the mountains and their fields were, the real signature of the vista out the train window was the cave dwellings. Singly, in pairs, or in clusters that made up whole villages, housing here on the rugged margins of the North China Plain was primarily designed around hollows dug out of the depths of wind-blown soil from the Ordos and Gobi deserts. The landscape was—as were so many of the prospects I and others in my group encountered—as we had read. We stood between the cars of the Beijing-Taiyuan train and stared in naive wonder at the number of people who found haven in the cool earth—the rain and wind diminishing our vision but not our awe at the economy of the Chinese peasant and his built environment. We also were ready for a Dazhai.

Arriving at the station, we alighted and found the customary half-dozen Shanghai automobiles awaiting our delegation. Somehow, one wanted to be led to Dazhai not in a car caravan but in the back of a truck half-filled with dynamite, ax handles, and peasant-lecturers returning from visits

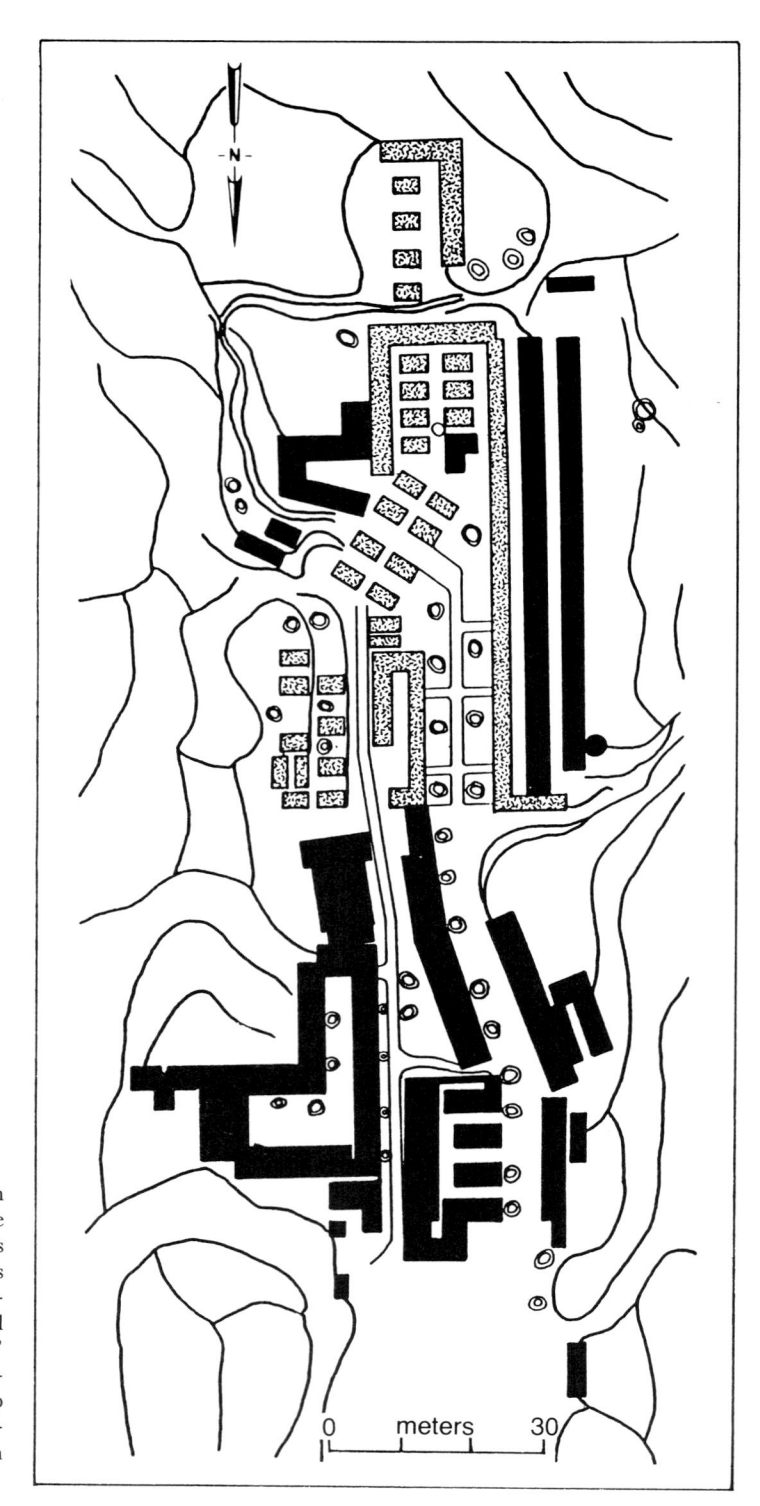

Figure 14.3. A map of Dazhai village reveals an extent and features that go beyond the needs of the eighty resident households. The gray area represents village residences; the black area includes facilities principally for visitors: a welcome hall and dormitories, a large restaurant, shops, a telephone and postal facility, as well as a Xinhua bookstore. Such visitors' facilities are more extensive than those shown in Figure 14.2. Note that north is at the bottom of the map for comparison with the perspective view of the village in Figure 14.2. [Source: Adapted from Yuan 1987, 102]

Dazhai Village, Shanxi 197

to other brigades. To have the first visions of the diorama come from the window of an automobile racing pell-mell through the well-trained and well-maintained fields of Xiyang county seemed a corruption of the initial sight of this already legendary landscape. But, in a schedule as highly orchestrated as ours, there was always justification for the more efficient mode of travel. The car saved time; hence the car made sense.

Passing through the outskirts of Xiyang and approaching Dazhai itself from the north, the cars passed three high domes of mounded limestone, just beginning to experience the fullness of early morning summer light. These were lime kilns, and the glow of flame and heat leaked through the walls of the stone ovens. Half talking to the Chinese host in my car and half recollecting the eerie image given to the lime burner in a Nathaniel Hawthorne short story, I felt that it was right that I first see these representatives of Dazhai's world-building labor force—these men who were already well into their day of labor by 7:00 A.M. Standing above us on their piles of limestone, burnt lime, and fuel, they were the creators of the mastic for the structure of Dazhai—the fertilizer, the mortar, the power to transform raw rock into workable materials for new dimensions of productivity. These firemen were the guardians of the gate that a national model village should have and should present. Technology as old as fire, energy as old as wood itself, and human ambition of like age: these are the proper traits to focus upon as one approaches Dazhai. Our mental images were not to confront visions of reality.

Figure 14.4. A view looking upslope through the village reveals the popularity of Dazhai Brigade as a place of pilgrimage for villagers from all over China, who came to learn and emulate Dazhai's experiences in the 1960s and 1970s. [Source: *Red Sun* 1969, 121]

Terraces

The Lore

The notes of any student of Dazhai are filled with mention of the labors of the 160 active workers of the production brigade in their battle to turn seven gullies and eight ridges into step terraces. The simple transformation from a slope of the loessial mountain flanks into neat bleachers of steady progression from valley bottom to the flanking hillcrest is what so much of the Dazhai history is about. The first two steps were to move the topsoil and to dig deep into the land in order to create a right angle where before there had been only a slope that carried away water, soil, and crops when the region's infrequent rains did fall. This new architecture was secured by either cleanly cut vertical earthen terrace faces or—as is more often cited in the literature of Dazhai—by solid stone walls of limestone cut and stacked with a simple geometry. Mortar was occasionally utilized, but more often the press releases and the associated photos told the reader of the skill with which the new masons created great walls with only sledge hammer, carrying pole, chain, and unprecedented determination. These terraces were the first steps in a visual understanding of the village.

The Landscape

As the cars wound their way up from Xiyang town, we passed a corvée group working on a reservoir a little more than a kilometer outside Dazhai village. Asking the driver to stop for a minute so that we could finally get a photo of the concerted effort of several hundred workers at one sight, we were told that we would get a chance later for such a photograph. The cars sped on toward the terraces in the distance. And, as is so painfully common in this sort of hasty tour, there was no second chance for the shot. There developed no opportunity for inspection.

You rise to Dazhai. Although the road sign that directs the final approach to the famed production brigade suggests nothing out of the ordinary, the tension induced by motoring upslope to the gray concrete wall proclaiming "Dazhai" created a special sensation. It is only a short drive through the village proper before visitors find themselves being swallowed up by the fully enclosed foreign guesthouse complex. Even as they are shown their rooms to put down their baggage in preparation for the obligatory "brief introduction," they can see that the guest accommodations are only inches away from a stone terrace face some 3 to 4 meters high. The village and its fields have been carved from living earth. All elements have become more productive in the process.

The actual tour through the stepped lands of the brigade took place by car. From level to level to level, our group of geographers ascended through examples of earthen walls that were, variously, raw earth, moss-covered mosaics of stone and earth, and completely stone. Wall heights varied from 1 meter to as much as 4 meters. Where earth would not bear the precious burden of soil—planted with maize, *kaoliang* (sorghum), or winter wheat—chunks, cubes, blocks, or fragments of limestone were wedged into the open fissures. The progression from earth to block stone suggested to me that the village goal was to have all of its terraces—even those that barely afford farming strips several meters wide—supported by stone walls of carefully wedged but unmortared rock quarried from the ridge of nearby Tigerhead Hill.

Two walls were being worked on during the day of our visit. One wall was just under a meter wide and half a meter deep. For its foundation, an earthen trench had been dug and blocks approxi-

Figure 14.5. A Dazhai terrace under construction in 1977. In the later rounds of terrace construction, villagers dug footings and created broad stone foundations for the terrace walls. The pattern of step terraces ascending a terraced stream bed is evident in this photo.

mately 30 centimeters square were being laid in a straight row. There was neither concrete underlying the blocks nor was there mortar used between the rocks. Like New England stone fences, the wall's elements were forced together by the patience and determination of the farmer-masons and by a sense of the benefit such construction would yield.

In the other project in progress, a wall was being sculpted around the base of the mountain-crest reservoir with rock being quarried from nearby. Already a height of nearly 2 meters had been reached. The stone walls descended in concentric rings, arching away in crescent fashion from the round stone water-storage pond that looked out over the entire Dazhai landscape.

At neither site was there a person to be seen. The tools of the transformers were arrayed on rock or earth, but there was an eerie quiet about this silent stone and absence of village workers.

The terraces that marched from the caves of the village to the upper reaches of the farmlands followed two general patterns. Initially the spurs of the local mountains had been transformed from slopeland into level land. These "man-made plains" curved around in an obvious symmetry and stretched from the margins of the brick kiln and pigsties by the village settlement up to the boundaries of the brigade's land. In a second phase of metamorphosis, control was focused on the seven streams and creeks that flowed between the mountain spurs jutting out toward the dwellings. It was in the battles to take this land from the stream system that Dazhai became so famous for its dogged self-reliance. Twice terraces were thrust up the stream beds. Twice flood waters washed away the terrace walls and the newly reclaimed fields.

In the third attempt, the terrace walls were put in with the gentle concave arc of an earthen dam, with deeper foundations and broader bases. By the time of my visit in 1977, these walls had withstood more than a decade of nature's attempts to regain use of the stream systems. The water of the rainy season thus far had only spilled over step after step, giving more useful moisture to each stratum and taking soil from none.

An initial and profound image is given to the whole brigade by these manufactured flatlands and their retaining walls. The tall stalks of maize and kaoliang stood right at the edge of these small plots, each averaging only a quarter of a *mu*, less than 200 square meters in size. In a few places, the earthen walls had slipped in summer rains and crop and soil were spilling out of the imposed geometry, but throughout most of the farmland, the order authored by Chen Yonggui—the originator of the village's battle with the mountain landscape—and put into effect by villagers was holding. It had the well-maintained look that a diorama should have.

Dwellings

The Lore

All students of China's loesslands have carried in their minds images of the traditional cave dwell-

Figure 14.6. Chen Yonggui and other villagers engaged in transforming nature are important parts of the lore of Dazhai. [Source: *Red Sun* 1969, 59]

ings carved out of the cliffs of windblown, compacted soil. Who among China geographers had not talked about the expedience of making one's home out of earth so that the dwelling would be relatively cool in summer and warm in winter, while at the same time pointing out that there was a danger in this plan because of the seismic activity of the Taiyuan Massif? In the literature that had been built up around the construction and presentation of the Dazhai diorama, the peasants' labors in the creation of their own new housing was second only to terracing in the inventory of man-made landscape projects. By 1977, a total of 770 rooms had been created for the eighty-some households, allowing most of the old cave homes either to be given over to expanded pigsties or to be abandoned altogether. The villagers had been creating new space for living as well as for farming.

The rebuilding of these new, stone-lined cave homes that helped create the Dazhai reputation was necessitated by the floods of the mid-1950s and early 1960s. Cascades of mud, stone, crops, and water ruined the terraces in the stream beds in those summer floods. This same slurry then ran through the village streets and devastated more than two-thirds of the peasants' homes in one flood. The elevation of the heroic qualities of Dazhai to unprecedented heights was wrapped in the epic stories of the rebuilding of these homes and the fashioning of farmland—all acomplished while maintaining crop production levels. The village became China's model village in 1964.

Figure 14.7. New courtyards have been created in Dazhai in which many of the facing dwellings are stone-lined caves. New row housing is visible in the rear.

The Landscape

Walking through one of the courtyards of the new Dazhai evoked a feeling curiously similar to that inspired by a Baltimore row-house block. Each arched doorway represented the sole entrance to a usually one-room complex with a vaulted ceiling, a concrete *kang,* one or two cabinets, storage urns, and perhaps a bicycle. A wooden lattice wall with window separated the hollowed out home from the outside elements. The units still incomplete showed that each cave had been lined with limestone—mortared, unlike the terrace walls—and then sealed with a thick application of finish plaster.

On the exterior, the foundations had been done in fired brick; the middle and upper portions of the facades (excluding the wooden jambs) were substantially made of cut stone. Communal kitchens and bathrooms were shared by several families. Running water was available in one or two standpipe faucets in each courtyard.

A setting of rustic simplicity was thus created in the shadow of the loess slopes, which had been redesigned to accommodate the intensified ambitions of the Dazhai brigade and its endlessly energetic members. The evidence of the rebuilding continued down into the shops of the community, which also were constructed of stone and brick with concrete floors as well as wooden door jambs and windows. Some courtyards were enclosed with brick walls with ornate door arches and entryways. In addition, a number of two- and three-story structures had been built in which the bottom floor was a lined cave and the upper floors were constructed totally from stone. Even the dining hall in the visitors' compound was set well back into a cave, giving the traveler some of the longed-for sense of "roughing it" in this model contemporary Chinese peasant settlement. A cave, even when limed and lit, has a sense quality that is very distinctive. Characteristics of dankness and crisp enclosure are perceived even in a big-as-life diorama.

Water Control

The Lore

The labors of Chen Yonggui included all manner of deeds. One of the contests he and his workers-in-arms waged that was not as widely chronicled as other efforts was the steady struggle for water control. Whereas the original Dazhai terraces primarily were built without the more complicated engineering associated with water delivery and drainage systems for aquatic crops, increasingly, new terraces were embraced within an irrigation net that made possible periodic irrigation of the maize and kaoliang.

More important, however, was the work done in the redirection of the streams that coursed between the spurs of the various hill systems spreading out from Tigerhead Hill. Although it was difficult to comprehend the transformation schemes in toto, it was clear that all of the earlier streams had been captured and that none of the gullies that were now home to ascending terraces had an associated stream channel. The waters had been removed entirely. Three rain-fed reservoirs crowned the transformed ridge crests of the village to supply water needed if summer rains were sparse or tardy.

Tunnels, conduits, canals, and drains all appear in the literature describing water control in Dazhai. The Dazhai model necessarily demanded full power over precious waters and earth—nothing wasted, nothing underutilized—in order to serve the needs of agriculture anywhere in China.

The Landscape

At the very apex of the Dazhai panorama sits the stone circle of water that fills so many needs in the

Figure 14.8. A view of terraces and dwellings across Dazhai's landscape creates a sense of virtually complete domination by man. Only high on the flanks of hills is there land left unterraced. Old residences dug into the loessial soil are observable in the rear.

brigade. Surrounded by a ring of rock walls still under construction, the reservoir was utterly still and unvisited when I came to it on a solo walk around the perimeter of the lands of this paradigmatic landscape. Leaning on the rim of the stone railing and looking out over the more than 40 hectares of totally modified farm base, I could see the impressive eight-arch stone aqueduct that stood some 2 meters high and spread across a valley for more than 60 meters. This reservoir must have played some part in feeding the system that coursed through the aqueduct.

Looking directly downslope toward the new buildings and the dormitory accommodations of the village center, the eye easily traced segments of a stone-bottomed-and-edged conduit system that carried water through some of the terraces lying below this stone tank. Like a karst stream, the ribbon of water disappeared into subterranean man-made vias only to resurface again at a lower elevation, running on its way toward a stream system below the fields of Dazhai village.

As I returned to the village, I saw further evidence of the brigade's dominion over water. A great drain nearly 3 meters in diameter stood off to the side of one of the major courtyards in the village. This impressive cut into the earth was fully stone-lined, surrounded by an iron railing, and connected with a storm drain some 6 meters below the grain-drying pad of the courtyard. Into that drain would rush the muddy flood waters that were able to spill over and through the terraces in magnitude adequate to reach the village. As the people of Dazhai had stolen the natural stream beds, good sense and perhaps a traditional desire for harmony with the forces of nature had compelled them to carry out this major task in hydraulic engineering. It also provided an excellent drain for newly accumulated waters in the village resulting from the massive increase of area in asphalt and concrete as the village expanded.

The villagers looked upon the storm drain with pride as a great achievement in their mastery of the waters. They had been defeated by the powers of mud and water too often to treat this resource lightly. With the completion of the drain, villagers had contained the life-giving and death-dealing force of water from its origins at the mountain ridge to its disappearance in a muddy swirl below the lowest point of the village.

Throughout the village, running water from communal taps, boiled water sitting ready in tall thermoses, and even hot water for washing the yellow dust out of the eyes and from the hair gave evidence of new demands the people of Dazhai were making on the most frightening holdover from the bad old days: For all too long in Dazhai's history, water had been the enemy that had most resisted transformation. Even during a visit in mid-August with a light rain falling, I could see continued respect in the eyes of the villagers as they studied the sky. They all knew that even a diorama can experience mechanical failure or material collapse.

Learning from the Landscape

The Lore

"In agriculture, learn from Dazhai." On Mao Zedong's birthday in 1964, Chen Yonggui personally brought news to Mao of the agricultural and social successes and the consequent political difficulties of his brigade. Mao could not have wished for a finer birthday present. Here was Chen Yonggui, a leader who had ascended from the poor and hired class of disenfranchised peasants of the Taihang Mountains and who had woven together a band of illiterate villagers with a new social cohesion and purpose. Together, they had been able to make changes in the life and lifestyle of every member of the village. Farmland had been remade, housing had been renewed and new units had been constructed. All the while, not only had grain yields steadily increased, making possible an improvement in the diet of villagers, but there was also sufficient surplus to augment sales of grain to the state. Virtually all had been done without any significant change in basic agrarian technology or implements, or, it was claimed, any significant state aid.

The only tradition that had been breached was the individualism that had made collective efforts at village improvement so difficult in the past. The only demand made on the state during two decades of transformation had been the request to form an irregularly large cooperative in the early 1950s. It is no wonder that Mao called on the Chinese masses to learn from this village's experience. If Dazhai could become so productive with only the little red book, *Quotations from Chairman Mao Zedong,* as its handbook and minor assistance from the People's Liberation Army, there was a chance for the realization of Mao's dream, a more productive and less class-conscious China.

The diorama was formally dedicated with the

Figure 14.9. Planted with weeping willows, the entryway to Dazhai village was marked with bulletin boards to welcome visitors. Both the painted billboards and the life-size statue of Mao Zedong express the revolutionary significance of this model brigade. [Source: *Red Sun* 1969, 18]

coining of "the great slogan," Mao's terse call, "In agriculture, learn from Dazhai."

The Landscape

As our delegation stood on the muddy shoulder of a hill overlooking the outskirts of the village center, a long line of Chinese youth, four abreast, emerged from the edge of the settlement and marched at a good pace upslope toward an open area some 300 meters from the last building. The progress of the marching troop could not but be noticed even as our own tutelage was going on by the brick kiln. As the first station on our circuit was completed with a discussion of the fact that the brigade's population happened to be exactly the same as had been reported a decade earlier, the distant snake of blue curled into new formation. The youths were seated across the valley from us as we were led back into our cars to drive the next 300 meters. Just as the car doors closed, the crack of the loudspeaker began and the high-pitched drone of yet another brief introduction began. Old and young alike were being educated through the medium of the landscape.

In our travels around the circuit of the terraced steps in cars, we geographers learned of sacrifice, ingenuity, persistence, and, finally, victory. We saw part of a gully left overrun with boulders, weeds, and ill-monitored maize—"the education plot" for instruction in what Dazhai fields used to look like. We saw some terrace margins left in disarray for the same purposes. Even the smoothly moving teams of night-soil carriers gliding up- and downslope were cited as workers who would be relieved of a difficult chore once there was more widespread use of chemical fertilizers in Dazhai farming.

The landscape was heuristic, designed for visitors to find things out for themselves. The villagers were the professors, and all visitors were students.

As we came to the penultimate stop on our tour, we stood on the brink of yet another terraced gully. To our rear were several hundred Chinese visitors being told the epic of Dazhai and Chen Yonggui as they sat in an amphitheater near the now defunct air-raid shelter commissioned by Mao's widow, Jiang Qing, in earlier days of her authority. In the immediate foreground were fruitless mulberry trees for a sericulture cottage industry that made up part of Dazhai's varied economic inventory. In the more distant foreground, the village was nestled in mist and the soft grays of an uncertain summer day. It occurred to me that lessons from the land could be taught here in all weather. If there was rain, instruct in the necessity of water control. If the sun burned holes in the attention span of visitors, speak of the benefit of cool cave shelters and the effectiveness of water delivery systems. Every day was a prime day. Every setting had its lesson.

Late in the day we were driven from the fields and structures of the community and transferred to a mammoth display center in Xiyang, the county seat, to continue our lessons. For two hours we were led through a high-ceilinged museum with thousands of items and paintings demonstrating the hardships in the life of Chen Yonggui and his campaign to transform Dazhai village into a model for all of agrarian China. At a distance from the reality of Dazhai's unique landscape, we were exhorted to appreciate the feats that new forms of human organization and determination had achieved. It was like standing outside the walls of the Forbidden City and being lectured on the grandeur of Ming palace construction.

The lessons of the locale were completed that evening when, after being feted for the second time that day with an extravagant meal and bottomless cups of *maotai* liquor and Chinese beer, we were ushered directly into a large room together with a group of African visitors and shown a seventy-minute film on new techniques in composting and soil management as developed by the Dazhai brigade. Knowing that we had to rise the next morning at 4:30 A.M. in order to make a train connection to Taiyuan, we went directly from the movie to bed.

The Enigma of Dazhai

How had it all happened? Who had done all of this work? Both written reports and brief introductions suggest a work force of approximately 160 people. There were supposedly no outsiders involved, no significant amount of external labor introduced even via one of the *xiafang,* or rustication of urban youth, campaigns that had an impact on rural development elsewhere in China. Heavy machinery did not arrive on the scene until the early 1970s, after most of the terrace construction had been completed for the third and final time. It was claimed that no money was accepted by the brigade to help in the rebuilding after the floods of the fifties or sixties. All landscape modification, so claimed the lore, was accomplished by local people using their own power.

The transformation of Dazhai occurred even as villagers (the same number and the same people as in the terrace-building work force) were increasing production tenfold from the early fifties to the mid-1970s. No miracles were claimed. Although newspapers told of transformations of poverty and marginal poverty in other areas of China, Dazhai alone rose to the national standard. Indeed, Dazhai became the national standard. Its influence spawned development in other brigades, communes, and even counties, not only the physical transformation of landscape and increases in grain production, but also the embracing of a political ideology of egalitarianism, self-reliance, and struggle.

The force responsible for this model building is not apparent in the image of Dazhai in lore or in landscape. In a three-hour walk on 17 August between 12:30 and 3:30 P.M., not one person was seen in the fields, at the stone walls, or at the reservoir. Admittedly, there was a light rain falling during that hike, and early afternoon is often a time for villagers to rest. Furthermore, all mental images of Chen Yonggui and villagers at work seem to have snow and storm settings, indicating work accomplished during the long winter slack season. The model was at full rest during my one opportunity to see building in process.

Even modest calculations of the kinds of labor done in the diorama provide overwhelming statistics. By determining the average plot size, one can approximate the length of stone terrace wall created by this eight-score labor brigade: each person stands responsible for approximately 600 meters of meter-high stone terrace wall. Such an achievement is not an impossibility, given the two-decade-long period of building and growth, but it does take on heroic attributes as you set these laboring forces in motion during the late fall and winter, after they have completed a crop year of unprecedented agricultural efficiency and expanded production.

Here, then, is the enigma of Dazhai. That all the tasks were accomplished is evident by the juxtaposition of actually viewed images with mental images carried to the scene. To believe at the same time that such monumental modification was authored by fewer people than in a good-sized introductory cultural geography class becomes more of a problem, however. To finally set these tasks in context by having them done in conjunction with an ever more productive general farming economy requires a further suspension of disbelief. The viewer of the reality of Dazhai cannot disbelieve the diorama or the model. The question arises in genesis.

I went to Dazhai very much an aficionado of Chen Yonggui, his model for self-reliance, as well as the traditional Chinese capacity to remold landscape. I felt the power of the terraces even from a car seat. I felt them considerably more intensely walking along the stone lips of earthen planting beds. The harmony created by the flowing water, the growing maize, and the upright pride of the night-soil carriers gave me still further reason to celebrate the labors of this brigade. Only the credits for the production left me nervous. Perhaps such feelings are the burden an academician carries into the field. Perhaps the only reality that should matter is the presence of the phenomenon of resculpted Dazhai itself. The disparity between the apparent magnitude of the creating force and the reported creating force is ultimately, after all, only academic.

Or, like an enigma, it is only a riddle for which we do not yet have all of the clues.

Dazhai Revisited: What Has the Model Taught Us?

In mid-1980—three years after the August 1977 trip that prompted the draft of the first part of this chapter—*Beijing Review* printed a self-criticism that made very clear the closing of the door on Dazhai as China's beacon landscape: "*Beijing Review* reported several times in the past how the Dazhai Brigade had transformed the mountain area through hard struggle. This is right. But owing to the influence of the erroneous line and lack of on-the-spot investigation, we described Dazhai as an advanced model in every respect. This is wrong, for which we should make a self-criticism" ("No Deification of Dazhai Brigade" 1980, 5).

There had been increasing slippage in the position of Dazhai after the death of Mao in 1976 and the reascendance of Deng Xiaoping, and this public announcement made overt a reality that had been whispered about increasingly since late 1977, the abandonment of the call "In agriculture, learn from Dazhai."

Chen Yonggui, the Dazhai village leader who had been the single most effective force in engineering the village's efforts at landscape transformation, had himself been transformed. In April 1969, he had been elected a member of the Ninth Central Committee of the Chinese Communist Party. In August 1973, he was elected a member of the Politburo of the Tenth Central Committee. And, in January 1975, he was appointed a vice-premier in conjunction with the Fourth National People's Congress (Tsou et al. 1982, 267). This ascent for a coal-mining and farming peasant of orphan background from upland China was extraordinary even for the heady times of the Cultural Revolution.

As the meaning and significance of Dazhai Brigade were called into question, so too was the political career of Chen. In late 1979, he was removed from his position as secretary of the Party committee in Xiyang county, and in September 1980 he resigned his vice-premiership. All during the summer and fall of 1980, press criticisms of Dazhai appeared, further sealing the fate of this model landscape (Tsou et al. 1982, 267–268). A February 1981 *Renmin ribao* [People's daily] newspaper report pointed out that "leftist errors . . . had [been] committed in guiding the movement to learn from Dazhai in [Shanxi] province." A commentary by the Party center was published alongside this self-criticism, asserting that since the beginning of the Cultural Revolution, Dazhai had become a model in "implementing 'the leftist line' and that the movement to learn from Dazhai had created serious consequences" (Tsou et al. 1982, 238).

The political changes that clouded the image of Dazhai led to profound structural and organizational changes in the Shanxi village as well. The strong images of this change are clearly at variance with the characteristics of change in the village that had been the foundation of its fame in the prior two decades:

Over the past ten years, tremendous changes have taken place in Dazhai. . . . In 1987, the total income of households exceeded 800,000 *yuan,* or 4.3 times as much as in 1978. The per-capita income was 653 *yuan,* a jump of 3.5 times higher than 1978 figures. . . . Agricultural production as a solo act is rapidly being supplemented by production of coal, transport and other sideline occupations. Since 1983, Dazhai has established two coal pits. . . . The village has also set up a cobblestone factory and a grain processing mill. . . . Of about 100 households, ten are engaged in commerce, transport service and stone processing. Moreover, hired labourers have emerged in the collective sector. For instance, among nearly 100 workers in village-owned enterprises, 40% are from other places. ("Changes in Dazhai Village" 1989, 39)

This return to coal mining and hired labor served as a further manifestation of changing rural policy and departure from practices that shaped China's development during the first quarter-century of the revolution. It also returned Dazhai to traditional patterns.

Although the economics of these changes have led to some interesting arguments in the pages of the *Monthly Review* (Hinton 1988; Deane 1989; Hinton 1989), for a geographer the real concern is, what really has happened to the village as a place? What has happened to its landscape?

Beijing Review, as in the past, continues to report on the village without on-the-spot coverage. The Chinese press still gives mention to Dazhai because of the tremendous notoriety the village gained in the 1960s and 1970s, "paraded as a national model for the other places to emulate, causing great suffering to the ordinary people" ("Changes in Dazhai Village" 1989, 39). Now, the use of the Dazhai model is related more to progressive ecological policy. In the past, the focus was on the single mountain village of Dazhai as a solitary environmental model. Over the past decade, the Chinese have made it very clear that no single ecological model can possibly serve the diverse landscape of the nation (Salter 1983; "No Deification of Dazhai Brigade" 1980).

What, then, should be the geographer's perspective on this village that is barely the size of an average college campus? What are we to make of a cluster of fewer than a hundred households that went from utter anonymity over hundreds of years of existence to become China's most sought after and reported upon landscape for a decade and a half? What are the lessons that exist in this drama that would serve a geographic observer today concerning the birth, life, and death of a "beacon landscape" for China's hero-hungry population?

1. Dazhai does serve as an effective village model for the remaking of an agrarian landscape. There was true and productive landscape modification achieved in the village.
2. The technology and human organization that remade the mountain flanks of Tigerhead Hill into a wall of terraces is a rich example of the Chinese capacity to focus labor and design on even the most reluctant landscapes.
3. Whenever any geographic phenomenon becomes a national model, the observer should be suspicious of its announced reality. The desire of the media (and, perhaps, the government) to find an ideal built by normal people and created from traditional landscape resources is likely to be so powerful that omissions and exaggerations will grow to obscure all but the most basic reality.
4. And, finally, the geographer can find grand examples of place, pattern, and progress in the evolution of a village such as Dazhai. Since knowing the reality of Chinese development is always going to be clouded by distance, by Chinese disinclination to tell the full story, and by waves of differing and often contradictory reportage, the village study should be seen as only one of many elements that must be understood to grasp

the complex reality of the Chinese cultural landscape.

Dazhai has served the discipline of geography well, for it has made students of China and the rural world look carefully at the continual battle between demanding nature and ambitious humankind. Even lacking the ultimate truth of what Dazhai was and is and what it was not and is not, there is tremendous geography to be learned by attempting to separate Dazhai's landscapes and lore.

CHAPTER 15

Suburban Weigang, Jiangsu
A Transformed Village

GREGORY VEECK

LOCATED south of the Zijin Mountains in the eastern suburbs of Nanjing city, Weigang—like much of the southern region of Jiangsu province (Sunan)—is comparatively affluent relative to most areas of rural China. A balanced mix of commercial agriculture, light industry, and government-supported military, academic, and research institutes has brought over time a sound economy with excellent social services and steady economic growth, creating a transformed village landscape. This diverse economy has largely come about because of the close proximity of Weigang to the city of Nanjing and the village's incorporation into the suburbs of this old and flourishing city, which served as the first capital of the Ming dynasty and more recently as the capital of Chiang Kai-shek's Republic of China from 1927 to 1949. In many ways, conditions in Weigang reflect a trend that is also apparent in other previously rural peri-urban areas of China. The following description will not only reflect the life and economy of a single suburban village, but will also suggest the broader context of the economic and cultural transformation occurring throughout China at the present time (Sun and Lin 1989, 43-44).

Weigang owes its existence and eminence to the hill for which it was named. An old place with a history residents say goes back at least to the Ming dynasty (1368-1644), the village received its name from the garrison stationed on the 60-meter rise that is the highest elevation for several kilometers along the main road. The garrison protected the southern entrance to the tomb of Zhu Yuanzhang (r. 1368-1398), the first emperor of the Ming dynasty. The character *wei* was originally associated with a garrison unit, although the current meaning is simply "to guard or protect." *Gang* is simply a small hill. Older residents recall when the village was referred to as one of the Zijin Mountain villages, but this administrative unit has not been used at least since 1949. Officially no longer classified as a village, Weigang is now administratively part of the eastern suburbs of Nanjing city, with some of its social services (electricity and postal services) supplied by the town of Xiaolingwei, and other services (higher education, ration coupons, health care) administered directly by the City of Nanjing.

If a militarily strategic position may be credited for the existence of Weigang, then its location on

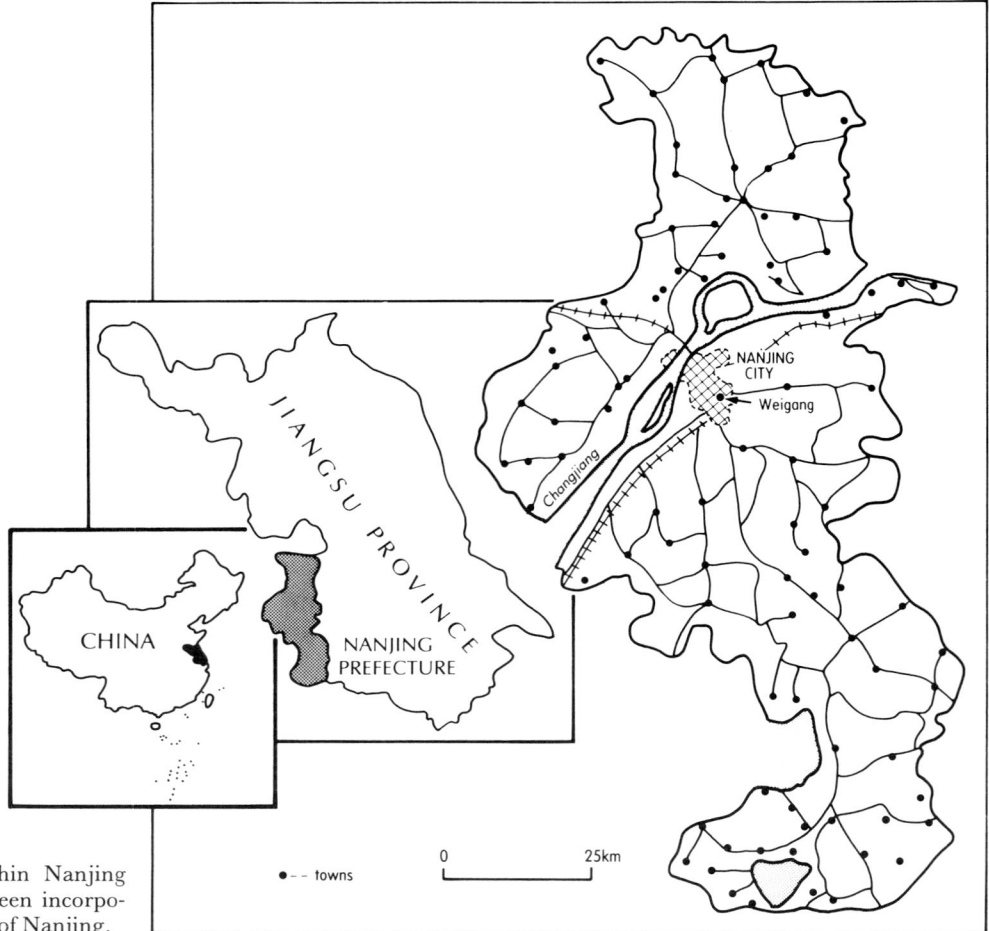

Figure 15.1. Located within Nanjing prefecture, Weigang has been incorporated into the municipality of Nanjing.

the main road to Nanjing must be credited for its prosperity and continued growth. The Ninghang road is the main eastern route that connects Nanjing to the cities of Sunan and then on to China's east coast. It is difficult to imagine how many times the route has been improved or widened over the centuries. The road has led to the Qixia monasteries built during the Sui dynasty (589–618), been a portion of the processional route taken to the tomb of the first Ming emperor, and even today passes through the great eastern gate of Nanjing, once called Chaoyang Gate ("Rising Sun Gate") but now called Zhongshan Gate ("Sun Yatsen Gate"). The area has harbored the gardens, guesthouses, and monuments of the Republican era elite, including a private villa of Madame Chiang Kai-shek.

The road from Nanjing to Weigang was repaved again in 1987, improved with the addition of a passing lane and paved shoulders in an effort to keep up with the relentless press of vehicles, tractors, carts, bicycles, and pedestrians going

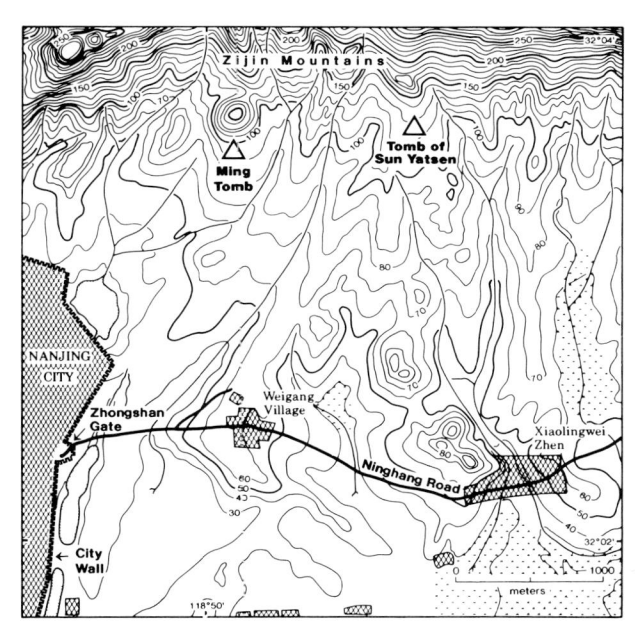

Figure 15.2. Weigang is located along the Ninghang highway between the Zhongshan gate of Nanjing city and the town of Xiaolingwei.

back and forth from the eastern peri-urban areas of Nanjing to the city center. The density of the traffic reflects the high level of economic integration between the city and the growing eastern suburbs. Perhaps more than any other feature, it is the road and its many implications that explain the form and function of the settlement of Weigang at the present.

Residential and industrial growth along the Ninghang road prompted the city to add a bus line as early as the 1960s, with a turnabout for the line at Xiaolingwei town, just 2 kilometers east of Weigang and only a fifteen-minute walk. Along this route, the Number 5 bus comes every ten minutes in daylight hours and is always filled to capacity with commuters as well as vendors and their vegetables and fowl. After dark, the buses continue to be crushingly full of students, moviegoers, and shoppers even to the last bus arriving from the city at midnight—an unseen hour in much of rural China.

The impact of the bus line cannot be overestimated. Because of the service, many families living in the research *danwei* (work units) in Weigang have members who work within the city. The bus route serves not only as a convenient means of transport for the people in Weigang but also as a conduit of all that is modern in Nanjing. Weigang's four stores and newspaper kiosk carry a better quality and a greater variety of goods than would generally be found in stores of more distinctly rural villages of similar size.

Contemporary Weigang and its environs provide few clues regarding what the original settlement was like when it was only a military garrison surrounded by peasant hamlets and fields. The early agricultural village of Weigang was bounded to the north by the Zijin Mountains, and the fields were watered from the small streams that flow from these low mountains. An irrigation and water control system built in the 1950s is now in place, fed in dry times by reservoirs located in these same hills. At present, most farmsteads are located north of the Ninghang road. As expansion of the village occurred, the more extensive paddy areas to the south of the road were co-opted either by newly arriving work units or as experimental fields for Nanjing Agricultural University. The loss of this paddy has meant that most farm families in Weigang can no longer be self-sufficient even if they wanted to be. They are now irreparably tied to the cash system intrinsic to commercial vegetable production—most certainly selected because it yielded higher profits than rice as well as because of characteristics of the land farmers still control. This transition to commercial agriculture has been found in many locations in southern Jiangsu (Fei 1986, 8–83). Although most farmers grow vegetables, a few farm households that have larger portions of land in the hilly

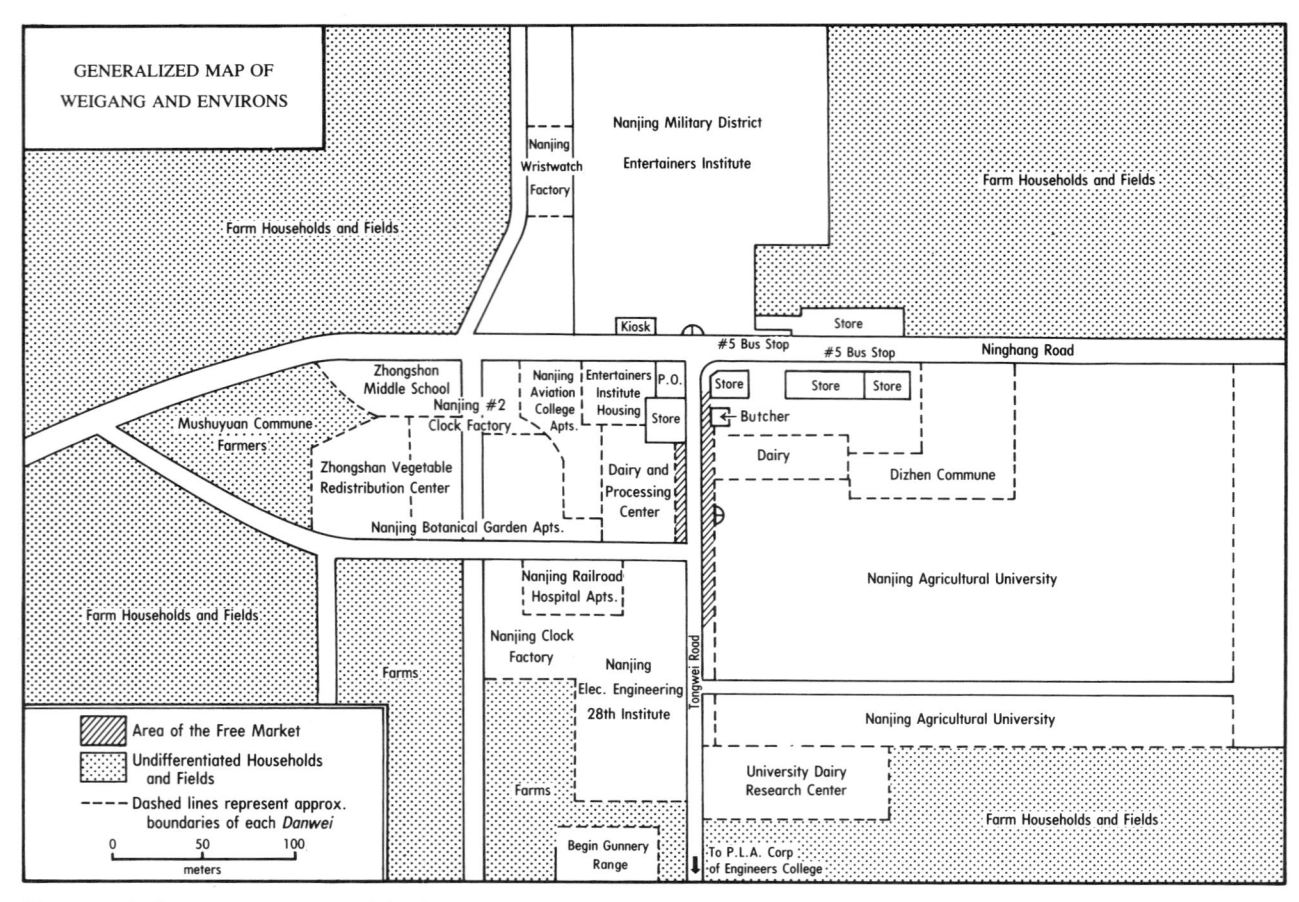

Figure 15.3. Contemporary map of the farm households and fields that surround the built-up section of Weigang. Here, *danwei* abut one another yet are separated by walls.

Figure 15.4. Lanes in Weigang, such as this one, are often paralleled by narrow canals. The single-story dwellings facing the lane and canal were built prior to 1979. Today, new dwellings are more dispersed, located closer to contracted land than to neighbors. [Photograph, 1987]

Figure 15.5. Raised vegetable gardens are typical of the Weigang area and help supply the food needs of greater Nanjing city. Plastic sheeting held over a bamboo frame allows planting to occur quite early in the spring. The scene here is in the western portion of Weigang, just north of the Ninghang road. [Photograph, 1987]

areas now raise tea or peaches. Almost all farm households have a small flock of ducks or chickens for family use and sale in the market. Many families keep two or three pigs as well as the fowl, and one or two pigs will be sold every six months. As commercial and industrial work units negotiate frontage on the main road, farmland and farm households are constantly being pushed to the periphery of the settlement.

Military personnel still reside in Weigang. The barracks that housed active troops during the Nationalist period became the Nanjing District Military Entertainers Institute after 1949. Talented performers of Jiangsu opera and more contemporary arts are trained there. Occasionally, the institute offers free shows to the people of Weigang. The largest and most popular drygoods store continues to be operated by the military, and Weigang's sole noodle stand is an annex to the store.

The arrival of light industrial collectives, such as the Nanjing Wristwatch Factory and the Nanjing Clock Factory, in the 1960s had a positive effect on the local economy. Most of the employees live within these collectives with their families. A number of these workers say they now wish to move back to the city, but the severe housing shortage throughout Nanjing makes such returns unlikely. Some work units, such as the Nanjing Railroad Hospital and the Nanjing Aviation College, which are actually located within the city, have also purchased land and built housing in Weigang because of lower acquisition costs.

For a variety of reasons, Weigang has become a center of education and research. As the competition for land within urban Nanjing increased in the 1960s and 1970s, growing or newly formed academic and research institutes were forced to look outside the city for suitable locations. When Nanjing Agricultural University and other research institutes expanded or were created, planning agencies located land with lower acquisition costs than in Nanjing. Weigang was such a place. The village was accessible by a good road, had

Figure 15.6. This view of the military store in Weigang shows the new surface on the Ninghang road and a small restaurant on the left. [Photograph, 1987]

Figure 15.7. Illegal housing along the Ninghang road right-of-way. The right-of-way is not controlled by any *danwei*, and local authorities did not take any steps to move these two houses in the one and a half years this author lived in Weigang. The house in the foreground is built without mortar, with bricks stacked simply to support a roof. It is likely that the household planned to save money in order to purchase mortar and complete the roof, dismantling the house and rebuilding it properly. Both dwellings were inhabited by childless elderly couples, who supported themselves by reselling paper, rags, and bottles. [Photograph, 1987]

open land held by politically weak agricultural communes, and was close enough to the city to promote city-suburban commuting patterns. Land-use change in many periurban areas of southern Jiangsu also reflects this spiraling pattern of land values, land-use intensity, and competition for use. The conflicting interests of the more recent arrivals in Weigang have resulted in almost continuous government arbitration regarding land use and the expansion of nonagricultural activities within the settlement. The resolution of these conflicts has generally entailed the appropriation of arable land for other uses and the transformation of settlements such as Weigang from a periurban agricultural village to a more developed, more integrated suburb of Nanjing.

The development and expansion of these industrial and academic work units have caused friction and resentment among farmers who have lost land, but the presence of these *danwei* has also brought improvements in infrastructure, education, health care and other social services. In

Figure 15.8. A well-stocked private store. In addition to the *baijiu* ("white liquor") and beer found in most village shops, this store sells wine, brandy, other spirits, daily staples such as rice, cooking oil, and condiments, as well as clothing, cloth shoes, and household sundries. [Photograph, 1987]

many ways, it is the *danwei* and not the village today that is the significant unit in the lives of the nonfarm population of Weigang. All of the academic and industrial *danwei* in Weigang have multipurpose residential areas that were established during the commune period, presenting an appearance quite similar to *danwei* found within cities. Walls frequently surround the *danwei,* and within housing is generally in the form of four- or five-story brick or concrete walk-up highrises. Each *danwei* has its own daycare, preschool, and primary school. The presence of factory workers and salaried personnel at the many academic, military, and research institutes has done much to stabilize the daily market and support the local economy of the larger Weigang community.

An indication of the new affluence of Weigang consumers is a roller-skating rink located between Weigang and Xiaolingwei town. The rink is a popular meeting place for students and workers from the universities and institutes. Local farmers, however, consider the place undesirable, an intrusion that promotes poor behavior. The rink presents an unusual sight, surrounded as it is by the paddy fields one expects in rural Jiangsu.

The "core" area of Weigang centers on the intersection of the Ninghang road and Tongwei Road, another paved road leading north to the Army Entertainers Institute and south to Nanjing Agricultural University. The branch post office, all of the stores, and the daily market are all near this intersection. The stores carry on a busy trade in the early morning, late afternoon, and early evening. Although at mid-day the village seems almost deserted, during market hours, the north-south road is noisy and always crowded with shoppers, commuters, and students. More than anything else, the "free" market seems to represent the tempo and cadence of daily life in Weigang. The market, located along Tongwei Road south of the main road, serves breakfast *youtiao* (deep-fried twisted dough sticks) and *yuanbing* (flat, circular baked biscuits) to commuters in the morning rush. By 10:00 A.M. the market disappears, not to return until mid-afternoon. Sales and attendance seem to peak around 5:00 or 5:30, as many residents return home from work (see Huang 1990, 203–205, for a concise discussion of the impact of "free markets").

Many more farmers from Weigang now choose to sell their produce at the afternoon market rather than in Nanjing or Xiaolingwei. It is said by many old timers that the growing influx of white-collar workers has slightly inflated the prices of meat, fish, and some vegetables. The steady sales of local specialties, such as delicious Nanjing salted duck, "five-fragrance tofu," and "knife fish," also attest to the affluence of at least some of the shoppers. Busy commuters buy from the local daily market rather than from the larger and slightly less expensive markets farther away. Farm families may purchase most of their staples at the less expensive market in Xiaolingwei, but the prices do not stop them from coming to the

Figure 15.9. The Weigang "free" market. [Photograph, 1987]

market for a visit over a glass of tea or a cigarette. The pleasant bustle of the daily afternoon market resembles that of its counterparts throughout much of rural China.

At mid-day, the market road at the center of Weigang is empty and still. The quiet is broken only by the loud gargle of the occasional power tiller hauling manure or freight. This impression of isolation is further enforced by the ubiquitous walls that surround all of the *danwei*. The high brick walls with gray metal gates bound each unit and run end-to-end along the main roads, obscuring activity and creating an impression that the village has suddenly vanished. Once the market is in session, however, the stark walls are muted by the flow of pedestrians and cars, and the vendors with their wares lining both sides of the road. When the market is in session, Weigang has the feel of a Chinese village. When the shoppers and sellers depart, the impression that Weigang is a specific place, rather than simply a cluster of isolated *danwei*, is lost as well.

Prosperity in the 1980s brought a construction boom to Weigang and has changed the face of the settlement. Housing built prior to 1978 was concentrated along the narrow lanes in a linear fashion. With few exceptions, the central entryway of the houses faced south. With the reforms of the 1980s, however, many new multistory farm houses were dispersed away from the core settlement, as many households preferred to build houses near their contracted fields.

It is not clear if Weigang will, in time, be engulfed by suburban sprawl or if it will remain as it is at the present—a mix of suburban and rural features possibly characteristic of an alternate form of settlement. Weigang is far from unique. As problems associated with urban growth, such as competition for land and housing, force suburban relocation of urban businesses and other *dan-*

Figure 15.10. Traditional housing has been concentrated along the narrow lanes. Most dwellings face south. [Photograph, 1990]

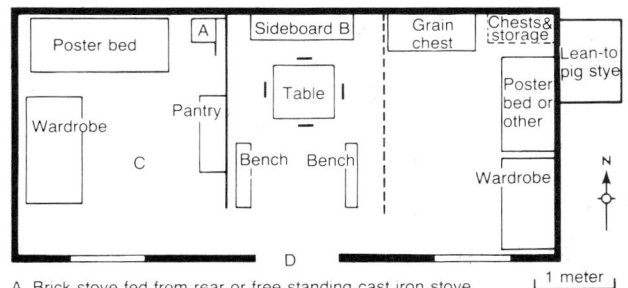

A. Brick stove fed from rear or free standing cast iron stove
B. Often with a small altar or pictures of political figures
C. Floors may be pounded earth, brick, or concrete slab
D. Doorway with raised threshhold closed off in evenings with slotted boards
------ Optional interior wall or curtain

Figure 15.11. Typical Weigang village residence. Plan, front, and side views.

wei, villages in peripheral zones are compelled to accept new residents and activities. Such infusions transform these places, converting what once were generally traditional rural places with limited ties to the city to hybrid suburban-commercial agricultural villages with strong economic and social links to the cities located nearby.

T. G. McGee, referring to such regions by the coined Bahasa Indonesian term "kotadesasi" (*kota* meaning "town," and *desa* meaning "village"), suggests that such regions may be a "persistent and important part of the spatial structures of developing countries" that have not been properly appreciated by policy makers (1987, 31). Chinese researchers have also argued for recognition of these economically distinct hybrid places. Zhou Yixing (1988) incorporates the Nanjing suburbs into what he calls the Nanjing-Shanghai-Hangzhou Metropolitan Interlocking Region. He supports McGee's hypothesis, emphasizing the mixed agricultural and industrial economies of such places as well as the need to develop policies that will allow the continued practice of both broad types of economic activities while also allowing the service sector to develop. Fei Xiaotong has called the growth of mixed economic regions in close proximity to major cities "short distance extension" (1986, 140). In supporting the contention that such places are neither urban nor rural, he argues that the mechanisms that created such areas are not simply economic but administrative as well, as provincial and city governments have initiated development beyond their jurisdictions.

The central issue for such hybrid places seems to be the question of permanence. Will places such as Weigang quickly lose their agricultural base and their physical form in the face of land demands by nonagricultural *danwei* that generally have more power in the political arena? Or will planners try to maintain agricultural land near large cities to minimize transport costs and congestion on the already overburdened distribution systems? These questions can only be answered with time. In theory, national policy will probably support the maintenance of arable land, but if local government is allowed to continue to arbitrate land-use decisions, valuable crop land will be lost and urban sprawl will carry the day. In the process, places such as Weigang will disappear, erasing a village and creating a hybrid settlement neither urban nor rural.

I thank the Committee on Scholarly Communication with the People's Republic of China for the funding that made possible this field-related work. I also thank Fred and Kay Krehbiel, who not only helped us along, but also through example taught us that we could make a living doing what we love.

CHAPTER 16

Lincun Village, Fujian
Harmony between Humans, Environment, and the Supernatural

HUANG SHU-MIN

SOUTHEASTERN China, especially the area along the coastal regions of Fujian province, was relatively well developed economically prior to 1949. Throughout much of the premodern period, this area was known for its experimentation with new crop varieties and its intensive use of rice paddies, yielding up to three crops per year (Ho 1955, 193–195; Rawski 1972, 38–44). Commercialization of agriculture in this region supported an active, cash-based market economy. Lucrative maritime trade with the European powers from the sixteenth century on brought prominence to such coastal cities as Quanzhou (Zayton) and Xiamen (Amoy), and linked them to the far-flung reaches of the globe, including the Philippines, Mexico, and Spain.

Despite these technological and economic achievements, Fujian province was never considered an easy location for human habitation. Though generally not high in elevation, the landscape of this region is characterized by steep slopes and treacherous rivers. Interspersed between the rugged hills and rapid streams—which may create a sudden deluge during rainy seasons—are small pockets of level basins, river valleys, and coastal plains. Through assiduous work and ingenuity, peasants in this region have transformed these patches into cultivated land, sometimes pushing all the way up the surrounding foothills to form contoured terraces for wet-rice cultivation and gentle slopes for dry fields or orchards.

Because of its geographic fragmentation and isolation, the Fujian region has also been known historically for its ethnic division and the weak political control exercised by the Chinese court. Difficulty in transportation was further aggravated by communication problems, in that people living on the other side of the hills might speak a totally different "dialect." Armed conflict across ethnic or regional lines was rampant, as was banditry (Lamley 1990). Intermittent local wars and banditry plus the weak governmental presence in this region made local autonomy and self-protec-

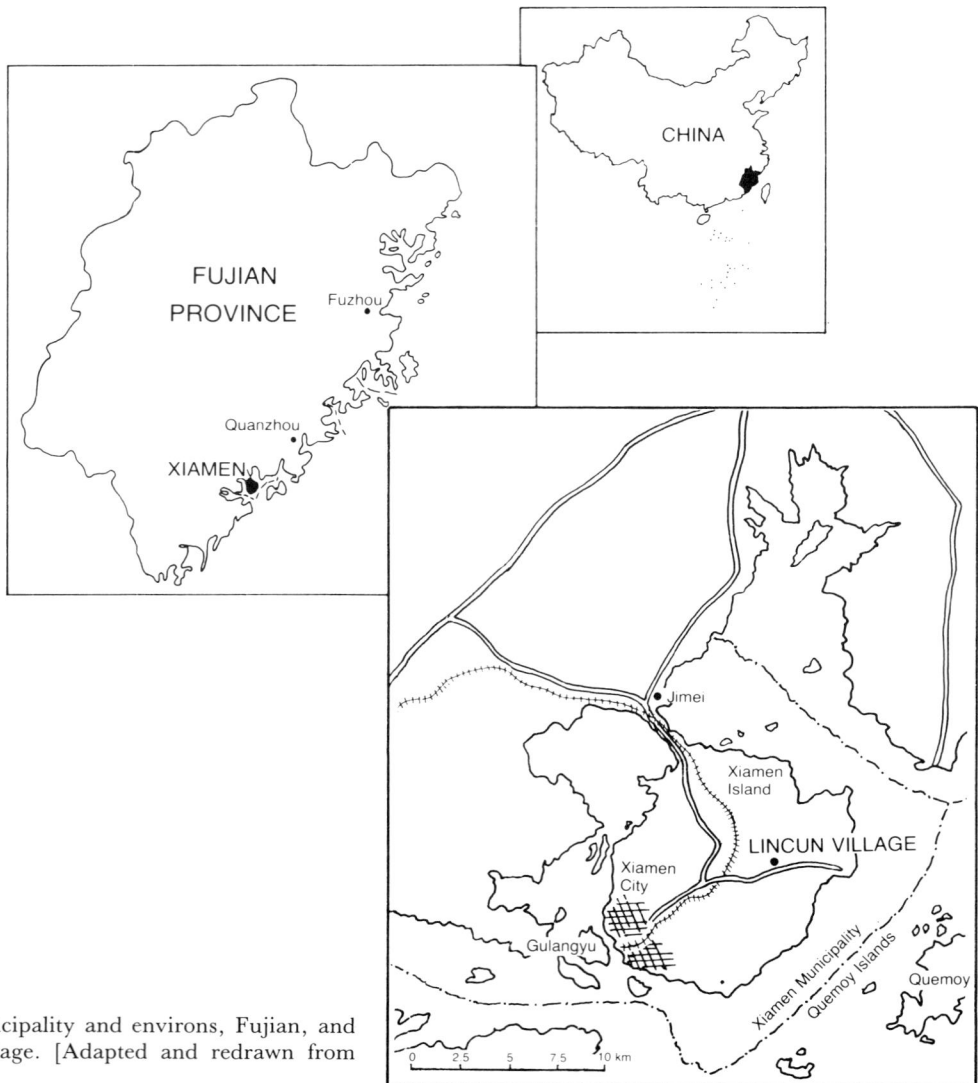

Figure 16.1. Xiamen Municipality and environs, Fujian, and the location of Lincun village. [Adapted and redrawn from Huang 1989, 15]

tion a necessity. Fujian's distinct socioecological conditions have had repercussions in human settlement patterns. For the purpose of self-defense, most rural communities in this region have been compact, and sometimes fortified villages formed on the basis of agnatic descent. The prominence of so-called single-surnamed lineage villages has made this region well known in the anthropological literature (Freedman 1958, 1966).

Lincun village, a compact settlement with a population of 1,047 in two hundred households, is located some 10 kilometers northeast of Xiamen city in southern Fujian. In this village with a total of 700 *mu* of farmland (1 hectare equals 15 *mu*),

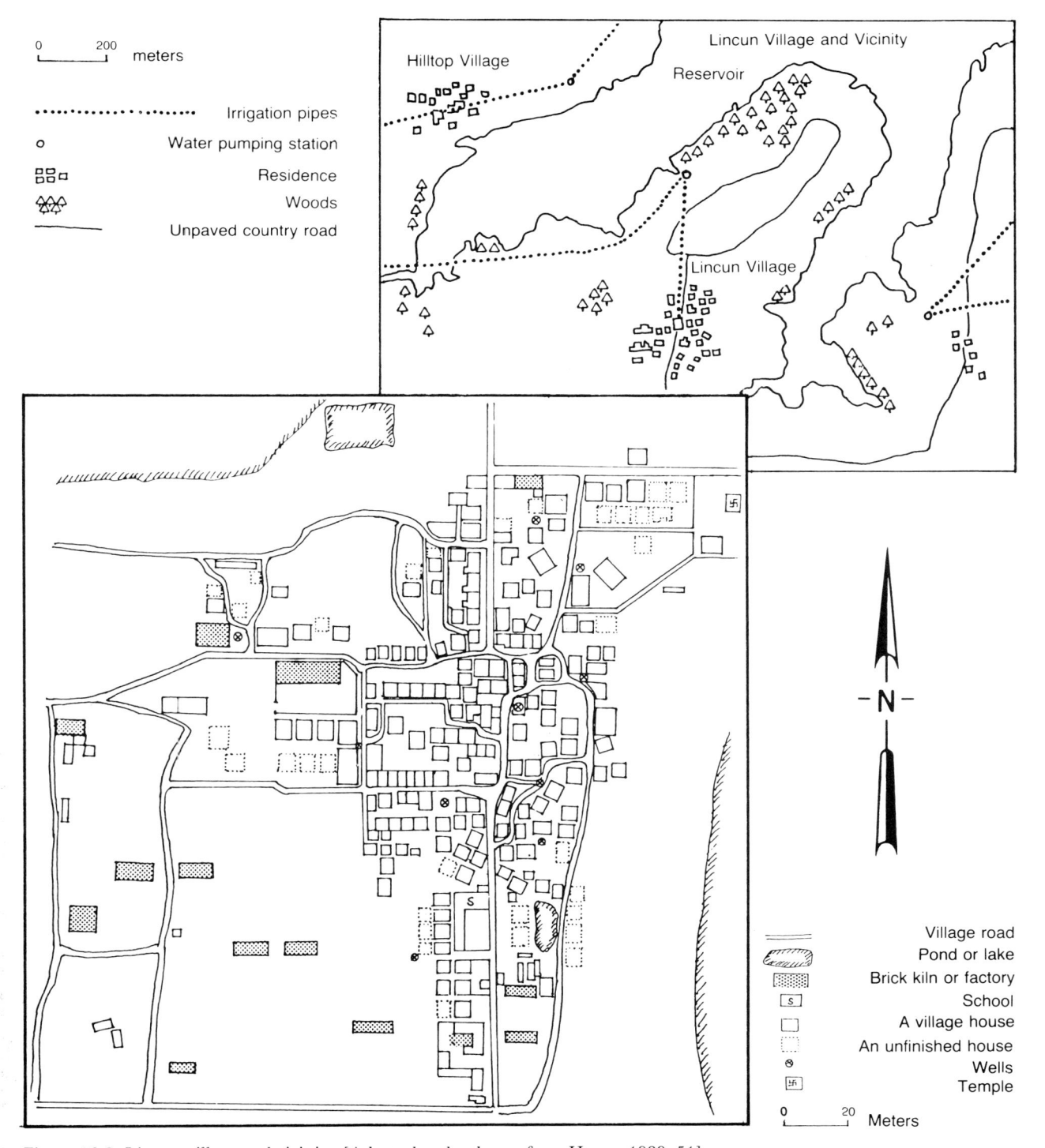

Figure 16.2. Lincun village and vicinity. [Adapted and redrawn from Huang 1989, 51]

agriculture traditionally has played a very important role in villagers' lives, changing only recently during the decade of reform that began in 1979. An asphalt road that connects Xiamen city and Hongshan village, about 1.5 kilometers south of Lincun village, is served by six scheduled buses daily. From Hongshan village it is just another twenty minutes' walk on a dirt road to Lincun.

Like most other rural settlements in this region, Lincun used to be a single-surname village with strong lineage organization that dominated almost every aspect of villagers' lives. Indeed, it was because the original inhabitants of this village were the Lins that the village came to be known as Lin village (Lincun). The ancestors of the Lins migrated to this place some two hundred years ago from Anhai township in Quanzhou prefecture, about 100 kilometers to the north. Local legend has it that during their heyday approximately 120 years ago, the Lins occupied a dominant position in this area, not only in present-day Lincun, but also in several adjacent villages. At that time, villagers assert, Lin village was much bigger than it is now, having perhaps a thousand cooking stoves, a loose measure of the number of individual Lin households actually present.

The Lins are said to have engaged in intermittent warfare with other surnames or lineages in neighboring villages. One of the Lins' archenemies was the Chen family of neighboring Mudhole village, about 2 kilometers from Lincun village. Most of the intervillage fighting involved irrigation water in ponds, graveyards, or petty theft. Because the Lins were numerous and strong, they abused others. For instance, they refused to let non-Lins live in the village, including their own tenant farmers. The Lins also charged fees for the right of passage when people passed through on their way to Xiamen city.

Today Lincun is bordered on three sides by the green, transparent water of a man-made reservoir built in 1961. The beach around the reservoir has a greenbelt of tropical pine *(Casuarina equisetifolia)*, a rare scene in southern China. About 1,000

Figure 16.3. Lincun's nearby farm plots and reservoir. When the reservoir was built in 1960, some twenty families were forced to tear down their dwellings and be resettled. [Photograph, 1985]

Figure 16.4. The main thoroughfare through Lincun village. [Photograph, 1990]

Figure 16.5. An older section of Lincun village. [Photograph, 1985]

meters to the south of the open side of the village is a chain of small hills with huge, exposed granite boulders. The grayish purple rock formations rise majestically above the green of the surrounding rice paddies, resembling traditional Chinese brush paintings.

Lincun village was situated by the early settlers amidst the tranquility and scenery of the surrounding area. When viewed from a distance, the village stands imposingly above the glittering, lushly green rice paddy. In spite of the village's scenic surroundings and colorful houses, the layout of the village itself is like that of most Chinese villages of this region, rather chaotic with an apparent lack of concern for planning and space utilization. Unpaved dirt roads and narrow alleys zigzag through back corners of haphazardly scattered houses or turn into field paths. A broad and straight street may suddenly bend or turn into a shoulder-wide narrow path simply because an old house protrudes into its open space. Pigpens and outhouses, unaesthetic in sight and stench in smell, block the main thoroughfare at the heart of the village. Uncovered sewers discharge household waste water and may run across road surface to reach another ditch. The heart of the village is thus like a maze. Even after three months in Lincun, I still had problems finding my way around. Only at the northern and western edges of the village, where most of the new houses have been built, has there been some attempt at community planning by making newly built houses into straight rows.

As one of the most prosperous villages in the township, Lin village boasts many impressive newly built houses, colorfully painted two-story buildings that attest to recent increases in villagers' incomes. Even though most of these new houses incorporate modern construction materials, such as steel beams, glass windows, and cement facades, they preserve many traditional architectural designs and elements, providing a tasteful blend of new and old.

The ground level of a typical house contains a walled-in court, with two pairs of smaller rooms at the front: a kitchen, a dining room, a washroom for bathing, and a storage room for farm tools and surplus grain. The rear of the house has three larger rooms arranged along an axis—in the middle, a living room or guest room; and on each side, a bedroom.

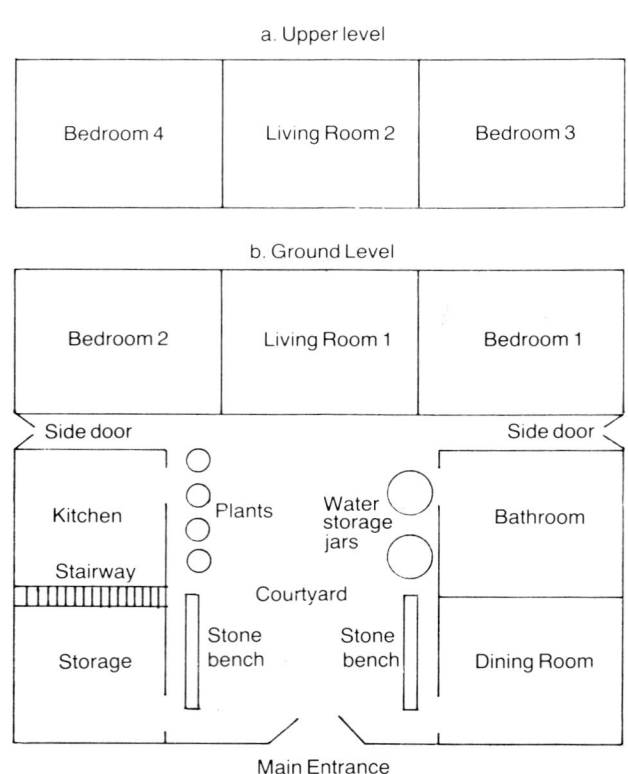

Figure 16.6. The traditional plan for Lincun village houses includes a rectangular core, a second floor above, and two single-story wings. The core contains the bedrooms and living rooms; the wings house the kitchen, storage rooms, bathroom, and dining room. The embraced courtyard is decorated with plants and contains jars for storing rainwater. [Adapted and redrawn from Huang 1989, 17]

In the open courtyard at ground level, many family activities take place. Here in the central court, many farmers grow dwarf kumquat plants in ceramic pots. These round or oblong-shaped fruits are not grown just for aesthetic or decorative purposes: Village women sometimes pick a handful of ripe kumquats and boil them in sugar and water to make a kind of orange-flavored syrup, the traditional remedy for children with minor coughs or men who carry home a hangover from a village banquet the night before.

Besides ornamental plants, most families keep large ceramic jars for water storage in this courtyard. Water is hauled daily from village wells and carried back with shoulder buckets to the house. Well water is mainly used for drinking or bathing. Most village women take their laundry to a nearby irrigation ditch or to the lakeside for washing.

The ground level of village houses is constructed mainly with granite slabs chipped out with hand chisels from nearby quarries. Villagers purchase the slabs to make floors, room parti-

Figure 16.8. A new multistory dwelling in Lincun. [Photograph, 1990]

Figure 16.7. Construction workers and masons build a new dwelling of cut granite and fired brick in Lincun. [Photograph, 1985]

tions, and sometimes even ceilings. Virtually no wood or steel is needed, reflecting the ingenious ways local people cope with the general shortage of wood and steel in the Fujian area. With these smoothly polished granite slabs piled up to build the wall, the lower level of the house is sufficiently strong to support the much lighter weight of the second floor.

The second story of village houses is generally built only above the back rooms of the ground floor, with one central living room and two bedrooms. Red bricks and white plaster are often used for the second floor to provide a sharp contrast to the grain-colored granite slabs of the lower level. One bold villager even added a colorful mosaic of a dragon and a phoenix, traditional symbols of good luck, to the front wall of the second story of his newly built house. Composed of green, red, and yellow painted 4-inch clay squares that were glazed over and fired into ceramic wall tiles, the mosaic—perhaps garish to art critics—is a strong statement of Lincun's recent prosperity.

Fengshui

Although villagers seem to be careless about their community layout, they actually pay a great deal of attention to certain environmental and topographic features in their settlement that figure in the practice of geomancy, or *fengshui*. Put simply, villagers apply the traditional beliefs in *yin-yang* dualism and the Five Phases to their environment and assign values to specific geographic features. For instance, in terms of cardinal orientation, according to folk belief, the most desirable direction is the south, for it symbolizes warmth, growth, and hence life. Next comes east, for the rising sun suggests birth and life. Less desirable after east is west, for the descending sun symbolizes the end of the day and hence termination of life. The worst direction is north, which receives blowing cold winds in the winter and faces perpetual darkness throughout most of the year.

Similarly, when Lin villagers look at a landscape, they scrutinize the composite features of the five elements: metal (rock formation), wood (forest or trees), water (ponds, rivers, or streams), fire (exposure to sun), and earth (soil) in this microcosm. Proper balance among all these elements ensures harmony. Deficiency in one or more of them, villagers believe, leads to environmental disequilibrium, and hence less than suitable sites for building their houses or even graves for their dead.

A third geomantic principle villagers traditionally have looked at is the shape and formation of the topography. Hills and mountain chains are designated as cosmological animals such as dragons, tigers, toads, and so on. A landscape dominated by an auspicious dragon ensures prosperity and proliferation of descendants for whatever family either builds a house or buries a recently dead ancestor there. A landscape dominated by a tiger means violence and bad fortune, and is to be avoided by everyone.

These simplified geomantic principles have been carefully observed by Lin villagers constructing houses and tombs. They also use geomancy to interpret some of the more dramatic events in the history of the village affecting the village's population composition and physical layout. An example is the village legend regarding the decline of the Lin lineage and the subsequent influx of other surname groups into this village. This decline occurred, it is explained, when the geomantic composition of the Lin lineage ancestral shrine was accidentally damaged over one hundred years ago.

The Lin lineage used to have an imposing ancestral shrine, which was situated on the slope north of the village but is now submerged under the reservoir. The ancestral shrine was owned by all Lins, who went there twice a year, on the fifteenth of the second month and at the winter solstice, to offer sacrifices to their ancestors. The ancestral shrine had its own trust land, approximately 5 or 6 *mu* of rice paddies, the best land in the village. The rents collected from the trust land, about 300 or 400 catties (one catty equals about half a kilogram) of unhusked rice every half year, were used to pay for the ancestral rites. The remaining funds were used to provide a feast for all the Lin descendants, called *chizu* ("eating the ancestors") in the local dialect. If there was still money left after the feast, it was used to purchase pork to be divided among all the male descendants of the Lins. The ancestral shrine was the focal point of all Lins, for it propagated all living lineage members, and it embodied unity and protection for them all.

The shrine was built along the slope, with the front door facing the low land toward the east and the back wall leaning against the high ground of the west, a reasonably auspicious location. During the rainy season, the running water gushing down the slope splashed against the back wall of the shrine and caused minor but visible damage. According to local legend, it was a scholar among the Lins who suggested that a ditch be dug at the back of the shrine so the running water would be channeled away from it. The suggestion was accepted by the Lin elders, who sent several laborers to dig the ditch. When the workers dug the ground at the back of the shrine, they hit a small spring that spouted red, bloodlike water that soaked the surrounding soil. The workers were frightened by this and fled, convinced that something horrible had happened. Legend has it that the digging had accidentally cut into the neck arteries of a reclining dragon that constituted the local topographic contour and had provided protection and prosperity to the Lins. Once the dragon was injured, the Lins were no longer protected by this favorable geomantic force. As a result, major disasters began to befall the Lins. The first calamity came to the village in the 1880s —an outbreak of bubonic plague, the black death. Nobody knows exactly how many people died, but a rough estimate was that about half the original village inhabitants died within one single year. Many surviving Lins were so frightened that they fled to other villages or to the Nanyang (South Seas), the term used by the Chinese to describe peninsular Southeast Asia.

Tragedy struck again about seventy-five years ago, around the end of the first decade of this century. Older villagers remember this second black death epidemic in vivid detail. It is recalled that when one person contracted the disease, all other family members would soon be infected and die. When the epidemic came, it was already late fall and the Lins had already harvested their sweet potato and rice crops. They were, moreover, preparing for the birthday celebration of the local patron god Lord Liu (Liufu *yuanshuai*) on the fourteenth day of the tenth month. As an opera troupe, hired from Zhangzhou city for three days' performance, carried wooden boxes and crates containing their paraphernalia to the village, the villagers were busy carrying wooden coffins out for burial. Again, large numbers of Lins died during this period, and many more fled the village, considering it a cursed place.

In between these two epidemics the Lins discovered an even more threatening problem: many Lin wives became barren. In this part of Fujian province people observed strict marriage rules that prohibited a man from marrying a woman of the same surname or from the same village. Men from the Lin lineage had always acquired spouses from villages with which they did not engage in warfare and were not agnatically related, about 60 kilometers due north in the hills in Anxi county. These women, used to a harsh living environment and industrious work, were strongly built and bore large numbers of sons for the Lins. After the first epidemic, however, many Lin wives stopped bearing children. Even those who were still able to conceive produced only daughters. The immediate threat was that without a son in the family, parents would have no one to depend upon in their old age. Even more threatening was that without a son to carry on the family line, parents would die without anyone to offer ritual sacrifice for them. Those uncared-for ancestral spirits would become wandering ghosts. Without male issue in the family, the lineage branch would be ended *(daofang)* and the "house (family) would collapse" *(daotang)*.

As the village experienced drastic depopulation at the turn of the century, many Lins began to lease out farmland to poor peasants from the hills in the interior. The influx of immigrants, especially those not related to the Lins, fundamentally changed the village composition and its social life. The first change was the appearance of internal strife. The newly arrived tenants, who constituted the majority of the village population, didn't like the Lin landlords and accused them of dishonesty. Initially, a Lin landlord would lease out an abandoned field to a tenant and charge only one-quarter of the annual yield as rent. After the tenant built up the terraces and improved the soil quality, the Lin landlord would raise the rent to one-third of the annual yield. If the tenant refused to pay, the landlord would revoke the lease and rent the field to other tenants who were willing to pay higher rent for this well-developed field. Because the Lins were rich and powerful, they bullied the non-Lins and created animosity within the village.

The second change in Lincun, the development of intravillage marriage patterns, was a consequence of the demise of the Lin lineage at the turn of the century. Before that time, the Lins strictly followed the rule of village exogamy. They had no choice, since all residents in the village were Lins and were related. The presence of the tenant families, whose surnames were not Lin and who were not related, altered this pattern. In a multisurname village, youngsters were able to seek spouses from within the village. Marrying within the village since the late 1940s has become the rule rather than the exception.

A second incident mentioned by villagers that involves geomantic factors and village settlement patterns is quite recent. This incident involves the cardinal direction of village houses. A few families that tried to circumvent the principles of direction brought misfortune and death to family members. As mentioned above, Chinese building their houses have always preferred southern exposures and directing the back of the house toward high ground while the front faces the low land. This position traditionally has been viewed as stable and secure, like a man squatting on the ground able to view the panorama of the surrounding area.

In attempting to observe these principles as houses were built, Lin villagers were confronted with a dilemma, because the village site itself is situated on a slope that tilts high to the south and descends to the north. In such a position, the villagers simply could not build their houses facing south, for the hills and high ground to the south would block air flow to the houses, and the backs of their houses would open to the low land. In local slang this kind of inverse geomantic orientation is called "tumbled upside down" *(daotousai)*. Houses built in this fashion, it has always been believed, would bring bad luck to the residents. Since villagers could not build their houses facing south, the second best option was east.

There were a few villagers in the post-Liberation era who tried to manipulate geomantic principles when building houses. Even though they knew they couldn't build their houses facing south, they figured that if they could slightly twist their houses in a southeasterly direction, they would still be able to enjoy the benefits of southern exposure. When they did that, according to local legends, unfortunate disasters befell their families. One of the owners of such an "irregular" house was a man named Li Ai, whose nickname was Shorty because of his diminutive body size. When Shorty built his house in 1968, he angled it slightly toward the south. When he hired a contractor to build the house, the latter advised against this plan and warned that bad fortune would descend on his family. But Shorty was stubborn, saying that since he was a Communist Party member, he didn't believe in such nonsense. He repeatedly ignored the plea by the contractor to change the house plan to due east.

During the construction process, there were

constant problems, including a wall at the back of the house that wouldn't hold up and collapsed repeatedly. It had to be built several times before it became stable. By 1969 the house was completed and Shorty's entire family moved in immediately. By the end of 1969, Shorty's thirty-nine-year-old wife died from a mysterious illness. Three months later, in January 1970, Shorty himself died from cancer, at forty-two. Another four months later, Shorty's mother, who had been living with them, also died from an unidentified illness. Thus, within one short year, all three adults died, leaving behind four children. The children and the neighbors were extremely sorrowful and fearful. People believed that the house, built against proper geomantic dictation, was cursed and was dangerous to live in.

Since Shorty's oldest child, a daughter, was only nineteen then, too young to take care of the entire family, his wife's brother came to live with the children as their guardian. Their maternal uncle reported experiencing many horrible things in the house. For instance, in the dark of night, he often heard howling and screaming on the roof. One day he went up to the attic to look around and found several pieces of spirit money, the kind of yellowish, straw-paper money people use on ceremonial occasions, stuffed under the house beam. Apparently, the contractor had left it to protect himself when building the house.

A few years later, more evidence showed up to indicate that this house was indeed cursed. It was in 1975, when the back wall of the house collapsed. When villagers looked through the rubble, they found a piece of human kneecap nailed to a miniature wooden shoe with a piece of red string tied around it—apparently another magical item hidden by the contractor during construction to harm Shorty's family.

Local legend has it that when a house is built against geomantic principles, either the builder or the occupants of the house will suffer from ill fortune. If the contractor wants to make sure that he will not be the one to suffer the consequences, the best strategy for him is to employ charms or spells as the house is built to spare the craftsmen and redirect the consequences to the owner's family. Once the kneecap and wooden shoe were discovered in Shorty's house, the last charms had been removed from Shorty's remaining children. The movement of the bad force was, at that point, redirected toward the contractor, who by then was living in another village. Villagers said that this man went out one night and got drunk. On his way home, he fell into a roadside pit that peasants used to store manure and was drowned.

Another village family that suffered a similar fate because of negative geomantic forces was the family of a very stubborn man who used to be the head of the brigade. When he built his house in 1968, a villager with some knowledge of geomancy warned him that the house site was not balanced with all five essential elements—wood, fire, metal, water, and earth. To correct the problem, the house owner was advised to dig a ditch behind the house. This person, again a Party member, dismissed the advice completely. A few months after the completion of his house, he lost his position as brigade head. Soon after, he died of cancer, but that was not the end of the family tragedy. In September 1983, his oldest son, driving a hand tractor and hauling earth from a mountain slope to make sand bricks, was buried alive in an avalanche. Villagers continue to believe that this house also is cursed.

Villagers furthermore are convinced that the construction of a large reservoir in 1961 drastically improved the geomantic composition of the locality that had been damaged over one hundred years ago. The body of the water, many say, provides a resting haven for the injured dragon. The two small embankments built for this reservoir

Figure 16.9. The Lincun village temple was reconstructed in the early 1980s on a new site in the northeastern section of the village. The old site was submerged after the construction of the village reservoir. [Photograph, 1985]

also stop the draining of spiritual essence from the village. Evidence for this, many believe, can be seen in the steady increase in the village's population since 1949, from about 400 to over 1,000 today. Even the Lins, whose women became sterile after the geomantic damage, today produce healthy, multiple sons.

For its residents, Lincun village constitutes their most intimate physical, social, and spiritual environment. They build and own houses here that provide warmth, protection, and a sense of belonging. They farm the land for the grain and vegetables that are the staples of their diet. Most village children attend the village elementary school up to fifth grade for their formal education.

Adolescents who dislike farming or, more likely, who simply cannot find enough work to do on the farm take jobs working in one of the dozen or so village manufacturing facilities as wage laborers. There, they will meet and date the opposite sex, and ultimately they will marry. Newlyweds first reside with the groom's family for a while and later on move out to build their own house. The circle of life repeats itself through these mundane events that provide meaning and excitement for the village as a community.

From an anthropological viewpoint, on yet another dimension the Chinese village is a body of cultural knowledge to be transmitted from one generation to the next. Perhaps it is unfashionable to use the term "little tradition" now to describe folk customs and beliefs in contrast to the high culture and philosophical tradition of the Chinese elite. Lin village's "local knowledge," to borrow the term from Geertz (1983), includes not only the oral history that depicts the origin and development of the community, but also the cosmological beliefs that provide meanings to behavior and form to habitat.

I am grateful for the support of the National Science Foundation (BNS-8317637) as well as a fellowship from the Committee on Scholarly Communication with the People's Republic of China during the 1984–85 academic year and sabbatical support from Iowa State University during the fall semester of 1985. The support of Dr. Gerald Klonglan, then anthropology department chair at Iowa State, and Dr. George Christensen, then vice-president for academic affairs, is appreciated.

CHAPTER 17

Fengjiacun Village, Shandong
A Corporate Community

STEWART ODEND'HAL

FORMING a peninsula that juts between the Huanghai and Bohai seas off the east coast of China, Shandong province is mountainous in the central and eastern sections, with vast flat lands wrapping the massif. Once Shandong was an island, but over millennia the extraordinary deposition of the Huanghe river has layered its perimeter with tons of alluvial sediment, forming a low and gentle terrain that has become part of the North China Plain—which covers more than 300,000 square kilometers of China's "good earth."

The northern region of the province occupies a portion of the delta of the Huanghe, and it is here that Fengjiacun village is located. Since the third millennium B.C., the alluvial plains of the Huanghe have been densely populated in spite of the floods, drought, soil alkalinization, and waterlogging that have been plagues to agriculture here. The capricious Huanghe itself has forced countless periodic out-migrations from the region. Yet, as George B. Cressey reminded us, the people continue to "dominate the geography" (1955, 270). Village settlements as well as large cities crowd the coastal and low areas of the province. Although Shandong is the third most populated province of China, it has a population density 2.7 times that of China's most populous province, Sichuan.

Fengjiacun means "the village *(cun)* of the Feng (surname) family *(jia)*." Over 70 percent of the 295 families residing in the village in 1989 had the last name Feng. With a population of 1,165 people, the basic population structure of the village cumulatively reflects the disaster of the Great Leap Forward and the natural catastrophes that occurred between 1960 and 1962 (Ashton et al. 1984). The institution of the one couple, one child policy in 1979 may have led to a curious sex imbalance of many more males than females in certain age cohorts (Odend'hal 1989b). Between 1987 and 1989, the annual growth rate of the village was less than 1 percent. Although the population is not expanding rapidly, the village is able to retain substantial cohesion based on strong familial ties.

Located some 35 kilometers south of the Huanghe and 80 kilometers from the provincial

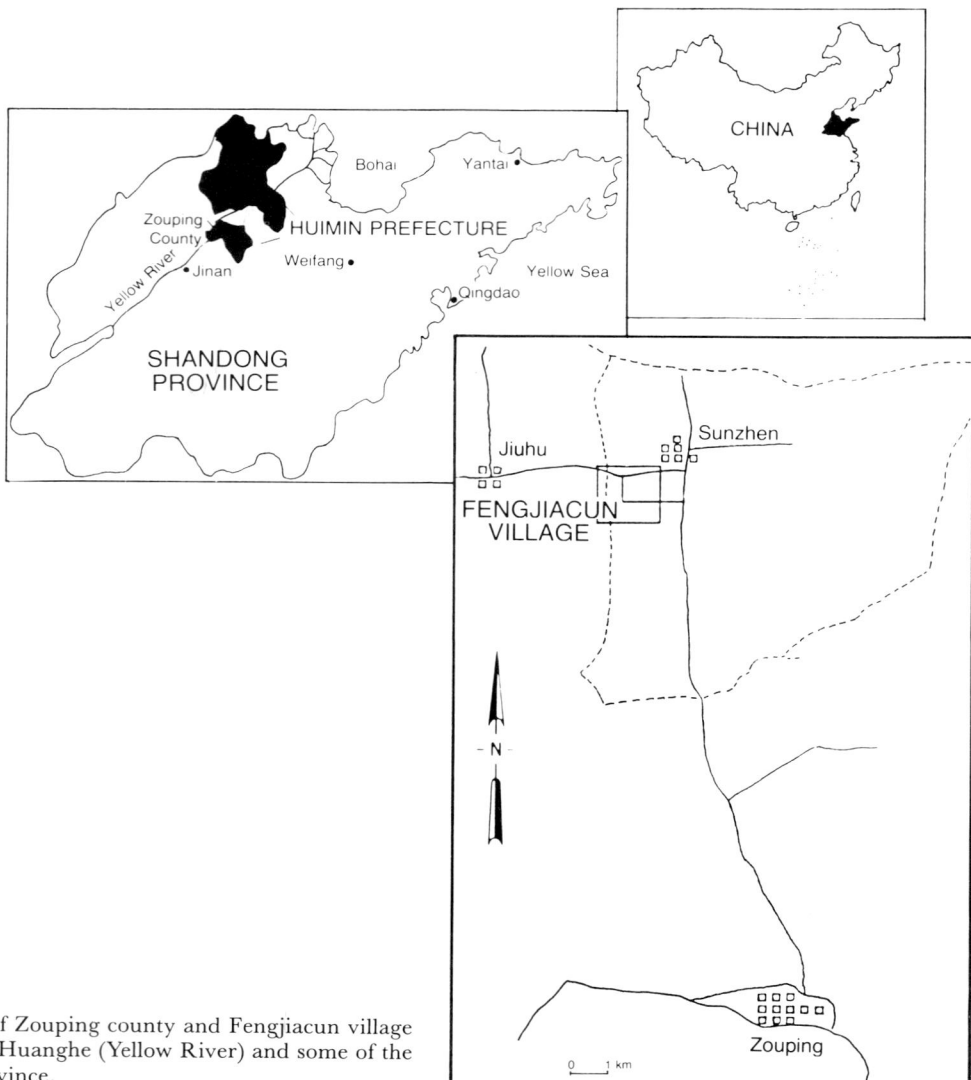

Figure 17.1. The locations of Zouping county and Fengjiacun village are shown in relation to the Huanghe (Yellow River) and some of the major cities of Shandong province.

capital, Jinan, Fengjiacun sits on a site that eons ago was either an inland sea or a lake bed, as the discovery of shells suggests. Even today the water table is only 7 meters below the surface. Fengjiacun is in the center of the land under its control. Canals and ditches form almost a complete border around the village, separating it from the land under the control of adjacent villages. Drought has not been a problem in recent decades. An irrigation canal, begun in 1958 and completed in 1974, brings water to the borders of the village from the Xiaoxing River, some 4 to 5 kilometers to the north. As a result, the cultivated land today is one hundred percent irrigated, supplementing the relatively meager average annual rainfall, which varies between 450 and 600 millimeters.

Fengjiacun's principal crops are wheat, corn, and cotton. Beans, peanuts, and a variety of vegetables are also grown. The wheat and corn are grown on the same land, using what is known as "relay planting." The corn is sown before the wheat ripens in June so that there will be enough growing time for the corn to mature before the fall frost. Approximately 1,200 *mu* are usually planted in wheat and corn and over 1,000 *mu* in cotton. Near the village are an apple orchard and several vegetable patches as well as two greenhouses. Trees are grown along the major roads and pathways of the land area under the village's control.

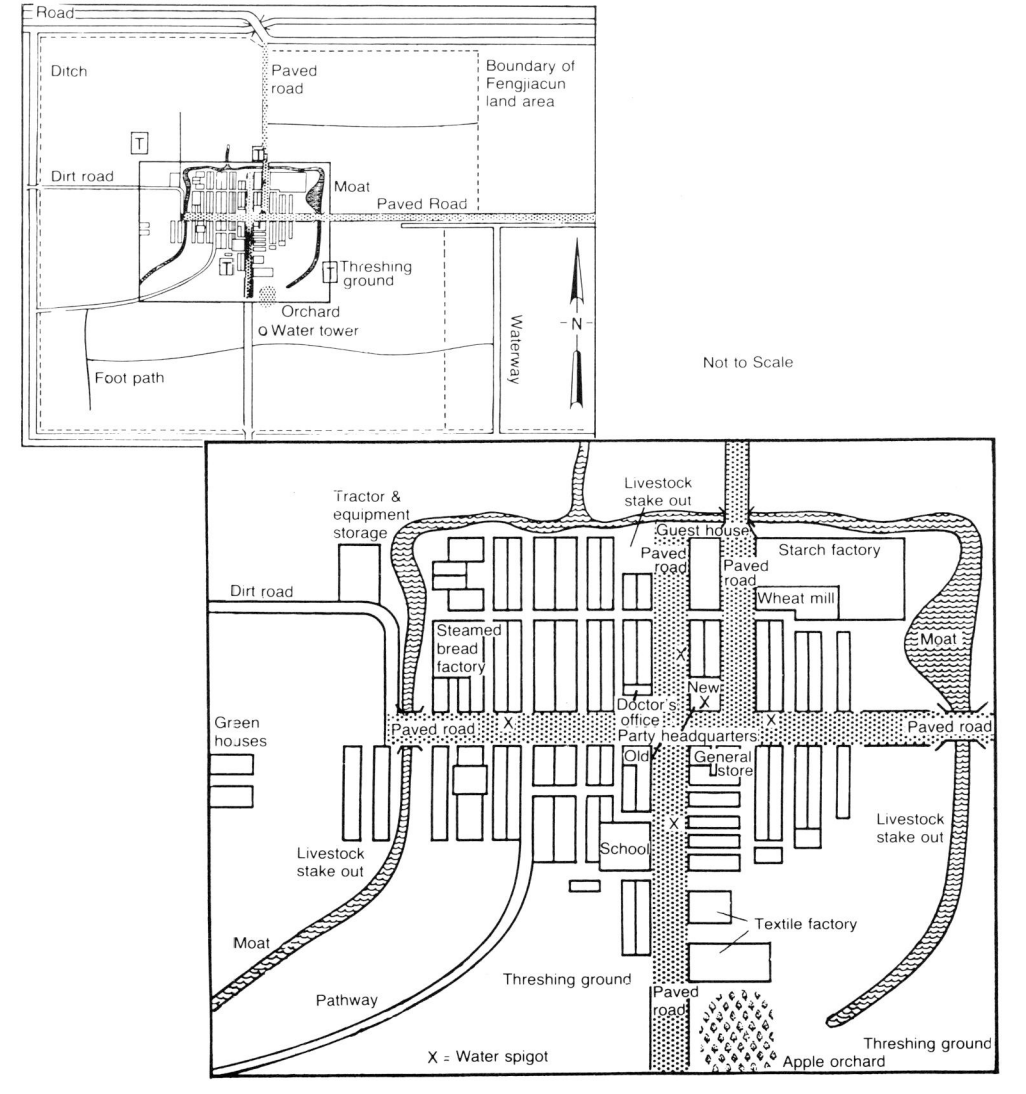

Figure 17.2. Fengjiacun village map, with inset.

Each household has responsibility for several plots of land. The land is fractionated so that one family has both good land and less desirable land; no one has all good land. This fractionation of family fields existed in the rural areas of Shandong well before 1949 (Yang 1945, 14–16).

Paved roads head east and north from Fengjiacun, and dirt roads lead west and south. Threshing grounds just outside the village are often cluttered with large stacks of wheat straw as well as corn and cotton stalks. The corn stalks are chopped up and transported to the courtyards to use as animal feed. This economical practice of feeding draft animals from the available crop residues has gone on for centuries in north China (Gamble 1954, 79). The cotton stalks, however, are used as cooking fuel. Although some wheat straw was said to be transported to a paper mill, there seems to be a problem regarding what to do with the bulk of it.

To serve the villagers' needs for water, Fengjiacun depends on an electrically powered well, which is 380 meters deep, and a water tower to supply water to six taps placed throughout the village. The water is very alkaline, and it is impossible to disguise the salty taste. Curiously, when one takes a bath using village water, it seems impossible to get dry; it always feels like there is a thin film of fluid on the surface of one's skin.

The moat that surrounds the village is not connected to the irrigation ditches. It was constructed during the 1940s to protect the village against the Communist threat of the time. Except for two blocks of houses and an equipment storage unit on the west side of town, most all of the buildings of the village are inside the moat. People wash their clothes and dishes in the moat on the west and north sides. Ducks and geese can be seen using the moat there also. The eastern side of the moat is not frequented, because it is heavily polluted by effluent from the starch factory. The immediate area near the eastern moat emits a very unpleasant smell. There are bridges over the moat on the east, north, and west sides.

Fengjiacun has good all-weather roads leading to township and county markets. The village itself is bisected by a paved east-west street that connects directly with the paved road leading to the major highway system for the county. The dirt road from the south becomes paved in the village, and this wide road forms an expansive open paved area where it crosses the main east-west street at the center of the village. Here, the doctor's office, the general store, and the party headquarters all face each other in this area. In addition, crops are dried at harvest time, announcements are posted, and collectively purchased materials are distributed to villagers at this important village junction.

With few exceptions, most of the other streets of the village are narrow lanes wide enough only for an animal cart to pass. One lane that bisects the northern half of the village is frequently filled

Figure 17.3. The main road that enters Fengjiacun from the east. The public water tap, on the left, is one of six in the village.

Figure 17.4. Fengjiacun's moat, which borders the village on three sides, freezes over in the winter.

Figure 17.5. Fengjiacun's village center. The doctor's office opens onto the area where cotton is being dried. The two-story building in the background is the party headquarters compound.

Figure 17.6. A typical narrow north-south running lane in Fengjiacun. Courtyards are entered through the doorways on both sides. Corn cobs are piled on the left and corn stalks lean against the walls.

with staked out draft animals. Groups of old men and old women gather separately, but not too far from each other. They swap stories among themselves and share the care of grandchildren periodically between the two groups as they sun themselves. During the rainy season, neighbors will gather in the lanes to pass the time of day in between the periodic showers.

The largest structure in the village is the starch factory in the northeast corner. It accounts for the most income and also for the pungent, unpleasant aroma that permeates the eastern side of town. Employing seventy people, the factory is operated twenty-four hours a day. The newest factory is the textile factory located on the southern edge of town, with seventy employees and an around-the-clock schedule. In 1989, the popsicle factory operated during the summer season, with out-of-town vendors lining up early in the morning. By the

Figure 17.7. Cattle are staked here along one of the east-west lanes that bisect the northern half of Fengjiacun. Cotton stalks are stored on the roof in the right foreground.

Figure 17.8. The old men of Fengjiacun gather along a lane to sun themselves and chat. Older women in the village gather a few yards down the lane.

Figure 17.9. Neighboring familes—men, women, and children—congregate outside their gates in the narrow lanes of Fengjiacun to catch up on local affairs.

summer of 1990, however, the popsicle factory had closed and its building had become part of the textile factory. Other less lucrative business enterprises include a steamed bread factory, a wheat mill, a general store, and two recently constructed greenhouses. Except for the starch and textile factories, which are managed by the village as a whole and thus resemble family businesses, the remaining enterprises are operated on a contractual basis.

The party headquarters building, located across from the general store and next to the open area that acts as the town square, has the only telephone and public toilet in town. Here also are meeting facilities, guest rooms, a washing machine, a television set, a kitchen, and a water spigot. Directly facing the open area is the doctor's office. Opposite is the old party headquarters building, which is now only used for storage.

The primary school, a two-story building with a large playground inside a walled compound, is located on the south side of the village, across the street from the textile factory. Athletic facilities here consist of a ping pong table as well as a basketball hoop and backboard. The middle school is in Sunzhen, the township seat a kilometer and a half away; the nearest high school is in Zouping county town, some 20 kilometers away.

Two guesthouses have been constructed to house the foreign visitors and dignitaries that come to the village during the summer months. These houses have indoor Western-style commodes, running cold and (at times) hot water, color television, and air conditioning. At other times of the year, guests are housed in rooms within the party headquarters building.

Housing units within the village are monotonously the same, built in a similar rectangular shape, of brick with tile roofs, and with a southerly orientation. Each unit consists of two or three nearly identical rooms off a courtyard. Rooms are dominated by either a large bed or a *kang* in one corner and a square table with two straight-backed chairs nearby. Most rooms include, in addition, one or two almirahs and two soft-cushioned chairs. Walls are usually decorated with pictures from calendars, and ceilings are left open to the rafters.

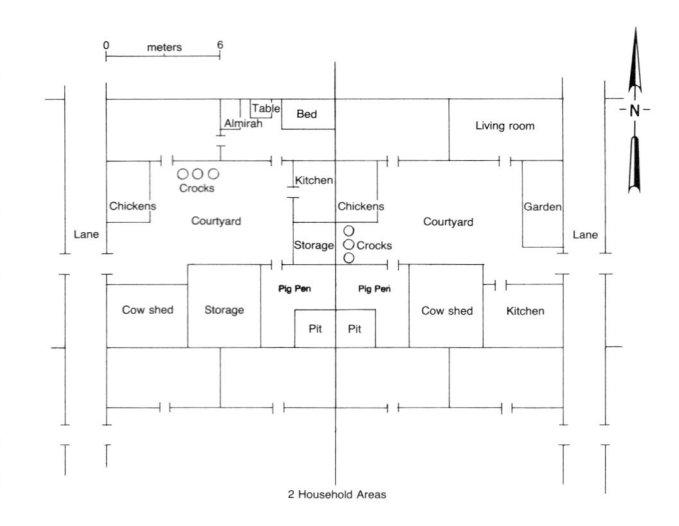

Most housing units were constructed during the 1980s, a boom time in Fengjiacun as in many other Chinese villages. Recently constructed housing includes fourteen units on the west side of town outside the moat, completed before 1987; four houses just within the moat on the northwest edge of the village, completed in 1988; and fourteen units just south of the school that were completed in early 1989. There is a plan to build additional housing units within the moat on the eastern side of town where draft animals are now staked out every day.

In addition to the main rooms that form the axis of each dwelling, there sometimes are additional rooms off the courtyard for various uses. Universally, there is a pigsty (with a pit) off every

Figure 17.11. A typical Fengjiacun living area with a ceiling open to the rafters. Sitting and eating areas are toward the front; the bed to the rear is enclosed by a mosquito net.

courtyard. This pit serves as the toilet for each household, and chamber pots are also emptied in the pit. Periodically throughout the year, each pit is cleaned out and the manure is spread onto the fields. Depending on the number of animals in the household, the pit may be cleaned out every two to three months.

The kitchen is always a separate room off the courtyard, with just enough room for the cook to sit in front of the box-shaped stove and operate the hand bellows from the side. The kitchen is usually filled with cotton stalks, the fuel for the stove. The demand for cotton stalks is reflected in the ubiquity of their storage throughout the village—on the rooftops, in the corner of every courtyard, and in large stacks bordering the threshing grounds.

In many households, a cow shed or draft animal quarters may be enclosed as a separate room

Figure 17.12. In the kitchen, a hand-operated push-pull-type bellows is used to stoke the fire. Cotton stalks, used in Fengjiacun for fuel, are piled high surrounding the stove.

or devised as a corner of the courtyard covered with a tin or thatched roof. Frequently, the cow shed is next to the pigsty, and a hole in the wall separates the two so that the fecal material produced by the draft animals can be shoveled into the pit daily. Each animal pen includes a concrete feed bunker to feed the animals.

Chickens, housed in assorted enclosures, are kept by at least 90 percent of the families of Fengjiacun. Ducks and geese are owned by only a few families and are not usually kept in distinct enclosures. They are allowed more free-ranging activities than chickens and are often found swimming in the moat.

The courtyards may be of concrete, brick, or dirt. Sometimes they are temporarily congested with harvested material. Many courtyards have a covered area where an animal cart is stored. There may be another room to store the chopped corn, which is the principal animal feed, as well. Some of the courtyards have small vegetable plots. Most families have large crocks in the courtyards where the pig food is stored. One of the main pig foods is a by-product of the starch factory.

There is a village in sight in every direction from the edge of Fengjiacun. Like Fengjiacun, most of these villages are similar in size and laid

Figure 17.13. A typical Fengjiacun courtyard during the fall harvest season. Corn cobs have been spread on the roof of the dwelling to dry, stacked on the window sills, and then piled up in preparation for storage. Just harvested cotton is tied in large bundles.

out in a gridiron fashion with intersecting paths and roads. Fengjiacun seems to be more affluent than most of them. Unlike Fengjiacun, whose dwellings are all of fired brick, some of the surrounding villages still have houses made of adobe and are in a state of disrepair. Some villages are not as clean as Fengjiacun, and the small business establishments are less well stocked.

Before the construction of the starch factory, most of Fengjiacun's income was derived from the production of raw agricultural crops. Now more than one half of the total annual income is derived from nonagricultural pursuits. Still, the basic pulse of the community continues to flow from the seasonal activities associated with agriculture. By some measures, the village appears to be even more of a farm village than it once was. In 1986, there were 155 draft animals cared for by a production team and kept in a few pens. On January 16, 1987, however, all of the draft animals were decollectivized. The pool of draft animals was sold to the highest bidders, and draft animals became private property overnight. Within a year, the number of draft animals in the village, including outside purchases of additional animals, more than doubled. By late 1989, about 65 percent of the households had their own work animals, penned or staked near the households throughout the village. It seems ironic that, despite China's desire to modernize agriculture, animal power has increased and the use of tractors has diminished in the fields (Nagarajan et al. 1985).

Dramatic changes have taken place in Fengjiacun in recent years: the institution of the responsibility system in agriculture, the construction and operation of the starch and textile factories, the development of contracts to manage previously owned village businesses, and the decollectivization of animals. Yet, Fengjiacun, like other surrounding villages, retains its inherited landscape, little affected by these changes in human lives.

My research in Fengjiacun was supported by the Committee on Scholarly Communication with the People's Republic of China.

CHAPTER 18

Dacaiyuan Village, Henan
Migration and Village Renewal

NANCY JERVIS

FROM the perspective of the road from Linxian town, in Linxian county, Henan province, Dacaiyuan village appears tiny and insignificant. If you were to drive fast along the blacktop, you might miss it altogether. Not only is it set relatively far back, but it is slightly sunken, the ground on which it stands being lower than the road. Most of the year it is almost hidden from view by the branches of trees. Only the small hill in back of it serves as a landmark reminding you where to look for the turnoff. Its hill notwithstanding, Dacaiyuan is considered one of the "flat villages" in the county, with a reasonably good, though not abundant, water supply and a relatively high population density.

About 3 kilometers out of Linxian town, a rutted dirt path jogs right and then continues along an irrigation ditch. Such paths become pools of mud after even a brief rainfall. At normally dry times, there is barely room for a jeep or a Shanghai brand car on such paths. After a rainfall, even the jeep has to stop on the main road. The bus, with frequent service to the city of Anyang or to Changzhi in neighboring Shanxi province, never stops here; you must catch it in the county town.

The road along the ditch takes you to the southwest corner of Dacaiyuan, where, on most ordinary days, a group of women can be seen washing clothes in the ditch. When I first arrived, they would stop their washing to stare at the strange foreigner on her way to or from town. Later, when I became more familiar, they would ask, "Chile meiyou?" ("Have you eaten?"), the polite greeting equivalent to "How are you?" "Chile" (yes, I have) I would reply, giving the polite reply regardless of whether I had or not.

Dacaiyuan (which means "Great Vegetable Garden" to contrast it with a nearby village called "Small Vegetable Garden") is divided into two halves, each of which in 1984 had three production teams with a combined population of approximately 1,800. The southern half, which is referred to as such *(nan bian)*, is closer to the Linxian county town. The northern half *(bei bian)* houses most of the public buildings: administrative offices, the health clinic, workshops, a meeting ground, and a small store. The two halves are connected by a narrow street, with private vegetable plots on one side and the village school on the other. Although you can walk from one end of the

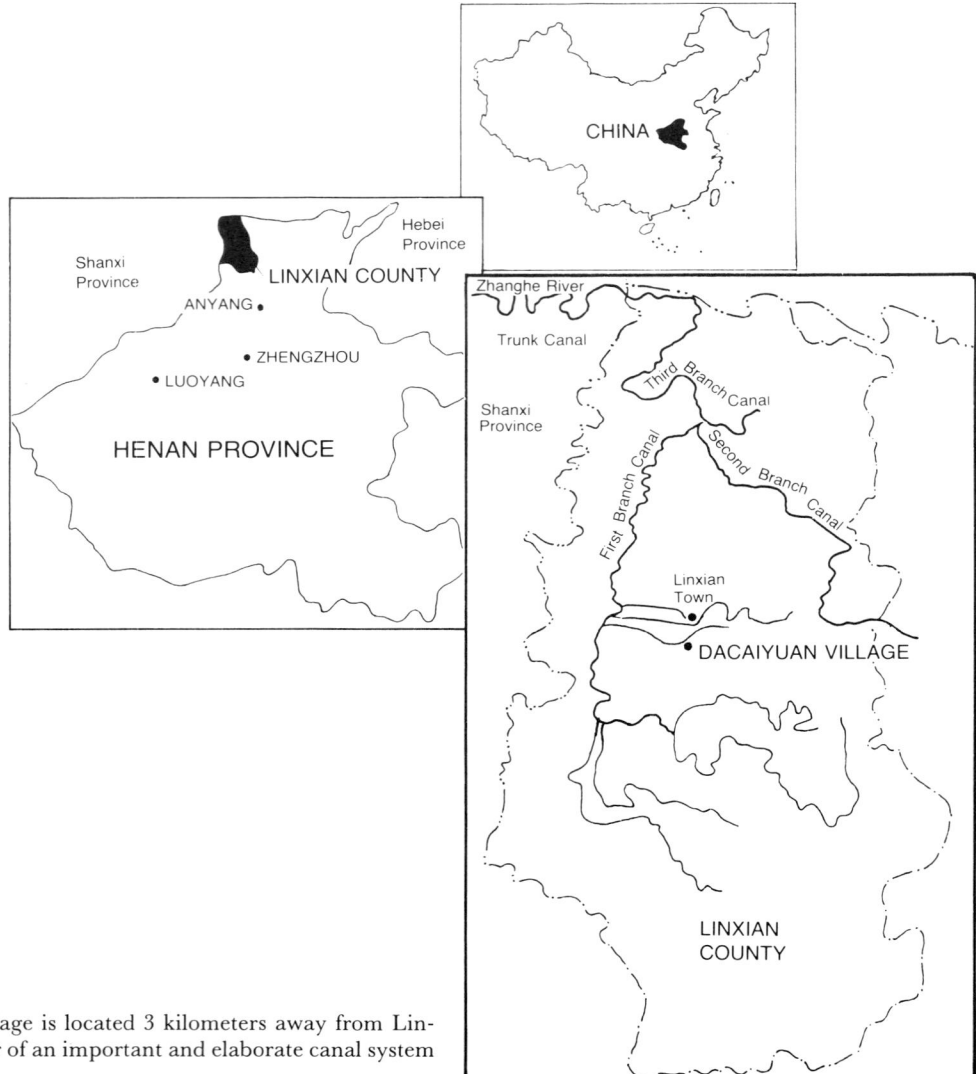

Figure 18.1. Dacaiyuan village is located 3 kilometers away from Linxian county town, the center of an important and elaborate canal system built during the 1960s.

village to the other in less than ten minutes, the north-south distinction is an important one. Only occasionally do people have personal business that might take them as far as the other half of the village.

Walking through its streets, one gets the impression that the village is squarely laid out. This impression, however, is deceptive, as narrow paths lead behind some compounds to the next ones, and smaller paths wind around the village, leading to yet another small neighborhood. Along the wider streets, there are piles of bricks, straw, cement beams, and other materials for houses soon to be built. Large willow and poplar trees,

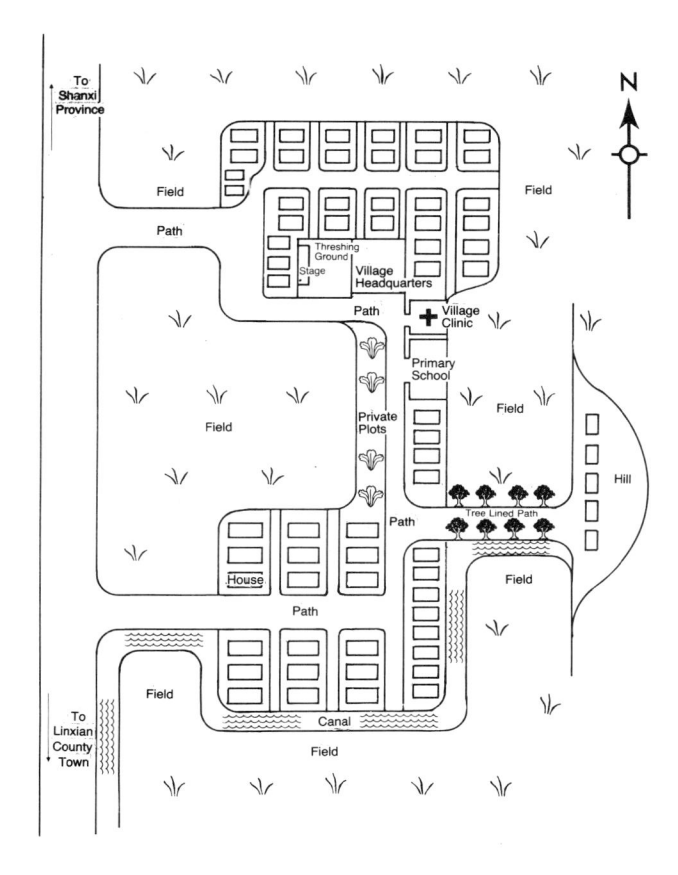

Figure 18.3. A corner of one of the paths that surrounds the village of Dacaiyuan. [Photograph, 1972]

their roots firmly planted in courtyards, protrude their branches over the walls, providing some shade to the paths.

Neighborhoods and houses in this compact village are tightly clustered. The walls of each family compound are contiguous, with gates that face inward toward village streets rather than outward toward the fields. The whitewashed courtyard walls give the whole village a walled appearance, adding to the feeling of a world within a world. Most of the living that goes on within these family compounds is thus hidden from public view.

The village on most days awakens slowly, in stages. The cock arises first, announcing the day before the light has come. Women are the next ones up, stepping out into the family's courtyard to light the charcoal stove and prepare breakfast. The noise picks up after 7:00 A.M. By then, everyone is up, the men getting ready to work and the children to go to school. At about 11:00, the streets are quiet again: The women are indoors cooking, the children are still at school, and everyone else is busy. Activity reappears at the noon mealtime. On a pleasant day, people take their bowls of food and eat outside the house, squatting on their haunches or sitting on a doorstep. Several old women or men may gather at a corner or at the doorway of a large family compound, exchanging gossip or eating quietly together. At around 6:00 P.M., everyone returns: the children from school, those who work from their jobs, the women from their chores. Supper is eaten late, as darkness falls, when everyone has gathered. Later, the streets will become busy again, as evening is the best time for seeing a neighbor on business or visiting a friend. By about 10:00 or 11:00, the village becomes quiet again, as people settle in for the night.

In the rhythms of its daily life, its walled compounds, and its dusty streets, Dacaiyuan is not unlike many other north China villages. As in

Figure 18.4. With the Taihang Mountains in the background, a lane leads into the village of Dacaiyuan. The writing on the wall on the right reads, "Long live the Chinese Communist Party." The lane jogs to accommodate a village well. [Photograph, 1972]

Figure 18.5. A typical village lane in Dacaiyuan with high whitewashed walls. Entry to family courtyards where most village life takes place is through the doorways. [Photograph, 1972]

Figure 18.6. A corner of a family courtyard. The stone slab stand holds a washbasin. In the 1980s in Dacaiyuan, water was still drawn from a well and stored in large vats in each courtyard, from which it was ladled into pots and washbasins. [Photograph, 1972]

other parts of north China, people eat the wheat, corn, and millet they grow themselves as staple crops. But agriculture has begun to lose its place as the economic mainstay of the village. Although Dacaiyuan produces an agricultural surplus, since the 1980s it has become primarily reliant on income earned by its mostly male members from work performed outside the village. Dacaiyuan's location in the remote northwestern corner of Henan province coupled with the reforms of the last decade have produced a pattern of life that increasingly challenges the insularity of both the village economy and village society.

Linxian, or Lin county, in which the village of Dacaiyuan is situated, is geographically separate and ecologically rather different from the low-lying plain of the rest of Anyang district in which it is located. The Taihang mountain range forms a backdrop in the distance, as the Red Flag Canal —an enormous irrigation project initiated during the Great Leap Forward and made famous during the Cultural Revolution—winds its way through the lower plains. Villages and terraced fields are

Figure 18.7. A wall of the central room of a Dacaiyuan dwelling in 1972. A portrait of Chairman Mao occupies the position traditionally used for the ancestors. Occasionally, mirrors or ordinary pictures occupied the central place in this invariably symmetrical layout.

carved into the Taihangs' vertical slopes, where occasionally the sight of open holes in the hillsides next to a village reminds one that these caves were once inhabited.

Linxian's relatively remote and rocky setting has had a major impact on the lives of its people. Even its "stories of origin," recorded in the

Figure 18.8. A portion of Red Flag Canal in 1972. In addition to irrigation water, the completion of this canal brought hydroelectric power to the Linxian area as well. The canal was built primarily by human labor, which was supplied on a corvée-type system by each village.

county gazetteer, reflect the importance of geography. *Lin* means "forest" in Chinese. Early accounts describe the region as heavily wooded, and perhaps this characteristic accounts not only for the county's name but also for the carpentry skills of villages, although the area is denuded today.

In yet another version of the county's origins, the present residents of Linxian are descendants of people who crossed over from Shandong province to the northeast and Shanxi province to the northwest. This claim perhaps reflects the prevailing pattern of trade and migration between Linxian and neighboring counties across the Taihang range. According to this story, Linxian was resettled by decree after a famine had depopulated the county. It is said that there is still a village in neighboring Shanxi called Lin village, from which Linxian's people are supposed to have migrated. But the gazetteer refers to this process in reverse: the people of Linxian migrated out in search of more land, thereby populating southern Shanxi. Whichever is correct, and probably both migrations occurred at different times, the stories of origin emphasize the local pattern of famine, depopulation, and migration. Taken together with the denuding of the landscape centuries ago, it is a pattern largely, though not exclusively, dictated by physical geography.

Linxian's location—remote from the administrative center of the province, yet near the borders of Shanxi, Hebei, and Shandong—made it relatively easy for people to flee when times were hard. Sometimes whole families were forced to migrate. Running away to avoid taxation is a traditional escape for families fallen on hard times, and this response continues in Linxian up to today. In 1981, in fact, a family with a fourth, unauthorized child fled the increased financial penalties for violating the birth control policy.

Although poverty often forced whole families to flee, by far the more common pattern was for individual men to leave their natal villages in search of employment in other cities and towns. Both cultural and regional factors contributed to migration as a likely response to poverty. The cultural practice of dividing up a family's property among the male heirs *(fen jia)* combined with the ever decreasing size of already small plots of dry and rocky soil made it imperative that in families with several male heirs, some leave. Sometimes these men returned; often they were never heard from again. For without land or wealth, it was virtually impossible for a man to obtain a bride and begin a family.

The land tenure system also contributed to the evolution of a pattern of temporary, or circular, migration, where men left for varying periods of time but always returned home. By the 1920s, the local practice—common throughout north China—of combining small peasant freeholding with tenancy meant that many peasant wives, in spite of strong cultural injunctions against it, remained at home tilling the fields while their husbands left to find work outside the village to pay the fixed village land rents to local landlords (Thaxton 1981, 12).

Men who migrated went wherever they could find work. Traditionally, this migration was westward, over the Taihang Mountains to Changzhi, the nearest large town in Shanxi, rather than to the provincial centers of Anyang or Zhengzhou. The existence of a relatively good highway connecting Linxian and Changzhi has ensured that this traditional pattern of exchange of populations would survive into the present. Many village families have sons or brothers who work in Changzhi's factories in state or temporary jobs.

But by far the most predominant form of circular migration in Dacaiyuan is to the large cities of Beijing, Tianjin, and even Urumchi in the far northwest. The prevailing attitude has been that able-bodied men ought to bring in large sums of cash in some kind of job other than agriculture. Women listed this ability as essential in a prospective husband. In my survey of 61 households in one "team" or neighborhood in Dacaiyuan, 16 men had spent most of 1981 working on construction projects in the large cities. Although no formal survey was conducted after 1982, my sense from repeated visits through the mid-1980s is that this number increased each year.

Construction work in China's large cities was the most likely choice as an "outside" occupation for several reasons. First, employment options remain very limited throughout China and most particularly in rural China because of a still underdeveloped market economy. Second, the regional geography—Dacaiyuan's location in the Taihang foothills—has forced people to become adept at manipulating a rocky environment, and stonemasonry, for example, is an important skill. But perhaps most important in the development of skills in the building trades has been the necessity—at least in the past, because they were so easily eroded—to build and rebuild rural homes every twenty to thirty years. For these reasons together with the need to expand houses to accommodate married sons and the custom of helping neighbors and relatives to build and rebuild, most men in Dacaiyuan have considerable experience in carpentry, bricklaying, stonemasonry, and other construction skills.

For the twenty-year period of the people's communes, from 1958 to the beginning of the 1980s, however, all forms of migration were halted in Dacaiyuan as they were throughout China. For those villages that had never relied on migration to supplement income or to solve problems of extreme poverty, perhaps this feature of the commune era was less significant. In Dacaiyuan and throughout Linxian county, the inability of peasants to leave, even temporarily, exacerbated the economic difficulties of the commune era, clearly affecting the village environment itself.

During the commune period, peasants remained locked up in their villages (then called "brigades" and "teams") because of an "official residence policy" *(hukou)* that actually began in 1949, right after Liberation. Originally conceived to prevent peasants from flooding the cities, over the years *hukou* became a rigid collection of rules determining an individual's rights of travel and residence.

The reasons for the increasingly rigid *hukou* system were cultural and historical as well as economic and political. Briefly stated, the *hukou* system evolved from a system of administrative control that dynastic rulers had earlier imposed on the rural populace in order to tax and control them. During the commune period, when grain production and labor power were strongly emphasized, the *hukou* system was in full force, and it became extremely difficult for peasants to get permission to leave their villages.

The household responsibility system that was introduced in 1978 was a collection of rural reforms that have been implemented differently and have consequently had different impacts, varying by locale throughout China. In Linxian and Dacaiyuan, as elsewhere in China, land was divided and collective plots became family plots.

But people in Linxian have always said that "a gift of land is no gift," because farming Linxian's dry soil yields a meager existence at best. Rather, it was another part of the reform "package"—the loosening of *hukou* restrictions—that has had the major effect on life in Dacaiyuan. Although formal migration still has to be officially approved, temporary rural-to-urban migration to the construction sites and other job markets of China's large cities has been a de facto result of the reforms.

"Going out" to work—which is how local people refer to circular migration—is a different experience for men today than it was in the 1930s or 1940s. The commune era, far from being erased, has left its imprint on the way work is organized in Dacaiyuan. Although individual men make the decision to migrate, the projects they will be involved in are organized collectively by the village, formerly the "brigade." In a sense, the village has taken on the role of labor contrac-

Figure 18.9. A family in Dacaiyuan weighing in its share of the wheat harvest after partial decollectivization in 1982.

tor. Arrangements with urban *danwei* (work units) in major cities are negotiated by village contractors, who guarantee both labor and materials for large projects. Usually, a management fee of 10 percent of the total contract paid to individual contractors is turned over to the village. This management fee, and often whatever can be skimmed off the purchase price of materials, is supposed to be used for local projects: a school, a local workshop, a social project, something to benefit the whole village.

Individual families could also accumulate a great deal of cash through the temporary migration of male members. The average migrant wage in the early 1980s was 7 to 10 *yuan* per day for an unskilled worker, or about 250 *yuan* per month, well above the average salary of a factory worker or cadre at that time. Skilled journeymen could make considerably more. Although households were supposed to contribute some of their earnings (2.60 *yuan* per day) to the village, most did not pay the fee and kept the entire amount. How families chose to spend this new cash income reveals much about how a seeming exodus actually worked to reinforce village and family solidarity.

Anthropologist Eric Wolf, in a short but very significant book, described a "ceremonial" fund that peasants must spend on important rituals, reflecting their participation in social life (1966, 7). With religion and ritual less apparent in the countryside of the People's Republic of China than in other peasant societies, it makes sense to term a "cultural" fund that fund from which individual households were required to draw in order to remain full participants in village life. In Dacaiyuan, money from this "cultural" fund was spent for weddings, funerals, and house building.

Weddings, a prime example of "cultural" spending, cost 1,000 to 1,500 *yuan* in 1982. At a minimum, modern-styled light-colored wooden

Figure 18.10. Part of a Dacaiyuan wedding procession bringing the bride to the groom's home, where she will live. Firecrackers celebrate her arrival and announce to all in the village that she has arrived and the feast will begin shortly.

furniture, *beizi* (cotton quilts), as well as bolts of cloth and clothing had to be readied beforehand and prominently displayed at the wedding. By the mid-1980s, the cost of getting married had risen considerably, and the requisite items included many consumer goods that could not be made locally, such as bicycles, radios, and watches. These items as well as the wedding feast are all paid for by the groom's family, which also organizes the procession that brings the bride to her new home. When a son was planning to marry, he and his father and perhaps a brother would most likely hire themselves out on one of the village-run construction projects.

Also drawn from the accumulation in the "cultural" fund were funds needed for funerals. Although a household could not "plan" for a funeral in the way they planned for a wedding, the requirements of the event had the effect of drawing the family increasingly into contact with the national economy. Necessary items included the purchase of a casket and fine silk burial clothes as

Figure 18.11. A *suona* and a *sheng* being played at a funeral in Dacaiyuan. The band is one of two that were hired by the mourning family. The more bands hired, the louder each was supposed to play, and the more the family had to pay each band.

well as the hiring of mourners and one or more traditional music bands usually brought in from Anyang.

By far the largest share of the cash income derived from the pattern of circular migration went for house building. Although building a new house may be a necessary part of survival, it was also a major life-cycle event in Dacaiyuan. Signs of its importance included the red material tied to door frames on a house being built, the *mantou* (steamed bread) buried in the foundation under the hearth, and the firecrackers that were lit as particular stages of construction were completed. If you asked the men of Dacaiyuan why they were not only willing but even eager to stay away from home for so many hard months, their ready answer would be that they were getting the money to finance the building of a house—the single greatest expense a family would incur.

Until the introduction of the responsibility system, there was not much house construction in Dacaiyuan village. Houses are private property, but the land they occupy is not, and permission must be obtained before building. During the commune period, county policy prohibited new house construction, except for a brief period between 1972 and 1974, when approximately twenty houses per year were permitted to be constructed. Concurrently, however, an ever-expanding village population, an increasingly earlier division of families brought about by married sons, and strict residence requirements all combined to increase demand. The backlog of housing requests created by increased demand probably prompted the village cadres to construct the unused cave dwellings in Dacaiyuan's backyard hill in 1975. By 1978, demand for housing had been bottled up for so long that it exploded in a veritable orgy of building.

Between 1979 and 1982, there was a 25 percent increase in "new housing starts" in Dacaiyuan. Sixty families in the village received permission to build, out of a total of 100 who had applied. In fact, the entire village resembled a construction

Figure 18.12. In the rear is Dacaiyuan's former village stage for opera, films, and other events. The space in front has been used also as a playing field, but here in 1982 it is shown being used as a storage space for house-building materials.

Figure 18.13. With the increase of house building in the early 1980s, the limits of the residential area of Dacaiyuan expanded onto land formerly used for growing crops. [Photograph, 1982]

site in the early 1980s. The already narrow streets had become even narrower, lined with building materials. Piles of bricks for walls and stones for foundations were piled up, and even the mixing and pouring of steel-reinforced cement beams often took place right out in the streets. Men carting wheelbarrows relayed back and forth, and the sound of dynamite blasting rocks out of the hillside went on all day and sometimes into the night.

Housing costs varied considerably. The cheapest house, built by the poorest member of the village, cost about 800 *yuan,* and the most expensive about 5,000 *yuan* in the early 1980s, with the cost of the average house about 3,000 *yuan.* Differences in cost are largely explained by choice of building materials. Houses with wooden beams, instead of steel-reinforced concrete, cost more. The lion's share of the building costs were earned and saved by the migrant workers during their contracted labor away from home. Much of the labor cost of the construction of the houses was covered by enlisting the help of relatives and friends on a labor exchange basis. Since the early 1980s, costs have risen dramatically, and they are at least double their 1980 value today.

Migration, as the pattern unfolded in Dacaiyuan, has tended to reinforce rather than loosen the roots of the village community. Because it is circular, it has not drawn away permanent residents. Rather, because the earnings return to the village and are spent either on village-organized projects or on family events such as house construction, weddings, or funerals, migration actually strengthens the family-village bond.

But the expansion of population and the neverending demand for house building are also creat-

Figure 18.14. A view of the Buddhist temple on the prominent hill on the east side of Dacaiyuan. [Photograph, 1972]

ing a problem that challenges not only the present inhabitants of Dacaiyuan but also future generations: the shrinking size of arable land available for farming. The story of the small hill behind Dacaiyuan—the landmark of the village—probably best illustrates both the desire for change and the resistance to it.

The hill has gone through several transformations in recent decades. In the more distant past, it was the site of a Buddhist temple. The Cultural Revolution closed the temple and the monks were dispersed. In 1972, when I first visited the village, the old temple buildings were still standing, but they were in the midst of being converted into a junior middle school In 1975, toward the end of the Cultural Revolution, the village leadership decided to raze the village and move its people to the cavelike dwellings, modeled after Dazhai, in order to gain more land for farming. So by 1981, when I next returned, all the old temple buildings were gone, and the top of the hill had been flattened out and brick cave houses dug into its front. But no one was willing to move. Everyone preferred the plain to the hill and the traditional walled courtyards to life in a cave.

One year later, in 1982, these original temple grounds had been turned into a construction site. The hill was now some meters shorter, as villagers blasted into its sides for rocks and gravel to build their own new but still traditional-style houses. By 1983, the hill was sold to a provincial cement factory, and the former cave houses were being remodeled by Dacaiyuan peasants, contracted for the project as part of the deal between the village and the cement factory.

When Mao Zedong retold the famous fable "The Foolish Old Man Who Removed the Mountain," he was surely imagining a process different from the one that took place at the small hill in back of Dacaiyuan. And yet, perhaps not. For both Mao's story and the story of the village of Dacaiyuan reflect a common theme: the elimination of the walls of insularity that have surrounded Chinese villages for millennia.

Figure 18.15. In the early 1980s, the site of Dacaiyuan's former Buddhist temple was converted to housing for nearby factory workers. [Photograph, 1982]

This research was supported by a Columbia University Traveling Fellowship and a grant from the Wenner-Gren Foundation for Anthropological Research. I am also grateful for the guidance and encouragement of the late Professor Morton H. Fried and the editorial suggestions of Wenjun Xing.

CHAPTER 19

MaGaoqiao Village, Sichuan
Habitat in the Red Basin

STEPHEN ENDICOTT

Local people say the original name of the settlement was Ma'anqiao, "Horse Saddle Bridge," from a twin-arched structure that spanned the converging Yellow Ox and Bridle Path rivers. The name changed to MaGaoqiao during the Qing dynasty (1644–1911), according to local lore, when a magistrate on an inspection tour of newly repaired bridges happened to see a boisterous wedding party crossing over. Thinking this coincidence a good omen, he declared on an impulse, "A new couple crosses over a new bridge," and renamed the bridge after the surnames of the families of the bride and groom, Ma and Gao.

MaGaoqiao village occupies 130 hectares of gently sloping land on the northern edge of the Western Sichuan plain. Its land is bisected in one direction by the eastward flowing People's Canal, part of a vast provincial irrigation project of the 1950s that eliminated the Yellow Ox and Bridle Path rivers, and in the other direction by a county railway and the main asphalt-topped highway built in the 1960s. To the north, distant on the horizon, tower the Longmenshan, the Dragon Gate Mountains. These snow-crested peaks, shrouded in mist and fog most of the year, store the glacial waters that feed the Shiting River, one of several streams that have shaped the alluvial plain on which the farmers here have sown and reaped for over two thousand years. A half-hour walk to the south is the nearest market town, where villagers sell their products and stock up on household necessities. It is a tranquil world, a world where no outsider could guess the course of storms and upheavals, both geological and human, that underlie its history.

According to scientists, the fertile soil of the basin was formed in the Mesozoic era. At that time, as the earth's crust settled, great earthquakes threw up deposits of red sandstone and purple shale, creating a soil type that would crumble into reddish loam under farmers' heavy hoes. It is these soils that make the *tianfu*, the "land of plenty" or "granary of heaven," as the Chinese call the Red Basin of this famed inland province of Sichuan.

When viewed from the distance of the railway embankment, MaGaoqiao village seems to have a steady, ancient rhythm, a unity that can be understood and described. Children cut grass for pig

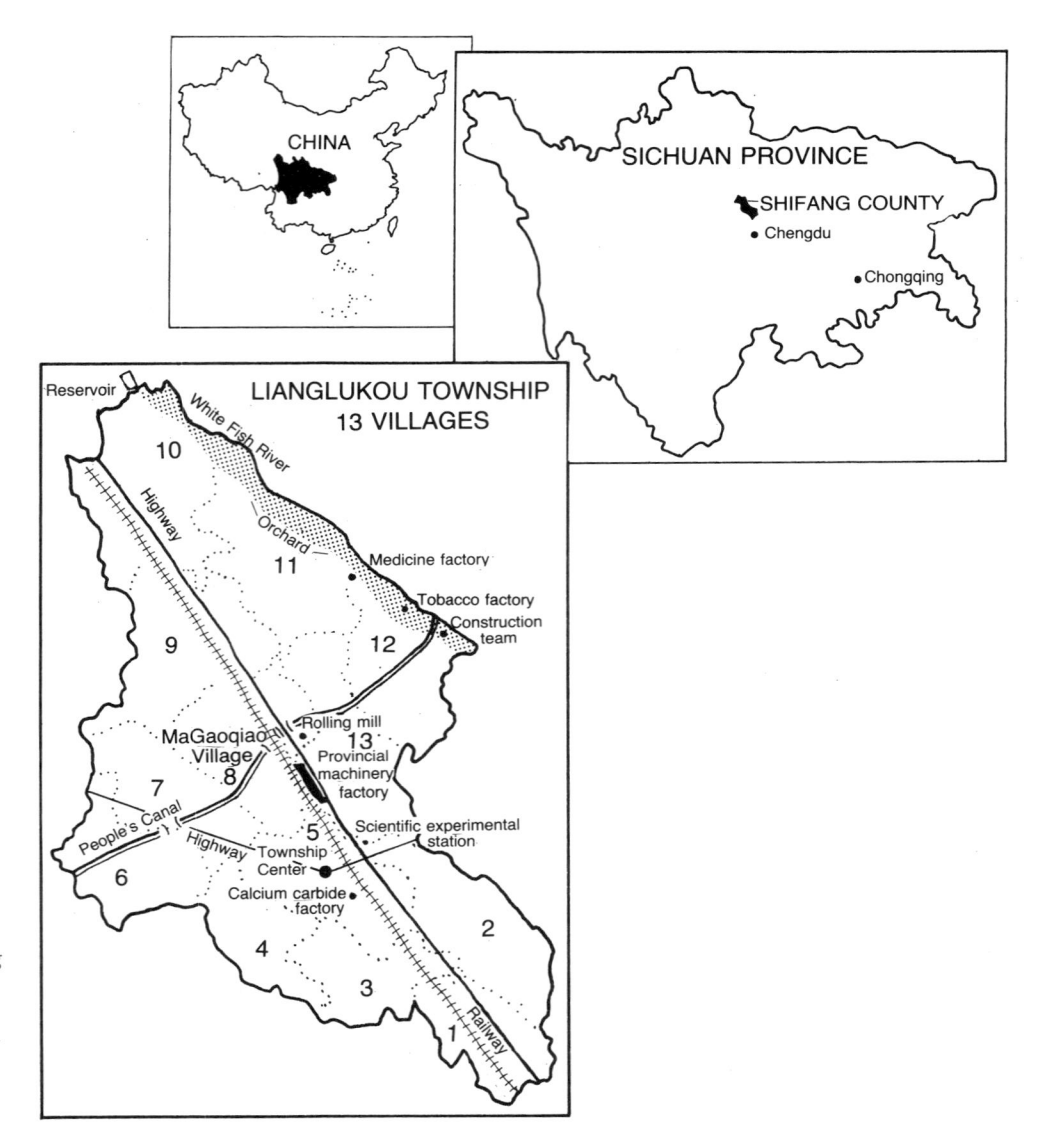

Figure 19.1. Shifang county, Sichuan province, embraces nineteen townships (formerly known as communes). Lianglukou ("Junction") township is 6 kilometers northwest of the Fangting county seat and contains thirteen villages (formerly brigades), of which MaGaoqiao is No. 8. [Adapted and redrawn from Endicott 1989, 69]

fodder, women chat as they wash clothes in a spring-fed stream, a blue-clad farmer with a wide straw hat guides the plow behind a slow-moving water buffalo, and a village tractor driver hauls in a load of coal. Narrow footpaths along the field edges act as connecting threads between the farmhouses, supplemented by bumpy, rutted tractor roads leading to the seven main centers of the village.

A feeling of physical dispersal pervades. Unlike the compact brown-walled villages of the North China Plain, with their network of lanes and roads, in Sichuan the rural population lives in scattered clusters of farmhouses called *yuanzi,* or

Figure 19.2. A general view of the large, reconstructed square fields surrounding MaGaoqiao, and in the distance one of the "island clusters" of village houses.

Figure 19.3. The main road into MaGaoqiao, suitable for driving tractors. The old school is on the left with the tiled roof of the village headquarters just beyond. [Photograph, 1981]

courtyards, that are shaded by bamboo groves or stands of eucalyptus. Typically four to six families live in one of these clusters, which might be termed "hamlets." At MaGaoqiao the forty or more leaf-hidden *yuanzi* appear to float in the surrounding paddy fields, small islands in a mirage of turquoise or light greens depending on the season. Without any main street, tower, tall building, or other distinguishing landmarks, it is hard to imagine that it is an integrated, organized community of 2,000.

Upon closer examination, it turns out that the village is divided into seven smaller groupings or hamlets. Under the Guomindang government prior to 1949, these were called *jia*, groups of ten households; since the Communists came to power, they have been "village groups," "production teams," and "cooperatives," depending on the changing central planning guidelines. The courtyards in these hamlets are linked together by proximity and by relationships of labor power, water supplies, and other matters vital to successful farm operations. During the period of the people's communes (1958 to 1982), production teams were the basic accounting unit of a three-tier structure of team, brigade, and commune corresponding here to the hamlet, village, and township, respectively. In 1982, after the summer harvest and following a national constitutional amendment adopted in Beijing that designated townships as the basic level of government organization, the villagers of MaGaoqiao gave up communal organizational forms and contracted the land out to individual families.

Memories go back twelve or thirteen generations at MaGaoqiao, to the fall of the Ming dynasty (1368–1644). At that time, the bloody suppression of a peasant rebellion in Sichuan decimated the native population; the land-hungry forebears of the present inhabitants trekked in from provinces in eastern China. The successful ones established new branches of their family clans, planted willow trees to mark out the boundary of their family holdings, and maintained shrines and ancestral graves.

At the time of the land reform, which occurred in MaGaoqiao in 1951, thirty-six families lived in No. 5 hamlet. They occupied nine separate courtyards and cultivated 435 *mu* (29 hectares) of land. Following a stormy political campaign to determine class status, three families fell into the "bad" landlord category (owning 250 *mu*), and fifteen families who owned no land could claim the "good" poor peasant class; in between were eighteen families of rich and middle peasants who together owned 185 *mu*. These class categories, as defined by the Central Committee of the Chinese Communist Party, replaced kinship ties in defining the political rights and social status among the villagers and remained strictly in force for the thirty years that followed.

Figure 19.4. Schematic map of No. 5 Hamlet at the center of MaGaoqiao village showing the scattered nature of the dwellings and the attention paid to building road and irrigation networks in recent years.

The land reform work team confiscated the properties of landlords and classified the land according to fertility. Each person was to have enough land to produce 500 *jin* (a *jin* is equal to 1.1 pounds or half a kilogram) of grain per year. A scientific land survey conducted by Shifang county years later determined that there were twelve distinct soil types at MaGaoqiao, but at the time of the land reform, the peasants counted only six different grades. They divided the land into 1.1 *mu* of class 1-A land, 1.2 *mu* of class 1-B, and so on to 1.6 *mu* of class 3-B. Every man, woman, and child, including members of the landlord families, received an equal share. In addition, the poor peasants kept control of 93 *mu* as a public reserve for future population growth. The distributive justice entailed in the land reform became the lasting basis of Mao Zedong's popularity and the grounds of legitimacy for the rule of the Communist Party in the hearts of the villagers in spite of many hardships that lay ahead.

By 1949, the Liao family in No. 5 Hamlet had become one of the most powerful clans in the village, with large landholdings and buildings to which others could only aspire. The dragon gate of their compound faced east in honor of their ancestors. A 2.5 meter wall, made of sun-dried bricks and plastered over, wound its way around the complex. At the back on the southwest corner was a fortified tower higher than the bamboo groves, about 9 meters to the top. The walls of the tower were nearly a meter thick and had gun portholes on all sides; it was a place of refuge for the landlord and his family in case the compound was broken into, and it served on occasion as a jail.

Inside the compound, the single-storied brick and tile living rooms, kitchens, and bedrooms formed around open spaces. The privy, thatched storage sheds for farm tools, as well as pens for the buffalo, pigs, and poultry were crowded against each other in a section of the compound. The open spaces had flower pots and small fish ponds, and could be used for sunning grain during fine weather. Large, gnarled willow trees surrounded the buildings. The burial ground, outside the compound on the west side in an extensive bam-

Figure 19.5. A view of widow Liao's *yuanzi*, a compound of traditional pounded-earth and thatched-roof housing in MaGaoqiao. [Photograph, 1981]

boo grove near the tower, had magnificent graves with stone facings and carved headstones. All these—graves, walls, tower, and eventually the trees as well—would be leveled to the ground when communization came in the Great Leap Forward of 1958. Former landlord Liao and his wife moved into one of the pounded-mud, thatched-roofed houses of the former tenants that clustered around their compound; their residence became in 1958 the headquarters of the Eighth Brigade of the newly formed people's commune in Lianglukou township, with some of the rooms becoming a primary school and a medical clinic.

A temperate climate and the agricultural cycle determine the rhythm of village life and culminate in three harvests each year. The smaller spring harvest is in April–May, when the wheat and rape crops planted in November ripen; the summer harvest of sun-cured tobacco takes place in July, and the all-important paddy rice crop is gathered in late August and September. Subsidiary crops in this area include medicinal herbs, potatoes, sweet potatoes, soya and broad beans, lotus root, and many varieties of green vegetables. About 20 percent of the collective land each year is sown in green manure and pig fodder. In addition, 10 percent of the arable land is reserved as private plots for each household the product from which is tax-free. Each family raises several pigs for sale in the market and as a source of valuable manure.

It takes but 70 days to cultivate the land assigned to each person. Since only half the people are able-bodied—the rest being too old, too young, or otherwise disabled—each able-bodied person needs to do approximately 150 days of field work. This leaves 200 days free for other kinds of work or leisure. How these days are used is crucial to the wellbeing of the community and its families.

During the years of Mao Zedong's leadership

Figure 19.6. Sun-cured tobacco storage shed in MaGaoqiao. At night the drying leaves are pushed under the roof by means of the rings that slide along the poles. [Photograph, 1986]

Figure 19.7. MaGaoqiao's old water-powered grist mill, which is no longer in use since electric power became available. [Photograph, 1983]

and taking as its inspiration the movement "In agriculture, learn from Dazhai" (the poverty-stricken north China village that raised itself up by self-reliant collective efforts discussed in Chapter 14), the village organized its surplus labor force for capital construction projects and invested its surplus in technological improvements.

In the 1960s the village had seventy-two wheelbarrows and twelve manually operated waterwheels but no tractors, pumps, or electricity. By the end of the 1970s, after strenuous work and investments in mechanized equipment, on the same area of land 70 percent more grain and 50 percent more cash crops were being harvested. The Eighth Brigade, as the village was known then, doubled its income between 1962 and 1972, and doubled it again in the next decade. To do this the villagers carried out capital construction on about one-third of their arable land. They changed small fields into big ones suitable for

Figure 19.8. Women washing clothes at the spring in MaGaoqiao's No. 5 Hamlet. [Photograph, 1984]

Figure 19.9. An open-air village meeting in MaGaoqiao to prepare for county and township general elections in 1984. The village party secretary and village head are seated at the table near the hydro pole on the right.

tractor plowing, leveling, and squaring them to make it easier to calculate fertilizer needs and production costs and results. They straightened and narrowed irrigation channels to save precious cropland, planted mulberry trees along the paths as well as fast-growing poplar for firewood, and built 7 kilometers of roads so that the tractors (of which they purchased nine), large carts with pneumatic tires, and machine-drawn plows and harrows could reach the land of all seven production teams.

"We were a little tired by all the labor," said village party secretary, Jiang Wenguang, shaking his head from side to side, "even exhausted at times. But we did the farmland reconstruction well. We have gathered in the fruits of this big effort, and we did it without taking on any loans or debts."

More recently, in an effort to create new employment opportunities, MaGaoqiao entered into an agreement with the provincial chemical fertilizer machinery factory that occupies a small corner of village land to build and operate a small steel rolling mill. When completed this rural enterprise will employ 150 workers and will generate new funds for social investments.

Festivals and life-cycle celebrations continue to play an important role in village life. The most popular occasion here, as in the rest of China, is Spring Festival, when everyone is in a holiday mood: The young men take part in colorful dragon dance competitions, and young women form

Figure 19.10. Team leader Wang standing beside a householder's methane gas pit. Animal and human wastes as well as organic household waste are "digested" here to create bacteria-free manure as well as fuel for cooking. Many villagers in MaGaoqiao feel these contraptions are clumsy to use and still prefer an open manure pit. [Photograph, 1981]

into a cinema for weekly shows and has established a "room of culture" with a color TV set and a small lending library. Illiteracy is rare among those under thirty-five years of age and is almost universal for those above that age. Since 1987 the village boasts a new two-story school that includes a junior high school section. The Women's Association has also organized a full-time daycare center.

Although the local Earth God shrine was demolished in the course of one of the mass campaigns for cultural change, in the privacy of their own homes many individuals keep up old practices, including the lighting of candles before ancestor tablets. Cremation when people die is a county government policy, and it appears to be universally obeyed, but for the funeral ceremony most villagers still invite Daoist priests to their homes to conduct conspicuous days of mourning.

The most recent change in MaGaoqiao has been the appearance of new private dwellings. As a result of the national drive for modernization, more capital remained in the countryside during the mid-1980s, and many villagers used it to

drum bands; households decorate their gates with poetic sayings and door gods and invite close relatives for meals; people make special trips to the county town to enjoy Sichuan opera, to gamble at cards, or to listen to storytellers in the teahouses.

To enhance leisure-time activities, the village has turned the meeting hall in its headquarters

Figure 19.11. MaGaoqiao team leader Wang's new brick and tile house built on the site of his former home in 1984.

Figure 19.12. A new house in MaGaoqiao of baked brick and tile under construction in 1984.

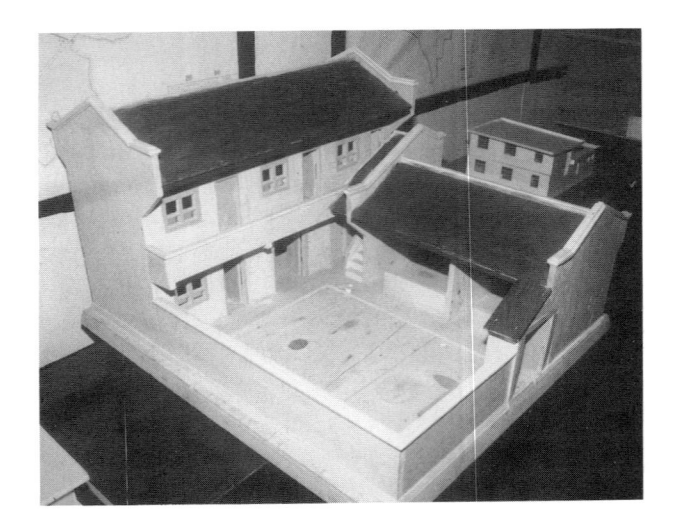

Figure 19.13. Model of new-style village housing being promoted in Shifang county that maintains the concept of a private courtyard. Subsidies are provided to farmers who build two-story houses in order to save arable land. [Photograph, 1984]

replace their pounded-earth, thatched homes by new brick and tile structures of the type that formerly only wealthy landlords could afford. Some of them have broken with tradition by having two stories. Mostly the new homes remain on the former sites, within the crowded island clusters, surrounded by paddy fields.

I am indebted to the Social Sciences and Humanities Research Council of Canada for financial support for this project and to Sichuan University, Chengdu, for practical help in making local arrangements for research.

CHAPTER 20

Longlin Village, Hainan
Cash Crops and New Houses

CATHERINE ENDERTON AND WEN CHANGEN

Longlin, a small village of 176 people in thirty-five families, is located in China's newest province, about 45 kilometers or two hours southeast of Haikou, Hainan's provincial capital. The first 37 kilometers of the trip from Haikou can be made on the paved two-lane Haiyu Dong Highway, one of Hainan's main roads, which passes Sanmenpo town, the small service center for Longlin, and the other villages of Longma district, Qiongshan county. The last 8 kilometers to Longlin are only accessible along a narrow dirt lane that passes through Hongming Provincial State Farm.

Hainan, a large island situated off the south China coast between Vietnam and Hong Kong, was a part of Guangdong province until 1988. Although Hainan is the same size as Taiwan and was also occupied by the Japanese during World War II, it has remained a relatively more remote and underdeveloped place compared to its more northerly sister island. The Beijing government has made repeated attempts to stimulate Hainan's development, and the recent designation of the island as a separate province is part of current development plans to make Hainan a major foreign investment and export zone. The island has a mountainous center with peaks just over 1,800 meters high that form the core for the broad coastal plains that rim the island in the north and east. A humid tropical climate with a dry winter season from November to April is experienced throughout most of the lowlands. Longlin, however, is located in the wetter and windier northeastern part of Hainan. Most of the 2,000 millimeters or more of precipitation each year falls between June and October and is related to periodic continental northeast monsoons, maritime southeast and southwest monsoons, and typhoons originating in the Pacific Ocean and the South China Sea. Hainan receives more typhoons than any other region of China. Longlin's inland position protects it from the worst of the typhoon destruction that can occur along Hainan's northeastern coast, especially between May and November; the most severe typhoons are apt to occur in September. The great typhoon of 1973 struck

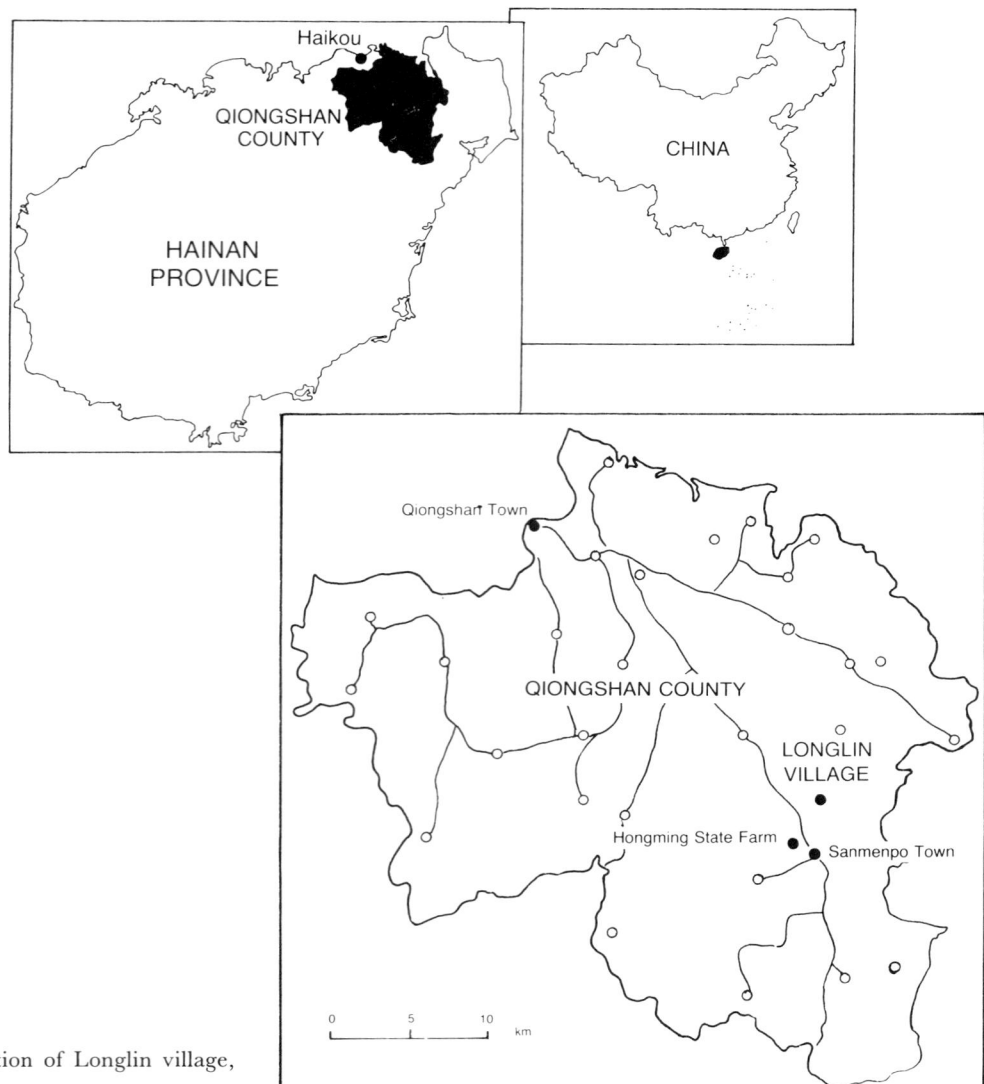

Figure 20.1. General location of Longlin village, Hainan province.

with winds in excess of 220 kilometers per hour, leveling houses and uprooting most of the rubber trees near the coast.

Longlin is a Han village in a Han region of Hainan and as such is similar to many other Han villages in the northern and eastern part of the island. Hainan, like many provinces on China's periphery, has a substantial ethnic minority population, principally the indigenous Li and more recently a substantial Miao population. The Li and Miao nationalities live in the central mountains and the southwestern part of Hainan; northern and eastern Hainan are now entirely Han. The isolated non-Han villages in the central mountains are quite different from the Han villages, with distinctive architectural forms. Such villages are usually poorer and less agricultural than Han villages. Although Longlin is far enough from town or city to be distinctively rural, other Han villages are more "suburban," with elements of urban form and function that tie their economies to nearby urban centers.

Longlin is neither a perfectly "average" village, nor is it a model village. The village was settled some two hundred years ago by migrants from Fujian province. Today, twenty-two families share the surname Liang, four are Huang, four Fu, and five are relative newcomers having come from Fujian in the early 1940s.

A distinctive characteristic of the settlement geography of Hainan is that a third of the arable land in the province belongs to state farms. State farms, as centers of rural housing and farming, tend to be more advanced technically, better off economically, and built more recently than many of the natural villages; they are styled for a more communally and centrally run living style. Longlin borders Hongming State Farm, established by the People's Liberation Army in the 1950s to grow rubber. Proximity to the state farm is an important element of Longlin's geography.

The Chinese government regards the district of Longma, which includes Longlin village, as having a relatively small rural population of less than one thousand and an abundance of arable land. Therefore, over half of the 11,000 *mu* in the district has been leased to the state farm. The remaining land is shared by seven villages. Longlin

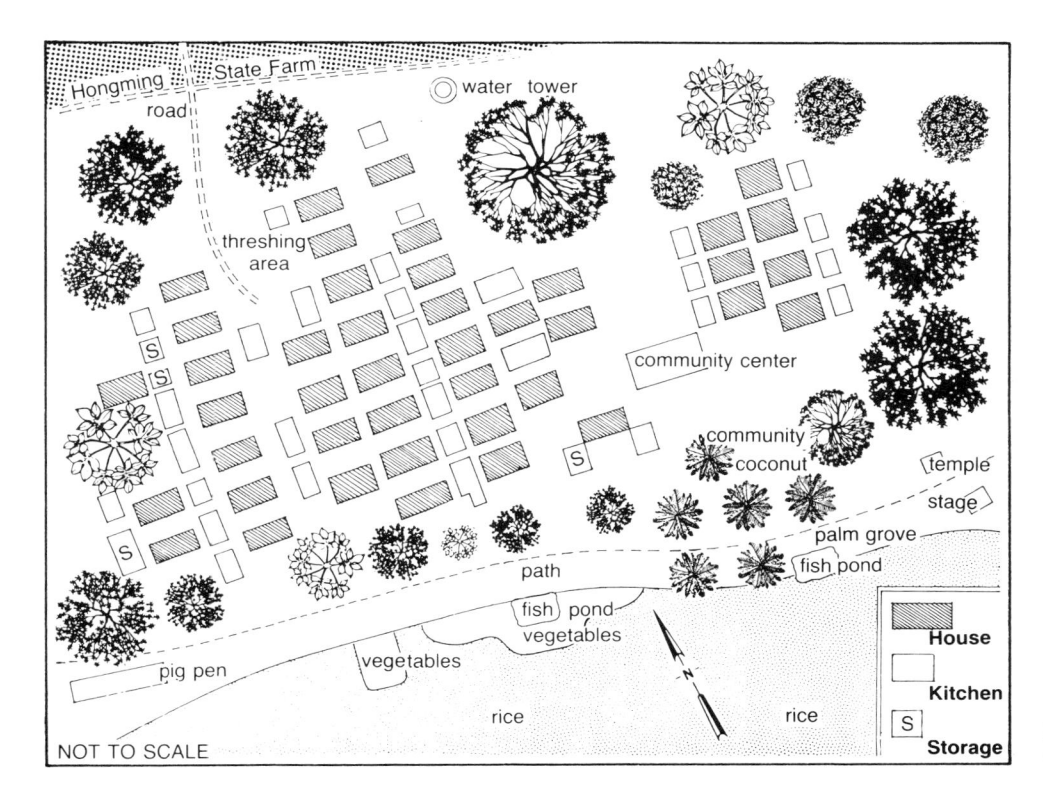

Figure 20.2. Longlin village plan.

villagers now feel, owing to changed agricultural and economic policies, that they are short of land. They now rent land from other villages in order to expand their agricultural activities. They nevertheless maintain good relations with neighboring Hongming State Farm and derive considerable benefit from Hongming's proximity. For instance, they take advantage of Hongming's more elaborate infrastructure, which includes an elementary school, a snack bar, dances, films, mail delivery twice a week, a doctor, and trucks. Some of the farmers in Longlin exchange work on the state farm for technical assistance and the occasional loan of a truck. Most of the work done by Longlin villagers for the state farm consists of helping protect state farm rubber trees from poaching.

In some areas of the island, villages and state farms have had considerable friction over land, but relations between the Hongming State Farm and Longlin appear generally to be good despite the state farm's lease on a substantial amount of Longlin's arable land. However, one conflict of interest that has come up concerns Hongming's control of the reservoir that village farmers depend on for irrigation water. Apparently, the state farm has procrastinated about reservoir and irrigation channel maintenance, since they don't themselves need the irrigation. Another Longma village also wants Hongming to build a footbridge across one of the irrigation channels so that the village children can get to school.

Longlin is an attractive nucleated village of brick and stone houses built close together on a slope that drains toward the rice paddies. In Longlin and in Longma district generally only a small part of the land is in paddy fields, 800 *mu* in all in the district. The rest is planted in tropical crops such as rubber, sugarcane, and tropical fruits.

Longlin village was originally oriented to the south by a local geomancer. Main houses traditionally have been aligned so that a breeze can blow through from the front door of one to the front door of the next. One can stand in the rear doorway of the northernmost house at the top of the slope and see straight through the doors of a row of houses down the slope to the paddy fields. Longlin has a tidy and prosperous appearance, with many new buildings, in part a reflection of the prosperity brought to the village with the economic reforms of the 1980s.

The village has a formal name, Longlin—or Dragon-scale—village, and a local spoken name, Tunlin village, which means Cane village, as in sugarcane. In the past, sugarcane was an important crop, but now little cane is grown because the market price is unfavorable. Until 1978, rice too was an important crop for Longlin farmers, even though production was often insufficient to meet their needs, and the villagers often had to buy additional state grain. Today, however, less than

Figure 20.3. A view through Longlin village with the front of the dwellings on the right facing the rear of dwellings on the left. A terrace runs between them. [Photograph, 1990]

Figure 20.4. Looking through a line of doorways in Longlin village from north to south. Generally oriented to the south to conform to dictates of local *fengshui*, the facing doors when opened facilitate interior ventilation. [Photograph, 1990]

half of Longlin's land is in rice production, because rice is comparatively more labor intensive and less profitable than tropical cash crops. Yet sufficient rice is grown to meet the state quota with a surplus available for sale on the free market. This productivity has been accomplished by a near doubling of rice yield on the village's double-cropped fields from 200 to 300 kilograms per *mu* in 1979 to 500 kilograms in 1989. Rubber is becoming one of Longlin's major cash crops and should increase in importance as the trees mature. Pineapples are interplanted with rubber—an intensive use of valuable land. Whereas rubber is sold to the state, the pineapples are sold on the free market. Other crops such as ginger, black pepper, coconuts, and sour apples contribute to the village's prosperity. Longlin villagers keep relatively few animals. They have 40 water buffalo; 70 pigs; 60 goats; 1,000 chickens, ducks, and geese; 20 dogs; and 10 cats. The animals are mostly for local consumption or, in the case of the water buffalo, for plowing local rice paddies that are too deep for the village's walking tractors. The village pigs used to wander about looking for scraps, but now the village has decided that for health reasons the pigs should be kept in pens. Penning also makes it easier to collect pig manure for fertilizer. There are almost no sideline activities carried on in the village except for a small degree of construction work associated with local housing. Some villagers now contract land in nearby villages to grow pineapples.

Longlin village is nearly self-sufficient in food, but in recent years villagers have reached to the outside world for goods and services. Salt and oil and some fish and pork are purchased in nearby villages or in the market in Sanmenpo as are chemical fertilizers, seeds, pesticides, clothes, pots, pans, and tools. Although the village doesn't have mail service, villagers can arrange to pick up mail at Hongming State Farm school twice a week. Since there is no bus service to the village, younger villagers depend on bicycles. Older villagers rarely venture far afield. Only two of the villagers questioned in 1990 had ever been to the China mainland. One Longlin family has recently purchased a motorcycle for 1,100 *yuan,* and their son often rides it to Haikou where he is looking for work. Several families have small walking tractors that are attached to wagons and used for

Figure 20.5. Much space in Longlin village is used informally and temporarily. Depicted here, the husking of fresh coconuts in order to obtain the coconut milk. [Photograph, 1990]

Figure 20.6. Longlin's children, like adults, usually relax outside their homes. Here children play cards in a shaded area on the edge of the village. [Photograph, 1990]

transportation. Longlin has no telephone, but there are radios as well as a color television set in the village's recreation room. One person in the village subscribes to a newspaper, which he picks up twice a week from the state farm. Few books besides the children's school texts reach the village.

Major improvements in Longlin have accompanied the introduction of piped water and electricity. Piped cold water was brought to the village in 1986 following the completion of a 30-ton water tower and a new well. It took the village three years to raise the 23,000 *yuan* needed for their water project. Today there are water taps in most of the courtyards and in some of the kitchens. Before 1986, the villagers, mostly the women, had to carry buckets of water uphill from the old well, an arduous task. Today the old well is used for a laundry area. The houses do not have either toilets or bathrooms, nor is there any toilet or bathhouse in the village.

The village has had electricity since 1981, and each house has several light sockets with 40-watt bulbs. Some have fixtures for fluorescent lights but no bulbs. Villagers say that the fluorescent bulbs give more light but are too expensive. Besides simple lighting, some of the houses also have small electric fans, but there are no other

Figure 20.7. Village women in Longlin continue to use the old well, but for laundry only instead of as a source of drinking water. [Photograph, 1990]

Figure 20.8. The water tower, built on the slope above Longlin, is now a landmark in the village. [Photograph, 1990]

electrical appliances except radios and the single community television set. Firewood is still the fuel used for cooking.

Besides basic electricity and the new water pipes, the most striking sign of modernization in the village is the presence of many new houses. To build a new house a family needs about 13,000 *yuan,* money that some borrow from relatives and others are able to save themselves. Imported timber, even some from the United States, is used in house construction by some rich families, although most families use local Hainan timber. Most of the new village houses have been built by carpenters from Fujian province since local carpenters are few.

Houses in Longlin all have the same floor plan —two long rooms and a central wide hallway with a door to the courtyard at each end of the hall so that the hall is well ventilated. The hall acts as a parlor or public room, whereas the two bedrooms can be closed off for more privacy. Many families park their bicycles in the main hall, where some families also have benches. Extra rice is stored in 2-meter tall woven basket containers in one of the rooms of each dwelling. The kitchen is a separate building off to one side containing a wood-burning stove, a cold-water faucet, and a table and chairs. Some families now have two houses, a new house for a married son or sons and an old house for the older generation. In several cases, the old place is used for storage, while the family actually lives in the newer house.

Longlin village has a small Buddhist temple on the southeast edge of the village. It is a single-room brick building with an altar that nearly fills the interior. The altar is covered with an assortment of colorful religious artifacts and plastic flowers. In front of the temple is a small enclosed courtyard. The temple was rebuilt recently, because the original one was destroyed during the Cultural Revolution. The temple is used mostly

Figure 20.9. Piped water from the tower has been brought to a standpipe in most of Longlin's housing courtyards. The buildings on the right and left are main houses; that in the back facing the courtyard is a kitchen. [Photograph, 1990]

Figure 20.10. Houses in Longlin share a common three-bay plan, with an entryway in the middle to a parlor off of which are two bedrooms.

Figure 20.11. A new village temple surrounded by a walled courtyard was constructed in Longlin in recent years to replace one destroyed during the Cultural Revolution. [Photograph, 1990]

on ceremonial occasions such as the New Year, weddings, or funerals. Longlin's graves are scattered through the fields, where the geomancers sited them in the traditional style, a practice that is still continued.

Other community structures include a recreation room with a 20-inch color television and a table tennis table. Villagers contributed 9,500 *yuan* and some 500 volunteer labor days to build the recreation room. Outside they built a volleyball court, a badminton court, as well as a large stage where visiting theater and opera groups perform. Young children travel to the state farm to attend elementary school; older ones attend junior and senior middle school in Sanmenpo as boarding students. They return to the village on weekends. So far only two village children have been able to go on to get advanced schooling.

Longlin is an upper-middle-income village compared to others in Hainan. Although individuals and families have resources, Longlin is short of the community capital necessary to carry forward projects such as water conservancy, road construction and maintenance, and bridge building, which would improve the village's economic infrastructure. Village leaders claim that Longlin still requires a bathhouse and a public lavatory as well as a fund for emergencies. Village leaders are optimistic about continuing improvement in village income. They figure that under good conditions one worker can produce about 3,000 *yuan* per year of tropical crops. Since only a small number of the rubber and pineapple plants are mature now, villagers expect to earn more from these crops in a few years. Although they acknowledge that they do not understand marketing, only a few of the more educated villagers have attempted to learn how to tap the competitive marketplace. Transportation remains a problem to be solved. Most Longlin villagers hope that the current policies will continue to allow them to use their creative abilities in order to diversify their local economic activities and improve life in the village.

We thank the Association of American Geographers, the International Studies and Overseas Programs of the University of California at Los Angeles, and the Guangdong Geography Institute for their generous funding. Among those who assisted and supported our research in the field are faculty, staff, and students of the Geography Institute and many officials and scholars in Hainan province. Special thanks to Ye Shuning and Zhou Chunyang of the Guangdong Geography Institute and Jack Williams of Michigan State University for field assistance and to Jack Ma of UCLA for the translation of documents.

CHAPTER 21

Hsin Hsing Village, Taiwan
From Farm to Factory

RITA S. GALLIN AND BERNARD GALLIN

When the Nationalist government retreated to the island province of Taiwan in 1949, it found a primarily agricultural island marked by conditions not all favorable to development. The policies it adopted to foster economic growth, which have been well documented (Ho 1978; Lin 1973), included strengthening agriculture to provide a base for future industrialization, pursuing a strategy of import substitution for a brief period during the 1950s, and in the 1960s adopting a policy of export-oriented industrialization. The export-oriented policy produced dramatic changes in Taiwan's economic structure. Agriculture's contribution to the net domestic product declined from 36 percent in 1952 to 7 percent in 1986, while the contribution of industry rose from 18 percent to 47 percent over the same period (Lu 1987, 2). As might be expected, industrialization was accompanied by rapid urbanization and migration from rural areas to the cities. Industrialization, however, was not restricted to a few urban centers. During the late 1960s, industry began to disperse to the countryside to gain access to labor and raw materials. By 1971, 50 percent of the industrial and commercial establishments and 55 percent of the manufacturing firms in Taiwan were located in rural areas, and the proportion of farm members working off-farm grew substantially (Ho 1979, 83). This chapter will discuss the relationship between these changing economic conditions and the village of Hsin Hsing (for other descriptions of this relationship, see Chen 1977; Cohen 1976; Harrell 1981; Huang 1981; and Wang and Apthorpe 1974).

Located on the west-central coastal plain in Chang-hua county, some 200 kilometers southwest of Taipei, Hsin Hsing was first settled in the late eighteenth century by Hokkien-speaking people from the Xiamen area of Fujian province. Throughout most of the village's history, its economy was founded on the family farm (B. Gallin 1966). During our 33 years of study, however, the community's economy changed dramatically from a system based almost purely on agriculture to a system founded predominantly on off-farm employment (Gallin and Gallin 1982; Gallin and Ferguson 1988). In addition, its population declined; in 1958, 509 people lived in 99 households

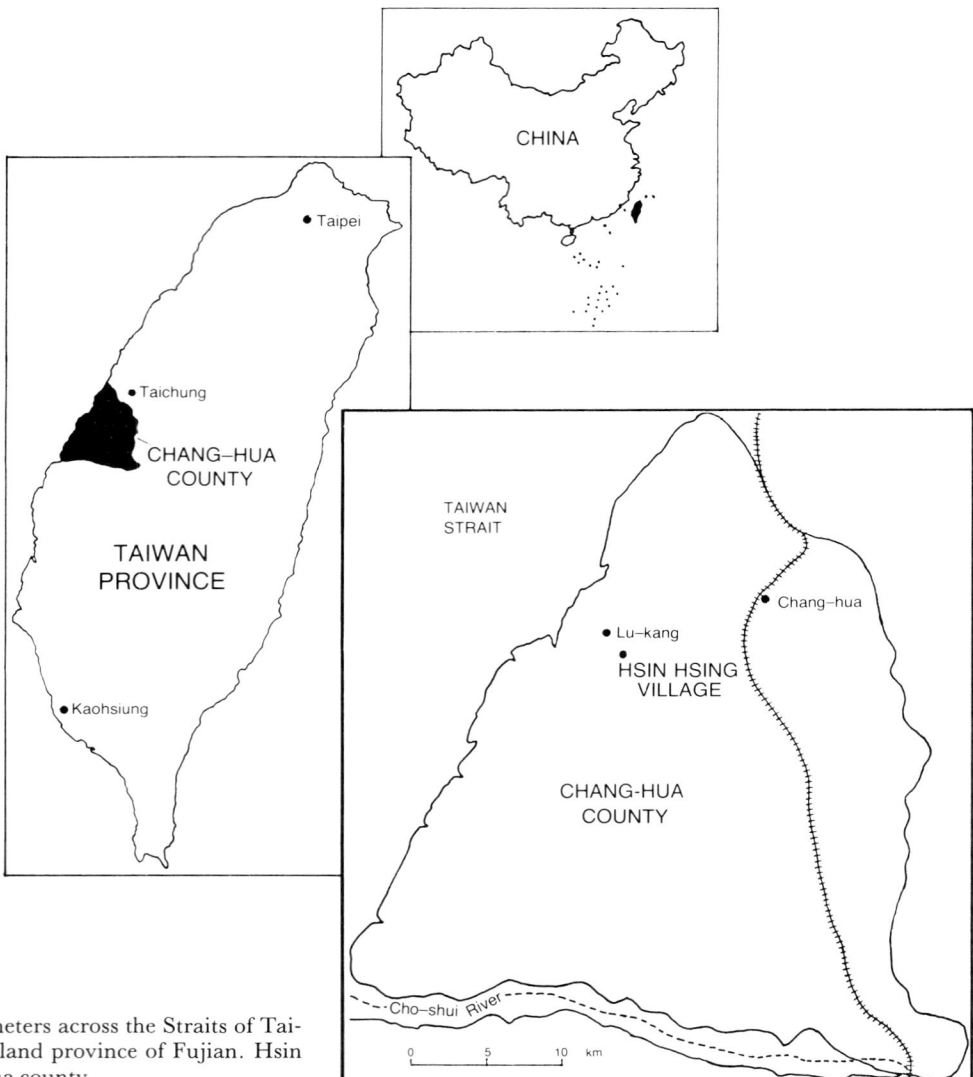

Figure 21.1. Some 100 kilometers across the Straits of Taiwan, Taiwan faces the mainland province of Fujian. Hsin Hsing is located in Chang-hua county.

within the village, whereas in 1979 only 383 people, living in 73 households, were resident in Hsin Hsing.

Hsin Hsing in the 1950s

In the late 1950s, travel to Hsin Hsing village was neither easy nor brief, requiring a four- to six-hour trip by train to Chang-hua and then a one-hour bus ride from Chang-hua to Lukang. From Lukang, which lies about 5 kilometers northwest of the village, the traveler boarded an old wooden Japanese bus for the fifteen-minute ride to the village. The ride, made along the unpaved county road running between Lukang and Hsi Hu, was dusty or wet, according to the season, but it was always bumpy, noisy, and crowded. As the bus moved along the road, it passed lush rice paddies as well as large areas of dry fields; a few menthol-distilling factories, brickworks, and small rice mills; clusters of houses that made up the district's villages; oxen pulling wheeled carts loaded with bundles of produce or farm supplies; and pedestrians or bicyclists, often transporting heavy loads.

The uncomfortable ride ended when the bus came to a halt across the road from the Hsin Hsing village store, where men congregated to talk and play chess, and adjacent to a small pond, where women washed the family laundry and water buffalo bathed and eliminated. The village store, the bus stop, and the washing area served at this time as important points for the dissemination of gossip and news; only four village families owned radios, none had a telephone, and just a few subscribed to newspapers.

Like most villages in Taiwan, Hsin Hsing was nucleated—a compact settlement with most dwellings facing south. To the north the community was bounded by a broad river that drained the area, and to the east, west, and south were farmlands, which separated Hsin Hsing from two villages, Lo Ts'e and Ta Yu, located 700 meters to the west and east, respectively.

With the exception of a few plots lying adjacent to the village or in the arable land separating Hsin Hsing from Lo Ts'e and Ta Yu, most of the fields farmed by Hsin Hsing's villagers were inconveniently located on the other side of the county road, as much as 5 kilometers distant from the village. The scattering of landholdings as well as fragmentation of the land was a product of two factors: Land insufficiency caused villagers to buy or rent land wherever it was available, and patterns of inheritance—in which land was bequeathed to sons in equal shares—generated a mosaic of tiny, irregularly shaped plots scattered throughout the surrounding countryside.

Village agriculture was focused primarily on wet-rice cultivation, watered via an intricate network of irrigation systems consisting of rivers, dams, pumping stations, earthen ditches, and dikes. Often, however, because Hsin Hsing lies as far as it does from the mountain headwaters of the water supply, rain alone made it possible to transplant the rice seedlings. In irrigated fields, villagers harvested three crops annually: two crops of rice and a third crop of wheat, soybeans, sweet potatoes, or vegetables. On dry land, two or possibly three crops were grown as well.

Such intensive cultivation was made possible by a favorable climate, irrigation facilities, the availability of chemical fertilizer, as well as an increasing population that provided additional labor to work the available land. Ironically, the increasing population that made intensive cultivation of land possible also created problems of land scarcity and village poverty. There was little industry in the area and thus insufficient demand for the labor of villagers who cultivated too little land to support their families. Some villagers peddled vegetables during the agricultural slack sea-

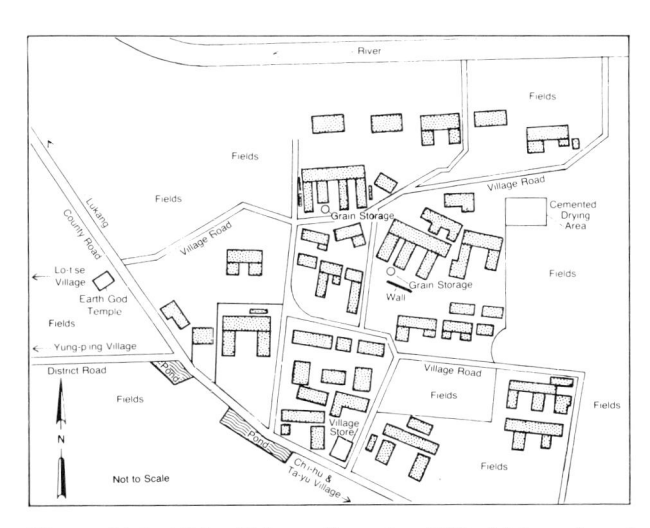

Figure 21.2. Hsin Hsing village in 1958. [Adapted and redrawn from Gallin 1966, 27]

son or found other seasonal work, but this was no real solution to the economic problem. The only alternative was for members of expanding families, and even whole households, to move to urban centers to earn a livelihood or to supplement the family farm income (B. Gallin 1967; Gallin and Gallin 1974a and 1974b). Remittances sent by these migrants often represented the only way families were able to secure livelihoods above the subsistence level.

The impoverished condition of the villagers' lives in the late 1950s was apparent in their dwellings. Most houses—even new ones—were constructed of bamboo, mud, and plaster. Heavy bamboo poles served as the main supports. The walls were constructed of a latticework of bamboo strips filled in with plaster, made of mud, straw, and cow dung, and the roofs were thatched. Only an occasional new house and the old homes of formerly wealthy families were constructed of fired brick and had roofs of clay tiles.

Village houses tended to be clustered together in small compounds, reflecting the fact that Hsin Hsing is a multisurname and multilineage *(zu* or *tsu)* village. Most houses, or at least the original sections built, were of one fundamental type, varying mainly in size. The basic structure consisted of a single length of rooms, with the ancestral-worship room *(gongting* or *kung t'ing)* in the center, flanked by one or two rooms on either side, which were used for sleeping and cooking. When the size of a family increased, as when it expanded through the marriage of sons, the house usually was enlarged by the addition of wings, which gave the dwelling an L shape or a U shape. As a family continued to extend, more and more wings might be added as finances permitted. Sometimes wings were added in a fairly orderly fashion, and sometimes they were added in such a random fashion that the house resembled a kind of maze. Each household or conjugal family then had its own "apartment" in the large house.

Figure 21.3. House building in Hsin Hsing in the late 1950s, a time at which the use of bamboo, mud or fired brick, and plaster was common.

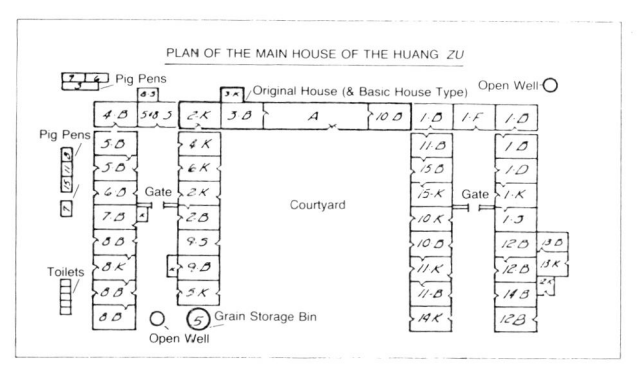

Figure 21.4. One of the three enlarged houses in Hsin Hsing in the late 1950s. The original rectangular core of the dwelling was enlarged with extensions and wings to provide "apartments" for fifteen households in the Huang *zu*. Note that the rooms of a household's apartment may not be contiguous. Most of the house depicted here was built of brick and cement with a tile roof; only a few sections had maintained bamboo and mud walls. The central *gongting* was used in common by the *zu* for ancestral worship. [Adapted and redrawn from Gallin 1966, 28]

Some families tended to build new dwellings near the original house rather than to add wings. Such new dwellings, over the years, expanded to fit the new needs of the growing family. Interspersed throughout the village were the smaller houses of families made up of very small groups and those completely unrelated to any other family in the village.

Pigsties—virtually all families in the village raised at least a few pigs—typically constructed with mud floors, bamboo sidewalls, and straw roofs, were either attached directly to the sides of houses or situated several meters away. Some households also raised water buffaloes, kept strictly as draft animals in pens abutting their owners' houses. Almost every family also raised some chickens, ducks, and geese; at night they were kept under bamboo cages, but during the day they were constantly underfoot as they roamed the village foraging for food.

Situated close to the animals' stalls were compost pits in which the dung of pigs and water buffalo, and biodegradable garbage were collected for use as fertilizer. None of the houses had indoor toilet facilities. Outhouses were located inside compounds or close to houses, and their contents were collected and also used as fertilizer. Village dwellings lacked running water—open wells were scattered around the village—and only about two-thirds had access to the electricity that came on erratically and primarily at night.

Perhaps because houses were dark and extremely cluttered, villagers tended to work and socialize outside their dwellings. During the busy agricultural season most able-bodied villagers spent their days in the fields, while, after the harvest, unhusked rice could be found drying on cement courtyards in preparation for its use in the payment of taxes, its sale, or its storage either inside the house or in bins dispersed throughout the village. During the slack seasons, however, the community was a beehive of outdoor activity. Men repaired houses, farm implements, and other accouterments of daily living. Women prepared, dried, and preserved vegetables; darned clothes; cared for young children; and made straw brooms and fiber hats for sale to brokers. Preserved and fresh vegetables, rice fertilizer, and even farm implements, together with the family's furniture, utensils, and debris accumulated over decades created a generally disordered appearance.

Because of kinship ties and physical proximity, villagers frequently cooperated in many aspects of their daily lives. Patrilineal relatives, particularly if they had recently divided into separate households, often shared expensive farm implements or bought them cooperatively. They also helped each other with jobs that demanded more labor than any individual family had available. Nevertheless, because of the small size of lineage groups in the village, joint ownership of machines and cooperative work efforts extended to nonkin neighbors and friends; agricultural operations that harassed farmers with deadlines and time limitations, such as the planting and harvesting of rice, necessarily required nonrelated villagers to join together in exchange-labor groups.

Hsin Hsing's lineages, then, were not economic groups. But they were ceremonial groups, and their members came together on a recurring basis to celebrate life-cycle events and to participate in religious and magical activities. Most of these activities took place in the ancestral worship rooms or *gongting* of individual dwellings. The appointments of the room—then and now—include an altar that stands against the wall opposite the main entrance. Above the altar hang two calligraphic scrolls flanking a painting depicting the Buddhist goddess Guanyin. Statues of the main Daoist gods and the ancestral tablets stand on top of the altar. Incense receptacles and wine cups are placed before the statues of the gods, whereas food offerings are placed on a large table in front of the altar. The last furnishing is an incense pot hanging from the ceiling a few feet from the entrance to the hall wherein the spirit of T'ien Kung, the highest god, is said to reside.

In many respects, the appointments of this room illustrate the eclecticism of the villagers' beliefs. Although elements of popular Daoism and ancestor worship (which is closely related to Confucianism) are the strongest and most apparent, there is a clear Buddhist influence. These elements have been merged into a single system that allows villagers to adjust to and achieve rapport with the spirits of natural objects, ancestors, deified heroes, and demons or evil spirits. In many respects, the uses to which the *gongting* are submitted also reveal the nature of village religion. Although the room was the most important single site for the performance of cyclical and noncyclical rituals *(baibai* or *pai pai)* as well as shamanistic practices, its use was not limited to the "sacred." Sacks of rice and fertilizer, mounds of sweet potatoes, farm equipment, and bicycles frequently were stored there.

The multiple uses to which the *gongting* was put were attributable to two factors: village houses had limited space, and Hsin Hsing, like other small communities in the area, had no large temple in which to house statues of gods such as the community god (Dashigong or Ta Shih Kung). Village-owned statues, therefore, were rotated among and maintained in the *gongting* of private homes. When it was necessary to worship many gods at one time, the gods were invited to come from their resident *gongting* to the single *gongting* that was to be the center of worship for the occasion.

The Earth God (Tudigong or T'u Ti Kung) was the only deity with his own small temple, located in the fields across the road from the village. Individuals worshiped Tudigong there on a daily basis. Some villagers also occasionally sacrificed food at the small "devil" temple near the edge of the village where demons were said previously to have congregated.

Although the observance of certain rites, for example, ancestor worship, and the participation in particular rituals, such as those organized for the purposes of shamanistic curing, were determined strictly by the *zu* group or individual family, other rituals were performed by the whole village on set days. Some religious or magical act was performed in the village almost every day, either by a family or by the community as a whole. The frequency of these observances, however, was not merely a symbol of the villagers' religiosity. Most Hsin Hsing villagers were very aware that religion and magic were functionally important in their lives.

Participation in rites and rituals helped to relieve the anxiety of people who were desperately seeking to survive in a world of uncertainty or were looking for solutions to insoluble problems. These observances also had "entertainment" value and offered a change in the daily routine of life. Some observances were filled with thrills and excitement. Others represented a rare occasion to invite outside guests formally and to be invited in turn. All provided an opportunity to overcome the community pressures for thrift, which on a day-to-day basis tended to standardize the villagers' diet. Finally, although divisive influences sometimes surfaced in the process of organizing and administering *baibai,* such rituals served as principal occasions for a show of cooperation and unity within and between families and the *zu* groups in the village (B. Gallin 1963).

Hsin Hsing in the 1990s

Improvements in Taiwan's communication system over the decades have produced striking changes in the amount of time and energy required to travel to Hsin Hsing. Two air-conditioned buses—one from Taipei to Lukang and the second from Lukang to the village—convey the traveler to the community in a mere three and a half hours. The first leg of the journey is made on a four-lane superhighway; the second consists of a ride along the two-lane county road, which is now paved with cement and clogged with motorcycles, automobiles, taxicabs, tour buses carrying Taiwanese on pilgrimages to the many famous and not-so-famous temples that dot the island, trucks transporting produce and products to Taiwan's markets, as well as containers packed with commodities destined for shipment overseas. The bus passes countless service and retail-sales shops, factories, and businesses that line the road, as well as cultivated and fallow fields crowded between the numerous commercial and industrial structures that dot the countryside.

The bus comes to a halt across the road from the old village store. The much-used pond where the traveler formerly ended the journey has disappeared. It has been reclaimed and converted to residential and industrial uses and provides the first sign that the boundaries of the village have been extended. New houses, several of which serve as both dwellings and business properties, line the south side of the county road in front of and to the east and west of the village. In addition, three houses stand on formerly cultivated fields to the village's south, a factory and a rice mill occupy arable land on the northwest side of the county road, and several multiuse dwellings obscure the fields that lie between the district road and the Earth God temple. This surge in construction has altered the village's configuration. Hsin Hsing is now a community in which most dwellings are compacted into a nucleated settlement, but some dwellings are distributed either in a linear or a scattered pattern. The broad drainage river still marks the village's northern boundary, but its water now is polluted, as is the water delivered, still in an unpredictable way, by the irrigation system.

The encroachment of buildings on the arable land surface has reduced the number of fields visible to the eye, but forces external to the village also have altered the local agricultural landscape and the nature of the farming process itself. The government's land consolidation program of the early 1960s mandated land repatterning, supplanting the patchwork of small fields with neat rows of somewhat larger, rectangular-shaped plots. This program, in addition to reducing the numerical and spatial distribution of individual farmers' fields, made possible the mechanization of farming. Other developments, such as the introduction of herbicides and the abolition of the government's enforced rice-fertilizer exchange system, contributed to the chemicalization

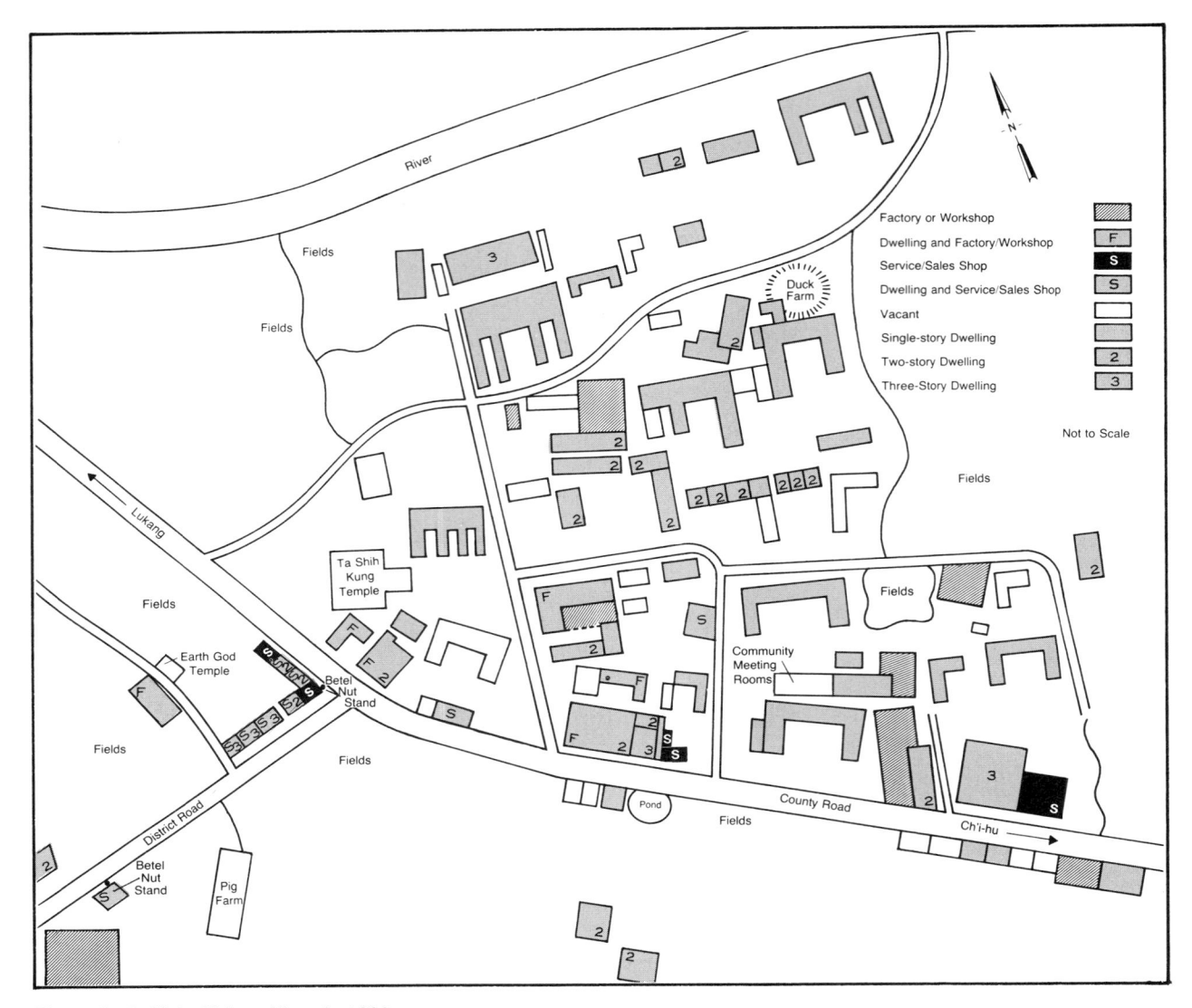

Figure 21.5. Hsin Hsing village in 1990.

of farming. Together with the development of tube wells operated by diesel engines or electric motors, these innovations have obviated the need for either a physically strong or a large agricultural labor force.

As a result, rice farming in Hsin Hsing today is technology-intensive rather than labor-intensive.

Exchange-labor groups organized to carry out operations such as planting and harvesting rice have been replaced by labor teams of specialists that are hired, along with their machines, by individual farmers to perform these strenuous and time-consuming tasks. Similarly, cooperative groups, which in the past were formed to main-

Figure 21.6. A 1950s vintage dwelling in 1990 Hsin Hsing village. A central core with a pair of wings embraces the littered courtyard.

tain the local irrigation system, have been made redundant by the advent of privately owned tube wells and the replacement of the earthen public irrigation system by cement waterways. Only a few tasks involved in the cultivation of rice are still performed manually by family members, and vegetables remain the sole crop cultivated primarily by hand labor.

Government policy and agricultural innovation made the reorganization of the farming process possible. But such reorganization also was brought about by the villagers' demand for and commitment to off-farm employment. Hsin Hsing's economy no longer has as its foundation the family farm, and fully 90 percent of the income of resident families' is derived from work in the industrial and commercial sectors. The majority of this income is earned outside the community. But in 1979, 36 businesses within Hsin Hsing offered employment to the members of the owners' families as well as to unrelated villagers: Seven villagers operated satellite factories that performed piecework for large parent companies, 3 villagers operated artisan workshops, and 26

Figure 21.7. Discarded and rusting farm implements in front of a partially abandoned 1950s vintage village house in Hsin Hsing. [Photograph, 1990]

residents operated retail service shops, small businesses, and itinerant marketing enterprises. Preliminary analysis of 1989–1990 data suggests that this number has increased by 20 percent.

The economic transformation of villagers' lives in Hsin Hsing has reshaped the physical features that define the village community. Only a few bamboo and plaster houses remain, and these are unoccupied. Some are owned by out-migrants

Figure 21.8. This Hsin Hsing dwelling also serves as a workshop for the family's business. Work takes place within the house and in front. [Photograph, 1990]

who occasionally return to the village for *baibai* or family events such as marriages and funerals; others were inhabited while new dwellings were being built and now stand abandoned in varying stages of decay as they gradually are destroyed by the elements. The homes that have replaced these reminders of the villagers' former poverty are of two types. Those built during the late 1960s and early 1970s are replicas of the traditional homes of the wealthy. They consist of a single length of rooms constructed of brick with roofs of clay tiles. Those erected more recently are two- or three-story buildings constructed of reinforced concrete —in some cases faced with small white ceramic tiles—with flat roofs.

Regardless of their type, all new dwellings include windows shielded by iron bars, a feature appended during the manufacturing process as a

Figure 21.9. A new multistoried dwelling fronts on an old dwelling and its littered forecourt. [Photograph, 1990]

deterrent to thieves, who are considered onmipresent in Taiwan. All houses also have access to electricity, and most families have used money earned in the cash economy to furnish their homes with refrigerators and color televisions; some have used disposable income to add VCRs, washing machines, and even a desk-top computer to their possessions. A good proportion of dwellings also include modern amenities: Four-fifths are equipped with telephones, more than half have running water piped in from storage tanks perched on the roofs, and about one-quarter contain indoor toilets. Today, most women cook using two-burner stoves fueled by propane gas delivered in canisters, rather than employing the less convenient traditional brick oven.

As in the past, households belonging to the same *zu* tend to live in close proximity. Many related families have built houses that are designed like duplex apartments. Families of brothers or patricousins each have their own homes in one of the several narrow buildings that abut each other. Some families have erected free-standing houses in sections of the village distant from the compound where their original apartments stood. In such cases, no house land was available near the site of the old and large *zu* house, and families were forced to build wherever space was available.

The proliferation of new buildings in the village is a result of several factors. First, wages earned off-farm and remittances from out-migrants living and working in distant cities produced the cash required to support their construction. Second, the expansion of families living in houses with finite amount of space necessitated their

Figure 21.10. An oil seal subcontracting factory in Hsin Hsing. [Photograph, 1990]

erection. Third, a family's switch from agriculture to entrepreneurship mandated that space be created for the unit's newly established or growing enterprise.

A number of these village-based enterprises are located in the first floor of multistoried buildings. Others occupy newly constructed structures that have been attached directly to or erected adjacent to the family dwelling. Still other businesses, either because of inadequate capital or the enterprise's small scale, are operated within preexisting space. In such cases, members of the family fulfill their responsibilities either in the *gongting* of the family house or, weather permitting, in the courtyard in front of the dwelling.

As might be expected, buildings affixed to the sides of houses or situated several meters away have supplanted animal pens. Although architectural change demanded the deletion of these crude pens, their displacement was more than a product of modifications in housing design. Other forces contributed to their elimination and to the virtual demise of animal husbandry in Hsin Hsing. The introduction of mechanized farm equipment made water buffalo superfluous, and the entry of villagers into the wage labor force reduced the time available for the breeding of pigs. In 1980, only one villager raised pigs and he did so as a business venture. Another villager is an entrepreneur specializing in raising over a thousand ducks for their eggs. Perhaps because poultry demand less attention than swine, women continue to raise a few fowl for their own families' consumption. But these animals are kept caged rather than allowed to range freely as in the past.

Compost pits maintained for their valuable fertilizer also have practically disappeared from the village. The chemicalization of agriculture has made them unnecessary. In their place, large mounds of discarded plastics, papers, bottles, and cans, as well as broken tools and furniture now accumulate. Often, the vagaries of wind, small children, and dogs carry away bits and pieces of the heaped debris, subsequently depositing the refuse and trash along the paths of the village and into nearby fields.

The cluttered condition of the paths is reproduced in the open areas surrounding many village houses. Piles of materials used in the production process are heaped on porches of dwellings. Lean-tos, constructed of wood, tin, or tarpaulin, conceal parts of homes; their contents, which range from decaying bamboo baskets to manufacturing materials and from unused bicycles to motorcycles, often spill out into the areas they adjoin, adding to the disorder. Farm implements, such as plows and harrows, abandoned to the weather, lie rusting in alcoves and courtyards. Cartons packed with products destined for local or foreign markets stand in rows waiting for the trucks that will carry them to their destinations. Motorcycles, cars, and trucks—all signs of relative affluence—block the pathways and yards in front of the buildings. The accumulations of relics and contemporary matter—as well as the incessant shrill of drill presses, electric motors, and other machinery—serve as compelling markers of the villagers' current pursuits.

Nevertheless, although off-farm employment engages most villagers full-time, they have not abandoned farming. In 1979, more than three-quarters of the village families farmed as well as pursued nonagricultural activities; an additional 6 percent farmed only. Nevertheless, to accommodate their dual roles as well as to compensate for the limited profits derived from the land, villagers have changed their patterns of land use. In 1979, only two-thirds cultivated rice during the first two crops. Two-fifths gave over part of their land surface to the cultivation of vegetables or sugarcane, and approximately one-sixth cultivated no rice at all. During the third crop, approximately one-third of the farmers allowed their land to lie fallow.

Modifications in Hsin Hsing's village economy were accompanied by changes in the community landscape. Early in the morning or at dusk, men hurry along the roads to the fields, either to tend to the irrigation water delivered through tube wells or to communicate with the specialists hired to work their land. During the day, women, according to the season, stoop in the fields picking vegetables or move slowly across courtyards wielding rakes over drying vegetables or rice.

With the exception of these female farmers, few young or middle-aged villagers are in evidence during the daytime as old men and women shuffle along the village's paths or sit daydreaming in the shade of houses. Grandmothers hover in doorways engrossed in piecework for local subcontractors, periodically looking up to scold the small children they care for while their mothers are at work. And women with children too young to attend school and no mothers-in-law to assume responsibility for their domestic work perch on chairs or squat on the ground, unremittingly sewing, cutting, folding, and assembling parts of products manufactured by their families or others (R. S. Gallin 1984a and 1984b).

A calm prevails in the village much of the time, a calm broken in the evening and on Sunday when off-farm workers and school-age children return to the village. Their presence signals the cessation of the workday, at least for those without chores to continue or to address, and marks one of the few occasions when villagers meet in groups. In part, the dearth of group activity in Hsin Hsing is a function of the villagers' preoccupation with their work off-farm as well as the changes in the agricultural process noted above. But in part, the lack of group activity is due to the decline in the importance of the *zu* as a ceremonial and social group. As the villagers disperse throughout the village, often locating in self-contained or

Figure 21.11. The plan for this enlarged dwelling accommodating fifteen households in the 1950s was shown in Figure 21.4. Today a three-story building with four apartments has been added in the rear for the families of four brothers (patricousins of people living in the older house in the foreground). [Photograph, 1990]

insulated living units, they find it increasingly inconvenient to cooperate in religious and magical activities. Furthermore, as the villagers' interests extend beyond the village and home area, they perceive less of a need to identify with and therefore to participate in rituals organized by the group.

The deterioration of the *zu* as a source of identification and solidarity as well as the breakdown of traditional village groupings based on economic necessity left, however, an urgent need for some firm means to instill a sense of cohesion in the people who remained in the community. Toward that end, a large, ornate temple dedicated to the village god, Dashigong (Ta Shih Kung), was erected in Hsin Hsing during 1989. Patterned after the numerous temples that dot the province, the structure serves as the locus for community religious activity and furnishes an important framework for unity and cooperation in village life. The organization of and participation in ritualistic festivals held there maintain a semblance of community life, and the glorification of the village deity that the temple heralds instills a sense of cohesion in villagers who remain in a geographic unit that has lost many of its marks of identity.

Government policies in Taiwan implemented during the 1950s and 1960s brought about changes in the island's economic structure, resulting not only in the stagnation of the agricultural sector and the spread of industry to rural areas, but also in the commodification of the domestic economy. In the absence of adequate income from the land and in the presence of the need for cash, village families increasingly turned to off-farm employment to earn the money needed to support their families or to secure their futures.

Although it is beyond the scope of this chapter

Figure 21.12. The Renxinggong (Jen Hsing Kung) temple, dedicated to the village god Dashigong, was erected in Hsin Hsing during 1989.

to examine the specific governmental actions that underlay this alteration of the agrarian economy, it is useful to highlight two factors that laid the base for change in the physical, economic, and social lives in Hsin Hsing and other villages in Taiwan's countryside. First, the state in Taiwan did not depend primarily on direct foreign investment to stimulate the export-oriented industrialization of the province. Rather, government planners relied on capital mobilization within the domestic private sector and an elaborate system of subcontracting to spearhead the growth of manufactured exports. As a result, the predominant form of economic activity in Taiwan has become the labor-intensive production of consumer goods within an intricate network of vertically integrated and geographically dispersed small-scale businesses and industrial firms.

Second, the state adopted policies and enacted laws that affirmed the ideological precepts of Chinese culture. By the 1970s, Taiwan occupied a semiperipheral position in the world economic system, and its industrial sector exhibited the features of competitive capitalism. Accordingly, to satisfy the economic imperatives implied by this form of capitalism, the government reinforced traditional culture, sustaining a matrix of values that cemented the integrity of the family as a work unit and reproduced a flexible labor force capable of exploiting simple and stable technologies.

The state, in sum, chose explicit policy options that created a favorable environment for the emergence and expansion of both a decentralized industrial structure composed of small firms and a dynamic private business sector dominated by a matrix of values emanating from familial culture. By its actions, the government successfully propelled Taiwan into the global economy and established the conditions for change in Hsin Hsing village. The villagers, however, were not passive objects in this process. Rather, they seized the opportunities created to modify family production and reproduction as well as to transform their community as a place to live.

We thank the following organizations that provided financial assistance over the years and made our field trips to Taiwan possible: the Foreign Area Training Fellowship Program, the Fulbright-Hays Program, the American Council of Learned Societies, the Asian Studies Center of Michigan State University, the Midwest Universities Consortium for International Activities, the Social Science Research Council, and the Pacific Cultural Foundation. We also acknowledge the Institute of Ethnology, Academia Sinica, Taiwan, for sponsoring us as visiting scholars and providing invaluable assistance that facilitated our research.

REFERENCES

American Society of Heating, Refrigerating and Air-conditioning Engineers, Inc.
   1972   *ASHRAE Handbook of Fundamentals.* Menasha, WI: George Banta Associates.

Anderson, Eugene and Marja
   1973   *Essays on the Cultural Ecology of South Coastal China.* Taipei: Orient Cultural Service.

Ashton, N., et al.
   1984   "Famine in China, 1958–1961." *Population and Development Review* 10 (4): 785–786.

Baker, Hugh D. R.
   1968   *Sheung Shui: A Chinese Lineage Village.* London: Frank Cass & Co., Ltd.
   1979   *Chinese Family and Kinship.* London: The Macmillan Press, Ltd.

"Banhao gonggong shitang" [Manage public dining halls well]
   1958   *Renmin ribao* [People's daily] 3760 (October 25): 4.

Barnett, A. Doak
   1963   *China on the Eve of the Communist Takeover.* New York: Praeger.

Bell, Mark S.
   1884   *China. Being a Military Report on the Northeastern Portions of the Provinces of Chihli and Shantung; Nanking and Its Approaches; Canton and Its Approaches; etc.* 2 vols. Simla: Government Central Branch Press.

Bennett, Gordon
   1978   *Huadong: The Story of a Chinese People's Commune.* Boulder: Westview Press.

Bennett, Steven
   1978   "Patterns of the Sky and Earth: The Chinese Science of Applied Cosmology." *Chinese Science* 3:1–26.

Bernstein, Thomas P.
   1977   *Up to the Mountains and Down to the Villages: The Transfer of Youth from Urban to Rural China.* New Haven: Yale University Press.

Bishop, Isabelle L.
   1899   *The Yangtze Valley and Beyond: An Account of Journeys in China.* London: J. Murray.

Blaser, Werner
   1979   *Courtyard House in China: Tradition and Present.* Basel: Birkhauser.

Bourdier, Jean-Paul, and Nezar AlSayyad, eds.
   1989   *Dwellings, Settlements and Tradition: Cross-cultural Perspectives.* New York: University Press of America.

Browne, George Waldo
   1901   *China: The Country and Its People.* Boston: D. Estes and Company, 1901.

"Building Temples—or Schoolhouses"
   1987   *China Daily* 1824 (June 1): 4.

Chan, Anita, Richard Madsen, and Jonathan Ungar
   1984   *Chen Village: The Recent History of a Peasant Community in Mao's China.* Berkeley: University of California Press.

Chance, Norman A.
   1984   *China's Urban Villagers: Life in a Beijing Commune.* New York: Holt, Rinehart and Winston.

Chang Hong
   1989   "Six Vices Are Listed in New Crackdown." *China Daily* 2588 (November 14): 1.

Chang, William Y. B.
1990 "Human Population, Modernization, and the Changing Face of China's Eastern Pacific Lowlands." *China Exchange News* 18 (December): 3-8.

"Changes in Dazhai Village"
1989 *Beijing Review* 32 (6): 39. February 6-12.

"Chaoyang renmin gongshe shitang zong gaobuhao" [The public dining hall in Chaoyang People's Commune has never been run well]
1959 *Gongshang guancha* [Economic herald] 12 (18): 28.

Chen Chung-hsien
1955 "Lu Fa and His Family." *China Reconstructs* 4 (August 1955):22.

Chen Chung-min
1977 *Upper Camp: A Study of a Chinese Mixed Cropping Village in Taiwan.* Taipei: Institute of Ethnology, Academia Sinica.

Chen Shaowen
1961 "Dalu nongcun gonggong shitang de fazhan" [The development of rural public dining halls in Mainland China]. *Zuguo zhoukan* [China weekly] 33 (13): 12.

Chen Yung-kuei [Chen Yonggui]
1966 "A Vivid Lesson on Bringing Politics to the Fore." *People's Daily.* In *Survey of China Mainland Press* No. 3675.

Chiang, Siang-tseh
1954 *The Nien Rebellion.* Seattle: University of Washington Press.

Chu Li and Tien Chieh-yun
1975 *Inside a People's Commune.* Beijing: Foreign Languages Press.

Chunyi Shuangxi jiacheng xu [Preface to the family history at Shuangxi, Chun county].
Qing N.p.

Cohen, Myron
1976 *House United, House Divided: The Chinese Family in Taiwan.* New York: Columbia University Press.
1990 "Lineage Organization in North China." *Journal of Asian Studies* 49 (3): 509-534.

Cressey, George B.
1934 *China's Geographical Foundations: A Survey of the Land and Its People.* New York: McGraw-Hill Book Co., Inc.
1955 *Land of the 500 Million: A Geography of China.* New York: McGraw-Hill Book Company, Inc.

Croizier, Ralph C., ed.
1970 *China's Cultural Legacy and Communism.* New York: Praeger.

Dazhai nongxueyuan, Shanxi nongxueyuan [Dazhai Agricultural Institute and Shanxi Agricultural Institute], eds.
1975 *Dazhai tian* [Dazhai fields]. Beijing: Renmin jiaoyu chubanshe.

"Dazhai Production Brigade"
1981 *Beijing Review* 24 (8): 3. February 23.

"Dazhai Takes on a New Look"
1988 *Beijing Review* 31 (45): 8-9. November 12-13.

Deane, Hugh
1989 "Mao's Rural Policies Revisited." *Monthly Review* 40 (10): 1-9.

de Groot, J. J. M.
1897 *The Religious System of China.* Leiden: E. J. Brill.

Diamond, Norma
1969 *K'un Shen: A Taiwan Village.* New York: Holt, Rinehart, and Winston.

Ding Zhong [Ting Chung]
1962 "Repairs of Temples and Preservation of Cultural Objects." *Southern Daily* (May 3, 1962). Translated by American Consulate General, Hong Kong. In *Survey of China Mainland Press,* No. 2742 (May 21, 1962):19-20.

Dixue tanyuan [An investigation into the origin of *fengshui*]
1986 Taibei: Liuyi chubanshe.

"Drive for Better Toilets Pays Off"
1991 *China Daily* 2987 (February 26): 3.

"Earth Buildings"
1991 *China Daily* 3009 (March 23): 5.

Eastman, Lloyd
1988 *Family, Field and Ancestors.* New York: Oxford University Press.

Ebrey, Patricia Buckley, and James L. Watson, eds.
1986 *Kinship Organization in Late Imperial China, 1000-1949.* Berkeley: University of California Press.

Endicott, Stephen
1989 *Red Earth: Revolution in a Sichuan Village.* Toronto: New Canada Publications.

Fairbank, John King
1983 *The United States and China.* Cambridge: Harvard University Press.

"Farmers Cut Expenses"
    1990   *Beijing Review* 33(12):39–40. March 19–25. Translated from *Zhongguo tongji xinxibao* [China's statistical and information daily], January 8, 1990.

Faure, David
    1986   *The Structure of Chinese Rural Society: Lineage and Village in the Eastern New Territories.* Hong Kong: Oxford University Press.
    1989   *The Rural Economy of Pre-Liberation China: Trade Increase and Peasant Livelihood in Jiangsu and Guangdong, 1870–1937.* Hong Kong: Oxford University Press.

Faure, David, James W. Hayes, and Alan Birch, eds.
    1984   *From Village to City: Studies in the Traditional Roots of Hong Kong Society.* Hong Kong: Centre of Asian Studies, Hong Kong University.

Feuchtwang, Stephen
    1974   *An Anthropological Analysis of Chinese Geomancy.* Vientiane: Vithagna.

Fei Hsiao-tung [Fei Xiaotong]
    1939   *Peasant Life in China: A Field Study of Country Life in the Yangtze Valley.* London: Routledge & Kegan Paul.
    1983   *Chinese Village Close-up.* Beijing: New World Press.
    1986   *Small Towns in China—Functions, Problems, and Prospects.* Beijing: New World Press.

Freedman, Maurice
    1958   *Lineage Organization in Southeastern China.* London: Athlone.
    1966   *Chinese Lineage and Society: Fukien and Kwangtung.* London: Athlone.

"Fujian yuanlou—zhuanji"
    1989   [Round buildings of Fujian—special issue]. *Hansheng zazhi* [Echo magazine] 22 (August): 1–75.

Gallin, Bernard
    1963   "Land Reform in Taiwan: Its Effect on Rural Social Organization and Leadership." *Human Organization* 22:109–112.
    1966   *Hsin Hsing, Taiwan: A Chinese Village in Change.* Berkeley: University of California Press.
    1967   "Chinese Peasant Values Toward the Land." In Jack M. Potter, May Diaz, and George Foster, eds., *Peasant Society: A Reader,* pp. 367–375. Boston: Little, Brown and Company.

Gallin, Bernard, and Rita S. Gallin
    1974a   "The Rural-Urban Migration of an Anthropologist in Taiwan." In George M. Foster and Robert V. Kemper, eds., *Anthropologists in Cities,* pp. 223–248. Boston: Little, Brown and Company.
    1974b   "The Integration of Village Migrants in Taipei." In Mark Elvin and G. William Skinner, eds., *The Chinese City Between Two Worlds,* pp. 331–358. Stanford: Stanford University Press.
    1982   "Socioeconomic Life in Rural Taiwan: Twenty Years of Development and Change." *Modern China* 8:205–246.

Gallin, Rita S.
    1984a   "Women, Family and the Political Economy of Taiwan." *Journal of Peasant Studies* 12:76–92.
    1984b   "The Entry of Chinese Women into the Rural Labor Force: A Case Study from Taiwan." *Signs* 9:383–398.

Gallin, Rita S., and Anne Ferguson
    1988   "The Household Enterprise and Farming Systems Research: A Case Study from Taiwan." In Susan Poats, Marianne Schmink, and Anita Springs, eds., *Gender Issues in Farming Systems Research and Extension,* pp. 223–235. Boulder: Westview Press.

Gamble, Sidney D.
    1954   *Ting Hsien: A North China Rural Community.* New York: Institute of Pacific Relations.

Gao Shangde and Zeng Hujiu, eds.
    1982   *Xincun guihua* [The planning of new villages]. Beijing: Zhongguo jianzhu gongye chubanshe.

Gao Zhenming, Wang Naixiang, and Chen Yu
    1987   *Fujian minju* [Folk dwellings of Fujian]. Beijing: Zhongguo jianzhu gongye chubanshe.

Geertz, Clifford
    1983   *Local Knowledge: Further Essays in Interpretative Anthropology.* New York: Basic Books.

Gillenkirk, Jeff, and James Motlow
    1987   *Bitter Melon.* Seattle: University of Washington Press.

Golany, Gideon
    1983   *Earth-Sheltered Habitat: Architecture and Urban Design.* New York: Van Nostrand Reinhold Company, Inc.
    1988   *Earth-Sheltered Dwellings in Tunisia.* Newark: University of Delaware Press.

1989 *Underground Space Design in China: Vernacular and Modern Practice.* Newark: University of Delaware Press.
1990 *Design and Thermal Performance: Below-Ground Dwellings in China.* Newark: University of Delaware Press.
1992 *Chinese Earth-Sheltered Dwellings: Indigenous Lessons for Modern Urban Design.* Honolulu: University of Hawaii Press.

Golas, Peter J.
1980 "Rural China in the Song." *Journal of Asian Studies* 39 (2): 291–325.

Gold, Thomas B.
1988 "Still on the Collective Road: Limited Reform in a North China Village." In Bruce L. Reynolds and Ilpyong J. Kim, eds., *Chinese Economic Policy,* pp. 41–65. New York: Paragon House Publishers.

Grunde, Richard
1976 "Land Tax and Social Change in Sichuan, 1925–1935." *Modern China* 2 (1): 23–48.

Guojia tongji ju nongcun shehui jingji tongji si [State Statistical Bureau, Rural Social Economic Statistics Department], ed.
1987 *Zhongguo nongcun tongji nianjian* [China's rural statistics yearbook]. Beijing: Zhongguo tongji chubanshe, 1987.

Han Pao-teh [Han Baode]
1983 *Guji de weihu* [The preservation of historic sites]. Taibei: Xingzhengyuan wenhua jianshe weiyuanhui.

Han Pao-teh [Han Baode] and Hung Wen-hsiung [Hong Wenxiong]
1973 *Banqiao Lin zhai: diaocha yanjiu ji xiufu jihua* [Banqiao Lin family compound: the survey, study, and restoration]. Taizhong: Donghai daxue.

Harrell, Stevan S.
1981 "Social Organization in Hai-shan." In Emily A. Ahern and Hill Gates, eds., *The Anthropology of Taiwanese Society,* pp. 125–147. Stanford: Stanford University Press.

Hartwell, George E.
1939 *Granary of Heaven.* Toronto: United Church of Canada.

Hase, Patrick
1981 "Notes on Rice Farming in Shatin." *Journal of the Hong Kong Branch of the Royal Asiatic Society* 21:196–206.
1983 "Traditional New Territories Farming Manuring." *Journal of the Hong Kong Branch of the Royal Asiatic Society* 23:241–247.
1988 "A Traditional New Territories Latrine." *Journal of the Hong Kong Branch of the Royal Asiatic Society* (forthcoming).

Hayes, James W.
1962 "The Pattern of Life in the New Territories in 1898." *Journal of the Hong Kong Branch of the Royal Asiatic Society* 2:75–102.
1963 "Movement of Villages on Lantau Island for Fung Shui Reasons." *Journal of the Hong Kong Branch of the Royal Asiatic Society* 3:143–144.
1969 "The Occupancy Level of Village Houses in the Hong Kong Region." *Journal of the Hong Kong Branch of the Royal Asiatic Society* 9:158–160.
1977 *The Hong Kong Region, 1850–1911: Institutions and Leadership in Town and Countryside.* Hamden, CT: Archon Books.
1983 *The Rural Communities of Hong Kong: Studies and Themes.* Hong Kong: Oxford University Press.
1985 "Specialists and Written Materials in the Village World." In David Johnson, Andrew J. Nathan, and Evelyn S. Rawski, eds., *Popular Culture in Late Imperial China,* pp. 75–111. Berkeley: University of California Press.

Hinton, William H.
1977 "Two Ways to Read the 'Red Book.'" *New China* 3 (2): 19–29.
1988 "Dazhai Revisited." *Monthly Review* 39 (10): 34–50.
1989 "A Response to Hugh Deane." *Monthly Review* 40 (10): 10–36.

Ho, Pingti
1955 "The Introduction of American Food Plants into China." *American Anthropologist* 57 (2): 191–201.

Ho, Samuel P. S.
1978 *Economic Development in Taiwan, 1860–1970.* New Haven: Yale University Press.
1979 "Decentralized Industrialization and Rural Development: Evidence from Taiwan." *Economic Development and Cultural Change* 28 (1): 77–96.

Hong Kong Government
1979 *Rural Architecture in Hong Kong.* Hong Kong: Government Information Services, Hong Kong Government Printer.

Hong Shixian, chief ed.
1789– *Guanyuan Hongshi zongpu* [Genealogy of the
1796 Hongs at Guanyuan]. 22 vols. N.p.

Hosie, Alexander
1922 *Szechuan: Its Products, Industries and Resources.* Shanghai: Kelly & Walsh.

Hou Jiyao, Ren Zhiyuan, Zhou Peinan, and Li Zhuanzi
1989 *Yaodong minju* [Subterranean folk dwellings]. Beijing: Zhongguo jianzhu gongye chubanshe.

Hsiao, Kung-chuan
1960 *Rural China: Imperial Control in the Nineteenth Century.* Seattle: University of Washington Press, 1960.

Hsu Min-fu [Xu Mingfu]
1990 *Taiwan chuantong minzhai ji qi difangxing shiliao zhi yanjiu* [Traditional dwellings in Taiwan and local research materials research]. Taibei: Hushi tushu gongsi.

Hu Chin
1974 "The People of Tachai." *Chinese Literature* 2:3-64; 3:15-84.
1975 *Learning from Tachai in Rural China.* Beijing: Foreign Languages Press.

Huang Hanmin
1984a "Fujian minju de chuantong tese yu difang fengge, shang" [The traditional character and local styles of the folk dwellings of Fujian, part 1]. *Jianzhushi* [The architect] 19:178-203.
1984b "Fujian minju de chuantong tese yu difang fengge, xia" [The traditional character and local styles of the folk dwellings of Fujian, part 2]. *Jianzhushi* [The architect] 21:182-194.
1989 "Rammed Citadels: Wonders of South Fujian Province." *Building in China* 2 (December): 29-36.

Huang Jin and Lu Huixing, eds.
1988 *Nongcun jianzhu shiji yu shigong tuji* [Drawings for rural architectural design and construction]. Shanghai: Shanghai jiatong daxue chubanshe.

Huang, Philip C. C.
1985 *The Peasant Economy and Social Change in North China.* Stanford: Stanford University Press.
1990 *The Peasant Family and Rural Development in the Yangzi Delta, 1350-1988.* Stanford: Stanford University Press.

Huang, Shu-min
1981 *Agricultural Degradation: Changing Community Systems in Rural Taiwan.* Washington, D.C.: University Press of America.
1989 *The Spiral Road: Changes in a Chinese Village through the Eyes of a Communist Party Leader.* Boulder: Westview Press.

Huc, Evariste-Régis
1855 *The Chinese Empire, Forming a Sequel to the Work Entitled 'Recollections of a Journey through Tartary and Thibet.'* 2d edition. 2 vols. London: Longman, Brown, Green, and Longmans.

Jervis, Nancy
1990 "Waste Not, Want Not." *Natural History Magazine* May 1990:70-74.

Jiang Zhengrong et al., eds.
1984 *Nongcun jianzhu shouce* [Handbook of rural building]. Beijing: Zhongguo jianzhu gongye chubanshe.

Jiang Zhongguang
1959 "Banhao gonggong shitang jige wenti" [Some problems in organizing public dining halls]. *Caijing kexue* [Financial and economic science] 1:153.

Jianzhubu Cunzhen jianshesi Xinxi yanjiuchu [Information Bureau, Rural Construction Department, Construction Ministry]
1989 "Zhongguo cunzhen jianshe fazhan sishi nian" [Forty years of town and village construction development in China]. *Cunzhen jianshe* [Town and village construction] 34 (October): 2-4.

Jin Qiming
n.d. "Zhongguo nongcun juluo de xingtai yu guimo" [The morphology and scale of Chinese rural settlements]. Mimeographed.
1982 "Nongcun juluo dili yanjiu—yi Jiangsu sheng weili" [A geographic study of rural settlements—using Jiangsu province as an example]. *Dili yanjiu* [Geographical Research] 1 (September): 11-20.
1984 *Juluo dili* [Settlement geography]. Nanjing: Nanjing shifan daxue, dilixi.
1985 "Nongcun juluo dili" [Rural settlement geography]. In Li Xudan, ed., *Renwen dilixue luncong* [Symposium on human geography]. Beijing: Renmin jiaoyu chubanshe.
1988 *Nongcun juluo dili* [Rural settlement geography]. Beijing: Kexue chubanshe.
1989 *Zhongguo nongcun juluo dili* [Chinese rural settlement geography]. Nanjing: Jiangsu kexue jishu chubanshe.

Jin Qiming, Dong Xin, and Lu Yuqi, eds.
1990 *Zhongguo renwen dili gailun* [An introduction to the human geography of China]. Xian: Shaanxi renmin jiaoyu chubanshe.

Knapp, Ronald G.
1986 *China's Traditional Rural Architecture: A Cultural Geography of the Common House.* Honolulu: University of Hawaii Press.
1989 *China's Vernacular Architecture: House Form and Culture.* Honolulu: University of Hawaii Press.

Knapp, Ronald G., and Shen Dongqi
1991 "Politics and Planning: Rural Settlements in Contemporary China." In Nezar Alsayyad, ed., *Adaptation and Evolution of the Physical Environment; The Politics of Planning,* pp. 1–45. Berkeley: Center for Environmental Design Research, University of California at Berkeley.

Kulp, Daniel H.
1925 *Country Life in South China: The Sociology of Familism.* New York: Teachers College, Columbia University.

Kunshan xian Zhouzhuang wenshi zhengji zu [Kunshan County, Zhouzhuang Historical Essays Editorial Committee], ed.
1986 *Jiangnan shuixiang gu zhen Zhouzhuang* [Zhouzhuang—a watertown in the Jiangnan region]. Report.

Lamley, Harry J.
1977 "Hsieh-tou: The Pathology of Violence in Southeastern China." *Ch'ing-shih wen-t'i* 3 (7): 1–39.
1990 "Lineage Feuding in Southern Fujian and Eastern Guangdong under Qing Rule." In Jonathan N. Lipman and Stevan Harrell, eds., *Violence in China: Essays in Culture and Counterculture,* pp. 27–64. Albany: State University of New York Press.

The Land Reform Law of the People's Republic of China
1950 Beijing: Foreign Languages Press.

Lee Chien-lang [Li Qianlang]
1980 *Taiwan jianzhu shi* [History of the architecture of Taiwan]. Taibei: Beiwu chubanshe.
1984 *Chuantong jianzhu rumen* [An introduction to traditional architecture]. Taibei: Xingzhengyuan wenhua jianshe weiyuanhui.
1988 *Yangmingshan guojia gongyuan chuantong juluo ji jianzhu diaocha yanjiu* [Research survey on traditional villages and architecture in the Yangmingshan National Park]. Taibei: Lee Chienlang Ancient Architecture Research Center.

Lee, Sang Hae
1986 *Feng-shui: Its Content and Meaning.* Ph.D. dissertation, Cornell University.

Lee, Yokshiu F.
1989 "Small Towns and China's Urbanization Level." *The China Quarterly* 120 (December): 771–786.

Li Cangjun
1988 *Zhongguo jixiang tu'an* [Chinese propitious patterns]. Hong Kong: Qinggongye chubanshe.

Li Chengrui
1985 "Economic Reform Brings Better Life." *Beijing Review* 28 (29): 15–22. July 22.

Li Fengwu and Wang Jingmo
1989 "Juzhai fengshui yu cunzhen guihua" [Housing *fengshui* and town and village planning]. *Cunzhen jianshe* [Town and village construction] 30:7.

Li Gui
1834 *Xiazhuang Li shi zongpu* [Genealogy of the Li clan at Xia village]. N.p.

Li Hong
1990 "Housing Boom in Rural Areas Cools Down." *China Daily* 2793 (July 12): 1.

Liang Chao
1990 "Rapid Land Shrinkage Is Under Control." *China Daily* 2634 (January 6): 1.

Lin, Ching-yuan
1973 *Industrialization in Taiwan, 1946–1972.* New York: Praeger.

Lin Min
1974 *Red Flag Canal.* Beijing: Foreign Languages Press.

Link, Perry, Richard Madsen, and Paul G. Pickowicz, eds.
1989 *Unofficial China: Popular Culture and Thought in the People's Republic.* Boulder: Westview Press.

Little, Alicia B.
1908 *The Land of the Blue Gown.* London: T. F. Unwin.

Liu Baozhong, Zhou Ruoqi, and Shao Xiaoguang
n.d. "Survey of Dang's Village." Unpublished manuscript.

Liu Baozhong
n.d. "Traditional Folk Houses of Shaanxi." Unpublished manuscript.
1981 *Gu jianzhu zhinan* [Guidebook to China's ancient buildings]. Beijing: Zhongguo jianzhu gongye chubanshe.

Liu Nan
1958 "How Big Willows Became Health Conscious." *China Reconstructs* 7 (June 1958): 15.

Liu Suinian and Wu Qungan, eds.
1986 *China's Socialist Economy—An Outline History (1949-1984)*. Beijing: Beijing Review.

Lu Min-jen
1987 "Promotion of Constitutional Democracy Government's Goal." *Free China Journal*, October 5, p. 2.

Lu Yuanding and Wei Yanjun
1990 *Guangdong minju* [Folk dwellings of Guangdong]. Beijing: Zhongguo jianzhu gongye chubanshe.

Lung, David
1979 "Fung Shui: An Intrinsic Way to Environmental Design, with Illustrations of Kat Hing Wai." *Asian Architect and Builder*, October, pp. 16-23.
1991 *China's Traditional Vernacular Architecture* [Zhongguo chuantong minju jianzhu], bilingual edition. Hong Kong: Regional Council, Museums Section.

Ma Hai-teh [George Hatem]
1959 "Wiping Out Disease by Mass Action." *China Reconstructs* 8 (August): 9.

Ma Yin, ed.
1989 *China's Minority Nationalities*. Beijing: Foreign Languages Press.

McGee, T. G.
1987 "Urbanasi or Kotadesasi? The Emergence of New Regions of Economic Interaction in Asia." Working paper, East-West Environment and Policy Institute, Honolulu. April.

Madsen, Richard
1984 *Morality and Power in a Chinese Village*. Berkeley: University of California Press.

Markert, Christopher
1986 *I Ching*. Wellingborough: The Aquarian Press.

Maxwell, Neville
1975 "Learning from Tachai." *World Development* 3 (7-8): 473-495.
1978 "China's New 'Learn from Tachai' Movement." In D. B. Miller, ed., *Peasants and Politics: Grass Roots Reaction to Change in Asia*. New York: St. Martin's Press.

Meisner, Mitch
1978 "Dazhai: The Mass Line in Practice." *Modern China* 4 (1): 27-62.

Moser, Leo J.
1985 *The Chinese Mosaic: The Peoples and Provinces of China*. Boulder: Westview Press.

Myers, Ramon H.
1970 *The Chinese Peasant Economy: Agricultural Development in Hopei and Shantung, 1890-1949*. Cambridge: Cambridge University Press.

Myrdal, Jan
1965 *Report from a Chinese Village*. New York: New American Library.

Nagarajan, K., S. Singh, and J. K. Wang
1985 "Optimal Allocation of Farm Power Resources in Multicrop Farming Systems." *Papers of the American Society of Agricultural Engineers*, No. 85-5056. Honolulu.

Nee, Victor, and Su Sijin
1990 "Institutional Change and Economic Growth in China: The View from the Villages." *The Journal of Asian Studies* 40 (1): 3-25.

Needham, Joseph
1971 *Science and Civilization in China*, vol. 4, *Physics and Physical Technology*. Cambridge: Cambridge University Press.

Nelson, Howard
1964 "The Chinese Descent System and the Occupancy Level of Village Houses." *Journal of the Hong Kong Branch of the Royal Asiatic Society* 9: 113-123.

Ng, Peter Y. L., and Hugh D. R. Baker
1983 *New Peace County: A Chinese Gazetteer of the Hong Kong Region*. Hong Kong: Hong Kong University Press.

Niu Weina
1988 "Nongcun zhuzhai sheji de huigu yu zhanwang" [Review and prospect concerning rural housing design]. In *Nongcun jizhen yu zhuzhai* [Rural towns and housing], pp. 25-47. Beijing: Zhongguo jianzhu jishu fazhan zhongxin, Cunzhen guihua sheji yanjiusuo.

"No Deification of Dazhai Brigade"
1980 *Beijing Review* 23 (31): 5. August 11.

"Nongcun zhufang jianshe shinian banshu nongju xiqian xinju" [In ten years of rural housing construction, half of all farming households have happily moved into new homes]
1990 *Renmin ribao—haiwai ban* [People's daily—overseas edition] 1824 (November 22): 1.

"Occupation of Arable Land Must Stop"
1990 *China Daily* 2882 (October 24): 1.

Odend'hal, Stewart
1989a "Effects of Decollectivization of Draft Animals in a Shandong Village of the People's Republic

of China." In *Proceedings of the Eleventh International Symposium on Asian Studies, 1989,* 131–137.
1989b "Population Changes in a Shandong Village Between 1987 and 1988 in Mainland China." *Asian Profile* 1 (4): 305–309.

Pan Lusheng, ed.
1990 Zhongguo Hanzi tu'an [Chinese characters patterns]. Hong Kong: Qinggongye chubanshe.

Parish, William L., and Martin K. Whyte
1978 *Village and Family in Contemporary China.* Chicago: University of Chicago Press.

Perry, Elizabeth J.
1980 *Rebels and Revolutionaries in North China, 1845–1945.* Stanford: Stanford University Press.

"Plans Laid for Towns, Villages of China"
1991 *China Daily* 2961(January 25):4.

Potter, Sulamith Heins, and Jack M. Potter
1990 *China's Peasants: The Anthropology of Revolution.* Cambridge: Cambridge University Press.

"Qunzhong xihuan nazhong xingshi de shitang?" [What type of dining hall do the masses prefer?]
1958 *Xinhua banyuekan* [New China semi-monthly] 22:88–89.

Rawski, Evelyn Sakakida
1972 *Agricultural Change and the Peasant Economy of South China.* Cambridge: Harvard University Press.

The Red Sun Lights the Road Forward for Tachai
1969 Beijing: Foreign Languages Press.

"Renlei wenming de 'huo huashi' " ["A living fossil" of human civilization]
1989 *Renmin ribao—haiwaiban* [People's daily—overseas edition], July 11, p. 1.

Richthofen, Ferdinand Paul Wilhelm von
1903 *Baron Richthofen's Letters, 1870–1872,* 2d edition. Shanghai: The North China Herald.

Ruan Yisan
1988 *Jiu cheng xinglu* [Notes on ancient cities]. Shanghai: Tongji University Press.

Ruan Yisan, Huang Pei, and Jiang Weiping
1989 "Shuixiang guzhen baozhenqu—lishi guzhen Kunshan Zhouzhuang de guihua" [Ancient market town in the watertown region—the plan of the historic market town Zhouzhuang in Kunshan]. *Jianzhushi* [The architect] 32 (3): 30–43.

Salter, Christopher L.
1976 "The Role of Landscape Modification in Revolutionary Nation Building." *The China Geographer* 4 (Spring): 41–59.
1977 "Tachai Beyond Tachai." *The China Geographer* 7 (Spring): 59–65.
1978 "The Enigma of Tachai: Landscapes and Lore." *The China Geographer* 9(Winter):43–64.
1983 "A Model Is Not a God." *Pacific Viewpoint* 24 (1): 1–10.

Schoppa, Keith
1989 *Xiang Lake—Nine Centuries of Chinese Life.* New Haven: Yale University Press.

Selden, Mark
1985 "Income Inequality and the State." In William L. Parish, ed., *Chinese Rural Development: The Great Transformation,* pp. 193–218. Armonk, NY: M. E. Sharpe.

"Shaanxi Hancheng faxian Ming-Qing jianzhu cunluo; zhong wai zhuanjia guanzhu rongwei yuwei Zhonghua guibao" [Ming-Qing dynasty village discovered in Hancheng, Shaanxi; Chinese and Western specialists praise it as a Chinese gem]
1989 *Renmin ribao—haiwaiban* [People's daily—overseas edition], November 4, p. 1.

Shan Deqi
1984 "Cunxi, tianjing, matouqiang—Huizhou minju biji" [Village streams, skywells, gable walls—notes on the vernacular architecture of Huizhou]. *Jianzhu shi lunwenji* [Treatise on the history of architecture] 6:120–134.
1987 "Yixian Hongcun guihua tanyuan" [Exploration of the plan for Hongcun, Yixian]. *Jianzhu shi lunwenji* [Treatise on the history of architecture] 8:87–97.

Shanhe xiangzhi [Shanhe village gazetteer].
Qing N.p.

Shan Shiyuan
1981 "Hangtu jishu qiantan" [Summary talk on the earth tamping technique]. *Keji shi wenji* [Collection on the history of science and technology] 7: 119–123.

Shenan Zhongcun jiacheng xu [Preface to the family history at Zhong village, She county].
Qing N.p.

Shen Dongqi
1988 "Zhejiang sheng nongcun zhuzhai fazhan qushi" [Trends in the development of rural housing in Zhejiang province]. In Niu Weina, ed., *Nongcun jizhen yu zhuzhai* [Rural towns and

housing], pp. 72-81. Beijing: Zhongguo jianzhu jishu fazhan zhongxin, Cunzhen guihua sheji yanjiusuo.
1991 *Nongcun zhuzhai jianzhu sheji* [The design and construction of rural settlements]. Beijing: Zhongguo jianzhu gongye chubanshe.

"Shenghuo zhengzai qibianhua" [Life is undergoing a change right now]
1958 *Zhongguo qingnian* [Chinese youth] 18:17-19.

Shils, Edward
1981 *Tradition*. Chicago: University of Chicago Press.

Siu, Helen F.
1989 "Recycling Rituals: Politics and Popular Culture in Contemporary Rural China." In Perry Link, Richard Madsen, and Paul G. Pickowicz, eds., *Unofficial China: Popular Culture and Thought in the People's Republic*, pp. 121-137. Boulder: Westview Press.

Skinner, G. William
1964 "Marketing and Social Structure in Rural China, Part I." *Journal of Asian Studies* 24 (1): 3-43.
1971 "Chinese Peasants and the Closed Community: An Open and Shut Case." *Comparative Studies in History and Society* 13 (3): 270-281.

Smil, Vaclav
1984 *The Bad Earth: Environmental Degradation in China*. Armonk, NY: M. E. Sharpe.

Smith, Arthur H.
1899 *Village Life in China*. London: Fleming H. Revell Company.

Song Zilong and Ma Shiyun, eds.
1990 *Huizhou zhuandiao yishu* [Engraved bricks in Huizhou district]. Hefei: Anhui meishu chubanshe.

Spencer, Joseph E.
1940 "The Szechwan Village Fair." *Economic Geography* 16 (1): 48-58.
1941 "Chinese Place Names and the Appreciation of Geographic Realities." *Geographical Review* 31: 79-94.
1971 *Asia, East by South: A Cultural Geography*. New York: John Wiley and Company.
1977 "The Transformation of the Traditional Rural Village." In Robert C. Eidt, Kashi N. Singh, and Rana R. B. Singh, eds., *Man, Culture, and Settlement*, pp. 160-169. New Delhi: Kalyani Publishers.

Steinhardt, Nancy Shatzman
1990 *Chinese Imperial City Planning*. Honolulu: University of Hawaii Press.

Sun Chingchih
1962 *Xinan diqu jingji dili* [Economic geography of southwest China]. Beijing: Kexue chubanshe. Translated by Joint Publications Research Service, No. 15,069, 1971.

Sun Jianai et al.
1905 *Shujing tu shuo* [Illustrations and notes to the *Shujing*], juan 32/2b. Beijing: n.p.

Sun Yinshe and Lin Yazhen
1989 "Rural Urbanization: Process and Types." *Chinese Geography and Environment* 2 (Summer): 42-59.

Tachai: Standard Bearer in China's Agriculture
1972 Beijing: Foreign Languages Press.

Tan Manni
1987 "A Taste of Rural Life." *China Reconstructs* 30 (June): 42-43.

Tang Ming-chao
1958 "The General Line for Socialist Construction." *China Reconstructs* 7 (September 1958): 2.

Tannenbaum, Gerald
1971 "The Real Spirit of Tachai." *Eastern Horizon* 10 (2): 5-36.

Thaxton, Ralph
1981 "The Peasants of Yaocun: Memories of Exploitation, Injustice, and Liberation in a Chinese Village." *Journal of Peasant Studies* 9 (1): 3-46.

Tongji daxue jianzhu chengshi guihua xueyuan [College of Architecture and Planning, Tongji University] and Jiangsu sheng Kunshan xian chengshi jianshe ju [Bureau of Urban Construction, Kunshan County, Jiangsu Province], eds.
1986 *Shuixiang gu zhen Zhouzhuang zongti ji baohu guihua* [A master plan and preservation study for the watertown Zhouzhuang]. Report.

Tongji daxue jianzhu chengshi guihua xueyuan [College of Architecture and Planning, Tongji University]
1986 *Zhouzhuang shuixiang jiexiang minju diaocha* [A survey of Zhouzhuang: its streets and dwellings]. Report.

Tsou, Tang, Marc Blecher, and Mitch Meisner
1982 "National Agricultural Policy: The Dazhai Model and Local Change in the Post-Mao Era." In Mark Selden and Victor Lippit, eds., *The Transition to Socialism in China*, pp. 266-299. Armonk, NY: M. E. Sharpe.

References

Tuan, Yi-fu
1989 "Traditional: What Does It Mean?" In Jean-Paul Bourdier and Nezar AlSayyad, eds., *Dwellings, Settlements and Tradition: Cross-cultural Perspectives*, pp. 27–34. New York: University Press of America.

"Twelve Million School Graduates Settle in the Countryside."
1976 *Peking Review* 19 (2): 11–13. January 9.

Unger, Jonathan, and Jean Xiong
1990 "Life in the Chinese Hinterlands under the Rural Economic Reforms." *Bulletin of Concerned Asian Scholars* 22(2):4–17.

Veeck, Gregory, ed.
1991 *The Uneven Landscape: Geographical Studies in Post Reform China*. Baton Rouge: Geoscience Publications.

Vermeer, Eduard B.
1982 "Income Differentials in Rural China." *The China Quarterly* 89 (March): 1–33.
1988 *Economic Development in Provincial China: The Central Shaanxi since 1930*. Cambridge: Cambridge University Press.

"A Visit to Huaxi Village"
1984 *China Pictorial* 11:34–36.

Voon Phin-Keong
1969 "The Origins of Chinese Place Names." *Geographica: Journal of the Department of Geography, University of Malaya* 5:34–47.

Wang Jinsuo
1990 "Modernizing Rural Production." *Beijing Review* 33 (18): 25–27. April 30–May 6.

Wang, Joseph Cho
1991 "Zoufang guzhen Zhouzhuang: jingguan Zhongguo shuixiang zhi mei" [A visit to old town Zhouzhuang: the tranquil beauty of Chinese watertowns]. *Yaqi* [Arch monthly] 6: 126–134.
1992 "Watertown Zhouzhuang: On the Brink." *Mimar* 42. Forthcoming.

Wang Kangsheng, ed.
1990 *Zhongguo ruishou tu'an* [Chinese auspicious animals patterns]. Hong Kong: Qinggongye chubanshe.

Wang Shuangwu
1984 "Ming-Qing jianzhu qun Hongcun cunluo minju" [Hongcun village residences: a Ming-Qing architectural ensemble]. *Jianzhu xuebao* [Architectural journal] 10:74–77.

Watson, James L.
1982 "Chinese Kinship Reconsidered: Anthropological Perspectives on Historical Research." *The China Quarterly* 92:589–622.

Williams, Samuel Wells
1883 *The Middle Kingdom: A Survey of the Geography, Government, Literature, Social Life, Arts and History of the Chinese Empire and Its Inhabitants*. Revised edition. 2 vols. New York: C. Scribner's Sons.

Wolf, Eric R.
1966 *Peasants*. Englewood Cliffs: Prentice-Hall.

Wolf, Margery
1968 *The House of Lim*. Englewood Cliffs: Prentice-Hall.

"Wo sheng liuge pinkun xian jiushiwan ren tuokun" [Nine hundred thousand have cast off poverty in Zhejiang's six poorest counties]
1989 *Zhejiang ribao* [Zhejiang daily] 14577 (April 22): 1.

Wright, Arthur F.
1977 "The Cosmology of the Chinese City." In G. William Skinner, ed., *The City in Late Imperial China*, pp. 33–73. Stanford: Stanford University Press.

Wu Maode and Jiao Liuquan
n.d. "Planning of Dangjia Village." Unpublished manuscript.

Wu, Nelson I.
1963 *Chinese and Indian Architecture*. New York: George Braziller, Inc.

Xiao Li
1991 "Problems Mar Boom in Housing." *China Daily* 3098 (July 5): 3.

Xiao Tihuan
1985 "Woguo cunzhen jianshe jiakuai mianmao gaiguan" [Increasing changes in the face of construction in the nation's villages and towns]. *Renmin ribao—haiwaiban* [People's daily—overseas edition], November 8, p. 1.

Xie Lansheng
1875– *Piling Xieshi zongpu* [General genealogy of the
1909 Xie clan at Piling]. 56 vols. N.p.

Xue Quli
1990 "Zhongguo chuantong yingzao yishi de xiangzhengxing" [The symbolism of China's traditional building ideas]. *Jianzhushi* [The architect] 38:1–13.

Yang, C. K.
1959 *A Chinese Village in Early Communist Transition*. Cambridge: M.I.T. Press.

Yang, Martin C.
1945 *A Chinese Village: Taitou, Shantung Province.* New York: Columbia University Press.

"Yige ban de henhao de gongshitang" [A well-run public dining hall].
1960 *Qiushi* [Search for truth] 3:46–49.

Yin Junke
1983 "Mingdai Beijing jiaoqu cunluo de fazhan." *Lishi dili* [Historical geography] 3:121–130.
1988 "The Development of Rural Settlements in the Beijing Area during the Ming Dynasty." *Chinese Geography and Environment* 1 (2): 3–20.

Yu Kunliang
1983 *Minsu yishu de weihu* [The preservation of folk arts]. Taibei: Xingzhengyuan wenhua jianshe weiyuanhui.

Yu Shengfang
1987 "Shuixiang gu zhen Zhouzhuang" [The old watertown Zhouzhuang]. *Jianzhu xuebao* [Architectural journal] 221:34–38.

Yuan Jingshen, ed.
1987 *Dangdai Zhongguo de xiangcun jianshe* [Contemporary rural development in China]. Beijing: Zhongguo shehui kexue chubanshe.

Yunnan sheng sheji yuan [Yunnan Provincial Design Institute]
1986 *Yunnan minju* [Yunnan folk dwellings]. Beijing: Zhongguo jianzhu gongye chubanshe.

Zhang Baixin
1991 "Shijiazhuang cun: 'haiwai guanxi duo' " [Shijiazhuang village: "many overseas connections"]. *Renmin ribao—haiwai ban* [People's daily—overseas edition] 1900 (February 19): 1.

Zhang Lin
1990 "Hazardous Schools on the Decline." *China Daily* 2692 (March 16): 3.

Zhang Tingwei
1986 "A Study of the Watertown Region in the Southeast." Unpublished paper, Department of Architecture, Tongji University. Report.

Zhang Yuhuan
1985 *Jilin minju* [Folk dwellings of Jilin]. Beijing: Zhongguo jianzhu gongye chubanshe.

Zhang Zhongyi et al.
1957 *Huizhou Mingdai zhuzhai* [Ming dynasty houses of Huizhou]. Beijing: Jianzhu gongcheng chubanshe.

Zhao Bonian
1983 "Rural Housing Boom: New Designs for Changing Lifestyles." *China Reconstructs* 32 (3): 53–56.

Zheng Shensheng
1989 "Huigu yu zhanwang" [Review and prospect]. *Cunzhen jianshe* [Town and village development] 30:2–4.

Zhongguo jianzhu jishu fazhan zhongxin, jianzhu lishi yanjiusuo [Center for Chinese Architectural Technology and Development, Research Unit for Architectural History]
1984 *Zhejiang minju* [Folk houses of Zhejiang]. Beijing: Zhongguo jianzhu gongye chubanshe.

Zhou Yixing
1988 "The Metropolitan Interlocking Region in China: A Preliminary Idea." Paper presented at the Conference on the Extended Metropolis in Asia, East-West Environment and Policy Institute, Honolulu, September 19–23.

"Zhouzhuang shuixiang jieshen minju diaocha"
1986 [A survey of the streets and dwellings of Zhouzhuang] Report.

Zurndorfer, Harriet T.
1989 *Change and Continuity in Chinese Local History: The Development of Hui-chou Prefecture, 800–1800.* Leiden: E. J. Brill.

Zweig, David
1989 *Agrarian Radicalism in China, 1968–1981.* Cambridge: Harvard University Press.
1990 "Evaluating China's Rural Policies: 1949–1989." *The Fletcher Forum of World Affairs* 14(1): 18–29.

CONTRIBUTORS

Catherine Enderton is a cultural and environmental geographer specializing in China's rural and wild environments. She has done extensive field work in southern and western China, especially Hainan, Sichuan, and Tibet. She is currently an administrator and lecturer at the University of California, Los Angeles.

Stephen Endicott, Senior Scholar, Atkinson College, York University, Canada, was born in Shanghai and grew up in China before 1949. His lengthy return visits to China began in 1972 and continued through 1988, during which time he carried out research in MaGaoqiao. His most recent book is *Red Earth: Revolution in a Sichuan Village* (1989).

Fan Wei, is an instructor at the Beijing Institute of Civil Engineering and Architecture. His publications include "The Type of *Fengshui* of Langzhong City—A Preliminary Explanation of *Fengshui* Theory and the Environmental Form of Ancient Cities" (in Chinese) and "Dwelling Hermeneutics—Chinese Settlement Studies" (in Chinese). His current research focuses on the dialogue between Eastern and Western architecture.

Bernard Gallin, Professor of Anthropology at Michigan State University, has been carrying out research on Hsin Hsing since 1957. His book *Hsin Hsing, Taiwan: A Chinese Village in Change* (1966) has been followed by many articles examining the interplay of elements of Taiwan's socioeconomic system, especially rural-urban migration and the industrialization of village communities in Taiwan.

Rita S. Gallin, Director of the Women and International Development Program and Associate Professor of Sociology at Michigan State University, is the editor of two books on women in the Third World and the author or coauthor of numerous articles about Hsin Hsing village. Her current research focuses on the relationship between rural industrialization and the position of women in the social structure.

Gideon Golany, Research Professor of Urban Design/Planning at Pennsylvania State University, is the author or editor of eighteen books focusing on earth-sheltered housing, urban design in arid zones, and new town design and planning throughout the world. He has been a visiting professor in Australia, England, India, and Israel, and is a recipient of an honorary professorship from the Chinese Academy of Sciences.

Contributors

Jonathan Hammond, Associate Professor in the Department of Landscape Architecture at the University of Illinois at Urbana-Champaign, first visited Taishan county in 1980, when he traveled there to design a hotel inspired by local vernacular architecture. He is the author of *Planning Solar Neighborhoods* (California State Energy Commission, 1981). With a master's degree in ecology from the University of California, Davis, he is a registered architect and landscape architect.

Patrick Hase, with a Ph.D. in medieval history from Cambridge University, has lived in Hong Kong since 1972. He has carried out research into local Hong Kong village history and life-styles since 1979 and authored a number of articles. He is a research assistant of the Centre of Asian Studies, University of Hong Kong, a member of the Council of the Royal Asiatic Society, Hong Kong Branch, and editor of the Society's *Journal*. He is currently an administrative officer for the Hong Kong government.

Huang Shu-min, Professor of Anthropology at Iowa State University, carried out research in Lin village in 1984–1985 supported by a fellowship from the Committee on Scholarly Communication with the People's Republic of China. He is currently completing a five-year (1987–1991) project on rural health care in Zouping county, Shandong. He is the author of *The Spiral Road: Change in a Chinese Village Through the Eyes of a Communist Party Leader* (1989).

Nancy Jervis, Vice President and Director of the School of Chinese Studies at China Institute in America in New York City, received her Ph.D. in anthropology from Columbia University in 1987. Her research in Henan province was carried out first in 1972, and then during repeated field trips between 1981 and 1985. She lived and worked in China from 1979 to 1982. In addition to contributing "Waste Not, Want Not" to the May 1990 issue of *Natural History Magazine,* she is working on a book about Dacaiyuan village.

Jin Qiming, Professor of Geography at Nanjing Normal University, is China's foremost authority on rural settlements. His numerous books include *Nongcun juluo dili* [Rural settlement geography] (1988), *Zhongguo nongcun juluo dili* [Chinese rural settlement geography] (1989), and *Zhongguo renwen dili gailun* [An introduction to the human geography of China] (1990).

Ronald G. Knapp, Professor of Geography at the State University of New York, College at New Paltz, is the author of *China's Traditional Rural Architecture: A Cultural Geography of the Common House* (1986) and *China's Vernacular Architecture: House Form and Culture* (1989), among other books and articles on China's cultural and historical geography. His current research focuses on the formation and change of four villages in Zhejiang province.

Olivier Laude, a graduate of Skidmore College in art history, has traveled widely in China, South and Southeast Asia, as well as Europe and Africa. He is preparing a book-length photographic essay *Minju: Traditional Rural Houses in China* on Chinese vernacular architecture.

Lee Man-yip is a fourteenth-generation inhabitant of Sheung Wo Hang village. He has a degree in Fine Arts from Kingston-on-Thames Polytechnic and teaches in the Kiangsu-Chekiang College, Sha Tin, Hong Kong. He has been interested in the history of his clan and village for fifteen years and has gathered together a fine collection of objects used by villagers in previous generations.

Li Wei, a Lecturer of Geography at Beijing University, is currently completing a doctorate at the University of Southern California. She is one of the younger generation of Chinese geographers researching topics on human geography. She is the author of "Agricultural Development in the Semi-arid Zone of the United States" (in Chinese) and coauthor of "The Southern Region of Taiwan," in *Economic Geography of Taiwan* (in Chinese).

Liu Baozhong, educated in architecture at the Dongbei Institute of Technology, is currently the Head of the Research Institute of Architecture at the Xi'an Institute of Metallurgy and Construction Engineering, where he has taught since 1956. In addition to being the author of five books and more than thirty-five articles that focus on Chinese and Western architecture, he has designed five buildings.

Stewart Odend'hal, Associate Professor in the Department of Anatomy and Radiology, College of Veterinary Medicine, University of Georgia, has carried out research concerning livestock in several countries. His ongoing research in Fengjiacun village is supported by the Committee on Scholarly Communication with the People's Republic of China.

Christopher L. Salter is Chair and Professor of Geography at the University of Missouri, Columbia. He began *The China Geographer* and edited it from 1975 until 1985. He did his undergraduate work at Oberlin College in Geology and Geography and his M.A. and Ph.D. at the University of California, Berkeley, in Geography. He has published works in cultural geography, landscape analysis, geographic education, and China.

Shan Deqi is Vice President of the School of Architecture at Qinghua University in Beijing, where he earned a bachelor's degree in 1960. His numerous publications include articles on vernacular architecture, landscapes, and design methods in *The Architect, Treatise on the History of Architecture,* and *Architectural Journal* (all in Chinese). He is currently the lead professor for the "Man and Dwelling Environment" project of the Chinese National Natural Science Research Foundation.

Shen Dongqi, Chief of Architects at the Zhejiang Urban and Rural Planning and Design Research Institute in Hangzhou, has lectured and written widely on rural planning in China. He is the author of numerous articles and the book *Nongcun zhuzhai jianzhu sheji* [The design and construction of rural dwellings] (1991) as well as a recipient of national awards for architectural designs and reports.

Gregory Veeck received a Ph.D. in geography from the University of Georgia and is now an Assistant Professor at the Louisiana State University. The author of articles on rural development in Jiangsu province, he has edited and contributed to *The Uneven Landscape: Geographic Studies in Post-Reform China* (1991).

Joseph C. Wang is Professor in the College of Architecture and Urban Studies at Virginia Polytechnic Institute and State University. A native of Suzhou, Professor Wang was educated on three continents: He has a B.Sc. in architecture from Cheng Kung University in Taiwan, an M. Arch. from the University of California, Berkeley, and a Ph.D. from the University of Bath, UK. His recent publications include "A Biographical Profile of Professor Liang Ssu-ch'eng (1901–1972)" and "Three Episodes-A Study of Urban Housing in China." His current research interests include design theory and methods, architectural education, and topics in Chinese architecture and planning.

James P. Warfield is an Architect and Professor of Architecture teaching in the graduate design studios at the University of Illinois at Urbana-Champaign. His written and photographic works in the field of vernacular architecture and the people who create it have been presented to international audiences for more than twenty years. His current project "ANTHEM: A Celebration of Vernacular Architecture" combines his own research in Bolivia, Borneo, China, Mexico, Thailand, and Turkey with that of other scholar-artists in a major exhibit.

Wen Changen is Research Professor and Director of the Guangdong Institute of Geography in Guangzhou. He has published extensively in Chinese on south China and Hainan, including a set of maps on Hainan's resources and an article titled "Land Resource Superiority and Its Rational Utilization in Hainan."

INDEX

References to illustrations are in **boldface**.

Agricultural Society of China, 56
Aiguo weisheng yundong (Patriotic Sanitation Movement), 48, **49**
Analytical (Compass) school of geomancy (*Liqizong*), 38-39, 177
Ancestral hall (*zongci* or *citang*), 9, 90, 94, 165, 169, 177, 228, 284
Anhui, 3, 5, 8, 25, 27, 28, 41, **42, 44,** 78, 119-127, 139
Anshan (table mountain), **40,** 43
Antu (settling the earth). *See Fengshui*
Anzhai (settling the earth). *See Fengshui*
Architectural Society of China, 56
Assembly halls, **53, 58, 59, 60**

Ba (hamlet in Sichuan), 3
Bagua. See Eight Trigrams
Baihu (white tiger), **38, 40,** 43, **45**
Banpo (neolithic settlement), 32, 41
Bao (village settlement), 3
Bathing, 61, 171, 202, 275, 278
Beijing and environs, 8, 9, 26, **67, 68**
Black tortoise, 43, **45**

Campaigns, effect of on settlements and housing, 48-49, **50,** 50-63, 72, 189, 193-210
Canal sites for rural settlements, 139-150, **146**
Cangpo Village, Zhejiang, 6, 76, 173-185
Cave dwellings. *See* Earth-sheltered housing and settlements
Chang (village market), 3
Chang (village settlement), 3
Chaoshan (worshiping mountain), **40,** 43
Chawan Village, 6, 76, 107-117
Church, 184, **184**
Citang (lineage or clan ancestral hall), 9, 54, 77

Cliffside dwellings and villages, 24, 156-158
Collectivization, effect of on settlements, 52-55
Commodity economy, effect of on settlements, 63-69, 211-220, 238-240, 252-257, 267-268
Commune (People's), 47, 50-56, **51, 179,** 251
Courtyard (*tingyuan, yuanluo, yuanzi*), 23, 26, 30, 60, **123,** 124, **126,** 133-134, **134,** 158, 168-169, 182-183, **201, 226,** 227, 240-241, **240,** 242, **249,** 257
Cultural center, 59, **59,** 69, 190
Cultural Revolution. *See* Great Proletarian Cultural Revolution
Cun (village settlement), 2-3
Cunzhen jianshe guihua (town and village construction plan), 64
Cunzhen zongti guihua (town and villages master plan), 64

Da (hamlet in Jiangnan area), 3
Dacaiyuan Village, Henan, 6, 190, 245-257
Dai (hamlet in Jiangnan area), 3
Daixiaodian (commission shop), 20, **179**
Dangjia Village, Shaanxi, 5, 76, 129-137
Dazhai model, 47, 56-63, **57,** 64, **180,** 193-210, 265
Dazhai Village, Shanxi, 6, 56-58, **57,** 193-210
Daizhuang (linear village), 15, **16**
Dian (village market), 3
Dili. See Fengshui
Dingxian, Hebei, 19
Dining halls, 52-54, 59
Directional orientation of settlements, 27, 35-45, 120, 176, 230
Dispersed rural settlements, **17,** 18, 98-99
Drill grounds (*lianbing chang*), 53, **59**

Dwellings, 8; effect of policies on, 47-72; North China types, 23-26; South China types, 26-31; West China types, 31-34

Earth God (*tudigong*), 9, 10, 91-92, **91,** 267, 284
Earth-sheltered housing and settlements, 24-25, 56-58, 151-161, 200-202
Eight Point Charter for Agriculture, 55
Eight Trigrams, 39, 135, **136**
Electricity, 71, 117, 190, 191, 236, 275-276, 289
Ethnic minorities. *See* Minority settlements

Factories, village, **58, 59,** 61, 67, 68, **69,** 190, 193, 215-217, **223, 235,** 238-240, **260,** 287, **288, 289,** 290
Fang (bedroom), **86,** 87
Fang (market), 3
Fei jianzhi zhen (undesignated towns), 3
Fengjiacun Village, Shandong, 6, 190, 233-243
Fengshui (geomancy), contemporary applications of, 70-71; and settlements, 4-5, 35-45, 70-71, 76, 84, 87-94, 98-99, 120, 132, 177-178, 190, 228-232, **273**
"Five Haves and Eight Cleans" campaign, 50
Five Phases (*Wuxing*), 39, **41, 136,** 177, 228
Fong. See Fang (bedroom)
Forms (Configuration) school of geomancy (*Xingshizong*), 38-39, 177
Fortified settlements, 8-9
"Four treasures of the studio" (*wenfang sibao*), 178-180, **178,** 185
Framing systems, 169, 182
Fujian, 3, 6, 9, 20, 29, **36,** 71, 76, 78, 163-172, 173, 221-232, 271
Fung shui. See Fengshui

311

Index

Gansu, 6, 24–25, 32–33, **50**, 151, **156**, **158**
Geomancer's compass *(luopan)*, **37**, 39
Geomancy. See *Fengshui*
Geometry of settlements, 2, 59–60, **98**, 99, 107–110, **109**, 189–190, 246–247
God of Earth and Grain *(She Ji zhi Shen)*, 95, 104
Grain, threshing and drying, 24, 93, 102–103, **103**, 109, **110**, 112–113, **113**, 168, 179
Grand Canal, 139
Great Leap Forward, 50–51, 53–54, **53**, 62, 233, 249
Great Proletarian Cultural Revolution, 47, 62–63, 249, 257, 276
Great Wall Rural Settlement Region, **21**, 23–24
Guangdong, 3, 6, 9, 29, 91–105, 107–117, 163, 269
Guangxi Zhuang Autonomous Region, 3, 9, 29
Guanzhong area. See Shaanxi
Guizhou, 3, 30–31

Hainan, 6, 29, 269–278
Hakka, 6, 9, 29, 76, 77, 79, 85, 88, 163–172
Half Moon Village, Beijing, 8, 9
Hang (village market), 3
Hangtu. See Tamped earth walls and dwellings
Health stations, **58**, **59**, **60**, 61, 71, **237**
Hebei, 3, 19, 23–24, 25–26, 55, 59, **60**, 250
Heilongjiang, 23
Hekeng Village, Fujian, 6, 76, 163–172
Henan, 3, 6, 24–25, 51, **55**, **56**, 151, **156**, 245–257
Hetang (communal rice drying area), 93
Homes for the aged, 54, 69
Hongcun Village, Anhui, 5, 28, 76, 119–127
Hong Kong, 5, 70, 76, 77, 79–94, 97, 102, 189
Hotien Village, Taiwan, 7, 10
Housing. See Dwellings
Housing design competition, 66–67
Housing policies and settlement patterns, 47–72
Hsin Hsing Village, Taiwan, 6, 11, 279–293
Huanzhuang (ring village), 15–18
Hubei, 2, 30–31
Huizhou, Anhui, 6, 28, 119–127
Hukou (residence certificate), 189, 251–252
Hunan, 3, 28, **43**
Huoqiang (heated wall), 23

"In Agriculture, learn from Dazhai." See Dazhai model
Inner Mongolia Autonomous Region, 23, 32

Ji (periodic market), 3
Jiangnan, 3, 20, 26–28, 139–150
Jiangsu, 3, 6, 8–9, 20, 25, 27, **58**, 61, **61**, **62**, **64**, 139–150, 211–220
Jiangxi, 3, 28, **38**, 41, 163
Jianzhi zhen (officially designated town), 3–4
Jicun (nucleated village), 14–15, **14**, **16**
Jie (village market), 3
Jiecun (street village), 15
Jilin, 23, **65**
Jizhen (market town), 2, 3, 13, 19, 26, 27, 139–150

Kaixiangong, Jiangsu, 9
Kang (heated brick bed), 23, **158**, 159, **161**
Kanyu. See *Fengshui*
Kindergartens, 61, 68

Lalajie (lala streets), 18
Landlords, confiscation of dwellings of, 52
Land Management Statute, 67
Land Reform Law, 48
Land-use planning, effect of on settlements, 50–72
Lanes, village, 95, 101–102, **103**, 110–112, **111**, 122, **123**, 125, 133, **133**, **134**, **147**, 181, **214**, **225**, **238**, **239**, **247**, **248**, 290
Latrine, 49, 59, 62, 87, 100, 145, **147**, 169, 179, 183, 185, 190, 241, **267**, 278. See also Toilets
Lianbing chang (drill grounds), 53
Liaoning, 23, 65, **66**
Lighting. See Electricity
Lincun Village, Fujian, 6, 76, 190, 221–232
Lineage or clan ancestral hall *(zongci* or *citang)*, 9, 54, 77, 180–181, **180**, 228, 284
Lineages, settlements and, 10, 79–80, 119, 129–132, 163, 173–175 222–224, 228–229, 262, 282–283
Linear village settlements, 15, **16**
Liqizong (Analytical or Compass school of geomancy), 38–39, 177
Livestock, **59**, **60**, 68, 87, 100, 113, 169, **175**, 179, 190, 193, 226, **238**, 240–242, 273, 283, 290
Loessial dwellings and settlements. See Earth-sheltered housing and settlements
Loess Plateau Rural Settlement Region, **21**, 24–25
Lofts, use of, **86**, 87, 115, **116**
Long (dragon), 40, **40**, 42
Longlin Village, Hainan, 6, 190, 191, 269–278
Lucun (road village), 15
Luopan (*fengshui* "compass"), **37**, 39

MaGaoqiao Village, Sichuan, 6, 8, 189, 190, 259–268

Manchuria. See Northeast China; Northeast China Rural Settlement Region
Manure pits, 49, 290
Maoliao (matshed), 88
Markets, 217–218, **218**
Market towns *(jizhen)*, 2, 3, 13, 19, 26, 27, 139–150
Mau liu. See *Maoliu*
Middle-Lower Yangzi River Rural Settlement Region, **21**, 26–28
Migration and rural settlements, 172, 184–185, 250–256
Mingtang ("the bright or cosmic court"), **38**, 39
Minority settlements, 23, 24, 30, 32, 33, 34, 270–272
Model villages, 48–50, **50**, 56–63, **57**, **59**, **60**, **61**, 189, 193–210
Mofan cun. See Model villages
Mongols, 18
Mountain sites of villages, 151–161, 194–197
Movements. See Campaigns
Multiple story dwellings, 27, 28, 54, **55**, **57**, **59**, **60**, **62**, 67, 101, **101**, 110, 116, 123, 137, 182, 202, 218, 226–227, **226**, **268**, **288**

National Conference on Rural Housing Construction, 71
Nian villages, 8–9
Ningxia Hui Autonomous Region, 23, 24–25, 151
Nongcun (generic term for "villages"), 3
North China Plain, 1, 6, 19–20, 23, 25–26, 27, 233–243
Northeast China (Manchuria), 19, 20, 23, 32
Northeast China Rural Settlement Region, **21**, 23
Northern Rural Settlement Region, **21**, 32
Northwestern Rural Settlement Region, **21**, 32–33
Nucleated village settlements, 14–15, **14**
Nursery schools, 54, **58**, **59**, **60**, 61, 68

Pagoda, 132
Pak Kung (Earth God shrine), 91, **91**
Patriotic Sanitation Movement *(Aiguo weisheng yundong)*, 48, **49**
People's Commune. See Commune
Phoenix Village, Guangdong, 8
Pigpens. See Livestock
Pit dwellings and villages, 24, 159–161
Planning, rural, 50–72, 182
Policies, impact of on rural settlement, 47–72, 193–210
Preservation efforts, 11, 77–78, 127, 135–137, 139, 140, 148–150, 185
Private plots, 60

Index

Pu (village market), 3
Public toilets. *See* Latrine; Toilets

Qi (life-force), 39
Qinghai, 32-33
Qinghai-Xizang Rural Settlement Region, **21**, 33-34
Qinglong (azure dragon), **38**, **40**, **43**, **45**
Quan (village settlement), 3

Rammed earth. *See* Tamped earth walls and dwellings
Renmin gongshe (people's commune). *See* Commune
Responsibility system, effect of on settlements, 63-69, 240, 252-256
Roads, village, 59, 84, 95, 101, 116-117, 141, 171, 191, 193, 195, 212, 213, **216**, **235**, 236, **236**, **260**, 280-281, 285
Roller skating rink, 217
Row houses, 58, **59**, 60, **62**, 66
Rural planning, 50-72
Rural settlements: patterns of, 13-34, 98-99; regions and characteristics of, 20-34, **21**; size of, 19-20; types of, 2-3. *See also* Villages

Sancun (dispersed village), **17**, 18
Schools, **58**, **59**, **60**, 61, 69, **69**, 71, 93, 94, 129, 145, 172, 180, 185, 240, 278
Settlements. *See* Rural settlements; Villages
Settlement systems, 20-34, **21**
Sha ("local eminence"), 42
Shaanxi, 6, 24-25, 30, 32-33, 41, 58, **59**, 129-137, 151, **159-161**
Shandong, 3, 6, 25, **49**, 233-243
Shanghai and environs, 55, 68, 76, 139-150
Shang shan, xia xiang ("up to the mountains, down to the villages" program), 62-63, **62**, 206-207
Shanxi, 6, 23, 24-25, **49**, 56-58, **57**, 151, **155**, 193-210, 250, 251
Shape of villages, 14-18
Shaqi ("undesirable forces"), 91
Shat hei. *See Shaqi*
She Ji zhi Shen (God of Earth and Grain), 95, 104
Sheung Wo Hang Village, Hong Kong, 5, 10, 11, 76, 79-94
Shi (village market), 3
Shimadao Village, Shaanxi, 6, 76, 151-161, **154**
Shops, **60**, 61, 68, 113-114, **179**, 180, 193, 215-216, **217**, 281, 285
Shrines, 54, 95, 104, **104**, 228-229
Shuikou ("the mouth of the waterway"), **40**, 41, 43, 122
Sichuan, 2, 3, 6, 20, 30, 41, 259-268

Siheyuan (residential quadrangle), 133-134, **134**
Sishen (Four Beings), 44, **45**
Sites of settlements, factors in choice of, 6-7, 9-12, 88-89, 90-93, 132-133, 211-212, 226, 228-232
Siting, 35-45. *See also Fengshui*
Skywells *(tianjing)*, 28, 85, 86-87, **86**, **99**, 100, **100**
South China, 1-2, 7-8, 19-20, 42
Southeast Coastal Rural Settlement Region, **21**, 29-30
Southwest Rural Settlement Region, **21**, 30-31
South Yangzi River Hill Areas Rural Settlement Region, **21**, 28-29
Standard Market Towns, 2
Subterranean settlements. *See* Earth-sheltered housing and settlements

Taishan, 137, 179
Taiwan, 6, 29, 70, 76, 189, 279-293
Tam. *See Tan*
Tamped earth *(hangtu)* walls and dwellings, 24, 28, 29, 33, 165-168
Tan (pool), 92
Temples *(simiao)*, 9-10, 54, 69, **69**, 77, **176**, 179, 191, **256**, 257, 276, **278**, 292, **292**
Third Plenary Session, 47, 63
Threshing floor, 93, 102-103, **110**, 112-113, 179
Tianjing. *See* Skywells
Tibet Autonomous Region. *See* Qinghai-Xizang Rural Settlement Region
Tin tseng. *See* Skywells
Toilets, 49, 59, 62, 68, 116, 159, 275, 283. *See also* Latrine
Tongji University, 139, 148-150, **149**
Towers, **98**, **102**, 104-105, **135**, **136**
Townships, 4, 19
Tradition, 75-78
Transition, 189-191
Tree planting, 50, 59, 92, 95, 98, 135, **205**, 246, 263
Trees and shrines in villages, 54, 98, 104, **104**, 112, **127**, 224
Tsuen. *See Cun*
Tuanzhuang (compact village), 14-15, **14**
Tudigong. *See* Earth God
Tulou (Hakka earth buildings), 29, 163-172
Tun (village settlement), 3
T'u Ti Kung. *See* Earth God

Ventilation, 60, **273**
Vermilion bird, 43, **45**
Villages: names of, 2-3; shapes of, 14-18; size of, 19-20; types of, 2. *See also* Rural settlements

Wai (walled village), 84, 87-88
Walls, around settlements, 8-9, 84, 87-88, **176**, 178
Water, provision of, 6, 49, **60**, 71, **98**, 103-104, **103**, 116, 121-122, **122**, 169, 190, 202-204, **224**, 231-232, 236, **250**, **265**, 275, **276**, **277**, 283
Weigang Village, Jiangsu, 6, 190, 211-220
West China, 18
Workshops. *See* Factories
Wo tong. *See Hetang*
Wuxing (Five Phases), 39, **41**, **136**, 177

Xia tang (main room), **86**, 87
Xin fangzi, lao yangzi ("new dwellings in old style"), 66
Xingshizong (Forms or Configuration school of geomancy), 38-39
Xinjiang Uygur Autonomous Region, 32-33
Xiqi Village, Guangdong, 6, 76, 95-105
Xu (periodic market), 3
Xue ("lair" or "cave," "central point" in geomancy), **38**, 39-40, 90

Yachuan Village, Gansu, 6, 76, 151-161
Yang (the male aspect), **38**, 39, 89-90, 125, 228
Yellow River Diagram, 135
Yi da er gong ("large in size and collective in nature"), 53
Yi ping er diao ("excessive egalitarianism as well as the indiscriminate transfer of natural resources"), 52
Yin (the female aspect), **38**, 39, 90-91, 125, 228
Ying (village settlement), 3
Yinyang xiansheng (geomancer or *yinyang* interpreter), **37**, 39
Yuanba (hamlet in Sichuan), 3
Yuanlou (round Hakka building), 29, 163-172
Yuanzi (courtyard), 262, **263**. *See also* Courtyard
Yuanzi (hamlet in Sichuan), 3, 30
Yuet. *See Xue*
Yunnan, 30-31, 71

Zhai (village settlement), 3
Zhejiang, 6, 20, 27, 28, 29, 41, 47, 49, **53**, **60**, **62**, **65**, 68, 139, 173-185
Zhouzhuang Market Town, Jiangsu, 6, 76, 139-150
Zhuang (manor house; village), 3
Zhuang (village settlement; market place; farmhouse), 3
Zijian gongzhu ("publicly funded, privately built"), 61
Ziran cun (natural village), 19
Zongsi (lineage or clan ancestral hall), 9, 54, 77